**Fodor's 2000**

# Boston

**The complete guide, thoroughly up-to-date**

Packed with details that will make your

**The must-see sights, off and on the beate**

What to see, what to skip

**Vacation itineraries, walking tours, day**

Smart lodging and dining options

**Essential local do's and taboos**

Transportation tips

**Key contacts, savvy travel advice**

When to go, what to pack

**Clear, accurate, easy-to-use maps**

Books to read, videos to watch

KT-434-503

Fodor's Travel Publications, Inc. • New York, Toronto, London, Sydney, Auckland

# Fodor's Boston

**EDITOR:** Jennifer J. Paull

**Editorial Contributors:** Robert Blake, Natalie Engler, Carolyn Heller, Robert Kahn, Mark Murphy, Lauren Gibbons Paul, William G. Scheller, Helayne Schiff, Linda Schmidt, Stephanie Schorow, Anne Stuart, Mark Zanger

**Editorial Production:** Nicole Revere

**Maps:** David Lindroth, *cartographer*; Steven K. Amsterdam, Robert Blake, *map editors*

**Design:** Fabrizio La Rocca, *creative director*; Guido Caroti, *art director*; Jolie Novak, *photo researcher*

**Production/Manufacturing:** Mike Costa

**Cover Photograph:** James Lemass

**Cover Design:** Pentagram

## Copyright

## Special Sales

Fodor's Travel Publications are available at special discounts for bulk purchases for sales promotions or premiums. Special editions, including personalized covers, excerpts of existing guides, and corporate imprints, can be created in large quantities for special needs. For more information, contact your local bookseller or write to Special Markets, Fodor's Travel Publications, 201 East 50th Street, New York, NY 10022. Inquiries from Canada should be directed to your local Canadian bookseller or sent to Random House of Canada, Ltd., Marketing Department, 2775 Matheson Boulevard East, Mississauga, Ontario L4W 4P7. Inquiries from the United Kingdom should be sent to Fodor's Travel Publications, 20 Vauxhall Bridge Road, London SW1 2SA, England.

PRINTED IN THE UNITED STATES OF AMERICA

10 9 8 7 6 5 4 3 2 1

## Important Tip

Although all prices, opening times, and other details in this book are based on information supplied to us at press time, changes occur all the time in the travel world, and Fodor's cannot accept responsibility for facts that become outdated or for inadvertent errors or omissions. So **always confirm information when it matters,** especially if you're making a detour to visit a specific place.

# CONTENTS

## Maps

# ON THE ROAD WITH FODOR'S

**E**VERY Y2K TRIP is a significant one. So if there was ever a time you needed excellent travel information, it's now. Acutely aware of that fact, we've pulled out all stops in preparing Boston 2000. To guide you in putting together your experience, we've created multiday itineraries and neighborhood walks. And to direct you to the places that are truly worth your time and money in this important year, we've rallied the team of endearingly picky know-it-alls we're pleased to call our writers. Having seen all corners of Boston, they're real experts. If you knew them, you'd poll them for tips yourself.

A zinc-topped table? An oversize Kohler tub? After visiting the Boston area's accommodations, lodging updater **Natalie Engler** was sorely tempted but decided that they weren't quite worth a second mortgage. Instead she sprang for a stylish polyester bedspread and miniature soaps. A former freelance writer whose work has appeared in publications ranging from the *Boston Globe* to *Fast Company* magazine, she is now a senior editor at *InformationWeek*. On weekends she can be found canoeing on Spy Pond or in-line skating on the Minuteman Trail near her Arlington home.

**Carolyn Heller,** who updated the Side Trips and Destination: Boston chapters, recruited her six-year-old twins to help research this edition. She reports that they loved the North Shore beaches and rated Plimoth Plantation "the best, especially when the Pilgrim lady told us they didn't take baths in winter." A travel writer who has lived in Cambridge since 1983, she covers the area's restaurant and arts scenes as the Boston bureau chief for "On the Road," an on-line city guide for business travelers. Her recent travel articles have appeared in the *Boston Globe,* the *Los Angeles Times,* the *Philadelphia Inquirer,* the *Miami Herald,* and *FamilyFun* magazine. She has contributed to several Fodor's New England guidebooks.

**Robert Kahn,** a native of Valley Stream, N.Y., has a case of wanderlust dating back to 1995, when he became a travel writer for the *Boston Herald.* His adventures took him 15 times to Europe and once to the Middle East and Australia. After more than two years in airplanes, hotels, and taxi cabs, he lucked into a steady gig writing headlines for the *Boston Sunday Herald.* In the midst of updating our Exploring Cambridge chapter, he relinquished his Cambridge address and moved to Boston's tony South End, where he's trying to decide if he prefers focaccia to Wonder Bread.

**Mark Murphy** brings the experience of a decade of sports writing for the *Boston Herald* to our Outdoor Activities and Sports chapter.

Our dining critic has been reviewing Boston restaurants anonymously (and pseudonymously) for 25 years. As **Robert Nadeau,** he has a longstanding dining column in the *Boston Phoenix.* As Mark Zanger (his real name), he has written a cookbook, *The American Ethnic Cookbook for Students,* which will be published in 2000. He is renowned as "the one critic in town who will publish a slam-dunk pan." He also edits a discount travel Web site, contributes regularly to food and business magazines, and moderates an on-line discussion group on current affairs for the Delphi computer on-line service.

Exploring Boston updater **Lauren Gibbons Paul** grew up on Cape Cod but has called the Boston area home since 1986. In spring she loves to stroll along Newbury Street and fritter away an hour or two at an outdoor café; the Huntington Theater is a year-round favorite. In her more productive mode, she's a reluctant computer geek, covering technology and business issues for a host of trade publications such as *CIO* and *PC Week.* From her vantage point as mother of a four-year-old boy, she addresses parenting topics for the *Boston Parents Paper* and *Family PC Magazine.* She is also a contributor to the *Boston Globe* and Boston Sidewalk Web site.

Shopping updater **Stephanie Schorow,** who has lived in the Boston area since 1989, knows the sweetest words in the English language are "on sale." A still-recovering shopper, she has a weakness for bookstores, designer boutiques, pottery studios, and consignment shops. When not maxing out her credit cards, she's a writer and editor for the *Boston Herald.* She has adopted some ferocious driving habits from cruising Boston streets, "but only out of self-preservation."

Nightlife scout **Anne Stuart,** a New Englander by choice rather than by birth, has lived and worked in the Boston area since 1986. Her work, which has won numerous regional and national awards, has appeared in the *Los Angeles Times,* the *Washington Post,* the *Boston Globe,* the *Boston Herald,* and *Boston* magazine, among others. She spends much of her free time in Boston's theaters and museums.

When you use Fodor's maps to find your way to Filene's, you won't have to worry about getting lost: map editor **Bob Blake** spent most of his life in Boston. Fortunately for Fodor's, Bob moved south to New York, where he labors to keep Fodor's maps as accurate as they are clear and easy to read.

## Don't Forget to Write

Keeping a travel guide fresh and up-to-date is a big job. So we love your feedback—positive and negative—and follow up on all suggestions. Contact the Boston editor at editors@fodors.com or c/o Fodor's, 201 East 50th Street, New York, New York 10022. And have a wonderful trip!

Karen Cure
*Editorial Director*

# Boston

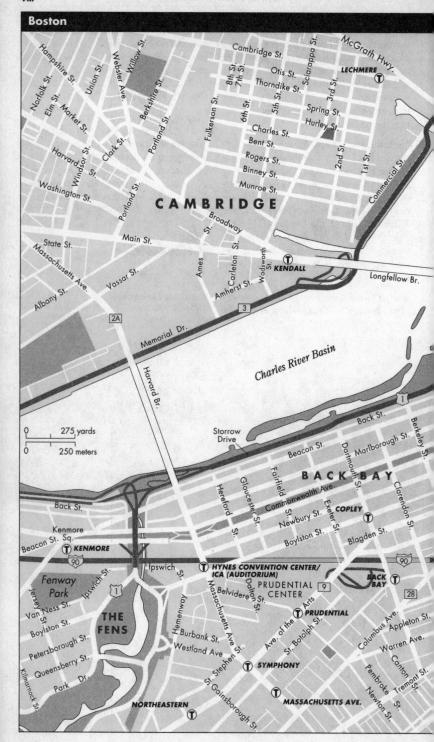

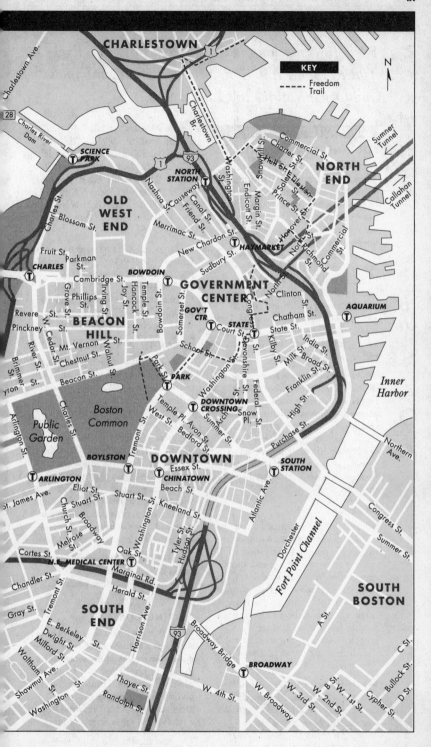

# ESSENTIAL INFORMATION

*Basic Information on Traveling in Boston, Savvy Tips to Make Your Trip a Breeze, and Companies and Organizations to Contact*

## AIR TRAVEL

### BOOKING YOUR FLIGHT

Price is just one factor to consider when booking a flight: frequency of service and even a carrier's safety record are often just as important. Major airlines offer the greatest number of departures. Smaller airlines—including regional and no-frills airlines—usually have a limited number of flights daily. On the other hand, so-called low-cost airlines usually are cheaper, and their fares impose fewer restrictions, such as advance-purchase requirements. Low-cost carriers as a group have a good safety record—about equal to that of major carriers.

When you book, **look for nonstop flights** and **remember that "direct" flights stop at least once.** Try to **avoid connecting flights,** which require a change of plane. Two airlines may jointly operate a connecting flight, so ask if your airline operates every segment—you may find that your preferred carrier flies you only part of the way.

### CARRIERS

When flying internationally, you must usually choose between a domestic carrier, the national flag carrier of the country you are visiting, and a foreign carrier from a third country. National flag carriers have the greatest number of nonstops. Domestic carriers may have better connections to your home town and serve a greater number of gateway cities. Third-party carriers may have a price advantage.

➤ MAJOR AIRLINES: **Aer Lingus** (☎ 800/223–6537). **Air Atlantic Canadian Partner** (☎ 800/426–7000). **Air Canada/Air Nova** (☎ 800/776–3000). **AirTran** (☎ 800/247–8726). **America West** (☎ 800/235–9292). **American Eagle** (☎ 800/433–7300.

**British Airways** (☎ 800/247–9297). **Continental** (☎ 800/525–0280). **Delta/Delta Express/Delta Shuttle** (☎ 800/221–1212). **Northwest** (☎ 800/225–2525). **TWA/TWA Express** (☎ 800/221–2000). **United** (☎ 800/241–6522). **US Airways/USAirways Shuttle** (☎ 800/428–4322). **Virgin** (☎ 800/862–8621.

➤ REGIONAL AIRLINES: **Business Express** (☎ 800/345–3400). **Cape Air** (☎ 508/771–6944 or 800/352–0714). **Colgan Air** (☎ 800/272–5488). **Comair** (☎ 800/354–9822). **Eastwind** (☎ 800/644–3592). **Midway/Midway Express** (800/452–2022).

### CHECK-IN & BOARDING

Assuming that not everyone with a ticket will show up, airlines routinely overbook planes. When that happens, airlines ask for volunteers to give up their seats. In return these volunteers usually get a certificate for a free flight and are rebooked on the next flight out. If there are not enough volunteers, the airline must choose who will be denied boarding. The first to get bumped are passengers who checked in late and those flying on discounted tickets, so **get to the gate and check in as early as possible,** especially during peak periods.

Always **bring a government-issued photo ID to the airport.** You may be asked to show it before you are allowed to check in.

### CUTTING COSTS

When flying within the U.S., **plan to stay over a Saturday night** and **travel during the middle of the week** to get the lowest fare. These low fares are usually priced for round-trip travel and are nonrefundable. You can, however, change your return date for a fee ($75 on most major airlines).

The least-expensive airfares to Boston must usually be purchased in advance and are non-refundable. It's smart to **call a number of airlines, and when you are quoted a good price, book it on the spot**—the same fare may not be available the next day. Always **check different routings** and look into using different airports. Travel agents, especially low-fare specialists (☞ Discounts & Deals, *below*), are helpful.

Consolidators are another good source. They buy tickets for scheduled international flights at reduced rates from the airlines, then sell them at prices that beat the best fare available directly from the airlines, usually without restrictions. Sometimes you can even get your money back if you need to return the ticket. Carefully read the fine print detailing penalties for changes and cancellations, and **confirm your consolidator reservation with the airline.**

When you **fly as a courier** you trade your checked-luggage space for a ticket deeply subsidized by a courier service. There are restrictions on when you can book and how long you can stay.

➤ CONSOLIDATORS: **Cheap Tickets** (☎ 800/377–1000). **Discount Airline Ticket Service** (☎ 800/576–1600). **Unitravel** (☎ 800/325–2222). **Up & Away Travel** (☎ 212/889–2345). **World Travel Network** (☎ 800/409–6753).

➤ COURIERS: **British Airways Travel Shops** (☎ 08706/061–133). **VEX Wholesale Express** (☎ 718/529–6814).

## ENJOYING THE FLIGHT

For more legroom **request an emergency-aisle seat.** Don't sit in the row in front of the emergency aisle or in front of a bulkhead, where seats may not recline. If you have dietary concerns, **ask for special meals when booking.** These can be vegetarian, low-cholesterol, or kosher, for example. On long flights, try to maintain a normal routine, to help fight jetlag. At night **get some sleep.** By day **eat lightly, drink water** (not alcohol), and **move around the cabin** to stretch your legs.

## FLYING TIMES

Flying time to Boston is one hour from New York, about 1½ hours from Washington, D.C., 2¼ hours from Chicago, 5½ hours from Los Angeles, 3¾ hours from Dallas, 1½ hours from Toronto, 7½ hours from London, and 21–22 hours from Sydney (including connection time). Delta and USAirways offer many daily shuttle flights to New York and Washington.

## HOW TO COMPLAIN

If your baggage goes astray or your flight goes awry, complain right away. Most carriers require that you **file a claim immediately.**

➤ AIRLINE COMPLAINTS: U.S. Department of Transportation **Aviation Consumer Protection Division** (✉ C-75, Room 4107, Washington, DC 20590, ☎ 202/366–2220). **Federal Aviation Administration Consumer Hotline** (☎ 800/322–7873).

## AIRPORTS & TRANSFERS

The major airport is **Logan International,** across the harbor from downtown Boston. Logan has five terminals, identified by letters A through E. Be aware that some airlines use different terminals for international and domestic flights. Most international flights arrive and depart from Terminal E. Most charter flights arrive and depart from Terminal D.

➤ AIRPORT INFORMATION: **Logan International** (☎ 800/235–6426). **Charter flights** (☎ 617/634–6270).

## TRANSFERS

For recorded information about traveling to and from Logan Airport, contact the airport's ground transportation hotline (☞ Airport Information, *above*). This is also your source for details on parking. The roadways in and around Logan remained under major construction through 1999; there is no curbside parking and little parking at terminals. However, a central garage is available.

Several **boat** companies make runs between the airport and downtown destinations. The Airport Water Shuttle makes seven-minute trips across Boston Harbor between Logan

S M A R T   T R A V E L   T I P S   A   T O   Z

Airport and Rowes Wharf downtown (year-round, every 15 minutes weekdays 6 AM–8 PM; every 30 minutes, Friday 8 PM–11 PM, Saturday 10 AM–11 PM, Sunday 10 AM–8 PM; ☞ Boat & Ferry Travel *and* Subways & Trolleys, *below*). A free shuttle bus runs between the airport ferry dock and all airline terminals. One-way fare is $10 for adults; purchase tickets on board. There's no service on July 4, Thanksgiving, Christmas, or New Year's. Connecting boats are available from Boston to Hingham on the South Shore (☞ Boat & Ferry Travel, *below*). The Harbor Express boat service takes passengers from Logan Airport to Long Wharf downtown (near the Aquarium) and to Quincy on the South Shore. The service makes 24 trips between 5 AM and 10 PM weekdays and 12 trips between 6 AM and 9:15 PM weekends. One-way fares are $8 between the airport and Long Wharf, $10 between the airport and Quincy. A seasonal Salem shuttle makes seven trips daily between downtown, Logan, and Salem on the North Shore; one-way fares are $8–$10. From April 1 though mid-October, the City Water Taxi offers on-call boat service between Logan Airport and several downtown locations. One-way fares to or from the airport are $10, $8 each for parties of two or more. ☞ Boat & Ferry Travel, *below*.

Six **bus** companies offer nonstop service between Logan Airport and South Station for $6 each way. Buses run daily every 15–30 minutes. Logan Express buses travel to the suburbs of Braintree, Framingham, and Woburn. One-way fares are $8 weekdays and $6 on weekends—a significant savings over a $35-minimum cab fare.

The **subway**'s Blue Line runs to downtown Boston in about 20 minutes; from there, you can reach the Red, Green, or Orange lines, or commuter rail. The MBTA (called the "T") costs 85 cents. Free shuttle buses connect the subway station with all airline terminals; they run from 5:30 AM to 1 AM. Shuttle bus 22 runs between Terminals A and B and the subway; shuttle bus 33 runs between the subway and Terminals C, D, and E.

**Taxis** can be hired outside each terminal. Fares to and from downtown should average about $15, including tip, via the most-direct route, the Sumner Tunnel, assuming no major traffic jams. The Sumner Tunnel is also the most direct route to Cambridge and the Massachusetts Turnpike (I-90). The Ted Williams Tunnel is the best bet for southbound travelers. It is usually open only to taxis and commercial traffic during the day on weekdays, but is open to all traffic after 10 PM daily. Lighted signs on major highways alert drivers to tunnel schedule changes.

US Shuttle provides door-to-door **van service** 24 hours a day between the airport and many Boston area destinations. Call and request a pickup when your flight arrives. To go to the airport, call for reservations 24–48 hours in advance. Sample one-way fares are $8 to downtown or the Back Bay, $15.50 to Cambridge.

➤ BOAT: The **Airport Water Shuttle** (☎ 800/235–6426). **Harbor Express** (☎ 617/376–8417). **Salem Shuttle** (☎ 978/741–3442).

➤ BUS: **Logan Express** or **Logan to South Station Service** (☎ 800/235–6426).

➤ SUBWAY: **MBTA** (☞ Subways & Trolleys, *below*).

➤ TAXI: **MASSPORT** (☎ 617/561–1751).

➤ VAN: **US Shuttle** (☎ 617/894–3100).

## BOAT & FERRY TRAVEL

Between April 1 and mid-October, water taxis ferry passengers between the World Trade Center, Congress St./Museum Wharf, Long Wharf, Rowes Wharf, North End/Burroughs Wharf, North Station/Fleet Center, Charlestown Navy Yard, Chelsea's Admiral's Hill, and other harbor destinations. One-way fares are $5 for non-airport stops, $10 to or from the airport. The service operates between 5 AM and 11 PM daily, but call ahead for reservations. Buy tickets on board.

Commuter boat service operates weekdays between Rowes Wharf and

Hewitt's Cove, off Route 3A in Hingham. Schedules change seasonally; call ahead.

➤ COMMUTER BOATS: **Boston Harbor Commuter Service** (✉ 60 Rowes Wharf, ☎ 617/439–4755). **Mass Bay Lines** (✉ 60 Rowes Wharf, ☎ 617/542–8000).

➤ WATER TAXIS: **City Water Taxi** (☎ 617/422–0392 or 800/235–6426).

## BUS TRAVEL TO AND FROM BOSTON

Greyhound has direct trips or connections to all major cities in North America. Peter Pan Bus Lines connects Boston with cities elsewhere in Massachusetts, Connecticut, New Hampshire, and New York. Plymouth & Brockton Buses link Boston with the South Shore and Cape Cod. The South Station terminal's multilevel bus deck simplifies making connections to other local public transportation.

➤ INTERSTATE BUSES: **Greyhound** (At South Station, ☎ 800/231–2222). **Peter Pan Bus Lines** (At South Station, ☎ 800/343–9999).

➤ INTRASTATE BUSES: **Plymouth & Brockton Buses** (At South Station, ☎ 508/746–0378).

## BUS TRAVEL WITHIN BOSTON

Buses of the Massachusetts Bay Transportation Authority (MBTA) crisscross the metropolitan area and travel farther into suburbia than subway and trolley lines. Some suburban schedules are designed primarily for commuters. Buses run roughly from 5:30 AM to 12:30 PM. Current local fares are 60¢ for adults; you must pay an extra fare for longer suburban trips. Smart Traveler provides current service updates.

➤ SCHEDULE AND ROUTE INFORMATION: **Massachusetts Bay Transportation Authority** (MBTA, ☎ 617/222–3200). **Smart Traveler** (☎ 617/374–1234).

## BUSINESS HOURS

Banks are generally open weekdays 9 to 4 (plus Saturday 9 to noon or 1 at some branches). Post office branches do business weekdays 8 to 5 and Saturday 9 to noon or 1, sometimes closing Thursday afternoon; the General Post Office (✉ 25 Dorchester Ave., behind South Station) is open around the clock. Public buildings are open weekdays 9 to 5.

## MUSEUMS & SIGHTS

Museums are generally open Monday through Saturday from 9 or 10 to 5 or 6 and Sunday noon to 5. Many are closed one day a week, usually Monday.

## SHOPS

Boston stores are generally open Monday through Saturday 9 or 9:30 to 6 or 7, later during the winter holidays. Mall shops often stay open until 9 or 10; malls and some tourist areas may also be open Sunday noon to 5 or 6.

## CAMERAS & PHOTOGRAPHY

➤ PHOTO HELP: **Kodak Information Center** (☎ 800/242–2424). *Kodak Guide to Shooting Great Travel Pictures,* available in bookstores or from Fodor's Travel Publications (☎ 800/533–6478; $16.50 plus $4 shipping).

### EQUIPMENT PRECAUTIONS

Always **keep your film and tape out of the sun.** Carry an extra supply of batteries, and **be prepared to turn on your camera or camcorder** to prove to security personnel that the device is real. Always **ask for hand inspection of film,** which becomes clouded after successive exposures to airport X-ray machines, and **keep videotapes away from metal detectors.**

## CAR RENTAL

Rates in Boston begin at about $30–$35 a day and $149 a week for an economy car with air-conditioning, an automatic transmission, and unlimited mileage. This does not include gas, insurance charges, or tax on car rentals, which is 5%.

➤ MAJOR AGENCIES: **Alamo** (☎ 800/327–9633; 020/8759–6200 in the U.K.). **Avis** (☎ 800/331–1212; 800/879–2847 in Canada; 02/9353–9000 in Australia; 09/525–1982 in New Zealand). **Budget** (☎ 800/527–0700; 0144/227–6266 in the U.K.). **Dollar**

(☏ 800/800–4000; 020/8897–0811 in the U.K., where it is known as Eurodollar; 02/9223–1444 in Australia). **Hertz** (☏ 800/654–3131; 800/263–0600 in Canada; 020/8897–2072 in the U.K.; 02/9669–2444 in Australia; 03/358–6777 in New Zealand). **National InterRent** (☏ 800/227–7368; 0345/222525 in the U.K., where it is known as Europcar InterRent).

### CUTTING COSTS

To get the best deal **book through a travel agent who will shop around.** Also **price local car-rental companies,** although the service and maintenance may not be as good as those of a major player. Remember to ask about required deposits, cancellation penalties, and drop-off charges if you're planning to pick up the car in one city and leave it in another. If you're traveling during a holiday period, also make sure that a confirmed reservation guarantees you a car.

### INSURANCE

When driving a rented car you are generally responsible for any damage to or loss of the vehicle as well as for any property damage or personal injury that you may cause. Before you rent see what coverage your personal auto-insurance policy and credit cards already provide.

For about $15 to $20 per day, rental companies sell protection, known as a collision- or loss-damage waiver (CDW or LDW), that eliminates your liability for damage to the car. However, **make sure you have enough coverage to pay for the car.** If you do not have auto insurance or an umbrella policy that covers damage to third parties, purchasing liability insurance and a CDW or LDW is highly recommended.

### REQUIREMENTS & RESTRICTIONS

In Boston you must be 21 to rent a car, and rates may be higher if you're under 25. You'll pay extra for child seats (about $3 per day), which are compulsory for children under five, and for additional drivers (about $2 per day). Non-U.S. residents will need a reservation voucher, a passport, a driver's license, and a travel policy that covers each driver, in order to pick up a car.

### SURCHARGES

Before you pick up a car in one city and leave it in another **ask about drop-off charges or one-way service fees,** which can be substantial. Note, too, that some rental agencies charge extra if you return the car before the time specified in your contract. To avoid a hefty refueling fee **fill the tank just before you turn in the car,** but be aware that gas stations near the rental outlet may overcharge.

### CAR TRAVEL

Driving is not easy in Boston. It's important to **look at a map first and have one with you at all times** due to the profusion of one-way streets and streets with the same names.

If you must bring a car, **keep to the main thoroughfares and park in lots**—no matter how expensive—rather than on the street. Also, remember that the massive highway reconstruction project, nicknamed "the Big Dig," disrupts downtown traffic, causing detours and delays.

### EMERGENCIES

**Dial 911** in an emergency to reach the police, fire, or ambulance services. If you are a member of the AAA auto club, you may reach their 24-hour help bureau.

➤ AAA EMERGENCY SERVICE:: AAA (☏ 800/222–4357 ).

### FROM THE AIRPORT

If you are driving from Logan to downtown Boston, the most direct route is by way of the Sumner Tunnel ($2 toll inbound; no toll outbound).

When there is a very serious traffic delay in the tunnel, one alternative is to take Route 1A north to Route 16 west, then to the Tobin Bridge and into Boston: From the airport, follow 1A north about 2½ mi. At a traffic light, the road will fork, with 1A bearing right toward Revere Beach and Lynn. Stay right as if you were continuing on 1A, but just past the traffic signal, immediately bear left to reverse direction, following the airport signs. As soon as you are back through the intersection, heading south on 1A, exit right at the sign for "16 West, Tobin Bridge/Chelsea." Follow 16 west to the Tobin Bridge ($1 toll) into Boston.

## GASOLINE

Gas stations are not plentiful in downtown Boston. Try Cambridge St. (behind Beacon Hill, near Massachusetts General Hospital), near the airport in East Boston, in Allston/Brighton along Commonwealth Ave. or Cambridge St., or off the Southeast Expressway in Dorchester. Cambridge service stations can be found along Memorial Drive, Massachusetts Ave., and Broadway. In Brookline, try Beacon St. or Commonwealth Ave.

## PARKING

Parking on Boston streets is a tricky business. Some neighborhoods have residents-only rules, with just a handful of two-hour visitors' spaces; others have meters (usually 25¢ for 15 minutes, one or two hours maximum). The meter maids are ruthless, and repeat offenders who don't pay fines may find the boot (an immovable steel clamp) secured to one of their wheels upon their return. In other words, **pay parking ticket fines** if you expect to come back to town.

Major public lots are at Government Center and Quincy Market, beneath Boston Common (entrance on Charles Street), beneath Post Office Square, at the Prudential Center, at Copley Place, and off Clarendon Street near the John Hancock Tower. Smaller lots and garages are scattered throughout downtown, especially around the Theater District. Most are expensive; expect to pay $10 to $12 for an evening and about $18 to park all day; the few city garages are a bargain at about $6–$10 per day.

## RULES OF THE ROAD

The speed limit on major highways in Massachusetts is 55 to 65 mph. Within the city of Boston and surrounding communities, speed limits on local streets are 20 to 30 mph. A right turn at a red traffic signal is permitted unless a NO TURN ON RED sign is posted. Rotary intersections are fairly common in Boston. When you are entering a rotary, state law dictates that you yield to any vehicle already in the rotary. Massachusetts state law requires all passengers in private cars to wear seat belts. Children under age 5 or weighing less than 40 pounds are required to ride in a child safety seat.

## CHILDREN & TRAVEL

### CHILDREN IN BOSTON

Boston is a great city for kids. It is home to world-class museums designed especially for children. Many of the historic sites in the city's compact and easily walkable center are outdoors along the Freedom Trail. The Boston Common and Public Garden, with boats and playgrounds, provide year-round fun for kids of all ages. Family-oriented value passes are available for many local attractions; contact the visitors bureau for information (☞ Visitor Information, *below*). Check out the *Boston Parents Paper* for events and resources; you'll find it at libraries, supermarkets, museums, children's shops, and nursery schools. If you are renting a car don't forget to **arrange for a car seat** when you reserve.

➤ LOCAL INFORMATION: Fodor's *Where Should We Take the Kids? Northeast* (available in bookstores, or ☎ 800/533–6478; $17). *Kidding Around Boston: What to Do, Where to Go and How to Have Fun in Boston,* by Helen Byers (John Muir Publications; $7.95).

### BABY-SITTING

➤ BABY-SITTING: **Parents in a Pinch** (45 Bartlett Crescent, Brookline, MA 02146, ☎ 617/739–5437).

### FLYING

If your children are two or older **ask about children's airfares.** As a general rule, infants under two not occupying a seat fly at greatly reduced fares or even for free.

Experts agree that it's a good idea to use safety seats aloft for children weighing less than 40 pounds. Airlines set their own policies: U.S. carriers usually require that the child be ticketed, even if he or she is young enough to ride free, since the seats must be strapped into regular seats. Do **check your airline's policy about**

SMART TRAVEL TIPS A TO Z

using safety seats during takeoff and landing. And since safety seats are not allowed everywhere in the plane, get your seat assignments early.

When reserving, **request children's meals or a freestanding bassinet** if you need them. But note that bulkhead seats, where you must sit to use the bassinet. may lack an overhead bin or storage space on the floor.

## LODGING

Most hotels in Boston allow children under a certain age to stay in their parents' room at no extra charge, but others charge them as extra adults; be sure to **ask about the cutoff age for children's discounts.** When planning your trip, **request a "Kids Love Boston" brochure** from the Greater Boston Convention and Visitors Bureau (☞ Visitor Information, *below*), which lists hotel packages for families and other discounts.

➤ BEST CHOICES: **Four Seasons Hotel** (200 Boylston St., Boston 02116, ☎ 617/338–4400). **Ritz-Carlton** (15 Arlington St., Boston 02117, ☎ 617/536–5700).

## SIGHTS & ATTRACTIONS

Places that are especially good for children are indicated by a rubber duckie icon in the margin.

### CONCIERGES

Concierges, found in many hotels, can help you with theater tickets and dinner reservations: a good one with connections may be able to get you seats for a hot show or prime-time dinner reservations at the restaurant of the moment. You can also turn to your hotel's concierge for help with travel arrangements, sightseeing plans, services ranging from aromatherapy to zipper repair, and emergencies. Always, **always tip** a concierge who has been of assistance.

### CONSUMER PROTECTION

Whenever shopping or buying travel services in Boston, **pay with a major credit card** so you can cancel payment or get reimbursed if there's a problem. If you're doing business with a particular company for the first time, **contact your local Better Business**

Bureau and the attorney general's offices** in your state and the company's home state, as well. Have any complaints been filed? Finally, if you're buying a package or tour, always **consider travel insurance** that includes default coverage (☞ Insurance, *below*).

➤ LOCAL BBBs: **Council of Better Business Bureaus** (✉ 4200 Wilson Blvd., Suite 800, Arlington, VA 22203, ☎ 703/276–0100, ℻ 703/525–8277). **Massachusetts Attorney General's Office, Consumer Division** (☎ 617/727–2200).

### CUSTOMS & DUTIES

When shopping, **keep receipts** for all purchases. Upon reentering the country, **be ready to show customs officials what you've bought.** If you feel a duty is incorrect or object to the way your clearance was handled, note the inspector's badge number and ask to see a supervisor. If the problem isn't resolved, write to the appropriate authorities, beginning with the port director at your point of entry.

### IN AUSTRALIA

Australia residents who are 18 or older may bring home $A400 worth of souvenirs and gifts (including jewelry), 250 cigarettes or 250 grams of tobacco, and 1,125 milliliters of alcohol (including wine, beer, and spirits). Residents under 18 may bring back $A200 worth of goods. Prohibited items include meat products. Seeds, plants, and fruits need to be declared upon arrival.

➤ INFORMATION: **Australian Customs Service** (Regional Director, ✉ Box 8, Sydney, NSW 2001, ☎ 02/9213–2000, ℻ 02/9213–4000).

### IN CANADA

Canadian residents who have been out of Canada for at least seven days may bring home C$500 worth of goods duty-free. If you've been away less than seven days but more than 48 hours, the duty-free allowance drops to C$200; if your trip lasts 24–48 hours, the allowance is C$50. You may not pool allowances with family members. Goods claimed under the C$500 exemption may follow you by mail; those claimed under the lesser exemptions must accompany you. Alcohol and tobacco products may be included in the seven-day and 48-hour exemptions but not in the 24-hour exemption. If you meet the age requirements of the province or territory through which you reenter Canada, you may bring in, duty-free, 1.14 liters (40 imperial ounces) of wine or liquor *or* 24 12-ounce cans or bottles of beer or ale. If you are 16 or older you may bring in, duty-free, 200 cigarettes and 50 cigars. Check ahead of time with Revenue Canada or the Department of Agriculture for policies regarding meat products, seeds, plants, and fruits.

You may send an unlimited number of gifts worth up to C$60 each duty-free to Canada. Label the package UNSOLICITED GIFT—VALUE UNDER $60. Alcohol and tobacco are excluded.

➤ INFORMATION: **Revenue Canada** (✉ 2265 St. Laurent Blvd. S, Ottawa, Ontario K1G 4K3, ☎ 613/993–0534; 800/461–9999 in Canada).

## IN NEW ZEALAND

Homeward-bound residents 17 or older may bring back $700 worth of souvenirs and gifts. Your duty-free allowance also includes 4.5 liters of wine or beer; one 1,125-milliliter bottle of spirits; and either 200 cigarettes, 250 grams of tobacco, 50 cigars, or a combination of the three up to 250 grams. Prohibited items include meat products, seeds, plants, and fruits.

➤ INFORMATION: **New Zealand Customs** (Custom House, ✉ 50 Anzac Ave., Box 29, Auckland, New Zealand, ☎ 09/359–6655, FAX 09/359–6732).

## IN THE U.K.

From countries outside the EU, including the United States, you may bring home, duty-free, 200 cigarettes or 50 cigars; 1 liter of spirits or 2 liters of fortified or sparkling wine or liqueurs; 2 liters of still table wine; 60 milliliters of perfume; 250 milliliters of toilet water; plus £136 worth of other goods, including gifts and souvenirs. If returning from outside the EU, prohibited items include meat products, seeds, plants, and fruits.

➤ INFORMATION: **HM Customs and Excise** (✉ Dorset House, Stamford St., Bromley Kent BR1 1XX, ☎ 020/7202–4227).

## IN THE U.S.

Non-U.S. residents ages 21 and older may import into the United States 200 cigarettes or 50 cigars or 2 kilograms of tobacco, 1 liter of alcohol, and gifts worth $100. Meat products, seeds, plants, and fruits are prohibited.

➤ INFORMATION: **U.S. Customs Service** (inquiries, ✉ 1300 Pennsylvania Ave. NW, Washington, DC 20229, ☎ 202/927–6724; complaints, ✉ Office of Regulations and Rulings, 1300 Pennsylvania Ave. NW, Washington, DC 20229; registration of equipment, ✉ Resource Management, 1300 Pennsylvania Ave. NW, Washington, DC 20229, ☎ 202/927–0540).

## DINING

The restaurants we list are the cream of the crop in each price category. Properties indicated by an ✕🏠 are lodging establishments whose restaurant warrants a special trip. *See also* Chapter 4, Dining.

| CATEGORY | COST* |
|----------|-------|
| $$$$ | over $40 |
| $$$ | $25–$40 |
| $$ | $15–$25 |
| $ | under $15 |

*\*per person for a three-course meal, excluding drinks, tip, and 5% sales tax*

## RESERVATIONS & DRESS

Reservations are always a good idea: we mention them only when they're essential or are not accepted. Book as far ahead as you can, and reconfirm as soon as you arrive. We mention dress only when men are required to wear a jacket or a jacket and tie.

## DISABILITIES & ACCESSIBILITY

### ACCESS IN BOSTON

In general, Boston has a number of two- and three-century-old buildings that are difficult to modify within the strictures of the Historical Commission. The Back Bay is flat with well-paved streets. Beacon Hill is steep and difficult, with uneven, often narrow brick sidewalks. Quincy Market's cobblestone and brick malls are crisscrossed with smooth, tarred paths. The downtown financial district, Charles Street, and Chinatown are reasonably accessible, while South Boston and the North End may prove problematic for wheelchair users.

➤ LOCAL RESOURCES: General information is available from the **Massachusetts Network of Information Providers for People with Disabilities** (☎ 617/642–0248 or 800/642–0249, TTY 800/764–0200). The **Massachusetts Office on Disability** (1 Ashburton Pl., 02108, ☎ 617/727–7440, TTY 800/322–2020) provides community outreach, advocacy, and education. The **Massachusetts Commission for the Deaf and Hard of Hearing** (210 South St., 5th Floor, 02111, ☎ 617/695–7500 or 800/882–1155, TTY 617/695–7600 or 800/530–7570, FAX 617/695–7599) provides an interpreter referral service and listings of recreational activities and events in the deaf community. They also have a 24-hour emergency number (☎ 800/249–9949 voice or TTY) for medical interpreters. The **Boston Center for Independent Living** (95 Berkeley St., 02116, ☎ 617/338–6665) is a self-help organization run by and for people with disabilities.

## LODGING

When discussing accessibility with an operator or reservations agent **ask hard questions.** Are there any stairs, inside *or* out? Are there grab bars next to the toilet *and* in the shower/tub? How wide is the doorway to the room? To the bathroom? For the most extensive facilities meeting the latest legal specifications **opt for newer accommodations.**

## SIGHTS & ATTRACTIONS

Many of Boston's most famous historic attractions are on or near the conveniently routed Freedom Trail, and most are wholly or partially accessible, as are most of the city's museums.

## TRANSPORTATION

Boston is filled with narrow, sometimes hilly, often winding and congested streets not conducive to car travel. The substantial number of curb cuts throughout the city is increasing steadily. Taxi travel is easier for wheelchair users in Boston than in most other places in the nation as a result of a recent law requiring a certain percentage of every cab company's taxis to be accessible.

Currently half the bus routes in Boston can handle people with disabilities. The Call/Lift Bus Program facilitates the remaining routes; to **arrange for special pickups, contact the MBTA bus system** by 1 PM on the day before you want to travel. Half the subway stations can accommodate people with disabilities; for complete information, **contact the subway system** (☞ Subways & Trolleys, *below*). The MBTA also offers a door-to-door pickup service called **The Ride.**

➤ AIRPORT TRANSPORTATION: The **Airport Handicapped Van** (☎ 617/561–1769) provides free service between terminals daily, on request.

➤ BUS/VAN TRANSPORTATION: Call **Lift Bus** (☎ 800/543–8287). **The Ride** (☎ 617/222–5123).

➤ COMPLAINTS: **Disability Rights Section** (✉ U.S. Department of Justice, Civil Rights Division, Box 66738, Washington, DC 20035-6738, ☎ 202/514–0301; 800/514–0301; 202/514–0301 TTY; 800/514–0301 TTY, FAX 202/307–1198) for general complaints. **Aviation Consumer Protection Division** (☞ Air Travel, *above*) for airline-related problems. **Civil Rights Office** (✉ U.S. Department of Transportation, Departmental Office of Civil Rights, S-30, 400 7th St. SW, Room 10215, Washington, DC 20590, ☎ 202/366–4648, FAX 202/366–9371) for problems with surface transportation. **Massachusetts Commission Against Discrimination** (✉ 1 Ashburton Place, ☎ 617/727–3990; TTY 617/720–6054.

## TRAVEL AGENCIES

In the United States, although the Americans with Disabilities Act requires that travel firms serve the needs of all travelers, some agencies specialize in working with people with disabilities.

➤ TRAVELERS WITH MOBILITY PROBLEMS: **Access Adventures** (✉ 206

Chestnut Ridge Rd., Rochester, NY 14624, ☎ 716/889–9096), run by a former physical-rehabilitation counselor. **CareVacations** (✉ 5-5110 50th Ave., Leduc, Alberta T9E 6V4, ☎ 780/986–6404 or 780/986–8332) has group tours and is especially helpful with cruise vacations. **Flying Wheels Travel** (✉ 143 W. Bridge St., Box 382, Owatonna, MN 55060, ☎ 507/451–5005 or 800/535–6790, FAX 507/451–1685). **Hinsdale Travel Service** (✉ 201 E. Ogden Ave., Suite 100, Hinsdale, IL 60521, ☎ 630/325–1335). ➤ TRAVELERS WITH DEVELOPMENTAL DISABILITIES: **Sprout** (✉ 893 Amsterdam Ave., New York, NY 10025, ☎ 212/222–9575 or 888/222–9575, FAX 212/222–9768).

## DISCOUNTS & DEALS

Be a smart shopper and **compare all your options** before making decisions. A plane ticket bought with a promotional coupon from travel clubs, coupon books, and direct-mail offers may not be cheaper than the least expensive fare from a discount ticket agency. And always keep in mind that what you get is just as important as what you save.

The Arts Boston coupon book offers 2-for-1 admission to 60 museums, attractions, and tour services in and around Boston. The booklets, which cost $9, can be purchased at Bostix booths in Copley and Harvard squares and in Faneuil Hall.

The CityPass is a reduced-fee combination ticket to six major Boston attractions: the John F. Kennedy Library and Museum, the John Hancock Observatory, the Museum of Fine Arts, the Museum of Science, the New England Aquarium, and the Isabella Stewart Gardner Museum. It is available at the Greater Boston Convention and Visitors Bureau information booths (☞ Visitor Information, *below*).

### DISCOUNT RESERVATIONS

To save money **look into discount-reservations services** with toll-free numbers, which use their buying power to get a better price on hotels, airline tickets, even car rentals. When booking a room, always **call the hotel's local toll-free number** (if one is available) rather than the central reservations number—you'll often get a better price. Always ask about special packages or corporate rates.

➤ AIRLINE TICKETS: ☎ **800/FLY–4–LESS.** ☎ **800/FLY–ASAP.**

➤ HOTEL ROOMS: **Accommodations Express** (☎ 800/444–7666). **Central Reservation Service (CRS)** (☎ 800/548–3311). **Hotel Reservations Network** (☎ 800/964–6835). **Quickbook** (☎ 800/789–9887). **Room Finders USA** (☎ 800/473–7829). **RMC Travel** (☎ 800/245–5738). **Steigenberger Reservation Service** (☎ 800/223–5652).

## PACKAGE DEALS

Don't confuse packages and guided tours. When you buy a package, you travel on your own, just as though you had planned the trip yourself. Fly/drive packages, which combine airfare and car rental, are often a good deal. In cities, ask the local visitor's bureau about hotel packages that include tickets to major museum exhibits or other special events.

## ELECTRICITY

Overseas visitors will need to bring adapters to convert their personal appliances to the U.S. standard: AC, 110 volts/60 cycles, with a plug of two flat pins set parallel to one another.

## EMERGENCIES

**Dial 911** for police, fire, ambulance.

➤ DOCTORS & DENTISTS: **Physician Referral Service** (☎ 617/726–5800); open weekdays 8:30–5. **Dental emergency** (☎ 508/651–3521). **Dental Referral** (☎ 800/917–6453).

➤ HOSPITALS: **Massachusetts General Hospital** (☎ 617/726–2000).

➤ 24-HOUR PHARMACIES: **CVS** (Porter Square Shopping Plaza, Massachusetts Ave., Cambridge, ☎ 617/876–5519); **CVS** (✉ 155 Charles St., Boston, ☎ 617/227–0437); **Osco** ( McGrath Hwy., Somerville, ☎ 617/628–2870); **Walgreens** (757 Gallivan Blvd., Dorchester, ☎ 617/282–5246).

➤ OTHER EMERGENCIES: **Poison control** (☎ 617/232–2120). **Traveler's Aid Society** (17 East St., ☎ 617/542–

7286; 617/737–2889; TTY 617/542–9482; FAX 617/542–9545); open weekdays 8:30–5; booths, open varying hours, at South Station (☎ 617/737–2880) and Logan Airport (✉ Terminal E, ☎ 617/567–5385); mayor's 24-hour traveler's aid hot line (☎ 617/635–4500).

### GAY & LESBIAN TRAVEL

Boston has a vibrant lesbian and gay populace, a large portion of whom live in the South End (☞ Chapter 2), one of the city's most racially and ethnically diverse neighborhoods. To find out what's the latest in Boston's lesbian and gay scene, **stop by Glad Day, New Words, or We Think the World of You bookstores** (☞ Books *in* Chapter 8), where you can **pick up a copy of *Bay Windows, IN Newsweekly,* and *Sojourner: The Women's Forum.***

➤ LOCAL RESOURCES: **AIDS Action Committee** (☎ 617/437–6200 or 800/235–2331). **Gay and Lesbian Helpline** (☎ 617/267–9001). **Cambridge Women's Center** (46 Pleasant St., Cambridge, ☎ 617/354–8807).

➤ GAY- AND LESBIAN-FRIENDLY TRAVEL AGENCIES: **Different Roads Travel** (✉ 8383 Wilshire Blvd., Suite 902, Beverly Hills, CA 90211, ☎ 323/651–5557 or 800/429–8747, FAX 323/651–3678). **Kennedy Travel** (✉ 314 Jericho Turnpike, Floral Park, NY 11001, ☎ 516/352–4888 or 800/237–7433, FAX 516/354–8849). **Now Voyager** (✉ 4406 18th St., San Francisco, CA 94114, ☎ 415/626–1169 or 800/255–6951, FAX 415/626–8626). **Yellowbrick Road** (✉ 1500 W. Balmoral Ave., Chicago, IL 60640, ☎ 773/561–1800 or 800/642–2488, FAX 773/561–4497). **Skylink Travel and Tour** (✉ 1006 Mendocino Ave., Santa Rosa, CA 95401, ☎ 707/546–9888 or 800/225–5759, FAX 707/546–9891), serving lesbian travelers.

### HOLIDAYS

Major national holidays include New Year's Day (Jan. 1); Martin Luther King Jr. Day (3rd Mon. in Jan.); President's Day (3rd Mon. in Feb.); Memorial Day (last Mon. in May); Independence Day (July 4); Labor Day (1st Mon. in Sept.); Thanksgiving Day (4th Thurs. in Nov.); Christmas Eve and Christmas Day (Dec. 24 and 25); and New Year's Eve (Dec. 31).

### INSURANCE

The most useful travel insurance plan is a comprehensive policy that includes coverage for trip cancellation and interruption, default, trip delay, and medical expenses (with a waiver for preexisting conditions).

Without insurance you will lose all or most of your money if you cancel your trip, regardless of the reason. Default insurance covers you if your tour operator, airline, or cruise line goes out of business. Trip-delay covers expenses that arise because of bad weather or mechanical delays. Study the fine print when comparing policies.

British and Australian citizens need extra medical coverage when traveling overseas.

Always **buy travel policies directly from the insurance company**; if you buy it from a cruise line, airline, or tour operator that goes out of business you probably will not be covered for the agency or operator's default, a major risk. Before you make any purchase **review your existing health and home-owner's policies** to find what they cover away from home.

➤ TRAVEL INSURERS: In the U.S. **Access America** (✉ 6600 W. Broad St., Richmond, VA 23230, ☎ 804/285–3300 or 800/284–8300), **Travel Guard International** (✉ 1145 Clark St., Stevens Point, WI 54481, ☎ 715/345–0505 or 800/826–1300). In Canada **Voyager Insurance** (✉ 44 Peel Center Dr., Brampton, Ontario L6T 4M8, ☎ 905/791–8700; 800/668–4342 in Canada).

➤ INSURANCE INFORMATION: In the U.K. the **Association of British Insurers** (✉ 51–55 Gresham St., London EC2V 7HQ, ☎ 020/7600–3333, FAX 020/7696–8999). In Australia the **Insurance Council of Australia** (☎ 03/9614–1077, FAX 03/9614–7924).

### LODGING

The lodgings we list are the cream of the crop in each price category. We always list the facilities that are available—but we don't specify whether they cost extra: when pricing accommodations, always ask what's included and what costs extra. Properties indicated by an ✕🔲 are lodging establishments whose restaurant warrants a special trip. *See also* Chapter 5, Lodging.

|  | BOSTON/ |  |
|---|---|---|
| CATEGORY | CAMBRIDGE | SIDE TRIPS |
| $$$$ | over $220 | over $180 |
| $$$ | $160–$220 | $130–$180 |
| $$ | $110–$160 | $80–$130 |
| $ | under $110 | under $80 |

*All prices are for a standard double room, excluding 9.7% tax and service charges.*

Assume that hotels operate on the European Plan (EP, with no meals) unless we specify that they use the Continental Plan (CP, with a Continental breakfast daily) or Breakfast Plan (BP, with full breakfast daily).

## APARTMENT RENTALS

If you want a home base that's roomy enough for a family and comes with cooking facilities **consider a furnished rental.** These can save you money, especially if you're traveling with a group. Home-exchange directories sometimes list rentals as well as exchanges. *See* the agencies listings for bed-and-breakfasts *in* Chapter 5, Lodging; often these agencies handle apartment rentals as well.

## B&BS

*See* the list of bed-and-breakfast agencies as well as select B&B reviews *in* Chapter 5.

## HOME EXCHANGES

If you would like to exchange your home for someone else's **join a home-exchange organization,** which will send you its updated listings of available exchanges for a year and will include your own listing in at least one of them. It's up to you to make specific arrangements.

➤ EXCHANGE CLUBS: **HomeLink International** (✉ Box 650, Key West, FL 33041, ☎ 305/294–7766 or 800/638–3841, FAX 305/294–1448; $88 per year). **Intervac U.S.** (✉ Box 590504, San Francisco, CA 94159,

☎ 800/756–4663, FAX 415/435–7440; $83 per year).

## HOSTELS

No matter what your age you can **save on lodging costs by staying at hostels.** In some 5,000 locations in more than 70 countries around the world, Hostelling International (HI), the umbrella group for a number of national youth-hostel associations, offers single-sex, dorm-style beds and, at many hostels, couples rooms and family accommodations. Membership in any HI national hostel association, open to travelers of all ages, allows you to stay in HI-affiliated hostels at member rates (one-year membership is about $25 for adults; hostels run about $10–$25 per night). Members also have priority if the hostel is full; they're eligible for discounts around the world, even on rail and bus travel in some countries. For a selection of hostels, *see* Chapter 5, Lodging.

➤ ORGANIZATIONS: **Hostelling International—American Youth Hostels** (✉ 733 15th St. NW, Suite 840, Washington, DC 20005, ☎ 202/783–6161, FAX 202/783–6171). **Hostelling International—Canada** (✉ 400–205 Catherine St., Ottawa, Ontario K2P 1C3, ☎ 613/237–7884, FAX 613/237–7868). **Youth Hostel Association of England and Wales** (✉ Trevelyan House, 8 St. Stephen's Hill, St. Albans, Hertfordshire AL1 2DY, ☎ 01727/855215 or 01727/845047, FAX 01727/844126). **Australian Youth Hostel Association** (✉ 10 Mallett St., Camperdown, NSW 2050, ☎ 02/9565–1699, FAX 02/9565–1325). **Youth Hostels Association of New Zealand** (✉ Box 436, Christchurch, New Zealand, ☎ 03/379–9970, FAX 03/365–4476). Membership in the U.S. $25, in Canada C$26.75, in the U.K. £9.30, in Australia $44, in New Zealand $24.

## HOTELS

All rooms have a private bathroom and no pets are allowed unless otherwise noted. Air-conditioning is noted only when it's unusual for the type of property, such as in historic buildings.

➤ TOLL-FREE NUMBERS: **Best Western** (☎ 800/528–1234). **Choice** (☎ 800/221–2222). **Clarion** (☎ 800/252–

7466). **Comfort** (☎ 800/228–5150). **Days Inn** (☎ 800/325–2525). **Doubletree and Red Lion Hotels** (☎ 800/222–8733). **Embassy Suites** (☎ 800/362–2779). **Forte** (☎ 800/225–5843). **Four Seasons** (☎ 800/332–3442). **Hilton** (☎ 800/445–8667). **Holiday Inn** (☎ 800/465–4329). **Howard Johnson** (☎ 800/654–4656). **Hyatt Hotels & Resorts** (☎ 800/233–1234). **Marriott** (☎ 800/228–9290). **Le Meridien** (☎ 800/543–4300). **Omni** (☎ 800/843–6664). **Quality Inn** (☎ 800/228–5151). **Radisson** (☎ 800/333–3333). **Ramada** (☎ 800/228–2828). **Renaissance Hotels & Resorts** (☎ 800/468–3571). **Ritz-Carlton** (☎ 800/241–3333). **ITT Sheraton** (☎ 800/325–3535). **Westin Hotels & Resorts** (☎ 800/228–3000). **Wyndham Hotels & Resorts** (☎ 800/822–4200).

## MONEY MATTERS

Sample costs: sandwich, $4–$7; slice of pizza, $1.50–$2.50; cup of coffee, $1–$2; bottle of beer, $3.50 and up; glass of wine, $4 and up. Museum entrance fees range from $7 to $13; many museums have one free-admission evening weekly.

Prices throughout this guide are given for adults. Substantially reduced fees are almost always available for children, students, and senior citizens. For information on taxes, *see* Taxes, *below.*

### CREDIT CARDS

Throughout this guide, the following abbreviations are used: **AE,** American Express; **D,** Discover; **DC,** Diner's Club; **MC,** Master Card; and **V,** Visa.

➤ REPORTING LOST CARDS: **American Express** (☎ 800/327–2177). **Discover Card** (☎ 800/347–2683). **Diners Club** (☎ 800/234–6377). **Master Card** (☎ 800/307–7309). **Visa** (☎ 800/847–2911).

### CURRENCY EXCHANGE

In the United States, it is not as easy to find places to exchange currency as it is in European cities. Currency may be exchanged at some bank branches, as well as at currency-exchange booths in airports and at foreign-currency offices such as Thomas Cook (check local directories for addresses and phone numbers). The best strategy is to **buy traveler's checks in U.S. dollars** before you come to the United States; although the rates may not be as good abroad, the time saved by not having to search for exchange facilities can often outweigh any financial loss.

For the most favorable rates, **change money through banks.** Although ATM transaction fees may be higher abroad than at home, ATM rates are excellent because they are based on wholesale rates offered only by major banks. You won't do as well at exchange booths in airports or rail and bus stations, in hotels, in restaurants, or in stores. To avoid lines at airport exchange booths **get a bit of local currency before you leave home.**

➤ EXCHANGE SERVICES: **International Currency Express** (☎ 888/842–0880 on East Coast; 888/278–6628 on West Coast). **Thomas Cook Currency Services** (☎ 800/287–7362 for telephone orders and retail locations).

### TRAVELER'S CHECKS

Do you need traveler's checks? It depends on where you're headed. If you're going to rural areas and small towns outside of Boston, be sure to bring cash; traveler's checks are best used in cities. Lost or stolen checks can usually be replaced within 24 hours. To ensure a speedy refund, buy your own traveler's checks—don't let someone else pay for them: irregularities like this can cause delays. The person who bought the checks should make the call to request a refund.

## PACKING

The principal rule on Boston weather is that there are no rules. A cold, overcast morning can become a sunny, warm afternoon—and vice versa. Thus, the best advice on how to dress is to **layer your clothing** so that you can remove or add garments as needed for comfort. Rain often appears with little warning, so remember to **bring a raincoat and umbrella.** Since Boston is a great walking city—with some picturesque but tough-on-feet cobblestone streets—be sure to **bring comfortable shoes.**

In your carry-on luggage **bring an extra pair of eyeglasses or contact lenses** and **enough of any medication you take** to last the entire trip. You may also want your doctor to write a spare prescription using the drug's generic name, since brand names may vary from country to country. In luggage to be checked, **never pack prescription drugs or valuables.** To avoid customs delays, carry medications in their original packaging. And don't forget to copy down and carry addresses of offices that handle refunds of lost traveler's checks.

### CHECKING LUGGAGE

How many carry-on bags you can bring with you is up to the airline. Most allow two, but not always, so make sure that everything you carry aboard will fit under your seat, and get to the gate early. Note that if you have a seat at the back of the plane, you'll probably board first, while the overhead bins are still empty.

If you are flying internationally, note that baggage allowances may be determined not by piece but by weight—generally 88 pounds (40 kilograms) in first class, 66 pounds (30 kilograms) in business class, and 44 pounds (20 kilograms) in economy.

Airline liability for baggage is limited to $1,250 per person on flights within the United States. On international flights it amounts to $9.07 per pound or $20 per kilogram for checked baggage (roughly $640 for a 70-pound bag) and $400 per passenger for unchecked baggage. You can buy additional coverage at check-in for about $10 per $1,000 of coverage, but it excludes a rather extensive list of items, shown on your airline ticket.

Before departure **itemize your bags' contents** and their worth, and label the bags with your name, address, and phone number. (If you use your home address, cover it so that potential thieves can't see it readily.) Inside each bag **pack a copy of your itinerary.** At check-in **make sure that each bag is correctly tagged** with the destination airport's three-letter code. If your bags arrive damaged or fail to

arrive at all, file a written report with the airline before leaving the airport.

### PASSPORTS & VISAS

When traveling internationally, **carry a passport** even if you don't need one; it's always the best form of ID. **Make two photocopies of the data page,** one to leave at home and another to be carried with you, separately from your passport. If you lose your passport, promptly call the nearest embassy or consulate and the local police.

➤ VISAS: **U.S. Embassy Visa Information Line** (☎ 01891/200–290; calls cost 49p per minute, 39p per minute cheap rate) for U.S. visa information. **U.S. Embassy Visa Branch** (✉ 5 Upper Grosvenor Sq., London W1A 1AE) for U.S. visa information; send a self-addressed, stamped envelope. Write the **U.S. Consulate General** (✉ Queen's House, Queen St., Belfast BTI 6EO) if you live in Northern Ireland. Write the **Office of Australia Affairs** (✉ 59th fl., MLC Centre, 19-29 Martin Pl., Sydney NSW 2000) if you live in Australia. Write the **Office of New Zealand Affairs** (✉ 29 Fitzherbert Terr., Thorndon, Wellington) if you live in New Zealand.

### PASSPORT OFFICES

The best time to apply for a passport or to renew is during the fall and winter. Before any trip, check your passport's expiration date, and, if necessary, renew it as soon as possible.

➤ AUSTRALIAN CITIZENS: **Australian Passport Office** (☎ 131–232).

➤ NEW ZEALAND CITIZENS: **New Zealand Passport Office** (☎ 04/494–0700 for information on how to apply; 04/474–8000 or 0800/225–050 in New Zealand for information on applications already submitted).

➤ U.K. CITIZENS: **London Passport Office** (☎ 0990/210–410) for fees and documentation requirements and to request an emergency passport.

### SENIOR-CITIZEN TRAVEL

To qualify for age-related discounts **mention your senior-citizen status up front** when booking hotel reservations (not when checking out) and before

**SMART TRAVEL TIPS A TO Z**

S M A R T   T R A V E L   T I P S   A   T O   Z

you're seated in restaurants (not when paying the bill). When renting a car ask about promotional car-rental discounts, which can be cheaper than senior-citizen rates.

➤ EDUCATIONAL PROGRAMS: **Elderhostel** (✉ 75 Federal St., 3rd fl., Boston, MA 02110, ☎ 877/426–8056, FAX 877/426–2166).

## SIGHTSEEING TOURS

### ORIENTATION TOURS

**Brush Hill/Gray Line** picks up passengers from hotels for 3½-hour Boston–Cambridge tours with stops at the USS *Constitution* and the Tea Party Ship, March through November. Other tours are available to Plymouth, Plimoth Plantation, Cape Cod, Salem and Marblehead, New Hampshire, and Newport. Reserve in advance. Adult fares range from $21 to $45, depending on the destination.

➤ BY BUS: **Brush Hill/Gray Line** (✉ Transportation Bldg., 14 Charles St. South, ☎ 617/236–2148 or 800/343–1328).

Narrated **trolley** tours last about 1½ hours and make frequent stops near Freedom Trail sites, other attractions, and hotels; you can get on and off as you wish. Hours of service listed are for summer; departures may be more infrequent and end earlier off-season.

➤ BY TROLLEY: The red **Beantown Trolleys** (✉ Transportation Bldg., 14 Charles St. S, ☎ 617/236–2148 or 800/343-1328) make 17 stops over two hours; cost is $18. Trolleys run every 20 minutes from 9 AM until 4 PM. **Old Town Trolley** (✉ 329 W. 2nd St., South Boston, ☎ 617/269–7010) runs every 30 minutes from 9 AM to 3 or 4 PM; adult fares are $21. Cambridge tours are also available. Call for details.

### THEME TOURS

➤ BANKING: The **Federal Reserve Bank** (✉ 600 Atlantic Ave., ☎ 617/973–3451) schedules free tours of its money-processing operations one Friday each month at 10:30 AM; reserve a week ahead. Children must be 12 or older and accompanied by an adult. No cameras are permitted.

➤ CHILDREN: **Make Way for Ducklings Tours** (✉ Historic Neighborhoods Foundation, 99 Bedford St., ☎ 617/426–1885) follow the route taken by the ducks in Robert McCloskey's eponymous children's book; designed for youngsters five and older, accompanied by adults, they're offered on Saturday in late spring and on Friday and Saturday from July 4 to Labor Day. Cost is $5 for kids, $7 for adults.

➤ GARDENS AND PARKS: **Beacon Hill Garden Club Tours** (✉ Box 302, Charles St. Station, 02114, ☎ 617/227–4392) are offered one day a year in mid-May. **Boston Park Rangers** (✉ Parks and Recreation Dept., ☎ 617/635–7383) lead free nature walks through many of the city's parks all year round.

➤ HISTORY: **Bay Colony Historical Tours** (✉ Box 9186, JFK Post Office, Boston 02114, ☎ 617/523–7303) offers prearranged private tours of the greater Boston area and Cape Cod for corporate clients, groups, and individuals.

➤ MANUFACTURING: *The Boston Globe* (✉ 135 Wm. T. Morrissey Blvd., ☎ 617/929–2653), the city's largest newspaper, gives free hourlong tours, by appointment, Tuesday and Thursday; participants must be at least 12 years old. The tiny **Commonwealth Brewing Company** (✉ 138 Portland St., ☎ 617/523–8383), which began making English-style ales and stouts by traditional methods in 1986, has free tours daily on request. The one-hour tours of the **Boston Beer Museum** and Samuel Adams brewery (✉ Boston Beer Company, 30 Germania St., Jamaica Plain, ☎ 617/368–5080), which end with a tasting, are given on Thursday and Friday at 2 and on Saturday at noon, 1, and 2. In July and August, there's an additional tour Wednesday at 2. A $1 donation is requested; it benefits a local charity.

### WALKING TOURS

➤ AFRICAN-AMERICAN: **Black Heritage Trail** (☎ 617/742–5415 or 617/739–2000; ☞ Chapter 2), a self-guided walk, explores Boston's 19th-century black community, passing 14 sites of historical importance on Beacon Hill. Brochures are available at the Visitor Information Center on the Boston Common (⊠ Facing Tremont St.). Rangers lead 90-minute guided walks from April to October a few times daily, and in winter by appointment.

➤ BEACON HILL: The **Society for the Preservation of New England Antiquities** (SPNEA; ⊠ 141 Cambridge St., ☎ 617/227–3956) conducts a walking tour of Beacon Hill that focuses on the neighborhood as it was in about 1810. Tours are given on most Saturdays May through October at 3 PM, with an extra 10 AM tour usually added in October. The cost is $10.

➤ HISTORIC NEIGHBORHOODS: The nonprofit **Historic Neighborhoods Foundation** (⊠ 99 Bedford St., ☎ 617/426–1885) covers the North End, Chinatown, Beacon Hill, the waterfront, and other urban areas on 90-minute guided walks Wednesday through Saturday from April through November. Tours cost at least $5.

➤ GENERAL-INTEREST: The 2½-mi **Freedom Trail** (☎ 617/242–5642) follows a red line past 16 of Boston's most important historic sites. National park rangers give free 90-minute guided tours daily from April to November. The nonprofit **Boston by Foot** (⊠ 77 N. Washington St., ☎ 617/367–2345 or 617/367–3766 for recorded information) offers guided 90-minute walks daily from May to October with specially trained volunteers. Most tours cost roughly $8.

➤ MARITIME HISTORY: **Harborwalk**, a self-guided tour, traces Boston's maritime history. Maps are available at the information center on Boston Common.

➤ SPECIAL-INTEREST: The **Boston Center for Adult Education** (⊠ 5 Commonwealth Ave., ☎ 617/267–4430) and the **Cambridge Center for Adult Education** (⊠ 42 Brattle St., Cambridge, ☎ 617/547–6789) periodically offer walking tours with themes ranging from contemporary art to Jewish Boston, Back Bay mansions, and the North End. **Victorian Society in America/New England Chapter** (⊠ Gibson House Museum,

137 Beacon St., ☎ 617/267–6338) tours specific sites, neighborhoods, and architecture representative of the Victorian era.

➤ WOMEN'S HISTORY: **Women's Heritage Trail** (☎ 617/522–2872) celebrates more than 80 accomplished women on four self-guided walks. The Old State House (⊠ 206 Washington St.) and the National Park Service visitor center (⊠ 15 State St.) sell maps for $5.

## WATER TOURS

➤ AROUND THE HARBOR: **Boston Harbor Cruises** (⊠ 1 Long Wharf, ☎ 617/227–4321) runs harbor tours from mid-April through October; other trips include sunset and evening entertainment cruises, a lunchtime ride, and trips to the Boston Harbor Islands (Memorial Day–Labor Day). **Massachusetts Bay Lines** (⊠ 60 Rowes Wharf, ☎ 617/542–8000) offers evening cruises with rock, blues, or reggae music and dancing, concessions, and cash bar, as well as daily harbor tours and sunset cruises.

➤ CHARLES RIVER BASIN: The **Charles Riverboat Co.** (⊠ 100 CambridgeSide Pl., Suite 320, Cambridge, ☎ 617/621–3001) offers a 55-minute narrated tour of the Charles River Basin. Tours depart from the CambridgeSide Galleria Mall on the hour from noon to 5 daily from June through August and on weekends in April, May, and September; the fare is $8. **Boston Duck Tours** (⊠ 790 Boylston St., Plaza Level, ☎ 617/723–3825) has 80-minute land-water tours that pair major Boston landmarks with a half-hour ride on the Charles River. Tours begin and end at the Huntington Avenue entrance to the Prudential Center (⊠ 101 Huntington Ave.). From April through November, tours leave every half hour, 9 AM till dark; the adult fare is about $20; less for children 3–12). Tickets are sold inside the Prudential Center 9–8 weekdays and Saturday, 9–6 Sunday; a limited number of tickets are available for purchase up to two days in advance.

➤ TO GLOUCESTER: **AC Cruise Company** (290 Northern Ave., ☎ 617/261–6633 or 800/422–8419) offers daily trips to Gloucester from Memorial Day through Labor Day, departing at 10 AM from its Northern Avenue pier; fare is about $18.

➤ WHALE-WATCHING: Most whale-watching cruises run between April and the end of October. Adult fares range from $18 to $25. Cruises are available from the following operators: **AC Cruise Company** (290 Northern Ave., ☎ 617/261–6633 or 800/422–8419); **Boston Harbor Cruises** (1 Long Wharf, ☎ 617/227–4321); **Massachusetts Bay Lines** (60 Rowes Wharf, ☎ 617/542–8000); **New England Aquarium** (Central Wharf, off Atlantic Ave., ☎ 617/973–5277). *See also* Chapter 7, Outdoor Activities and Sports.

## STUDENTS IN BOSTON

Reduced student admission prices are offered at some historic attractions and museums.

➤ STUDENT I.D.s & SERVICES: **Council on International Educational Exchange** (CIEE, ✉ 205 E. 42nd St., 14th fl., New York, NY 10017, ☎ 212/822–2600 or 888/268–6245, ℻ 212/822–2699) for mail orders only, in the U.S. **Travel Cuts** (✉ 187 College St., Toronto, Ontario M5T 1P7, ☎ 416/979–2406 or 800/667–2887) in Canada.

## SUBWAYS & TROLLEYS

The Massachusetts Bay Transportation Authority (MBTA)—or "T" for short—operates subways, elevated trains, and trolleys along four connecting lines. Call the 24-hour hotline (*below*) for information on bus, subway, and train routes; schedules; fares; wheelchair access; and other matters. Free maps are available at the MBTA's Park Street Station information stand, which is open daily 7 AM–10 PM.

➤ SUBWAY INFORMATION: **MBTA** (617/222–3200 or 800/392–6100, TTY 617/722–5146 ).

## FARES & SCHEDULES

Trains operate from about 5:30 AM to about 12:30 AM. Current T fares are 85¢ for adults, 40¢ for children ages 5–11. An extra fare is required heading inbound from distant Green Line stops and both inbound and out-bound on the most distant Red Line stops (for example, fare each way from Braintree is $1.70). Fares on commuter rail—the Purple Line—vary widely; check with the MBTA.

## ROUTES

The **Red Line** originates at Braintree and Mattapan to the south; the routes join near South Boston and proceed to suburban Arlington. The **Green Line,** a combined underground and elevated surface line, uses trolleys that operate underground in the central city. It originates at Cambridge's Lechmere, heads south and divides into four routes; these end at Boston College (Commonwealth Avenue), Cleveland Circle (Beacon Street), Riverside, and Heath Street (Huntington Avenue). Buses connect Heath Street to the old Arborway terminus. The **Blue Line** runs weekdays from Bowdoin Square and weeknights and weekends from Government Center to the Wonderland Racetrack in Revere, north of Boston. The **Orange Line** runs from Oak Grove in north suburban Malden to Forest Hills near the Arnold Arboretum. Park Street Station (on the Common) and State Street are the major downtown transfer points.

## VISITOR PASSES

MBTA visitor passes are available for unlimited travel on city buses and subways for one-, three-, and seven-day periods (fares $5, $9, and $18 respectively). Buy passes at the following MBTA stations: Airport, South Station, North Station, Back Bay, Government Center, and Harvard Square. Passes are also sold at the Boston Common Information Kiosk (☞ Visitor Information, *below*) and at some hotels.

## TAXES

**Sales tax** of 5% is added to restaurant and take-out meals and to all other items except non-restaurant food and clothing valued less than $175. Hotel room charges in Boston and Cambridge are subject to state and local taxes of up to 12.45%.

## TAXIS

Cabs may be hailed on the street; they're available around the clock. It's easiest to **go to a hotel taxi stand** or **call for a cab.** A taxi ride within the city of Boston starts at $1.50, plus 25¢ for the first quarter mile and 25¢ for each eighth of a mile thereafter. One-way streets often make circuitous routes necessary and increase your cost.

➤ CAB COMPANIES: **Boston Cab Association** (☎ 617/536–3200). **Checker** (☎ 617/536–7000). **Green Cab Association** (☎ 617/628–0600). **Independent Taxi Operators Association or ITOA** (☎ 617/426–8700). **Town Taxi** (☎ 617/536–5000). In Cambridge, **Ambassador Brattle Cab** (☎ 617/492–1100). **Cambridge Checker Cab** (☎ 617/497–1500).

## TELEPHONES

### DIRECTORY & OPERATOR INFORMATION

For assistance from an operator, dial "0". To find out a telephone number, call directory assistance, 555–1212 in every locality. These calls are free even from a pay phone. If you want to charge a long-distance call to the person you're calling, you can call collect by dialing "0" instead of "1" before the 10-digit number, and an operator will come on the line to assist you (the party you're calling, however, has the right to refuse the call).

### INTERNATIONAL CALLS

International calls can be direct-dialed from most phones; dial "011," followed by the country code and then the local number (the front pages of many local telephone directories include a list of overseas country codes). To have an operator assist you, dial "0" and ask for the overseas operator. The country code for Australia is 61; New Zealand, 64; and the United Kingdom, 44. To reach Canada, dial "1", followed by the area code and number.

### LOCAL CALLS

The area code for Boston, Cambridge, Brookline, and the innermost ring of suburban towns is 617. Communities in the next ring of suburbs, from Duxbury and Kingston to the south, Wellesley and Lincoln to the west, to Salem and Marblehead north of Boston, are in the 781 area. The area code for towns farther south, including those on Cape Cod, is 508, while communities to the north are in the 978 area.

### LONG-DISTANCE CALLS

Competitive long-distance carriers make calling within the United States relatively convenient and let you avoid hotel surcharges. By dialing an 800 number, you can get connected to the long-distance company of your choice.

➤ LONG-DISTANCE CARRIERS: **AT&T** (☎ 800/225–5288). **MCI** (☎ 800/888–8000). **Sprint** (☎ 800/366–2255).

### PUBLIC PHONES

Local calls from public phones cost between 25–35¢. Instructions for pay telephones should be posted on the phone. If you dial a long-distance number, the operator will come on the line and tell you how much more money you must insert for your call to go through.

## TIME

Boston is in the Eastern Standard Time zone. It is three hours ahead of Los Angeles, one hour ahead of Chicago, five hours behind London, and 15 hours behind Sydney.

## TIPPING

In restaurants, the standard gratuity is 15%–20% of your bill. Many restaurants automatically add a 15%–20% gratuity for large groups, so if your party includes six or more, ask if a service charge is included. Tip taxi drivers 15% of the fare, airport and hotel porters at least $1 per bag.

## TOURS & PACKAGES

On a prepackaged tour or independent vacation everything is prearranged so you'll spend less time planning—and often get it all at a good price.

### BOOKING WITH AN AGENT

Travel agents are excellent resources. But it's a good idea to collect brochures from several agencies because some agents' suggestions may be influenced by relationships with tour and package firms that reward them for volume sales. If you have a special interest **find an agent with expertise in that area**; ASTA (☞ Travel Agencies, *below*) has a database of specialists worldwide.

Make sure your travel agent knows the accommodations and other services of the place they're recommending. Ask about the hotel's location, room size, beds, and whether it has a pool, room service, or programs for children, if you care about these. Has your agent been there in person or sent others whom you can contact?

Do some homework on your own, too: local tourism boards can provide information about lesser-known and small-niche operators, some of which may sell only direct.

### BUYER BEWARE

Each year consumers are stranded or lose their money when tour operators—even large ones with excellent reputations—go out of business. So **check out the operator.** Ask several travel agents about its reputation, and try to **book with a company that has a consumer-protection program.** (Look for information in the company's brochure.) In the United States, members of the National Tour Association and United States Tour Operators Association are required to set aside funds to cover your payments and travel arrangements in case the company defaults. It's also a good idea to choose a company that participates in the American Society of Travel Agent's Tour Operator Program (TOP); ASTA will act as mediator in any disputes between you and your tour operator.

Remember that the more your package or tour includes the better you can predict the ultimate cost of your vacation. Make sure you know exactly what is covered, and **beware of hidden costs.** Are taxes, tips, and transfers included? Entertainment and excursions? These can add up.

➤ TOUR-OPERATOR RECOMMENDA-TIONS: **American Society of Travel Agents** (☞ Travel Agencies, *below*). **National Tour Association** (NTA, ✉ 546 E. Main St., Lexington, KY 40508, ☎ 606/226–4444 or 800/ 682–8886). **United States Tour Operators Association** (USTOA, ✉ 342 Madison Ave., Suite 1522, New York, NY 10173, ☎ 212/599–6599 or 800/ 468–7862, FAX 212/599–6744).

## TRAIN TRAVEL

Boston is served by Amtrak at South Station and Back Bay Station, which accommodates frequent departures for and arrivals from New York, Philadelphia, and Washington, D.C. New high-speed trains scheduled to debut in late 1999 or 2000 will cut the travel time between Boston and New York from 4 ½ hours to 3 hours. South Station is also the eastern terminus of Amtrak's *Lake Shore Limited,* which travels daily between Boston and Chicago by way of Albany, Rochester, Buffalo, and Cleveland. An additional Amtrak station is based just off Route 128 in suburban Canton.

The MBTA runs commuter trains to points south, west, and north. Those bound for Framingham, Needham, Franklin, Providence (RI), and Stoughton leave from South Station and Back Bay Station; those to Fitchburg, Lowell, Haverhill, Ipswich, and Rockport operate out of North Station (✉ Causeway and Friend Sts.) MBTA's Old Colony commuter line connects Boston's South Station with points south, running through Braintree to Plymouth and Middleboro; a third line to coastal Scituate was in the works at press time. (☞ Subways & Trolleys, *above*.)

➤ TRAIN INFORMATION: **Amtrak** (☎ 617/482–3660 or 800/872–7245). **MBTA** (☎ 617/222–3200). **South Station** (Atlantic Ave. and Summer St., ☎ 617/345–7451).

## TRANSPORTATION AROUND BOSTON

Most of the Boston area was laid out long before the automobile, so streets—particularly in older neighborhoods such as Beacon Hill and the North End—can lose their charm when you're a driver frustrated by the lack of parking. Boston's public transportation system, the T (☞ Subways & Trolleys, *above*) is superlative; it is easy and inexpensive and can get you quickly from one end of the city to another or from Boston to Cambridge or other outlying towns. If you're planning to try an out-of-the-way restaurant at an odd hour, a car will be helpful, and it will also make visiting Boston's farther-flung sights—such as those in the "streetcar suburbs" (☞ Chapter 2)—easier. For excursions outside the city, a car is practically required.

## TRAVEL AGENCIES

A good travel agent puts your needs first. Look for an agency that has been in business at least five years, emphasizes customer service, and has someone on staff who specializes in your destination. In addition, **make sure the agency belongs to a professional trade organization.** The American Society of Travel Agents (ASTA), with 27,000 agents in some 170 countries, is the largest and most influential in the field. Operating under the motto "Integrity in Travel," it maintains and enforces a strict code of ethics and will step in to help mediate any agent-client disputes if necessary. ASTA also maintains a Web site that includes a directory of agents. (Note that if a travel agency is also acting as your tour operator, *see* Buyer Beware in Tour Operators, *above*).

➤ LOCAL AGENT REFERRALS: American Society of Travel Agents (ASTA, ☎ 800/965–2782 24-hr hot line, ℻ 703/684–8319, www.astanet.com). **Association of Canadian Travel Agents** (✉ 1729 Bank St., Suite 201, Ottawa, Ontario K1V 7Z5, ☎ 613/521–0474, ℻ 613/521–0805). **Association of British Travel Agents** (✉ 55–57 Newman St., London W1P 4AH, ☎ 020/7637–2444, ℻ 020/7637–0713). **Australian Federation of Travel Agents** (✉ Level 3, 309 Pitt St., Sydney 2000, ☎ 02/9264–3299, ℻ 02/9264–1085). **Travel Agents' Association of New Zealand** (✉ Box 1888, Wellington 10033, ☎ 04/499–0104, ℻ 04/499–0786).

## VISITOR INFORMATION

Before you go, contact the city and state tourism offices below for general information. The National Park Service has a Boston office where you can watch an eight-minute slide show on Boston's historic sites and get maps and directions. For general information when you get to Boston, look for the Welcome Center and Boston Common Information Kiosk. The Traveler's Aid Society helps distressed travelers.

➤ CITY: **Greater Boston Convention and Visitors Bureau** (2 Copley Pl., Suite 105, Boston 02116, ☎ 617/536–4100 or 800/888–5515). **Boston Common Information Kiosk** (Tremont St., where the Freedom Trail begins, ☎ 617/426–3115); open Monday–Saturday 8:30–5 and Sunday 9–5. **Boston Welcome Center** (140 Tremont St., Boston 02111, ☎ 617/451–2227); open Sunday–Thursday 9–5 and Friday–Saturday 9–6 in winter, open till daily 9–7 (except Sunday 9–5) in summer. **Traveler's Aid Society** (☞ Emergencies, *above*).

➤ CAMBRIDGE: **Cambridge Tourism Office** (✉ 18 Brattle St., ☎ 617/441–2884 or 800/862–5678).

➤ NATIONAL PARKS: **The Boston National Historical Park Visitor Center** (15 State St., across from Old State House, ☎ 617/242–5642) is open daily 9–5 in winter, daily 9–6 in summer.

➤ STATE: **Massachusetts Office of Travel and Tourism** (100 Cambridge St., 13th floor, Boston 02202, ☎ 617/727–3201 or 800/447–6277, ℻ 617/727–6525).

➤ IN THE U.K.: **First Public Relations** (Molasses House, Clove Hitch Quay, Plantation Wharf, London SW11 3TN, ☎ 020/7978–5233, ℻ 020/7924–3134).

## WEB SITES

Do check out the World Wide Web when you're planning your trip. Fodor's Web site, **www.fodors.com**, is a good place to start your on-line travels. The **Greater Boston Convention and Visitors Bureau** Web site (www.bostonusa.com) is a great general resource, covering seasonal events, discount passes, attraction information, and more. The **Massachusetts Office of Travel and Tourism** site (www.mass-vacation.com) also provides trip planning and events information, plus fun features like a "lobster tutorial." For more information about Cambridge sights, events, and visitor services, including a section on bookstores, visit the **Cambridge Office for Tourism** site (www.cambridge-usa.org).

On the **Central Artery/Tunnel Project** site (www.bigdig.com) you can check on the current status of the mammoth construction project with updates on traffic detours. The *Boston Globe*'s site (www.boston.com) includes newspaper articles, local directories, etc. For edgy entertainment listings and reviews, head to the *Boston Phoenix* site (www.bostonphoenix.com/indexo.html). The monthly *Boston* magazine's site (www.bostonmagazine.com) has a rich stock of feature articles and reviews, plus the results of its annual "Best of Boston" awards.

## WHEN TO GO

Where the weather is concerned, it's best to **visit Boston in late spring and in September and October.** Like other American cities of the northeast, Boston can be uncomfortably hot and humid in high summer and freezing cold in the winter. Yet the city is not without its pleasures in these seasons. In summer, there are concerts on the Esplanade, harbor cruises, and sidewalk cafés. In winter there is Christmas shopping, First Night festivities on New Year's Eve, and music season. And a lot can be said for winter afternoon light on red brick.

Each September, Boston and Cambridge welcome thousands of returning students. University life is a big part of the local atmosphere, and it begins to liven considerably as the days grow shorter.

Autumn is a fine time to visit the suburbs. The combination of bright foliage and white church steeples will never become clichéd.

For a classic shore vacation, summer is the only time to go, but make your reservations early in the year.

### CLIMATE

| Jan. | 36F | 2C | May | 66F | 19C | Sept. | 71F | 22C |
|---|---|---|---|---|---|---|---|---|
| | 20 | −7 | | 49 | 9 | | 55 | 13 |
| Feb. | 37F | 3C | June | 75F | 24C | Oct. | 62F | 17C |
| | 21 | −6 | | 58 | 14 | | 46 | 8 |
| Mar. | 43F | 6C | July | 80F | 27C | Nov. | 49F | 9C |
| | 28 | −2 | | 63 | 17 | | 35 | 2 |
| Apr. | 54F | 12C | Aug. | 78F | 26C | Dec. | 40F | 4C |
| | 38 | 3 | | 62 | 17 | | 25 | −4 |

➤ FORECASTS: **Weather Channel Connection** (☎ 900/932–8437), 95¢ per minute from a Touch-Tone phone.

# 1 DESTINATION: BOSTON

# THE CITIES NAMED BOSTON

WO DESTINATIONS NAMED Boston occupy the clutch of irregularly shaped peninsulas at the westernmost recess of Massachusetts Bay. The tourist's Boston is the old city, far older than the republic it helped to create, soul and anchor of that peculiar thing called New England civilization, and the cradle of American independence. Its most famous buildings are not merely civic landmarks but national icons; its great citizens are not the political and financial leaders of today but the Adamses, Reveres, and Hancocks who live at the crossroads of history and myth.

The other Boston, built no less by design than the original, is barely three decades old. This is the business traveler's destination, the new Boston created by high finance and higher technology, where granite and glass towers rise along what once had been rutted village lanes. In this new city, Samuel Adams is the name of a premium beer, and John Hancock is an insurance company with a dramatic headquarters tower designed by I. M. Pei.

It is entirely possible to come to Boston intent on visiting either the Freedom Trail or the 48th floor of Amalgamated Software and to get exactly what you want out of the experience. With a little extra time and effort, though, you can appreciate both the old and the new Boston and understand why they are really one and the same American city.

Boston is where the Mystic and the Charles flow together to form the Atlantic Ocean. That's the old attitude, and it has been reinforced by local anecdotes, such as the one about the Boston lady who said she had driven to the West Coast "by way of Dedham," and the one about the two Bostonians who blamed a spate of hot San Francisco weather on the fact that the sea was 3,000 mi distant.

The sayings and stories reinforce the popular notion that Boston is exceedingly self-important. Yet Bostonians are not the only people who take the place so seriously. Boston, in reality and in myth, surely looms larger than any other settlement of close to 600,000 souls in the United States, with the possible exception of San Francisco. The reason for this is hard to come by, but it has to be more than merely the result of masterful self-promotion on the part of a city where "the Lowells speak only to the Cabots, and the Cabots speak only to God" and the common folk used to vote "often and early for James Michael Curley."

Boston has an odd combination of reputations to live up to. For years, the standard line was that it was staid, respectable, and quick to raise its eyebrows at anything or anyone smacking of impropriety. It was a town in which the Watch and Ward Society recommended the books and plays that ought to be banned, where the major social outlets were evenings at the Symphony and afternoons at the Club, and where the loudest noise was the sound of dust and interest collecting on old Yankee money. More recently, word has gone around that Boston's enormous population of undergraduate and graduate students, artists, academics, wealthy Europeans, and smart young professionals who graduated and stayed on has made the town a haven for foreign movies, late-night bookstores, racquetball, sushi restaurants, unconventional politics, and progressive rock bands.

Neither view is closer to the truth than the other, and neither will do on its own. For all its age and small physical size, Boston is one of the least socially homogeneous cities on earth. Sure, men with three last names sit in leather wing chairs at the Somerset Club, but in most of the city the prevailing idea of a club is the Holy Name Society or the Sons of Italy. Yes, you will see lampposts plastered with ads for performances by radical dance collectives, but Boston's big political concerns revolve around which shade of Democrat is running for high city office (a Republican would as soon swim to Provincetown) and how he or she will dispense help to the homeless, asphalt to the potholes, and goodwill to the high-tech barons. Despite its small size, Boston compartmentalizes itself so neatly that you can come here and find as staid or as hip a city as you desire.

In considering the roots of the Boston image and the Boston reality, we have to recognize two overwhelming influences on the Boston we know today. The first is definitely Anglo-Saxon, which can be either Yankee or Brahmin. The second is unquestionably Irish. Though there may never have been much love lost between the two factions, Boston is their mutual creation.

Most of the Yankees' ancestors left England in the 17th or the 18th century with little more than the clothes on their backs. There was nothing aristocratic about them then, and there is nothing aristocratic about them today—assuming we encounter them as the unspectacular yeomen and urban-suburban bourgeoisie who constitute the base coat of New England's overlay of populations. In the 1700s and early 1800s, however, some of them began to acquire fortunes to go with their ancient lineage, and thus the Brahmin was born. The term was first used by Dr. Oliver Wendell Holmes in *The Autocrat of the Breakfast-Table*: "He comes of the Brahmin caste of New England. This is the harmless, inoffensive, untitled aristocracy." Holmes himself was a sterling example of a Brahmin, as was his son and namesake the Supreme Court justice. Although not spectacularly wealthy, the Holmeses were vastly learned and endowed with a sense of civic responsibility. When combined with pedigree, these qualities counted as much as money in establishing the Brahmin mystique.

Money counted less and less as the years separated the Brahmins from their merchant-prince and industrialist ancestors who provided them with their China-trade porcelain, Back Bay town houses, and summer homes in Nahant. It became something you had but didn't talk about, something you devoted no great amount of time to multiplying. One theory as to why Boston lost out to New York in the struggle for financial supremacy in post–Civil War America credits the practice of tying up family legacies in trusteeships so that potential venture capital was inaccessible to one's heirs. Making money with gusto began to seem gauche, a frenetic activity best left to ostentatious New Yorkers. It was thought far better to husband your resources and live a seemly life.

At worst, this attitude created a race of "cold-roast Bostonians," thin-lipped and tight with a dollar, as conservative in the realm of social and aesthetic ideas as they were with their portfolios. At best, it produced an atmosphere in which people spent their energies on public beneficence and the cultivation of the life of the mind. Such organizations as the Appalachian Mountain Club were talked into vigorous existence over sherry and biscuits in the homes of comfortable men. Colonel Henry Lee Higginson founded the Boston Symphony and financed it for years out of his own pocket. And men like Thomas Appleton cultivated salons in which good conversation for its own sake was the prized commodity.

**M**OST IMPORTANT, the old Yankee fortunes poured into education; putting money into college endowments was the logical extension of the acute concern with education that the Puritans brought to Boston in 1630 and that manifested itself during that first decade in John Harvard's donation of his library to form the cornerstone of Harvard College. Finally, it was the means by which the idea of Boston as stodgy, intolerant, and unchanging was laid to rest. The strains of liberality evident in the intellectual and economic climate today are owed to the tremendous influx of fertile minds that the great investment in education made possible.

As Boston is a city of colleges, it is also a city of neighborhoods. Neighborhoods are the bastions of continuity in a big city, places where a certain outlook and sense of parochial identity are preserved. Ironically, Boston's ethnic groups, the Irish in particular, have managed to maintain the conservative, tradition-minded neighborhood spirit cultivated by the Yankees when all Boston was the neighborhood. If any custom replaced beans and brown bread on Saturday night in the Back Bay, it was fish-and-chips during Lent in Charlestown and Southie. The Irish, in this century, have been the keel of Boston.

**T**HE IRISH BEGAN to arrive in the late 1840s, when the potato famine devastated their home island. Boston had never seen such an invasion of immigrants and was anything but ready. The famous "No Irish Need Apply" signs went up, although the rapid growth of the city made it necessary for the locals to give the Irish jobs. There were only so many farm girls willing to come to the city and enter domestic service, and few businesses during the boom time of the Civil War era could afford the Waltham Watch Company's "Yankees only" employment strictures.

The Irish found their way into jobs and into the social structure. Two avenues appealed to them especially: the civil service, particularly in the police and fire departments, and local politics. The venture into politics was in large part a defensive maneuver, a means of consolidating power in municipal institutions when it was denied them in the social and economic spheres. The first Irish mayor was elected in 1886, and by 1906 John F. Fitzgerald, the legendary "Honey Fitz," held the office. He was fiercely Irish, the most flamboyant and assertive Boston politician until Mayor Curley himself appeared and defined big-city machine politics.

The wresting of political power from the Yankees allowed the Irish and their more recently arrived ethnic allies to take care of their own, and loyalty and votes were the mortar in the agreement. Similarly, civil service and other relatively secure blue-collar positions were a path to the kind of security that translated itself into stable, parish-oriented neighborhoods made up of row upon row of triple-decker apartment buildings, the wooden monoliths known in Boston as "Irish battleships."

The Irish and other ethnics, then, are the heirs and guardians of the old Boston insularity and stability. It was neighborhood (not just Irish) discomfiture at the violation of this state of affairs that produced the terrible antagonisms associated with court-ordered school busing in the early 1970s. The new minorities—blacks, Hispanics, Asians—often find themselves in a situation similar to that faced by the new arrivals in the last century.

Nowadays working-class white enclaves and poor minority neighborhoods alike worry about the effects of gentrification, loosely defined as the migration of upper-middle-class, white-collar workers and professionals (including many gay men and lesbians and couples who haven't yet had children) into the core of the city, where there are town houses to be restored and apartments to be converted into condominiums. Places like Union Park in the South End and some of the streets around the Bunker Hill Monument in Charlestown look better than they have in years, and the city can certainly use the tax base. New businesses flourish, often selling gourmet scones and the *Wall Street Journal* across from Hispanic bodegas and tired old luncheonettes. There are people who insist that such blocks are pretty but sterile and that the old neighborhood identities have gone. One thing is certain: we have not seen the end of this movement.

The new gentry is evidence of the success of Boston's 30-year attempt to redefine its place in New England and the world. By the 1950s, Boston was living on its past. The industrial base had eroded, the population had begun to decrease (it is still about 100,000 below its peak), and the high-tech era had yet to begin. To successive mayors Hynes, Collins, and White, and to the fiscal nabobs who made up the private advisory group known as "the Vault," it seemed to make sense to play up the service aspects of the local economy and at the same time to launch vast tear-down-and-start-over projects like the Prudential Center and Government Center. By the '70s the emphasis had shifted from new construction to the recycling of old buildings, except downtown, where office towers rose at a frantic pace in the '80s.

To a significant degree the plan has worked, and the legions of condo buyers and townhouse restorers are part of a new order only temporarily slowed by the recession of the early '90s. What remains are the questions of how the old neighborhoods will fit in, whether the public school system can be salvaged, and whether there will be a middle class of any size in Boston as the new millennium unfolds.

Given a population with such divergent antecedents, it is difficult to point to a "typical" Bostonian, although you see a number of types—Cambridge academics, North Shore Brahmin ladies in town for the Friday afternoon symphony, business-suited young women with rucksacks and running shoes. Even the famous old Boston accent is hard to pin down, beyond a few broad *A*s and dropped *R*s; there are so many immigrants from other parts of the country that the native speech has become hopelessly diluted. (One thing is certain: *no one* talks like the Kennedys, who developed an Irish Brahmin accent all their own.)

Your essential Bostonian does love sports and politics, probably because both are vehicles for argument. The disputations could well be carried past recent Red Sox trades and the City Council to questions of whether Boston is on its way up or down, whether it is forward-thinking or preoccupied with the past, whether Boston is fashionable or dowdy, progressive or conservative, wise to the world or just kidding itself. Go into a bar, and pick your topic. You may well decide that it is sheer contentiousness, often mixed with respectable intelligence and more than a little rectitude, that put Boston on the map.

–William G. Scheller

The author of *More Country Walks Near Boston* and *New Hampshire: Portrait of the Land and Its People*, William Scheller contributes frequently to national and regional publications.

# NEW AND NOTEWORTHY

Downtown Boston is in the midst of a massive multiyear construction project, known locally as the **Big Dig.** When completed, the elevated Central Artery that bisects the downtown area will be redirected underground, and the city center will be reunited with the North End and the waterfront. In the meantime, traffic delays and street closings abound. Allow extra time when traveling in this area.

Construction is also under way at Boston's **Logan Airport.** Most visible in 2000 will be the continuing expansion and renovation of Terminal E, the international arrivals building, as well as ongoing construction on the airport access roads, which is expected to continue through 2003.

Getting to Boston by train may get easier in 1999–2000, when Amtrak introduces the long-awaited **high-speed rail service** along the Northeast Corridor. Travel time between New York and Boston should be cut to 2¾ hours.

The stained-glass **Mapparium** in the world headquarters of the Christian Science Church closed for renovations in March 1998 and is scheduled to reopen in February 2000. The colorful globe depicts the world as it was in 1932. Tours of the Mother Church and other church exhibits will continue.

The **New England Aquarium,** which celebrated its 30th anniversary in 1999, is also in the midst of a multiyear expansion effort. It plans to begin construction on an IMAX theater in 2000, which would open the following year. In the meantime, a major exhibit about East Africa's Lake Victoria, the world's second largest lake, is slated for 2000.

If you're interested in whales, you've come to the right place. There are now numerous options for **whale-watching trips** leaving from Boston, from Plymouth (south of Boston), and from the North Shore towns of Gloucester and Newburyport. You may also want to journey one hour south to the **New Bedford Whaling Museum,** where from 1999 to 2000 the skeleton of a 66-ft blue whale is being rebuilt.

Good news for food lovers: Boston's **restaurant** scene is still booming. The downside of this restaurant renaissance is that weekend reservations for the city's newest spots are hard to come by unless you book at least a couple of weeks in advance.

Finally, as you plan your trip to Boston, be sure to book a hotel or B&B room as far in advance as you can. Although the Boston area is in the midst of a **hotel building boom,** with more than a dozen new hotels slated to open in 1999, the city still has one of the highest hotel occupancy rates of any city in the nation—and increased rates at many of the city's better hotels. Peak times of year when rooms can be particularly hard to come by are the graduation months of May and June and the fall foliage season. Among the hotel developments under construction for 2000 is the **Millennium Project,** the largest mixed-use development in Boston since Copley

Place opened in 1984. Located opposite Boston Common between Tremont and Washington streets, this complex will include a 300-room hotel, as well as an 18-screen movie theater and a large shopping center.

# WHAT'S WHERE

Boston, at least north and east of Massachusetts Avenue, is a compact city whose neighborhoods can be divided along precise lines. They share only their passion for the Red Sox, zip codes beginning with 02, and the "T," as they call the Massachusetts Bay Transportation Authority, which unites them via trolleys, subways, elevated trains, and conventional buses. In many instances, their names recall their situation centuries ago, before land reclamations beginning after the American Revolution forever changed the shoreline.

## The Back Bay

Extending along the Charles opposite Cambridge as far as Kenmore Square, south and west of Beacon Hill, it's the epitome of propriety, a veritable open-air museum of urban Victorian residential architecture, by turns French-influenced, Italianate, and reflecting revivals of Gothic and other styles. Its streets recall Paris boulevards, which Baron Haussman had laid out not long before the Back Bay was developed on 19th-century landfill. The Public Garden, also built on landfill, is in character truly a part of the Back Bay, although just across Charles Street from the Common (which is more properly part of Beacon Hill). Copley Place, the Prudential Tower, and Symphony Hall are also here.

## Beacon Hill

Earth scraped off the top of this height of land, named for the light that topped it in the 17th century, was put to use as landfill not far away. What remains is redolent of old Boston, with its gas lamps, shade trees, brick sidewalks, and stately brick town houses built between 1800 and 1850 in Federal style; many are now broken up into condominium apartments. Two of the loveliest thoroughfares are

Chestnut and Mt. Vernon streets; the latter opens out onto Louisburg Square, where William Dean Howells and the Alcotts once lived.

## Charlestown

This neighborhood on the north end of the Charlestown Bridge, across from the North End, is home to Bunker Hill and the USS *Constitution*, a tangle of masts and rigging moored at the Charlestown Navy Yard, now a National Historic Site for its long and continuous involvement in the American shipbuilding industry. Charlestown is becoming increasingly gentrified; you can glimpse home computers and house plants through newly gleaming windows, while the neighborhood eateries are developing devoted followers among the "Townies."

## Downtown Boston and Chinatown

The city's retail and financial districts constitute downtown, anchored by Faneuil Hall and Quincy Market on the north; Chinatown, the Theater District, and South Station on the south; Tremont Street and the Common on the west; and the harbor and the New England Aquarium on the east. The main commercial thoroughfare is Washington Street. Elizabeth Pain, the model for Nathaniel Hawthorne's scarlet-letter-wearing Hester Prynne, is buried at King's Chapel, not far from the Theater District, the Old State House, and those monuments to the mercantile mentality, Filene's and Macy's.

## East Boston

With the airport, it's across the inner harbor to the north and east. Once a uniformly Italian neighborhood, East Boston is now also home to a thriving Latino population. Santarpio's Pizza is famous here, with a line stretching down Chelsea Street every night.

## The Fens

This is the former swampland, south of Kenmore Square and southwest of the Back Bay, that Boston planners filled with green space rather than pavement, commissioning 19th-century American landscape architect Frederick Law Olmsted to do the work. In his hands, the landscape retains an aura of its marshy origins, by way of irregular, reed-bound pools. But between them are wide meadows, trees, and gardens of flowers. Nearby is a baseball stadium, Fenway Park—built in 1912 and still with a field that's real turf—plus two celebrated art museums, the immense, important Boston Museum of Fine Arts and the idiosyncratic, Venetian palazzo–inspired Isabella Stewart Gardner Museum.

## The North End and Government Center

The northernmost tip of the peninsula, cut off from Boston's other neighborhoods by the Central Artery and Government Center, this is one of the city's oldest sections, and many of its earliest structures went up in the 17th century, when Shakespeare was a contemporary figure, albeit recently dead, and Louis XIV had just ascended to the French throne. The Old North Church, made famous in Longfellow's "Paul Revere's Ride," is here, along with—despite creeping gentrification—a lively Italian population and the businesses that serve the neighborhood: restaurants, groceries, bakeries, churches, social clubs, and cafés.

## The Old West End

Just a few brick tenements are all that remain of this area north of Beacon Hill across Cambridge Street and west of the Central Artery. Landmarks include the Charles River Park apartment and retail development, the Suffolk County Jail, and Mass General, as the local public hospital is known. However, you're more likely to find yourself in the area to visit the Museum of Science, to share a pint of Guinness with your mates at the Harp, or to watch the Celtics play basketball at the FleetCenter.

## South Boston

This area juts due east toward the outer harbor and its cluster of islands; it is not to be confused with the South End. Another landfill project of the mid-1880s, it came into its own around 1900 with the influx of Irish immigration, and the Irish are still an important presence. It's the site of the Boston Children's Museum and the world's only Computer Museum, adjacent. Hundreds of artists have descended on A Street, once a stretch of abandoned warehouses next to the post office, now transformed into posh lofts and galleries.

## The South End

Not to be confused with South Boston, this area hugging the Huntington Avenue flank of the Back Bay, southeast of the Back Bay and due south of Chinatown, is another 19th-century development. But with its park-centered squares and blocks of extravagantly embellished bowfront Victorian houses, it's less Parisian in style than English. Today it's multiethnic and polyglot, both Spanish and Asian, with Middle Eastern groceries along Shawmut Avenue and some gentrification, including a booming restaurant row along Tremont Street. Rainbow flags and window boxes decorate many of the brownstones, heralding its large gay population.

## Cambridge

A kissing cousin just across the Charles River from Boston, Cambridge has long been a haven for writers, radicals, free thinkers, and iconoclasts of all kinds. Home to two of the world's best universities—Harvard and MIT—and a huge population of students, Cambridge has an eclectic mix of cafés, bookstores, record shops, funky clothing outlets, and crafts galleries. Its Harvard University museums—the Fogg and the Peabody, most notably—are among the nation's best. Despite its rarefied reputation, Cambridge also has concentrated ethnic and working-class neighborhoods in East Cambridge and Cambridgeport, seemingly light-years from the Colonial-era mansions on tony Brattle Street near Harvard Square.

## Urban "Suburbs"

South of the Back Bay Fens is Roxbury, a largely black neighborhood that merges along its eastern border with multiracial but poorly integrated Dorchester, and Jamaica Plain, one of the first of the "streetcar suburbs" brought into existence by turn-of-the-century trolley lines. West of Kenmore Square is the separate municipality of Brookline, which almost completely cuts off Allston and Brighton, two residential and industrial Boston neighborhoods, from the rest of the city. Brookline, long home to many of the Boston area's Jewish families, now shares with Allston and Brighton an increasing number of Asian residents.

Farther south still are West Roxbury, Roslindale, Hyde Park, and Mattapan—virtual suburbs within the city. People here are more likely to identify themselves as coming from these neighborhoods than as hailing from Boston itself. After all, parts of them are farther from Beacon Hill than Cambridge, Medford, or Winthrop.

# PLEASURES AND PASTIMES

### Colleges

More than anything else, the Yankee investment in scores of colleges and universities in and around Boston has helped establish its present character. People come here for schooling and never go home. And every year in August and September, fleets of trucks, vans, and overloaded family sedans converge on the city as BC, BU, Harvard, MIT, Northeastern, and more than a dozen others welcome back the thousands of students who help rouse the city from its summer rest.

### Day Trips

You've only to travel a short distance to visit sites connected with historic figures you started reading about back in grade school. *See* Chapter 9 for the many different destinations nearby.

### History

Perhaps no one today would speak of the Boston State House as "the hub of the solar system," as Oliver Wendell Holmes once did, yet it is very much at the heart of American history, both past and present. So much of the political ferment that spawned the nation took place here. The earthly remains of Cotton and Increase Mather, the 17th-century Boston theocrats, are in Copp's Hill Burying Ground; the chips in the headstones came about during British soldiers' target practices, and you can still see the pockmarks of musket balls. It was at Faneuil Hall that Samuel Adams first suggested, in 1772, that the colonies organize a Committee of Correspondence to maintain lines of communication in the face of British oppression. In the North End is the Old North Church, famous for the two lanterns that glimmered from its steeple on the night of April 18, 1775, warning Americans of British troop movements by sea. Heroes of the American Revolution are buried in its Granary Burying Ground: Samuel Adams, John Hancock, James Otis, Paul Revere. American portraitist Gilbert Stuart is buried in the Central Burying Ground, along with scores of British casualties of the Battle of Bunker Hill. Moored in Fort Point Channel is a replica of one of the ships whose forcible unloading occasioned the famous Boston Tea Party. And all around these sights and sites are vintage buildings, both maintained and restored, so that the feeling of history surrounding you is almost palpable.

### Parks and Gardens

The Boston Common, the oldest public park in the United States, is only one of Boston's green spaces. The Boston Public Garden, which abuts it across Charles Street, is the country's oldest botanical garden; the irregularly shaped pond in the center is famous for the swan boats that cruise it in warm months. The Fens, a landscape of meadows, trees, gardens, and reed-bound pools designed by noted landscape architect Frederick Law Olmsted, marks the beginning of Boston's famous Emerald Necklace, a chain of parks that extends along the Fenway, Riverway, and Jamaica Way to Jamaica Pond, the Arnold Arboretum, and Franklin Park. This loosely connected necklace of green has made Boston famous among 20th-century urban planners.

### Walking

Boston is on a human scale, and it is best experienced by walking. The North End, Boston's Italian neighborhood, just a 20-minute walk from Beacon Hill, is quite another world. The highlight of any visit to Boston should be the memory of walks and sights around town: along the redbrick sidewalks of Beacon Hill (particularly Pinckney, Mt. Vernon, Chestnut, and Beacon streets), along the Freedom Trail through the crannied lanes of the North End, catching the Charles River breezes from the Esplanade, along the shores of the Public Garden's pond, along the Boston Harbor waterfront at the back side of the New England Aquarium, and through the Arnold Arboretum, especially in spring, when its lilacs, azaleas, rhododendrons, and fruit trees are in full bloom. Another memorable walk: from the Ritz-Carlton Hotel, down Newbury Street to Gloucester Street, right on Gloucester to Commonwealth Avenue, and right on Commonwealth to the Public Garden.

# GREAT ITINERARIES

You could easily spend two weeks exploring Boston and its surrounding towns, but if you're here for just a short period you need to plan carefully so you don't miss the must-see sights. The following suggested itineraries will help you structure your visit efficiently. *See* the Boston neighborhood exploring tours in Chapter 2 and the Cambridge neighborhood exploring tours in Chapter 3. As small in size as it is large in history, Boston can be thoroughly explored by foot. Bring sturdy walking shoes and be prepared for the ever-unpredictable weather.

## If You Have 2 Days

DAY 1➤ Start with a stroll through the **Public Garden.** Wander through the narrow streets of **Beacon Hill,** with a stop at the **Statehouse,** the **Granary Burying Ground,** and **King's Chapel.** Follow Beacon Street toward the Back Bay; after lunch on Charles Street, cross the **Boston Common** into **Downtown Crossing.** From there, follow the **Freedom Trail** to **Faneuil Hall** and **Quincy Market** (stopping for a late-afternoon drink) and into the North End for a visit to **Paul Revere's home** and the **Old North Church.** Dine at one of the neighborhood's trattorias, followed by cappuccino and cannoli at a pastry shop.

DAY 2➤ Spend the morning at the **Museum of Fine Arts,** accessible by the MBTA. Lunch in the **Gardner Museum.** Or spend the morning at the **New England Aquarium** and **Computer Museum.** In the afternoon, go by T into Cambridge to explore **Harvard Square,** or take the Green Line back to **Back Bay** for some elegant shopping on **Newbury Street.** As night falls, head for the Prudential Center's **Skywalk** for a romantic view of the city at sunset. Then it's time for dinner in the **Theater District,** followed by a late-night comedy show.

## If You Have 5 Days

DAY 1➤ Walk **Beacon Hill** and explore the **Black Heritage Trail.** Shop for antiques on

**Charles Street.** Explore the **Boston Common** and the **Public Garden,** and then take a stroll along the **Esplanade.** Dine in the evening in the **Theater District,** and follow that with a show.

DAY 2➤ Visit the **Museum of Science,** and then take a stroll along the **Charles.** Hop the T into **Kenmore Square** for dinner and spend the evening club-hopping on Landsdowne Street. Or, on a more sedate Wednesday night, spend the evening at the **Museum of Fine Arts** with dinner in the Fine Arts Restaurant.

DAY 3➤ Walk the **Freedom Trail,** pausing to shop at **Downtown Crossing** and **Faneuil Hall.** After visiting the **USS** *Constitution* in Charlestown, catch the water shuttle to downtown. Walk into the **North End** for dinner.

DAY 4➤ Visit **Plimoth Plantation** and the *Mayflower II* in Plymouth, south of Boston.

DAY 5➤ Walk through **Back Bay** to marvel at its mansions, with stops at the **Boston Public Library** and the **Gibson House.** Stroll along **Newbury Street** for fine shopping and dinner.

## If You Have 8 Days

You may wish to use an extended visit to linger at many sites. Although a car isn't necessary to explore Boston or Cambridge, you'll need it to get to sites some distance from the city. And if you don't venture out at rush hour, it takes just a short time to get outside the city limits.

DAY 1➤ Walk the **Freedom Trail** from the **Boston Common** to the **USS** *Constitution.*

DAY 2➤ On Boston's waterfront, visit either the **New England Aquarium,** the **Children's Museum,** or the **Computer Museum.** Top any of these off with the **Boston Tea Party Museum.** In the early summer, consider a whale-watching tour that leaves from the **Aquarium.**

DAY 3➤ Drive north to **Salem** for a day at the **House of Seven Gables,** the **Peabody Essex Museum,** and the **Salem Witch Museum.**

DAY 4➤ Explore **Beacon Hill** and the **Public Garden.** Take the kids for a swan boat ride. On a fine day, walk to the **Charles River** and watch the sailboats. In inclement weather, spend the day at the **Museum of Science.** Dine in the **South End** on Tremont

Street and take in an avant-garde play nearby at the **Boston Center for the Arts.**

DAY 5➤ Visit **Plimoth Plantation** and the **Mayflower II.** Or, if the weather is good, pack a picnic lunch and spend the day swimming, sunning, and exploring **Walden Pond** in Concord. In the fall, do some leaf peeping at Walden Pond, and stop off in **Lexington** on the way back.

DAY 6➤ After exploring the grand mansions in **Back Bay** and shopping on Newbury and Boylston streets, stop off at the **Institute of Contemporary Art.** Make your way back to **Copley Square** for a peek at **Trinity Church** and the **Boston Public Library.** Have dinner in **Chinatown,** and then catch a show in the **Theater District.**

DAY 7➤ Ride the T into Harvard Square and explore **Harvard Yard** and its museums. Take kids to the university's complex of cultural and natural history museums; take yourself to the **Sackler** and **Fogg** art museums. Ride the T to **Kendall Square** for a stroll around the **MIT** campus; have dinner in one of the many ethnic restaurants in **Central Square** and check out the music scene at one of Central Square's funky night spots.

DAY 8➤ Take in a Red Sox game at **Fenway.** Or pack the kids off to the **Franklin Park Zoo** or **Arnold Arboretum.**

# FODOR'S CHOICE

No two people will agree on what makes a perfect vacation, but it's fun and helpful to know what others think. We hope you'll have a chance to experience some of Fodor's Choices yourself while visiting Boston. For detailed information about each, refer to the appropriate chapters within this guidebook.

Quintessential Boston

★ **Commonwealth Avenue when the magnolias are flowering.** The curved lines of these tree branches and the round shapes of their soft white-and-pink blossoms echo the elaborate detailing of the avenue's dark stone Victorian facades with their lacy wrought-iron balconies. Magnolia time happens during the middle of May.

★ **Concerts at the Isabella Stewart Gardner Museum.** Having built the Venetian palazzo of her dreams and stuffed it with innumerable curios and Old Masters, the celebrated Mrs. Gardner invited the rich and famous of her day—J. Pierpont Morgan, Henry James, Edith Wharton—to concerts in her resplendent Tapestry Room. Today, you, too, can be lulled by Bach and Scarlatti at the Gardner's Saturday and Sunday afternoon concerts, offered between October and April.

★ **Fourth of July along the Esplanade.** Everyone becomes a Liberty belle or beau at the Boston Pops's gala concert—the highlight: fireworks and *Stars and Stripes Forever.*

★ **The John Singleton Copleys at the Museum of Fine Arts.** Colonial Boston's most famous portraitist is represented by dozens of paintings on view here, including his famous image of Paul Revere—but don't miss his spectacular *Watson and the Shark.*

★ **Louisburg Square under a blanket of newly fallen snow.** It's easy to imagine former residents Jenny Lind and Louisa May Alcott emerging from one of the oh-so-prim-and-proper houses facing this tiny park. Mt. Vernon Street, which gives you access to this most decorous rectangle, is the home of the stateliest of the stately old Beacon Hill Houses, with their brilliantly polished brass door knockers.

★ **Paul Revere's Ride on Patriot's Day.** The ultimate Pony Express is reenacted every third Monday in April to celebrate Revere's speedy ride to salvation.

★ **The Public Garden in spring with the tulip beds in full bloom.** Best seen, perhaps, from the aptly named swan boats, the Public Garden is celebrated as the country's first botanical garden.

★ **The reflection of Trinity Church in the John Hancock Tower at Copley Square.** This capacious public gathering place, a harbor until it was filled in at the end of the 19th century, offers one of the most striking juxtapositions of 19th- and 20th-century building styles: the Renaissance Revival Boston Public Library (1885), designed by the American firm of McKim, Mead & White; architect H. H. Richardson's powerful Romanesque Revival Trinity Church (1877), an American masterpiece that's solid as the rough-textured, multihued stone of which it's built; and, just adjacent, the rhomboid, I. M. Pei–designed John Hancock Tower (1976), whose 60 stories of shiny black glass brilliantly mirror its neighbor. From its observatory, you can get a fine bird's-eye view of the square and beyond.

## Buildings and Monuments

★ **Christian Science Church's Reflecting Pool.** The cool expanse of this mammoth pool and the surrounding plaza can be a refreshing pleasure on a hot summer's day.

★ **Holocaust Memorial.** The glass-and-steel structure of this tribute to Hitler's victims seems jarring against the 18th-century backdrop of Blackstone Block, but a walk through its disquieting configuration is a moving experience.

★ **Longfellow National Historic Site, Cambridge.** This splendid Colonial mansion with period furnishings and elegant grounds is a reminder of the time when poets were the celebrities of the day.

★ **"Make Way for Ducklings" statue in the Public Garden.** If you have small children, run, do not walk, to the most child-friendly sculpture in the city.

★ **Paul Revere's statue in the Prado, North End.** Maybe this patriot overly benefited from Longfellow's poetic license. Still, few can match his record for revolutionary derring-do and sheer silver artistry.

★ **The State House seen from Boston Common at night.** Often described as a "beacon on the hill," the golden dome of the State House is a magnificent sight when illuminated at night.

★ **USS Constitution.** "Old Ironsides" upheld her nation's honor in battle and continues to do her proud as both a compelling exhibit and a fully commissioned warship.

## Bars

★ **The Bay Tower Room.** By day, it's a private club, but after dark it opens to the public for panoramic views of the Boston harbor and the music of a jazz trio.

★ **The Burren, Somerville.** Here you'll find a distillation of a great Irish bar—well-drawn Guinness, comfort food, and live Irish music nightly.

★ **The Cantab Lounge, Central Square, Cambridge.** In this seedy but stately dive, Harvard professors and down-and-outs hold animated debates about Karl Marx. Live music plays upstairs and down.

★ **Doyle's Café.** This Boston institution opened more than a century ago; local politicos still stop by to sample the Scotch and glad-hand.

★ **Mercury Bar.** Sink into a plush red booth and choose a few spicy tapas to accompany your cocktail.

## Hotels

★ **The Boston Harbor Hotel at Rowes Wharf.** At one of Boston's newer and most elegant hotels, guest rooms have views of either the city or the harbor. The hundred or so paintings and other artwork in the lobby and other public spaces celebrate the city's historical and artistic traditions. $$$$

★ **The Ritz-Carlton.** In the old Yankee manner, this perennial favorite still stands for luxury combined with understatement. Coveted rooms and suites have fireplaces and views of the Public Garden across the street. $$$$

★ **The Lenox Hotel.** Built in 1900 and now renovated, it is better than ever—a first-rate choice for its traditional decor, original architectural details, and handsome, ornate lobby. $$$$

★ **The Gryphon House.** Rooms in this 19th-century brownstone are rich with amenities. Even the staircase is extraordinary—it's wrapped in a 19th-century wallpaper mural. $$$–$$$$

★ **Harborside Inn.** A former mercantile warehouse near Faneuil Hall has been transformed into a plush, hushed property. $$–$$$

★ **The John Jeffries House.** Stays at this small hotel in a turn-of-the-century building across Charles Circle from Massachusetts General Hospital come complete with a graceful double parlor and Charles River views. $–$$

## Restaurants

★ **Biba.** The restaurant all Boston just keeps talking about: chef-owner Lydia Shire serves up giant portions of personality in the postmodern decor, surreal comfort food, desserts to study and devour, and a cross-cultural wine list. $$$$

⭑ **Julien.** Gilded cornices, weighty silver, and Queen Anne wing chairs help make this the handsomest dining room in the city. You half expect to see George Washington in such regal surroundings—and you just might: he figures in an N. C. Wyeth mural that adorns the adjacent bar. $$$$

⭑ **L'Espalier.** Set within a lovely Victorian Bay town house that has been updated with modern art and a "truffle"-hued color scheme, this restaurant serves what some say is the greatest dessert in Boston: the Chocolate Observatory Tower. $$$$

⭑ **Rowes Wharf Restaurant.** Unruffled elegance, a view of the harbor, impeccable cuisine based on New England foodstuffs, and an extraordinary list of American wines make this a standout. $$$$

⭑ **Hamersley's Bistro.** In a Red Sox cap instead of a toque, Gordon Hamersley runs one of the city's top dining rooms; it has the hearty spirit of a Parisian bistro. $$$–$$$$

⭑ **East Coast Grill.** A classic Cambridge restaurant, it serves often atypical species of fresh fish, grilled in unusual herbal crusts by informal masters of condiments and barbecue. $$$

⭑ **Pomodoro.** The playful decor and the winning country-Italian wine list make this bright, dynamic trattoria one of the nicest places in Boston's "Little Italy," the North End. $$$

⭑ **Legal Sea Foods.** Once a tiny adjunct to a fish market and now the chief resource for Bostonians who like their seafood straight from the sea, Legal has locations in the Prudential Center, Chestnut Hill, Park Square, Kendall Square in Cambridge, and Logan Airport among others, and they're always busy. $$–$$$$

⭑ **Elephant Walk.** The cuisine of France meets Southeast Asia's at these Brookline and Cambridge favorites. $$–$$$

⭑ **Lala Rokh.** Come here for a memorable experience of Persian cuisine amid treasured medieval maps, calligraphy, and miniatures. $$–$$$

⭑ **Chau Chow.** Head to Chinatown for incredible, Chiu Chow–style seafood-based cuisine. $–$$

# FESTIVALS AND SEASONAL EVENTS

The **Massachusetts Office of Travel and Tourism**'s events hot line (☎ 800/227–6277) lists upcoming events in Boston and surrounding communities. Additional event listings are posted on its Web site (www.mass-vacation.com).

➤ EARLY DEC.: **Thousands of tiny lights** are illuminated in the trees on Boston Common and on the big evergreen in front of the Prudential Center (☎ 617/635–4505). The **Newbury Street Holiday Stroll** (☎ 617/267–7961) entertains shoppers with music, food, and holiday activities.

➤ MID-DEC.: At the Boston Tea Party ship and museum, a **Boston Tea Party Reenactment** (☎ 617/338–1773) takes place, and in Cambridge at Harvard's Sanders Theater, **Christmas Revels** (☎ 617/621–0505) celebrate the winter solstice with music, dance, and folk plays from around the world.

➤ NEW YEAR'S EVE: Bostonians turn out in force for the city's **First Night Celebration** (☎ 617/542–1399), a full day and night of outdoor and indoor concerts and festivities, culminating in fireworks over Boston Harbor.

➤ NEW YEAR'S DAY: To warm your spirit, stop by South Boston's Carson Beach to see the L Street Brownies, a group of elderly swimmers—many in their eighties and nineties—take their **annual icy plunge.**

➤ LATE JAN.–EARLY FEB.: Boston's Chinatown celebrates **Chinese New Year** (☎ 617/542–2574) with firecrackers and special cakes. The **Boston Wine Festival** (☎ 617/330–9355; held at the Boston Harbor Hotel at Rowes Wharf) runs through April and includes a rare wine auction, cooking demonstrations, special wine dinners, and the Anthony Spinazzola Gala, New England's premier culinary event.

➤ FEB.: The Museum of Afro-American History, in conjunction with the New England Conservatory of Music, sponsors the Roland Hayes/Marian Anderson Music Series to celebrate **Black History Month** (☎ 617/739–1200) on several Sundays through the month. Hockey fans enjoy the annual **Beanpot Hockey Tournament** (☎ 617/624–1000) between area college teams.

➤ MID-MAR.: The **Annual Spring New England Flower Show** blooms at the Bayside Expo Center (☎ 617/536–9280).

➤ MAR. 17: All of Boston turns out for the **St. Patrick's Day Parade** (☎ 888/733–2678). It's also officially **Evacuation Day,** which commemorates the expulsion of British troops from South Boston by General Washington in 1776 and which is observed as the de facto legal holiday.

➤ EARLY APR.–EARLY MAY: In conjunction with the **Children's Museum** (✉ 66 Summer St., ☎ 617/439–7700), the **Big Apple Circus** comes to town.

➤ APR.: The **Red Sox** (☎ 617/267–1700 for tickets) open yet another hopeful season at historic Fenway Park.

➤ MID-APR.: Bostonians know it's really spring when the **swan boats** return to the **Public Garden** (☎ 617/635–4505). On **Patriot's Day** (the Mon. nearest Apr. 19), celebrants reenact Paul Revere's ride from Hanover Street in Boston's North End to Lexington (☎ 888/733–2678). On the same day, the **Boston Marathon** (☎ 617/236–1652, Boston Athletic Association) fills the streets from Hopkinton to the Back Bay. On the weekend of April 14–16, Lexington will stage elaborate **battle reenactments** to celebrate the 225th anniversary of the events; the skirmishes and ceremonies will involve more than 1,500 participants—including units from Britain.

➤ MID-MAY: Franklin Park is the site for the **Greater Boston Kite Festival** (☎ 617/635–4505). The **Arnold Arboretum** (☎ 617/524–1718) celebrates the 400 varieties of lilac in bloom with Lilac Sunday. Everyone "makes way for ducklings" during their

**Mother's Day** waddle over Beacon Hill to the Public Garden lagoon (☎ 617/635–4505).

SUMMER

➤ EARLY JUNE: **Scooper Bowl** (☎ 617/439–7700) is an all-you-can-eat ice cream festival; proceeds benefit the cancer-fighting Jimmy Fund.

➤ MID-JUNE: A weekend of activities culminates in a parade on **Bunker Hill Weekend** (☎ 617/242–5641), which recalls the battle in Charlestown. The **Boston Globe Jazz and Blues Festival** (☎ 617/929–2649) starts on Father's Day and gets everyone swinging for more than a week at venues throughout the city. From mid-June to mid-July the **Rockport Chamber Music Festival** (☎ 978/546–7391) draws music lovers to the seaside town on the North Shore.

➤ LATE JUNE–EARLY JULY: Boston's annual weeklong Fourth of July celebration, **Harborfest** (☎ 617/227–1528), takes place along the waterfront. It includes a concert synchronized to fireworks over the harbor, as well as **Chowderfest** on City Hall Plaza, which lets you sample New England clam chowder from Boston's best restaurants.

➤ JULY 4: There's a pyrotechnic show above the Esplanade for the annual **Boston Pops Concert and Fireworks Display** (☎ 617/266–1492), a musical extravaganza at the Hatch Shell.

➤ MID-JULY: On the weekend closest to July 18, at the Robert Gould Shaw and 54th Regiment Memorial on the Common, the National Park Service and the Museum of Afro-American History re-create the **Battle of Fort Wagner** (☎ 617/742–5415 or 617/739–1200), the Civil War battle fought by the first black regiment to be recruited in the North. From July 11–16, Boston will host an international fleet of tall ships for **Sail Boston 2000.**

➤ LATE JULY: More than 100,000 music lovers make their way to Lowell for the **Lowell Folk Festival** (☎ 978/970–5000). Marblehead's **Race Week** (usually the last week of July; ☎ 781/631–2868) attracts boats from all along the Eastern seaboard.

➤ MID–LATE AUG.: A dragon parade enlivens Chinatown for the **August Moon Festival** (☎ 617/542–2574).

AUTUMN

➤ MID-SEPT.: Numerous events take place along the Charles River for the **Cambridge River Festival** (☎ 617/349–4380). September is also a huge month for **North End "feasts"** honoring a variety of saints with great food, great music (Italian), and great people-watching.

➤ EARLY OCT.: A big **Columbus Day Parade** (☎

888/733–2678) moves from East Boston to the North End. On Columbus Day weekend south of Boston, the **Massachusetts Cranberry Harvest Festival** (☎ 508/295–5799, in service May–Oct.) is held in both Plymouth and neighboring South Carver's Edaville Cranberry Bog. Lowell honors its native son with **Lowell Celebrates Kerouac** (☎ 978/970–5000), presenting music, readings, and "Beat Tours." The nation's oldest county fair, the **Topsfield Fair** (☎ 978/887–5000), harks back to our farm heritage.

➤ OCT.: The **Bruins** and **Celtics** (☎ 617/624–1000; 617/931–2000 Ticketmaster tickets for both) both open their seasons in October.

➤ MID-OCT.: College crew teams and spectators bearing blankets and beer come from all over for the **Head of the Charles Regatta** (☎ 617/864–8415). **Haunted Happenings** turns Salem into a witchy brew, climaxing on Halloween (☎ 978/744–0013).

➤ LATE NOV.–LATE DEC.: Modern-day Pilgrims stroll through **Plymouth**'s historic homes the weekend before Thanksgiving (☎ 508/747–7533 or 800/872–1620). The **Boston International Antiquarian Book Fair** celebrates old tomes (☎ 800/447–9595). There's live Christmas music at **Faneuil Hall** (☎ 617/338–2323).

➤ LATE NOV.–EARLY JAN.: The Boston Ballet's **Nutcracker** (☎ 617/695–6950) heralds the return of another holiday season.

# 2 EXPLORING BOSTON

Genteel streets lined with elegant brick town houses, acres of public greens and gardens, more colleges than are found in many states, and a church on almost every corner: Boston serves up slices of history and culture at every turn. Savvy spin doctors of centuries past have made the town that cradled independence our nation's history and myth capital. More than ever, America's mother city serves up the bold and new with the old and true—reflecting skyscrapers mirror Colonial steeples, and expressways zip around buildings whose hand-etched look recalls the scrimshaw era. Few places in America display their history so lovingly.

By Stephanie Schorow and William G. Scheller

Updated by Lauren Gibbons Paul

**L**IKE A MULTITIERED WEDDING CAKE, the city of Boston consists of discrete layers. The deepest layer is the historical base, the place where musket-bearing revolutionaries vowed to hang together or hang separately. The next layer, a dense spread of Brahmin fortune and fortitude, might be labeled the Hub. The Hub saw only journalistic accuracy in the hometown slogan "the Athens of America" and felt only pride in the label "Banned in Boston." Over that lies Beantown, home to the Red Sox faithful and the raucous Bruins fans who crowded Boston GAHden or order chow-DAH; this is the city whose ethnic loyalties—Irish, Italian, Asian, and African-American—account for its many distinct neighborhoods. Crowded on top are the students who throng the city's universities and colleges every fall, infuriating not a few but pleasing the rest with their infusion of high spirits and dollars from home.

The best part for a visitor is that all these Bostons can be experienced within a day or two. This is a remarkably compact city, whose labyrinthine streets will delight the walker, although they can—and often do—push drivers over the edge. An hour's stroll will take you from sites in the North End—where bewigged icons from dusty high school history books are transformed into flesh-and-blood heroes—to Beacon Hill's mansions where the Lowells spoke only to the Cabots and the Cabots spoke only to God. You can explore the country's oldest public park, the Boston Common, in the morning, tour a Back Bay Victorian in the afternoon, and in the evening dine on Szechuan seafood in Chinatown or gnocchi in the North End. Even following the Freedom Trail—a self-guiding walking tour of famous American historic sites—traverses the layers: historical, Hub, and Beantown.

Some have accused Bostonians of being as frosty as their city's winter. But it's not that the natives are cold; it's rather that this city has all the reserve associated with New England. Instead of a hail-fellow-well-met bonhomie, there is a deep, abiding affection Bostonians have for old friends, family, and the city itself; they take perverse pride in mastering their M. C. Escher–like traffic patterns, in their frigid winters, and in their derring-do drivers. Boston has been first too many times—the first public library, the first public schools, the first subway system—to concede an inch of civic pride to bigger and bolder cities. It still sees itself as a pioneer in culture—both popular and rarefied. This is the city that created First Night (a massively popular public participation showcase of arts and cultural events) as an alternative activity on New Year's Eve. It's still going strong after 20 years and has inspired a string of imitators. And in the past few years, downtown Boston has started to simmer with change. The infamous, multiyear "Big Dig" project will sink the main highway underground; a new Federal courthouse opened on Fan Pier in fall 1998. Business buildings and hotels are in the works, including an office tower slated to stretch higher than the Prudential Center.

In 1858, Oliver Wendell Holmes—philosopher and author of *The Autocrat of the Breakfast-Table*—called Boston "the hub of the solar system"; social inflation, however, soon raised the ante to "hub of the universe." For Bostonians that still feels about right.

# BEACON HILL AND BOSTON COMMON

Enclave of Old Money grandees, contender for the "Most Beautiful" award among the city's neighborhoods, and hallowed address for many of its literary lights, Beacon Hill is Boston at its most Bostonian. As if with a flick of a Wellsian time machine, the redbrick elegance of its narrow streets wafts visitors back to the 19th century. But make no mistake: Beacon Hill is no Williamsburg clone; here, people aren't living *in* the past, but *with* it. Increasingly, the district is less old guard than catch-you-off-guard: residents are more likely to be college professors married to stockbrokers than D. A. R. matrons whose forebears were acquainted with Justice Oliver Wendell Holmes.

Even so, the Brahmin air of the Hill's cobbled streets still seems rarefied. From the splendidly gold-topped State House to mansions with neoclassical panache, Beacon Hill exudes power, prestige, and a calm yet palpable undercurrent of history. Once the seat of the Commonwealth's government, it was originally called "Tremont" or "Trimount" by the early colonists. It had three summits: Cotton Hill, Beacon Hill, and Mount Vernon. Beacon, the highest, was named for the warning light (at first an iron skillet filled with lighted tallow and suspended from a mast) set on its peak in 1634. The location of the old beacon was directly behind the State House, on land now occupied by the building's 19th-century additions.

The classic face of Beacon Hill comes from its brick row houses, nearly all built between 1800 and 1850 in a style never diverging far from the early Federal norm. Even the sidewalks are brick and will remain so by public fiat; in the 1940s, residents staged an uncharacteristic sit-in to prevent conventional paving. Since then, public law, the Beacon Hill Civic Association, and the Beacon Hill Architectural Commission have maintained tight control over everything from the gas lamps to the colors of front doors. Beacon Hill was finished quite nicely a century and a quarter ago, and as the Yankees say, "If it ain't broke, don't fix it."

When the fashionable families decamped for the "new" development of the Back Bay, not everyone left; enough residents remained to ensure that the south slope of the Hill never lost its Brahmin character. What is less well known, but no less interesting, is that Beacon Hill's north slope played a key part in African-American history. A community of free blacks lived here in the 1800s; many worshiped at the African Meeting House, established in 1805 and still standing, which came to be called the "Black Faneuil Hall" for antislavery activism. The area also housed a substantial Jewish population. Now both groups are among the inhabitants of both sides of the hill, but the south side retains its Brahmin character in the form of extremely high housing prices.

By the middle of the 20th century natives and newcomers alike realized that this was suitable ground for the new urban gentry. In what other city can one live on such an elegant plane within a 10-minute walk of the central business district? Thus, the unchanged facades of Beacon Hill were converted to condominium and apartment units rather than multistory single-family dwellings. These survive, too, but at prices in excess of a million dollars.

Today, Beacon Hill is the area bounded by Cambridge Street on the north, Beacon Street on the south, the Charles River Esplanade on the west, and Bowdoin Street on the east. Within these borders, residents distinguish three informal districts: the **"flat"** (the area west of Charles Street), the **south slope** (the area east of Charles Street and south of Pinckney Street), and the less architecturally distinguished **north slope** (the area east of Charles Street and north of Pinckney Street).

In contrast to Beacon Hill, the Boston Common, the country's oldest public park, exudes an attitude that is for, by, and of the people. From its first use as public land for cattle grazing, the Common has always accommodated the needs and desires of its citizens—whether for First Night, ice cream festivals, the Corporate Challenge run, or rousing political rallies. Public hangings, however, have gone the way of the Puritans.

A good place to begin an exploration of the Common or Beacon Hill is at the Visitor Information Center on Tremont Street just east of the Park Street Station (☞ *below*). Here you can pick up a free map to Boston's Freedom Trail or buy a more extensive guide. The red line of the self-guiding trail begins just outside, in Parkman Plaza with its 1950s bronze monuments extolling religion, industry, and learning. Note that ranger-led tours leave frequently from the **National Park Visitor Cénter** on State Street in spring, summer, and fall (☎ 617/242–5642).

*Numbers in the text correspond to numbers in the margin and on the Beacon Hill and Boston Common map.*

## A Good Walk

Few cities on earth are so ideally suited to walking, and few sections of Boston are as tailored for a leisurely amble as the Boston Common–Beacon Hill nexus. Boston has a way of turning every stroll into a historical adventure, and this suggested tour is as much a journey back in time as it is a conveyor belt of interesting sights. Your starting point is the **Visitor Information Center** ① on Tremont Street. From here, head into **Boston Common** past the Parkman Bandstand and toward the Central Burying Ground—where Tories and Patriots are buried side by side (to skip a tour of the Common, head directly to the Park Street Church on Tremont Street). Walk back toward the bandstand, turn left, and head for the Common's highest ground to take a look at the Soldiers and Sailors Monument. Immediately below and to the north is the renovated Frog Pond—once a watering hole for cows and now a picturesque spot, especially in winter when it becomes a small but glittering patch of ice for skating. From the pond, walk uphill to reach Augustus Saint-Gaudens's moving Robert Gould Shaw Memorial—a commemoration of Boston's Civil War unit of free blacks (a regiment depicted in the 1989 Hollywood film *Glory*). Here at the corner of Beacon and Park streets is where Beacon Hill—called "the Hill" by residents—the Common, and downtown Boston converge. If you head down Park Street along the Common—passing the Ticknor Mansion, the exclusive Union Club, and the Roman Catholic Paulist Center—you'll find the block ends at the **Park Street Church** ② and the **Granary Burying Ground** ③— final resting place of some of Boston's most illustrious figures, including John Hancock and Paul Revere (not to mention "Mother" Goose).

If you wish to view some of the grandest interiors in Boston, head up to **Beacon Street** and take a tour of the first two floors of the august **Boston Athenaeum** ④. From the **State House** ⑤—Charles Bulfinch's neoclassical masterpiece—continue along Beacon Street to soak up the local atmosphere; notable abodes include the Appleton Mansions and the third **Harrison Gray Otis House** ⑥. Turn right on Charles Street, then right on Chestnut Street and left on Willow to find **Acorn Street** ⑦— Boston's most photogenic byway—on your left. Continue on Willow across Mt. Vernon to reach quaint **Louisburg Square** ⑧, one of the few corners of Boston where Henry James would have little difficulty in recognizing his whereabouts. Turn right on **Pinckney Street** and follow to Joy Street: two blocks to the left on **Smith Court** is the **African Meeting House** ⑨, a moving testament to Boston's historic African-American community. Next door, in the Abiel Smith School, is the **Museum of Afro American History** ⑩. A visit to the north slope of the Hill should include a walk down Revere Street and glances into Rollins Place, Phillips Street, and Bellingham Place. These trim residential courts all dead-end at a hidden cliff; the shuttered, white clapboard house at the blind end of Rollins Place is not a house at all but a false front masking a small precipice. You can follow Revere to Charles Street or backtrack on Joy Street to **Mt. Vernon Street,** passing the historic **Nichols House** ⑪, its bow window elegantly beveled. Take Mt. Vernon back to the main artery of **Charles Street.**

TIMING

Beacon Hill, one of the more compact areas of Boston, can be easily explored in an afternoon; add an extra few hours if you wish to linger on the Common and in the shops on Charles Street or plan to tour the Black Heritage Trail. It's a particularly lovely walk in spring and summer. In winter, the cobblestone streets can be difficult to navigate, but it's an especially beautiful neighborhood during the holidays—the Common is lit with Christmas lights and on Christmas Eve carolers and bell-ringers fill elegant Louisburg Square. Other seasons bring other pleasures, particularly cherry blossoms on the Common in spring and Boston Pops concerts on the nearby Esplanade in July.

## Sights to See

★ ❼ **Acorn Street.** Surely the most photographed street in the city, Acorn is Ye Olde Colonial Boston at its best. The cobblestone street is considered by motorists to be Boston's roughest ride (it's also so narrow that only one car can squeeze through). Delicate, jewel-size row houses line one side, and on the other are the doors to Mt. Vernon's hidden gardens. Nineteenth-century artisans and small tradesmen once called these row houses home; today they are every bit as prestigious as their larger neighbors around the corners on Chestnut and Mt. Vernon streets.

❾ **African Meeting House.** Built in 1806 and centerpiece of the historic Smith Court African-American community (☞ *below*), the African Meeting House is the oldest black church building still standing in the United States. It was constructed almost entirely with African-American labor, using funds raised in both the white and the black communities. The facade is an adaptation of a design for a town house published by the Boston architect Asher Benjamin. In 1832 the New England Anti-Slavery Society was formed here under the leadership of William Lloyd Garrison. When the black community began to migrate at the end of the 19th century to the South End and Roxbury, the building became a synagogue. In 1972, it was purchased by the Museum of Afro American History, but that year a fire destroyed the slate roof and original pulpit. After its reconstruction, it was designated a historic site in 1974 and reopened in 1987 (☞ Black Heritage Trail®, *below*). At press time, the African Meeting House and the Museum of Afro American History (in the Abiel Smith School building) were closed for extensive renovations, due for completion in late 1999 and 2000. Call ahead for the latest information. In the meantime, the administrative offices have been relocated to the Boston suburb of Brookline. ⊠ *8 Smith Ct. (off Joy St., between Cambridge and Myrtle Sts.),* ☎ *617/739–1200.* ✆ *Suggested contribution $5.* ☉ *Late May–early Sept., daily 10–4; weekdays rest of yr. T stop: Park St., Charles/MGH.*

**Appalachian Mountain Club.** The bowfront mansion that serves as the headquarters of one of New England's oldest environmental institutions draws nature lovers from all over the world. The club is a great source of useful information on outdoor recreation throughout the region, including cross-country skiing and hiking. (You don't have to be a member to hit up its resources.) Architecturally, the building is no-

# Beacon Hill and Boston Common

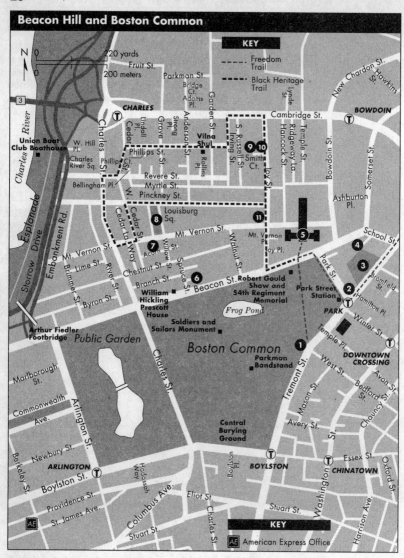

table for its carved cornices and spectacular oriel window decorated with vines and gargoyles. The club is around the corner from the **Nichols House** (☞ *below*). ✉ *5 Joy St.,* ☎ *617/523–0636.* ⊗ *Weekdays 8:30–5:15. T stop: Park St.*

**Beacon Street.** In New England, it used to be said wealth was a burden to be borne with a minimum of display. Happily, the residents of Beacon Street were all for showing off and lined the street with elegant architectural statements, from the magnificent State House to grand patrician mansions. Here you'll find some of the most important buildings of Charles Bulfinch—the ultimate designer of the Federal style in America—dozens of bowfront row houses, the Somerset Club (the Parnassus of Boston's First Families), and the grand and glorious Harrison Gray Otis House.

After the **Boston Athenaeum** (☞ *below*), Beacon Street highlights begin with the headquarters of **Little, Brown.** Based at the corner of Beacon and Joy streets, this venerable mainstay of Boston's publishing trade brought us Louisa May Alcott's *Little Women* and *Bartlett's Famous Quotations.* At 33 Beacon Street, the **George Parkman House** greets the eye, its gracious facade hiding more than a few secrets. One of the first sensational "Trials of the Century" involved the murder of Dr. George Parkman, a wealthy landlord and Harvard benefactor. He was bludgeoned to death in 1849 by Dr. John Webster, a Harvard medical professor and neighborhood acquaintance who allegedly became enraged by demands that he repay a personal loan. At the conclusion of the trial, the professor was hanged; he is buried in an unmarked grave on Copp's Hill in the North End. Parkman's son lived in seclusion in this house overlooking the Common until he died in 1908. The building is now used for civic functions.

Be sure to note the windows of the twin **Appleton Mansions,** built by the pioneer textile family, at Numbers 39 and 40. These are the celebrated purple panes of Beacon Hill; only a few buildings have them, and they are as valuable as an ancestor in the China Trade. Their amethystine mauve color was the result of the action of sunlight on the imperfections in a shipment of glass sent to Boston around 1820. The mansions are not open to the public.

The quintessential snob has always been a Bostonian—and the **Somerset Club,** at 42 Beacon Street, has always been *the* inner sanctum of blue-nosed Cabots, Lowells, and Lodges. The mansion is a rare intrusion of the granite Greek Revival style into Beacon Hill. The older of its two buildings (the newer was built to match) was erected in 1819 by David Sears to a design by Alexander Parris, the architect of Quincy Market. Just a few doors down you'll find the grandest of the three houses Harrison Gray Otis built for himself during Boston's golden age (☞ Harrison Gray Otis House, *below*).

If you wish to continue eastward along Beacon, an elegant coda to your stroll can be **Fisher College,** housed in a stately bowfront (1903) whose Classical Revival style epitomizes turn-of-the-century elegance. Inside—and you can go inside—the marble stairway with its gold-plated balustrade, the Circassian walnut–paneled dining room, and the library's hand-carved rosewood doors with sterling silver knobs are among the many genteel touches. ✉ *118 Beacon St.,* ☎ *617/236–8800.* ✇ *Free.* ⊗ *Weekdays 8:30–4:30. T stop: Arlington.*

★ ❹ **Boston Athenaeum.** One of the cofounders of the Boston Athenaeum is credited with coining an expression that has made politicians and newspaper editorialists rejoice ever since: William Tudor first compared Boston with Athens in an 1819 letter, and Bostonians now jealously

# FREE AT LAST:
# THE BLACK HERITAGE TRAIL®

**T**HE MENTION OF BEACON HILL conjures up images of opulence, wealth, and proper Boston Brahmins. Yet until the end of the 19th century, its north side was home to a vibrant community of free blacks—more than 8,000 at its peak—who built houses, schools, and churches that stand to this day. In the African Meeting House, once called the Black Faneuil Hall, orators railed against slavery. The streets were lined with black-owned and -operated businesses. The black community now has shifted to other parts of Boston, but the 19th-century legacy can be rediscovered on the Black Heritage Trail®.

Established in the late 1960s, the self-guiding trail stitches together 14 sites in a 1½-mi walk. Park rangers give tours daily from Memorial Day through Labor Day and by special request the rest of the year at 10 AM, noon, and 2 PM starting from the Shaw Memorial. Or you may follow directions in brochures available at the ☞ **Museum of Afro American History** or the **National Park Service Visitor Center** (✉ 14 Beacon St., ☎ 617/742–5415); park officials recommend you follow the brochure, as signs or plaques may be wrong or confusing. All but two houses on the trail remain private residences, but walking the twists and turns of the trail—often far less crowded than the better-known Freedom Trail—makes it easy to visualize an era when slavery was the nation's burning moral question.

Start at the stirring **Robert Gould Shaw and 54th Regiment Memorial** in the Boston Common. As depicted in the movie *Glory*, Shaw, a young white officer from a prominent Boston abolitionist family, led the first black regiment to be recruited in the North during the Civil War. From here, walk up Joy Street to 5–7 Pinckney to see the 1797 **George Middleton House**, the oldest existing home built by blacks on Beacon Hill. Nearby, the **Phillips School** at Anderson and Pinckney streets was one of Boston's first integrated schools. The **John J. Smith House,** 86 Pinckney, was a rendezvous point for abolitionists and escaping slaves, and the elegant **Charles Street Meeting House,** at Mt. Vernon and Charles streets, a former black church and community center. In 1876, the building became the site of the African Methodist Episcopal Church, which was the last black institution to leave Beacon Hill in 1939. The **Lewis and Harriet Hayden House,** 66 Phillips Street, the home of freed slaves turned abolitionists, was a stop on the Underground Railroad. Harriet Beecher Stowe, author of *Uncle Tom's Cabin,* visited here in 1853 for her first glimpse of fugitive slaves. The Haydens reportedly kept a barrel of gunpowder under the front step, saying they'd blow up the house before they'd surrender a single slave. At 2 Phillips Street, **John Coburn,** a clothing dealer and co-founder of a black military company, ran a gaming house, described as a "private place for gentlemen."

The five residences on **Smith Court** are typical of African-American Bostonian homes of the 1800s, including Number 3, the 1799 clapboard house where William C. Nell, America's first published black historian, boarded from 1851 to 1865. At the corner of Smith Court and Joy Street, the **Abiel Smith School,** the city's first public school for black children, is the permanent home for the ☞ **Museum of Afro American History,** which jointly administers the trail with the Park Service. Next door is the venerable ☞ **African Meeting House,** which served as the community's center of social, educational, and political activity. The ground level now houses a gallery; in the airy upstairs, you can relax in the seats and imagine the fiery sermons that once rattled the upper pews.

At press time, the Abiel Smith School and the African Meeting House were undergoing extensive restorations targeted for completion in 2000. Most of the collections have been moved to a temporary home in Brookline.

guard the title "Athens of America." Tudor, the first editor of the *North American Review,* would surely have cited the Athenaeum, one of the oldest libraries in the country, as proof. Founded in 1807 from the seeds sown by the Anthology Club (headed by Ralph Waldo Emerson's father), it moved to its present imposing quarters—modeled after Palladio's Palazzo da Porta Festa in Vicenza, Italy—in 1849. Only 1,049 proprietary shares exist for membership in this cathedral of scholarship, and most have been passed down for generations (accredited researchers with references may, however, apply for annual memberships).

The public is permitted to walk through the first and second floors, to marvel at the marble busts, the exquisite porcelain vases, lush oil paintings, and leather-bound books of this Brahmin institution. A second-floor gallery has revolving art shows, most with a literary bent. A guided tour affords one of the most marvelous sights in the world of Boston academe, the fifth-floor Reading Room. In the words of critic David McCord, it "combines the best elements of the Bodleian, Monticello, the frigate *Constitution,* a greenhouse, and an old New England sitting room." Among the Athenaeum's holdings are most of George Washington's private library and the King's Chapel Library sent from England by William and Mary in 1698. (In reference to most of these volumes' uncut pages, a librarian once pointed out, "It appears that probably nobody ever read them, and now it is quite certain, I should say, that nobody ever will.") With a nod to the Information Age, an on-line catalog now offers more than 600,000 volumes. ⊠ *10½ Beacon St.,* ☎ *617/227–0270.* ☕ *Free.* ☉ *Sept.–May, weekdays 9–5:30, Sat. 9–4; June–Aug., weekdays 9–5:30. Free guided tours 3 PM Tues. and Thurs. by appointment 24 hrs ahead. T stop: Park St.*

| | |
|---|---|
| NEED A BREAK? | Choose a green tea, blended fruit juice, or espresso at the **Curious Liquids Café** (⊠ 22B Beacon St., ☎ 617/720–2836). Then plump down into an overstuffed sofa—the café's vantage point at the corner of Beacon and Park streets across from the State House makes it a great spot to people-watch. |

**Boston Common.** Nothing is more central to Boston than the Boston Common, the oldest public park in the United States and undoubtedly the largest and most famous of the town commons around which New England settlements were traditionally arranged. Boston Common is not built on landfill like the adjacent Public Garden; nor is it the result of 19th-century park planning, as are Olmsted's Fens and Franklin Park. It is simply the Common: 50 acres where the freemen of Boston could graze their cattle. (Cows were banned in 1830.) Dating from 1634, it is as old as the city around it. Latin names are affixed to many of the Common's trees; it was once expected that proper Boston schoolchildren would have no problem translating them.

Although no building of substance ever stood here, the Common contains a variety of noteworthy sites. The **Central Burying Ground** may seem an odd feature for a public park, but remember that in 1756, when the land was set aside, this was a lonely corner of the Common. It is the final resting place of Tories and Patriots alike, as well as many British casualties of the Battle of Bunker Hill. The most famous person buried here is Gilbert Stuart, the portraitist best known for his likenesses of George and Martha Washington; he died a poor man in 1828.

The Common's highest ground, near the park's Parkman Bandstand, was once called **Flagstaff Hill.** It is now surmounted by the Soldiers and Sailors Monument honoring Civil War troops. The Common's most famous body of water is the **Frog Pond,** a tame and frogless concrete depression used as a children's wading pool during steamy summer days and for ice skating in winter. It marks the original site of a natural pond that inspired Edgar Allan Poe to call Bostonians "Frogpondians." In 1848, the pond was the focal point for the inauguration of Boston's municipal water system, when a gushing fountain of piped-in water was created.

On the Beacon Street side of the Common sits the splendidly restored **Robert Gould Shaw Memorial,** executed in deep-relief bronze by Augustus Saint-Gaudens in 1897. It commemorates the 54th Massachusetts Regiment, the first Civil War unit made up of free blacks led by the young Brahmin Robert Gould Shaw, a stirring saga that inspired the 1989 movie *Glory.* Colonel Shaw died with nearly half of his troops in an assault on South Carolina's Fort Wagner. The monument—first intended to depict only Shaw until his abolitionist family demanded the monument honor his black regiment as well—figures in works by the modern poets John Berryman and Robert Lowell, both of whom lived on the north slope of Beacon Hill in the 1940s. In Lowell's moving poem "For the Union Dead" he writes, "at the dedication, / William James could almost hear the bronze Negroes breathe." This magnificent memorial makes a fitting first stop on the National Park Service's Black Heritage Trail® (☞ *above*).

Also note the 1888 **Boston Massacre Memorial** on Tremont Street, near Boylston; the sculpted hand of one of the victims has a distinct shine from years of sightseers' caresses. *T stop: Park St.*

**The Cathedral Church of St. Paul.** Even a cursory comparison of this somewhat austere Episcopal church with its majestic Tremont Street neighbor, Park Street Church, underscores the difference between 18th- and early 19th-century architectural aesthetics as they applied to large public buildings. Built just 10 years after the Park Street Church, St. Paul's is topped with an uncarved entablature; as with New York's Metropolitan Museum of Art, similarly adorned with uncut blocks of stone, the money ran out before stone carvers could be engaged. ⊠ *138 Tremont St.,* ☎ *617/482–5800.* ⊘ *Weekdays noon–6. Sun. services at 8 and 10; daily services at 12:10 and 5:15; Holy Eucharist in Chinese at 12:30 Sun. Luncheon concerts Oct.–May, Thurs. at 12:45. T stop: Park St.*

**Charles Street.** With few exceptions, Beacon Hill lacks commercial development, and Charles Street more than makes up for it. The street is chockablock with antiques shops, bookstores, small restaurants, and flower shops. However, you won't see any glaring neon; in keeping with the historic character of the area, even the 7-Eleven storefront has been made to conform to the prevailing aesthetic standards. Check out the **chiropractor's sign** (⊠ 83 Charles St.)—an unfleshed human spine. The contemporary activity would present a curious sight to the elder Oliver Wendell Holmes, the publisher James T. Fields (of the famed Bostonian firm of Ticknor and Fields), and many others who lived here when the neighborhood belonged to establishment literati. Charles Street sparkles at dusk from gas-fueled lamps, making it a romantic place for an evening stroll.

**Chestnut Street.** With Mt. Vernon, Chestnut is one of the two loveliest streets in the city. Delicacy and grace characterize virtually every structure, from the fanlights above the entryways to the wrought-iron boot scrapers on the steps. Author and explorer Francis Parkman lived here, as did Richard Henry Dana (of *Two Years Before the Mast* fame) and 19th-century actor Edwin Booth. Booth's sometime residence, 29A, dates from 1800 and is the oldest house on the south slope of the Hill. In particular, note the **Swan Houses,** at Numbers 13, 15, and 17, commissioned from Charles Bulfinch by Hepzibah Swan as dowry gifts for her three daughters. Complete with Adam-style entrances, marble columnettes, and recessed arches, they are Chestnut Street at its most beautiful.

**Club of Odd Volumes.** The second-oldest book collectors' club in America is open to the public only for special exhibitions. An early 19th-century town house serves as its headquarters. ⊠ *77 Mt. Vernon St.,* ☎ *617/227–7003. T stop: Park St.*

★ ❸ **Granary Burying Ground.** "It is a fine thing to die in Boston," A. C. Lyons, that old Boston wit, once remarked—alluding to Boston's cemeteries, among the most picturesque and historic in America. If you found a resting place here at the Old Granary, as it's called, chances are your headstone would have been impressively ornamented with skeletons and winged skulls. Your neighbors would have been mighty impressive, too: Samuel Adams, John Hancock, Benjamin Franklin's parents, Paul Revere, and, last but not least, Elizabeth "Mother" Goose (whose nursery ditties were published by Thomas Fleet, who decided to illustrate the tome with a picture of a long-necked goose—an allusion to his mother-in-law's constant chattering—thereby creating her nom de plume). Note the winged hourglasses carved into the stone gateway of the burial ground; they are a 19th-century addition, made more than 150 years after this small plot began receiving the remains of Colonial Bostonians. *Entrance on Tremont St.* ⊙ *Daily 8–4:30. T stop: Park St.*

❻ **Harrison Gray Otis House.** Harrison Gray Otis, one of the Mount Vernon Proprietors, a U.S. senator, and Boston's third mayor, built in rapid succession three of Boston's most splendidly ostentatious Federal-era houses, all designed by Charles Bulfinch and all still standing. This, the third Harrison Gray Otis House, at 45 Beacon Street, was the last of these mansions—and the grandest. Here, Mr. Otis breakfasted on pâté de foie gras every morning (somehow he lived to a ripe old 80), fussed over his Simon Willard rocking-horse clock, and hosted musicales at the same pianoforte that Beethoven had used to compose his *Eroica* symphony. Now operated as the headquarters of the American Meteorological Society, the house was once freestanding and surrounded by English-style gardens. The **Second Otis House,** built in 1800 at 85 Mt. Vernon Street, is today a private home. The **First Otis House**—built in 1796 and the only one open to the public (☞ The Old West End, *below*)—is on Cambridge Street near the Old West Church. Otis moved into 45 Beacon Street in 1805 and stayed until his death in 1848. His tenure thus extended from the first days of Beacon Hill's residential development almost to the time when many of the Hill's prominent families decamped for the Back Bay, which was just beginning to be filled at the time of Otis's death.

★ ❽ **Louisburg Square.** "Be unimpressed by reference to its being like London," essayist A. C. Lyons once wrote. "It is Boston to the hilt." One of the most charming corners in a neighborhood that epitomizes charm, Louisburg Square was an 1840s model for town-house development that was never repeated on the Hill because of space restrictions. Today, the grassy square—enclosed by a wrought-iron fence and considered the very heart of Beacon Hill—belongs collectively to the owners of the houses facing it. The statue at the north end of the green is of Columbus, the one at the south end of Aristides the Just; both were donated in 1850 by a Greek merchant who lived on the square. The houses, most of which are now divided into apartments and condominiums, have seen their share of famous tenants: author and critic William Dean Howells at Numbers 4 and 16, the Alcotts at Number

10 (Louisa May not only lived but died here, on the day of her father's funeral). In 1852 the singer Jenny Lind was married in the parlor of Number 20.

There is no water in Louisburg (proper Bostonians always pronounce the "s") Square today, and the ground level is some 60 ft below the height of the original hill, yet the legend long persisted that this was the location of the Rev. William Blackstone's spring. Blackstone was the original Bostonian, having come here to live with his books and his apple trees four or five years before the arrival of the Puritans in 1630. It was he who invited them to leave Charlestown and come to where the water was purer, he who sold them all but 6 acres of the peninsula he had bought from the Indians. He left for Rhode Island not long after, seeking greater seclusion; a plaque at 50 Beacon commemorates him. (The name "Boston," given by the Puritans, comes from Boston, England, originally St. Botolph's Town.)

The square still boasts celebrity residents. One of the largest houses on the square was acquired several years ago by the woman dubbed the Ketchup Heiress—Teresa Heinz, who married Senator John Kerry (D-Mass.). The house was purchased for a reported $2 million—unrenovated. The couple caused a flurry of sniffs when they pushed to have a fire hydrant moved from the front of their abode—apparently Ms. Heinz had been getting too many tickets. *T stop: Park St.*

**Mt. Vernon Street.** With Chestnut Street, Mt. Vernon has some of Beacon Hill's most distinguished addresses. Mt. Vernon is the grander of the two streets, with houses set back farther and rising taller; it even has a freestanding mansion, the Second Otis House, at Number 85 (☞ Harrison Gray Otis House, *above*). Henry James once wrote that Mt. Vernon Street was "the only respectable street in America," and he must have known, as he lived with his brother William at 131 in the 1860s. He was just one of many literary luminaries who resided on Mt. Vernon, including Julia Ward Howe, who composed "The Battle Hymn of the Republic" and lived at 32, and poet Robert Frost, who lived at 88.

⑩ **Museum of Afro American History.** Ever since Crispus Attucks became one of the famous victims of the Boston Massacre of 1770, the African-American community of Boston has played an important part in the city's history. In the 19th century, Walt Whitman noted that "black persons" enjoyed a higher status in Boston than in New York. Throughout the century, abolition was the cause célèbre for Boston's intellectual elite, and during that time, blacks came to thrive in neighborhoods throughout the city, including Smith Court and Joy Street. The Museum of Afro American History was established in 1964 to promote this history. Its headquarters normally occupies the **Abiel Smith School** (1835), the first public school for black children in Boston. However, at press time the building was undergoing a major renovation due for completion in 2000. In the meantime, the museum has interim offices in Brookline; call ahead for the most recent information. Park service personnel continue to lead tours of the **Black Heritage Trail®** (☞ *above*) starting from the Shaw Memorial. The museum also hosts a variety of activities during February, Black History Month, and in July stages a reenactment of the Civil War's black 54th regiment. ⊠ *46 Joy St.,* ☎ *617/739–1200.* ▣ *Donations suggested.* ☉ *Weekdays 10–4. T stop: Park St., Charles/MGH.*

⑪ **Nichols House.** Complete with a deep window seat straight out of a Henry James novel, the Nichols House is the only Mt. Vernon Street home open to the public. Beacon Hill eccentric, philanthropist, peace advocate, and one of the first female landscape designers, Rose Stan-

# WHERE IT ALL BEGAN: THE FREEDOM TRAIL

**T**HE FREEDOM TRAIL is much more than a 2½-mi route of historic sites. As an eager army of curious visitors discovers every year, it's a walk into history, to the events that exploded on the world during the Revolution, an odyssey whose 16 way stations allow you to reach out and touch the very wellsprings of American civilization. (And for those with a pinch of Yankee frugality: only three of the sites charge admission.) You may follow the route marked on the neighborhood maps. Try to allow a full day to complete the entire route comfortably, although some have been known to cram it into a few aerobic-paced hours. Perhaps some of its sights are more interesting than others, and perhaps it lacks the multimedia bells and whistles now becoming the norm at historic attractions. But that's what makes the Freedom Trail unique: it allows history to speak for itself.

With one foot in front of the other—just like the fledgling nation—begin at the very hub of the Hub, ☞ **Boston Common,** America's oldest public park. Get your bearings at the Visitors Information Center on Tremont Street and then head for the ☞ **State House,** Boston's finest piece of Federalist architecture; its 23-karat gilded dome looms magisterially above Beacon Hill. Several blocks away is the ☞ **Park Street Church,** whose steeple is considered by many to be the most beautiful in all of New England; here, the anthem "America" was first sung. Reposing in the church's shadows is the ☞ **Granary Burying Ground,** final resting place of Samuel Adams, John Hancock, Paul Revere, and "Mother" Goose. A short stroll beyond the **statue of Benjamin Franklin** will bring you to ☞ **King's Chapel,** built in 1754 and a hotbed of Anglicanism during the Colonial period. One of the poetry readings here in "the King's English" will prep you for the ☞ **Old Cor-**

**ner Bookstore,** onetime publisher of Hawthorne, Emerson, and Longfellow. Nearby is the ☞ **Old South Meeting House,** where pre-tempest arguments over a tax on tea were heard in 1773, leading to the Boston Tea Party. Overlooking the ☞ **site of the Boston Massacre** is the earliest known public building in Boston, the ☞ **Old State House,** a stately Georgian beauty that houses a museum devoted to the city's yesteryears.

If it's midday, fuel up at **Faneuil Hall** (☞ *below*)—the first floor has numerous eateries—then explore its Assembly Room upstairs, the virtual "Cradle of Liberty," where Samuel Adams fired the indignation of Bostonians during those times that tried men's souls. Explore Quincy Market, and then pass under the expressway to enter the North End. Taking one step forward, into ☞ **Paul Revere's House,** takes you back 200 years—here are the hero's own saddlebags, toddy-warmer, and a pine cradle made from a molasses cask (Paul was papa to 16 children). Full-day trekkers might want to rest about now at the tranquil Paul Revere Mall, nearby. Next, tackle a place guaranteed to trigger a wave of oh-gosh patriotism: the ☞ **Old North Church** of "One if by land, two if by sea" fame— sorry, the 154 creaking stairs leading to the belfry are out of bounds for visitors. From ☞ **Copp's Hill Burying Ground,** cross the bridge over the Charles and check out that revered icon the ☞ **USS Constitution,** nicknamed "Old Ironsides" (cannonballs bounced off her copperplated hull). The photo finish? A climb to the top of the ☞ **Bunker Hill Monument** for the incomparable vistas. Finally, head for the nearby Charlestown water shuttle, which goes directly to the downtown area, and congratulate yourself: You've just finished a unique cram course in American History.

dish Nichols (1872–1964) made this house—built in 1804 and attributed to Charles Bulfinch—her lifelong home. Although the Victorian furnishings passed to Miss Nichols by descent, she added a number of Colonial-style pieces to the mix, such as an American Empire rosewood sideboard and a bonnet-top Chippendale highboy. The result is a delightful mélange of styles. Nichols made arrangements in her will for the house to become a museum, and gracious and knowledgeable volunteers from the neighborhood have been playing host to visitors since then. ⊠ *55 Mt. Vernon St.,* ☎ *617/227–6993.* ⊡ *$5 for tours only.* ⊘ *May–Oct., Tues.–Sat. noon–4:15; Nov.–Dec. and Feb.–Apr., Mon., Wed.–Thurs., and Sat. noon–4:15. Tours on the ¼ hr; closed Jan. T stop: Park St.*

**❷ Park Street Church.** If the Congregationalist Park Street Church, at the corner of Tremont and Park streets, could talk, what a joyful noise it would make. Inside the church, which was designed by Peter Banner and erected in 1809–10, Samuel Smith's hymn "America" was first sung on July 4, 1831. The country's oldest musical organization, the Handel & Hayden Society, was founded here in 1815; in 1829 William Lloyd Garrison began his long public campaign for the abolition of slavery. The church—called "the most impressive mass of brick and mortar in America" by Henry James—is earmarked by its steeple, considered by many critics to be the most beautiful in New England. Just outside Park Street Church at the intersection of Park and Tremont streets (and the main subway crossroads of the city) is **Brimstone Corner.** Does the name refer to the fervent thunderation of the church's preachers, the fact that gunpowder was once stored in the church's crypt, or the amazing story that preachers once scattered burning sulfur on the pavement to attract the attention of potential churchgoers? Historians can't agree. ⊠ *0 Park St.,* ☎ *617/523–3383.* ⊘ *Tours mid-June–Aug., Tues.–Sat. 9:30–3:30. Sun. services at 9, 10:45, and 5:30. T stop: Park St.*

**Park Street Station.** Look out for Charlie, that poor soul immortalized in the 1950s Kingston Trio hit about a man "who never returned" for lack of a five-cent subway fare. The Park Street Station was one of the first four stops of the first subway in America; the line originally ran only as far as the present-day Boylston stop. It was opened for service in 1897 against the warnings of those convinced it would make buildings along Tremont Street collapse. The copper-roof kiosks are national historic landmarks—outside the kiosks cluster flower vendors, street musicians, and partisans of causes and beliefs ranging from Irish nationalism to Krishna Consciousness, all making for a general dither and considerable litter.

**Pinckney Street.** Almost all the wooden houses on the north slope of Beacon Hill are gone now. Exceptions may be found at 5 and 7 Pinckney Street, near the corner of Joy Street, where a 1791 structure stands.

**William Hickling Prescott House.** A modest but intriguing house museum has been installed in this five-story, 1808 Federal structure designed by Asher Benjamin, home to historian William Hickling Prescott from 1845 to 1859. Some rooms are furnished with period furniture, including the former study with Prescott's desk and "noctograph," which helped the nearly blind scholar write. Ask about his secret staircase, which allowed Prescott to escape into his study from boring guests in the parlor. Now the headquarters for the Massachusetts Society of Colonial Dames of America, the house also has a fine costume collection. ⊠ *55 Beacon St.,* ☎ *617/742–3190.* ⊡ *$4.* ⊘ *Tours only, Tues.–Wed. and Sat. noon–4.*

★ **Smith Court African-American Community.** One of Boston's most important 19th-century African-American communities flourished in the neighborhood surrounding the African Meeting House (☞ *above*); today, you can soak up the historic atmosphere by viewing picturesque 3-ft-wide **Holmes Alley** (⊠ Between Joy and S. Russell Sts. at the end of Smith Ct.) and the five residential structures typical of the homes of African-American Bostonians in the 1800s. They include Number 3, a home built in 1799 and now a National Historic Landmark; it's one of the most gracious clapboard structures remaining in Boston. William Nell, the historian and famed crusader for school integration active in William Lloyd Garrison's circle, lived here. Together, these sites bring Boston's African-American past very close.

❺ **State House.** It is hard to imagine a prouder or more hopeful moment: the nation was at peace, Massachusetts ships sailed every sea in pursuit of ever more lucrative trade, and the surviving fathers of the Revolution were on hand to enshrine the ideals of their new Commonwealth in a handsome and graceful State House designed by Charles Bulfinch. It was the Fourth of July, 1795. Governor Samuel Adams laid the cornerstone. Paul Revere made a speech; later, he would roll the copper sheathing for the dome.

Bulfinch's State House is one of the greatest works—perhaps the greatest—of classical architecture in America, so striking that it hardly suffers for having had appendages added in three directions by bureaucrats and lesser architects. It is arguably the most architecturally distinguished seat of state government in America; it was built well before the trend turned toward designs based on the Capitol in Washington. (Charles Bulfinch later held the position of architect of the U.S. Capitol.) The neoclassical design is poised between Georgian and Federal; its finest features are the delicate Corinthian columns of the portico, the graceful pediment and window arches, and the vast yet visually weightless golden dome (gilded in 1874). During World War II, the dome was painted gray so that it would not reflect moonlight during blackouts and thereby offer a target to anticipated Axis bombers.

Bulfinch's work would have stood splendidly on its own, but the growth of the state bureaucracy necessitated additions. The yellow-brick annex extending to the rear is clumsily ostentatious, but at least it is invisible from Beacon Street. The light-colored stone wings added to either side of the original structure early in this century serve no aesthetic purpose.

Inside the State House are Doric Hall, with its statuary and portraits, a part of the original structure; the Hall of Flags, hung with battle flags from all the wars in which Massachusetts regiments have participated; and the chambers of the General Court (legislature) and Senate, including the carved wooden *Sacred Cod* that symbolizes the state's maritime wealth. In 1933, *Harvard Lampoon* wags stole the Cod; the uproar was so great it was speedily returned. (These rooms are open to the public during business hours.) Check out the giant, modernistic clock in the Great Hall designed by New York artist R. M. Fischer. Its installation in 1986 at a cost of $100,000 was roundly slammed as a symbol of legislative extravagance. There's also a wealth of statuary: figures of Horace Mann, Daniel Webster, and, added in 1990, a youthful-looking President John F. Kennedy in full stride.

Two statues of American women stand on the front lawn. One is Anne Hutchinson, who challenged the religious hierarchy of the Massachusetts Bay Colony. She was excommunicated in 1638 and sentenced to banishment; after leaving the colony she became one of the founders of Rhode Island. Her supporter Mary Dyer was also excommunicated; she later converted to the Quaker faith and was finally hanged for defending her beliefs. Her statue on the State House grounds overlooks the spot on the Boston Common where she mounted the gallows. ⊠ *Beacon St. between Hancock and Bowdoin Sts.,* ☎ *617/727–3676.* ⊡ *Free.* ☉ *Tours weekdays and Sat. 10–4, last tour at 3:30. Research library:* ☎ *617/727–2590.* ☉ *Weekdays 11–5. T stop: Park St.*

**Vilna Shul.** As the oldest remaining synagogue in Boston, this historic treasure is the focus of both renovation and research. The two-story brick synagogue was completed in 1920 by Jews from Vilna in what is now Lithuania. Of the more than 50 synagogues that once dotted Beacon Hill, it's the last intact example. The distinctive, L-shape second-floor sanctuary has separate seating for men and women in keeping with Orthodox tradition. The building, abandoned in 1985, was bought by the Vilna Center for Jewish Heritage, which is overseeing its restoration. ⊠ *14–18 Phillips St.,* ☎ *617/523–2324.* ⊡ *Donation.* ☉ *Apr.–Nov., Sun. 1–3; hrs may vary, call ahead. T stop: Charles/MGH.*

**❶ Visitor Information Center.** Information Central, this center is adjacent to the Common's Parkman Plaza. It's well supplied with stacks of free pamphlets about Boston, and the staff can field all questions. ☎ *617/ 536–4100 or 888/733–2678, general Boston information; center takes no incoming calls.* ☉ *Daily 9–5.*

# THE OLD WEST END

When Boston's 18th-century architects decided to go vertical with tall church steeples, they had no idea that their graceful edifices would one day be reposing in the shadow of 40-story skyscrapers. In this city, the startling contrast of old and new side by side is nowhere more evident than in the Old West End. Just a few decades ago, this district—separated from Beacon Hill by Cambridge Street—resembled the typical medieval city: thoroughfares that twisted and turned, maddening one-way lanes, and streets that were a veritable hive of laboring populations. Then, progress—or what passes for progress—all but eliminated the thriving communities of Irish, Italians, Jews, and Greeks to make room for a mammoth project of urban renewal, designed in the 1960s by that magnate of modernism, I. M. Pei. Today, little remains of the *Old* West End except for a few brick tenements and a handful of historic monuments, including the first house built for Harrison Gray Otis. But rambling around the Old West End can be a fascinating experience: here, time seems to zoom by and then, a minute later, magically stand still. For sports fans, the Old West End is nirvana: the FleetCenter draws in crowds by the thousands. And across from the neighborhood, at Science Park, sits the innovative Museum of Science.

The only surviving structures in the Old West End with any real history are two public institutions, the now disused **Suffolk County** (or Charles Street) **Jail** and the much-used **Massachusetts General Hospital.** Both are near the Charles Street Circle, where the Longfellow Bridge—called the Salt and Pepper Bridge because of the shakerlike stone shapes that ornament it—begins its reach across the Charles to Cambridge. The former jail is interesting chiefly for its central building, dating from 1849, designed by Gridley Bryant at the close of Boston's Granite Age. That made it too old for a secure jail, as well as terribly crowded and miserable for the inmates. The new Nashua Street Jail opened in 1991.

Behind Mass General and the sprawling Charles River Park apartment complex is a small grid of streets recalling an older Boston. Here are furniture and electric-supply stores, a good discount camping-supply house (Hilton's Tent City, on Friend Street; ☞ Sporting Goods *in* Chapter 8), and the Commonwealth Brewing Company on Portland Street (☞ Sightseeing *in* the Gold Guide). The main drag here is Causeway Street. North Station, on Causeway between Haverhill and Canal streets, provides service to commuters from the northern suburbs and can be jammed when there's a game at the FleetCenter.

*Numbers in the text correspond to numbers in the margin and on The Old West End map.*

## A Good Walk

As this walk proves, Boston allows you to enjoy both the 21st and the 19th centuries in the space of a few hours. From Beacon Hill walk along the scenic paths of the **Esplanade** bordering the Charles River to reach the giga-mega-techno wonders of the **Museum of Science** ① and the **Charles Hayden Planetarium.** For views of old Boston, backtrack via Fruit Street and **Massachusetts General Hospital** ② to Cambridge Street for a visit to the neoclassical salons of the first **Harrison Gray Otis House** ③ and the **Old West Church** ④. A visit to the **FleetCenter** ⑤ is best done via the T (North Station) or by car.

TIMING

Even with a kid or two in tow, it shouldn't take more than an hour to reach the Museum of Science via the Esplanade. The walk is not recommended in cold weather, but the locale is readily accessible by the MBTA's Green Line. After taking in the museum, head to the sights on Cambridge Street, and then catch dinner in the neighborhood. You can return to the museum's Hayden Planetarium for an evening laser show or follow the throngs of arriving sports fans to the nearby Fleet-Center to see the Celtics or Bruins in action.

## Sights to See

**Esplanade.** At the northern end of Charles Street is one of several foot-bridges crossing Storrow Drive to the Esplanade and **Hatch Memorial Shell.** The Boston Pops, made immensely popular by its former maestro, the late Arthur Fiedler, gives free concerts in summer up to and including the Fourth of July. For the almost nightly entertainment throughout the rest of the summer, Bostonians haul lawn chairs and blankets to the lawn in front of the shell; bring a picnic basket, find an empty spot—no mean feat, so come early—and you'll feel right at home, too. An impressive head, in stone, of the late Fiedler watches over the walkers, joggers, picnickers, and sunbathers who fill its paths on pleasant days. The Esplanade is home port for the fleet of small sailboats that dot the Charles River Basin. They belong to Community Boating, which offers membership on a monthly or seasonal basis. Here, too, is the turn-of-the-century **Union Boat Club Boathouse,** headquarters for the country's oldest private rowing club.

⑤ **FleetCenter.** At first, when the name for the facility replacing aging Boston Garden was announced, hard-core fans swore that only the words "New Boston Garden" would ever pass their lips. But gradually, the name FleetCenter has won acceptance. For starters, this grand facility on Causeway Street, where the Celtics (basketball) and the Bruins (hockey) play their home games, is nothing like the old creaking, leaking Garden, the only court in the NBA where basketball games could be called on account of rain. Opening in 1928, the Garden hosted acts from the Beatles to the Grateful Dead, from Liberace to Frank Sinatra. Larry Bird made his NBA debut there in 1979; Bobby Orr's Number 4 was

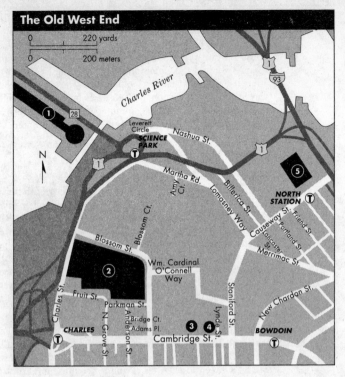

### The Old West End

retired in 1979. The old Garden will continue to be mournfully honored at after-game beer sessions in bars clustered around North Station. But since 1995 those same mourners have enjoyed the benefits and creature comforts of FleetCenter's amenities—air-conditioning, increased seating capacity, improved food selection, a 1,200-vehicle parking garage, and nearly double the number of bathrooms. The Bruins now play on a regulation-size rink, and there are no obstructed views. ⊠ *Causeway St. at Canal St.,* ☎ *617/624–1000 for recorded information on sports events and ticket availability. T stop: North Station.*

**❸ Harrison Gray Otis House.** This is the first of three houses built for and bearing the name of Harrison Gray Otis, Boston's third mayor and prominent citizen and developer. It's now the headquarters for the Society for the Preservation of New England Antiquities (SPNEA), an organization that owns and maintains dozens of historic properties throughout the region. The society has restored the Otis House (1796) and opened two of its floors as a museum. The furnishings, textiles, wall coverings, and even the interior paint, specially mixed to match old samples, are faithful to the Federal period, circa 1790–1810. You may be surprised to see how bright and vivid were the colors favored in those days and to learn that closets as we know them had not quite made their appearance. The dining room is set up as though Harry Otis were about to come in and pour a glass of Madeira; one gets the feeling he would have been good company. But Otis lived here only four years before moving to more sumptuous digs, designed by Charles Bulfinch, on Beacon Hill (☞ Harrison Gray Otis House *in* Beacon Hill and Boston Common, *above*). The SPNEA also conducts a Beacon Hill walking tour that originates here (☞ Sightseeing *in* Smart Travel Tips A to Z). ⊠ *141 Cambridge St.,* ☎ *617/227–3956.* ☞ *$4.* ⊘ *Wed.–*

*Sun. 11–5; guided tours only, on the hr; last tour at 4. T stop: Charles/MGH, Bowdoin.*

**❷ Massachusetts General Hospital.** For doctors and medical students, paying a visit to Mass General is akin to art historians' visiting the Louvre. Incorporated in 1811 and the site of one of the most important breakthroughs in modern surgery—the use of ether—it has traditionally been regarded as the nation's premier general hospital. The domed, granite **Bulfinch Pavilion** was designed in 1818 by Boston's leading architect, Charles Bulfinch. It was in the hospital's amphitheater that, on October 16, 1846, Dr. John Collins Warren performed the first operation on a patient anesthetized by ether; the place was promptly nicknamed "The Ether Dome." You may visit the amphitheater today when it is not in use (use the hospital's North Grove Street entrance) and see a display describing the procedure that made modern surgery possible.

Mass General once housed the Harvard Medical School, and it was in a laboratory here around Thanksgiving 1849 that one of Boston's most notorious murders took place. Dr. George Parkman, a wealthy landlord and Harvard benefactor, was bludgeoned to death by Dr. John Webster (☞ George Parkman House *in* Beacon Hill and Boston Common, *above*). After several days of mystery over Parkman's disappearance, Webster's doom was sealed when part of the victim's jaw was discovered in the laboratory stove. Other grisly evidence turned up in the cesspool beneath Webster's privy. ✉ *55 Fruit St.* 🕿 *Free.* ☉ *Amphitheater daily 9–5. T stop: Charles/MGH.*

**★ ☾ ❶ Museum of Science.** With 15-ft lightning bolts in the Theater of Electricity and a 20-ft-high *Tyrannosaurus rex* model, this is just the place to ignite any child's Jurassic spark. Occupying a compound of buildings that stands north of Mass General, the museum sits astride the Charles River Dam and its boat locks. Its collections date from 1830; its development as a rich educational resource evolved under the recent directorship of the explorer-mountaineer-cartographer Bradford Washburn, who is still active on the board. More than 600 exhibits cover astronomy, astrophysics, anthropology, progress in medicine, computers, the organic and inorganic earth sciences, and much more. Washburn and his curators made the Museum of Science a strong leader in hands-on education; "Investigate," a permanent exhibit, lets kids explore such scientific principles as gravity by balancing objects—there are no wrong answers here, only discoveries. Kids can learn the physics behind everyday play activities such as swinging and bumping up and down on a teeter-totter in a new permanent exhibit, "Science in the Park." Other exhibits invite the participation of children and adults: the Transparent Woman's organs light up as their functions are described, and whole families can play "virtual volleyball." Shows planned for 2000 include "Reptiles: Real and Robotic" (January–May), "Secrets of Aging" (April–September), and "Powers of Nature" (October—March 2001), and an exhibition devoted to twisters, hurricanes, storms, and earthquakes. At press time, there were plans to combine the Computer Museum (☞ Downtown Boston, *below*) and the Museum of Science. ✉ *Science Park at the Charles River Dam,* 🕿 *617/723–2500.* 🕿 *$9. Reduced-price combination tickets available for museum, planetarium, and Omni Theater.* ☉ *July 5–early Sept., Sat.–Thurs. 9–7, Fri. 9–9; mid-Sept.–July 4, daily 9–5. T stop: Science Park.*

The Museum of Science's **Charles Hayden Planetarium** (🕿 617/523–6664), with its sophisticated multimedia system based on a Zeiss planetarium projector, produces exciting programs on astronomical discoveries. Laser light shows, with laser graphics and computer animation, are scheduled Thursday through Sunday evenings. The shows are probably best for children older than five. Admission costs $7.50.

The Museum of Science also contains the **Mugar Omni Theater,** which has state-of-the-art film projection and sound systems. The 76-ft-high, five-story domed screen wraps around and over you, and 27,000 watts of power drive the 84 loudspeakers. Try to get tickets in advance; you can get them two days ahead for weekends and holidays (V, AE, and MC are accepted for phone orders with a $1.50 handling fee). ☎ 617/ 723–2500. ▣ *Shows only: $7.50. Reduced price combination tickets available for museum, planetarium, and Omni Theater.* ◎ *Shows from 10 AM.*

❹ **Old West Church.** Built in 1806 to a design of the great builder and architect Asher Benjamin, this imposingly elegant United Methodist church stands, along with the Harrison Gray Otis House (☞ *above*) next door, as a reminder of the days when the West End near Bowdoin Square was a fashionable district. In the early 1960s, when the church served as a public library and polling place, Congressman John F. Kennedy voted here. ✉ *131 Cambridge St. (at Staniford St.),* ☎ *617/ 227–5088.* ◎ *Generally weekdays 9–5, but call to confirm. Sun. service at 11. T stop: Bowdoin, Government Center.*

# GOVERNMENT CENTER

This is the section of town Bostonians love to hate. Not only does **Government Center** house that which they can't fight—City Hall—it also contains some of the bleakest architecture since the advent of poured concrete. The sweeping brick plaza that marks **City Hall** and the twin towers of the **John F. Kennedy Federal Office Building** begins at the junction in which Cambridge becomes Tremont Street, an area once known as Scollay Square. An ambitious urban renewal project in the 1960s completely obliterated the raffish, down-at-the-heels square— a bawdy, raucous place where sailors would go when they came into port—that was also famous for its burlesque houses (such as the storied "Old Howard") and its secondhand-book stores. It is remembered more and more fondly as years go by.

The curving six-story **Center Plaza** building, across from the Government Center T stop and the broad brick expanse of City Hall Plaza, emulates the much older Sears Crescent, a curved commercial block next to the Government Center T stop. (A small plaque in the square behind the crescent-shape building marks the site of the old Howard Theater's stage.) The Center Plaza building separates Tremont Street from the higher ground to the west: Pemberton Square and the old and "new" courthouses.

The stark, treeless plain surrounding City Hall—like a man-made tundra of brick—has been roundly jeered for its user-unfriendly aura, but in recent years the expanse has been enlivened by feisty political rallies, free summer concerts, and the occasional festival. On the corner of Tremont and Court streets, the bleakness is partly mitigated by the local landmark Steaming Kettle, a gilded kettle cast in 1873 that once boiled around the clock. (It now marks a Starbucks.) More gracious buildings are just a little farther on: 18th-century Faneuil Hall and the feeding frenzy of Quincy Market.

Separating the North End from the Government Center area—and the rest of Boston—is the **Fitzgerald Expressway,** which appears to be not long for this world. At some point it is due to be replaced with an underground highway as part of the multibillion-dollar Central Artery/Tunnel project (dubbed "The Big Dig"), whose master plan includes the creation of the Ted Williams Tunnel, a third underwater tunnel to Logan Airport now open but restricted to commercial vehicles. All of this is intended to improve traffic flow; in the meantime, calling the area a mess is putting it mildly. Signs and maps explaining the project can be found posted on construction zones along Surface Artery. Driver alert: the rerouting of traffic and shifts in one-way signs are constantly changing what was once a conquerable maze into a nearly impenetrable puzzle. Trust no maps.

*Numbers in the text correspond to numbers in the margin and on the Government Center and the North End map.*

## A Good Walk

The modern, stark expanse of Boston's **City Hall** ① and the twin towers of the **John F. Kennedy Federal Office Building** ② introduce visitors to Boston in the urban renewal age, but just across Congress Street is **Faneuil Hall** ③, a site of political speech-making since Revolutionary times, and just beyond that is **Quincy Market** ④, where shop-till-you-droppers can sample a profusion of international taste treats. For more Bostonian fare, walk back toward Congress Street to the city's oldest restaurant, the **Union Oyster House** ⑤. Near the restaurant is the recently dedicated **Holocaust Memorial** ⑥, a six-tower construction of glass and steel. Follow Marshall Street north and turn onto Blackstone Street to pass the open-air stalls of **Haymarket** ⑦, a flurry of activity on Friday and Saturday. To sample Italian goodies, make your way through a pedestrian tunnel underneath Fitzgerald Highway—destined to be a construction zone for the next few years due to Boston's massive Central Artery project—and enter the **North End** (☞ *below*) at Salem Street.

TIMING

You can easily spend a whole day hitting the stores, boutiques, and historic sites of the Faneuil Hall and Quincy Market complex. On Fridays and Saturdays, you'll be able to join in the frenzied activity of the Haymarket. Nearly all the historic sites and plenty of the local stores and restaurants are open on Sunday.

## Sights to See

❶ **City Hall.** Over the years, various plans—involving gardens, restaurants, music, and hotels—have been floated to make this area a more people-friendly site. Whether anything would ameliorate Bostonians' collective disregard for the chilly setting of Government Center is anyone's guess. But City Hall, an upside-down ziggurat design on a vast, sloping redbrick plaza, remains one of the most striking structures in the Government Center complex. The design by Kallman, McKinnell, and Knowles confines administrative functions to the upper floors and places offices that deal with the public on the street level: despite those democratic intentions, the building is not much loved. ⊠ *Congress St. at North St. T stop: Government Center.*

★ ❸ **Faneuil Hall.** In some ways Faneuil Hall is a local Ark of the Covenant; a considerable part of Boston's spirit resides here. Learning to pronounce its name is the first task of any newcomer—say "Fan'l" or "*Fan*-yuhl." Like other Boston landmarks, Faneuil Hall has evolved over many years. It was originally erected in 1742, the gift of wealthy merchant Peter Faneuil, who wanted the hall to serve as both a place for town meetings and a public market. It burned in 1761 and was immediately reconstructed according to the original plan of its designer, the Scottish portrait painter John Smibert (who is buried in the Granary Burying Ground). In 1763 James Otis helped inaugurate the era that culminated in American independence when he dedicated the rebuilt hall to the "cause of liberty."

In 1772 Samuel Adams stood here and first suggested that Massachusetts and the other colonies organize a Committee of Correspondence to maintain semiclandestine lines of communication in the face of hardening British repression. In later years the hall again lived up to Otis's dedication when Wendell Phillips and Charles Sumner pled for support of the abolitionist cause from its podium. The tradition continues to this day: in presidential election years, the hall hosts debates between contenders in the Massachusetts primary.

Faneuil Hall was substantially enlarged and remodeled in 1805 according to a Greek Revival design of the noted architect Charles Bulfinch, and this is the building we see today. Its purposes remain the same: the balconied Great Hall is available to citizens' groups on presentation of a request signed by a required number of responsible parties; it also plays host to regular concerts. (When the grand hall itself is closed to the public—for an event like a concert—a closed-circuit TV gives visitors a glimpse of the famous podium.)

Inside Faneuil Hall are the great mural *Webster's Reply to Hayne,* Gilbert Stuart's portrait of Washington at Dorchester Heights, and dozens of other paintings of famous Americans. On the top floors are the headquarters and museum of the **Ancient and Honorable Artillery Company of Massachusetts,** the oldest militia in the nation (1638). Its status is now strictly ceremonial, but it is justly proud of the arms, uniforms, and other artifacts on display.

Brochures about Faneuil Hall's history, distributed by the National Park Service, make light-hearted references to the ongoing commercialism nearby by reprinting a 1958 ditty by Francis Hatch: "Here orators in ages past / Have mounted their attack / Undaunted by the proximity / Of sausage on the rack." Faneuil Hall has always sat in the middle of Boston's main marketplace: men like Andrew Jackson and Daniel Webster debated the future of the Republic here while the fragrances of bacon and snuff—sold by merchants in Quincy Market across the road—greeted their noses. Today, the aroma of cinnamon wafts throughout Faneuil Hall from a gourmet coffee and snack bar. There are still shops at ground level, but they cater mainly to the tourists seeking New England bric-a-brac. If you want an authentic Boston souvenir, visit the **City Store** (enter on the north side of the hall), which sells surplus municipal items ranging from real fire hydrants to hard hats to banners from past Boston Marathons to vintage street signs (profits from City Store support neighborhood youth programs).

Why is the gold-plated weather vane atop the cupola in the shape of a grasshopper? One story has it that Sir Thomas Gresham—founder of London's Royal Exchange—had been discovered in 1519 as a foundling babe by children chasing grasshoppers in a field and placed an image of the insect over the Exchange to commemorate his salvation. Peter Faneuil liked the critter (it's the traditional symbol of good luck) and in his turn had one mounted over Faneuil Hall. The 8-pound, 52-inch-long insect remains as the only unmodified part of the original structure. Just across the way from Faneuil Hall is Quincy Market (☞ *below*), also known as the shopping extravaganza called Faneuil Hall Marketplace. ⊠ *Faneuil Hall Sq.* 🖾 *Free.* ☉ *Daily 9–5. T stop: Government Center, Aquarium.*

❼ **Haymarket.** The Haymarket is an exuberant maze of a marketplace, packed with loudly self-promoting vendors who fill Marshall and

Blackstone streets on Fridays and Saturdays from 7 AM until mid-afternoon. Pushcart vendors hawk fruits and vegetables against a backdrop of fish, meat, and cheese shops. The accumulation of debris left every evening has been celebrated in a whimsical 1976 public arts project—Mags Harries's "Asaroton," a Greek word meaning unswept floors—consisting of bronze fruit peels and other detritus smashed into pavement. It is now temporarily removed from the intersection of Blackstone and Hanover streets due to the Central Artery project; officials promise to reinstall Ms. Harries's piece when the project is over. Another Harries piece, in bronze depicting a gathering of stray gloves, tumbles down the escalators in the Porter Square T station in Cambridge.

Not far from the Haymarket—between North and Hanover streets—lies Boston at its time-machine best: the **Blackstone Block,** now visited mostly for its culinary landmark, the Union Oyster House (☞ *below*). Named for Boston's first settler, William Blaxton, it is the city's oldest commercial block, for decades dominated by the butcher trade. As a tiny remnant of Old Boston, the Blackstone Block remains the city's "family attic"—to use the winning metaphor of critic Donlyn Lyndon: more than three centuries of architecture on view, ranging from the 18th-century Capen House to the modern Bostonian Hotel. A Colonial-period warren of winding lanes—Scott Alley, Salt Lane, and Creek Square—surrounds the block, bursting with surprises and anachronistic storefronts at every turn.

Facing the Blackstone Block, in the vest-pocket-size **Union Park** framed by New Congress Street and Dock Square, are two bronze figures, one seated on a bench and the other standing eye to eye with passersby. Both represent James Michael Curley, mayor, governor, congressman, and questionable model for all urban bosses. It is just as well that he has no pedestal; the so-called Rascal King was much more a man than an idol. Strongly supported by the working classes, he pursued many public works projects and was known as a particularly persuasive speaker. In 1946, he was sentenced to serve time in a federal penitentiary for fraud, but he refused to resign from his dual posts as mayor and congressman. His sentence was eventually commuted—his popularity only marginally diminished by the scandal—and he served out his term as mayor.

At Creek Square, near the Haymarket, can be found the **Boston Stone,** set into the brick wall of the gift shop of the same name. Older than the 1737 date the inscription suggests, it was long used as milepost zero in measuring distances from Boston.

**❻ Holocaust Memorial.** At night, its six 50-ft-high glass-and-steel towers glow like ghosts who vow never to forget. During the day, the monument seems at odds with the 18th-century streetscape of Blackstone Square behind it. Shoehorned into the north end of Union Park, the Holocaust Memorial is the work of Stanley Saitowitz, whose design was selected through an international competition; the finished memorial was dedicated in 1995. Recollections by Holocaust survivors are set into the glass-and-granite walls; the upper levels of the towers are etched with 6 million numbers in random sequence symbolizing the Jewish victims of the Nazi horror. In the granite base, grates, aswirl in manufactured steam, cover pits of fiery electronic embers that make for a particularly haunting scene after dark.

**❷ John F. Kennedy Federal Office Building.** Looming up at the northwest edge of City Hall Plaza, these twin towers are noted structures for architecture aficionados: they were designed by the founder of the

# Government Center and the North End

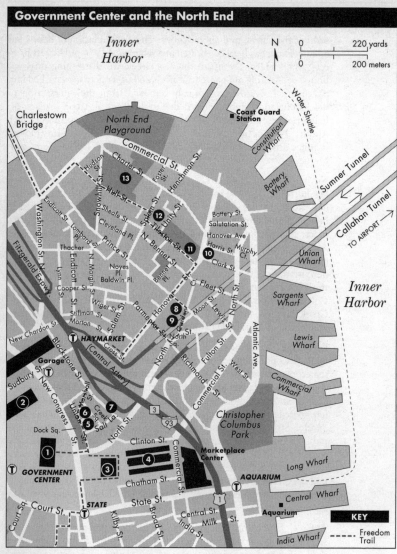

City Hall, **1**

Copp's Hill Burying Ground, **13**

Faneuil Hall, **3**

Haymarket, **7**

Holocaust Memorial, **6**

John F. Kennedy Federal Office Building, **2**

Old North Church, **12**

Paul Revere House, **8**

Paul Revere Mall (Prado), **11**

Pierce-Hichborn House, **9**

Quincy Market, **4**

St. Stephen's, **10**

Union Oyster House, **5**

Bauhaus movement, Walter Gropius, who taught at Harvard toward the end of his illustrious career. **Gropius's house,** designed by him in textbook Bauhaus style, is in nearby suburban Lincoln (☞ Lincoln *in* Chapter 9).

❹ **Quincy Market.** Not everyone likes Quincy Market, also known as **Faneuil Hall Marketplace;** some people prefer grit to polish and disdain the new cafés and boutiques. But there is no denying that this pioneer effort at urban recycling set the tone for many similar projects throughout the country and that it has brought tremendous vitality to a once-tired corner of Boston. More than two decades after its inauguration, Quincy Market continues to attract huge crowds of both tourists and locals throughout the year. In the 1970s, demolition was a distinct possibility for these historic yet decrepit buildings. Fortunately, the primitive idea that urban renewal was accomplished with a bulldozer was beginning to yield to the more progressive idea of "recycling." With the participation of the Boston Redevelopment Authority, architect Benjamin Thompson planned a renovation of all three Quincy Market buildings, and the Rouse Corporation of Baltimore undertook their restoration. Try to look beyond the shop windows to the grand design of the three monumental market buildings themselves; they represent a vision of the market as urban centerpiece, an idea whose time has certainly come again.

The market consists of three block-long annexes: **Quincy, North,** and **South Markets,** each 535 ft long and across a plaza from historic **Faneuil Hall** (☞ *above*). The structures were built to the 1826 design Alexander Parris conceived to alleviate cramped retailers' conditions then common to Faneuil Hall. The central structure—of handsome granite, with a Doric colonnade at either end and topped by a classical dome and rotunda—has kept its traditional market-stall layout, but the stalls now purvey international and specialty foods: raw shellfish, cold pasta salads, frozen yogurt, bagels, calzone, sausage-on-a-stick, Chinese egg rolls, brownies, and baklava, plus all the boutique chocolate-chip cookies your heart desires. This is perhaps Boston's best locale for grazing, the hardest part being choosing what to sample. Along the arcades on either side of the Central Market are vendors selling sweatshirts, photographs of Boston, and other arts and crafts—some schlocky, some not—along with a couple of open-air bars and restaurants. The North and South Markets house a mixture of chain stores and specialty boutiques. Quintessential Boston remains here only in Durgin Park, the traditional New England dining experience. At the waterfront end of Quincy Market is **Marketplace Center,** another shopping complex.

A favorite tourist site for photos is the tacky but beloved bronze Bugs Bunny statue standing outside the **Warner Bros. Store.** An outdoor flower market on the north side of Faneuil provides a splash of color; at Christmastime, trees along the cobblestone walks are strung with thousands of sparkling lights. In summer, up to 50,000 people per day descend on the market; the outdoor cafés are an excellent spot to watch the hordes. Year-round, these pedestrian walkways draw street jugglers and magicians—Peruvian instrumentalists often add their lilting sounds to the scene. Some people consider Quincy Market to be mall-style trendy, but you'll want to decide for yourself. ⌧ *Quincy Market/Faneuil Hall Marketplace,* ☎ *617/338–2323.* ⏱ *Mon.–Sat. 10–9, Sun. noon–6. Restaurants and bars generally open daily 11 AM–2 AM; food stalls open earlier. T stop: Haymarket, Government Center, State, Aquarium.*

**⑤ Union Oyster House.** Self-billed as the oldest restaurant in continuous service in the United States, the Union Oyster House first opened its doors as the Atwood & Bacon Oyster House in 1826. Charles Forster of Maine was the first American to use the curious invention of the toothpick on these premises. And John F. Kennedy was among more contemporary patrons; his favorite booth has been dedicated to his memory. The charming facade is constructed of Flemish bond brick and adorned with Victorian-style signage. In 1796, the seignorial Duke of Chartres (who would later assume the French throne as Louis-Philippe) helped pay rent for his accommodations on the second floor by teaching French. With its scallop, clam, and lobster dishes—as well as the de rigueur oyster—the menu hasn't changed much from the restaurant's early days (though the prices have). The distinctive semicircular oyster bar is open until midnight daily. ⊠ *41 Union St.,* ☎ *617/227–2750.* ⊙ *Sun.–Thurs. 11–9:30, Fri.–Sat. 11–10. T stop: Haymarket.*

# THE NORTH END

This warren of small streets on the northeast side of the Central Artery that extends to the end of the peninsula was Boston before there was a Boston. Men and women walked these narrow byways when Shakespeare was not yet 20 years buried and Louis XIV was new to the throne of France. The town of Boston bustled and grew rich here for a century and a half before the birth of American independence. In the 17th century the North End *was* Boston, for much of the rest of the peninsula was still under water or had yet to be cleared.

Today's North End is almost entirely a creation of the late 19th century, when brick tenements began to fill up with European immigrants—first the Irish, then Central European Jews, then the Portuguese, and finally the Italians. For more than 60 years the North End attracted an Italian population base, so much so that one wonders whether wandering Puritan shades might scowl at the concentration of Mediterranean verve, volubility, and Roman Catholicism here. This is not only Boston's haven for Italian restaurants (there are dozens) but also for Italian groceries, bakeries, boccie courts, churches, social clubs, cafés, and street-corner debates over home-team soccer games. July and August are highlighted by a series of street festivals, or *feste,* honoring various saints, and by local community events that draw visitors from all over the city.

But although you'll see hordes of tourists following the redbrick ribbon of the Freedom Trail through the North End, there's still a neighborhood feeling to the jumbled streets, from the grandmothers gossiping on fire escapes to the laundry strung on back porches. Gentrification has made inroads—it is a rare block in which one or more tenements have not received the exposed-brick and track-lighting treatment—but it is unlikely that the North End will relinquish its ethnic strength any time soon; the people speaking with Abruzzese accents on Salem and Hanover streets are not paid actors, and they are not—fortunately—going to disappear tomorrow. If you wish to study up on this fascinating district, head for the North End branch of the Boston Public Library on Parmenter Street, where a bust of Dante acknowledges local cultural pride.

*Numbers in the text correspond to numbers in the margin and on the Government Center and the North End map.*

## A Good Walk

History on two feet a day—that's the best way to view the sights of the North End: parking is practically nonexistent here, so most people do this neighborhood by foot power, arriving via the T (Haymarket or Government Center). If you arrive by car, you can park at any of several garages near Quincy Market and cross under the Central Artery through a pedestrian tunnel that connects with **Salem Street.** (Be leery—the underpass is often a haven for the city's homeless.) The area between Faneuil Hall and the North End is ground zero of the massive Central Artery project; it's filled with construction equipment, pits, fences, and ever-changing routes for cars and foot traffic. Plan to cross into the North End only by the pedestrian tunnel; otherwise, you'll have to make heart-pounding dashes through traffic. Once through the tunnel, turn right on Cross Street and left on **Hanover Street,** one of the North End's main thoroughfares. Take Hanover to Parmenter Street and turn left at North Square, following the Freedom Trail, to reach the fascinating (especially for kids) **Paul Revere House** ⑧—as the brochures state, "If Paul Revere were alive today, he'd still have a home in Boston." Right next door is the **Pierce-Hichborn House** ⑨, another venerable brick building. Take Prince Street back to Hanover Street and continue on Hanover to reach **St. Stephen's** ⑩, the only remaining church designed by the influential architect Charles Bulfinch. Directly across the street is the **Prado,** or **Paul Revere Mall** ⑪, dominated by a statue of the patriot and hero. At the end of the mall is the **Old North Church** ⑫, of "one if by land, two if by sea" fame, from which twin lanterns warned of the invading British on the night of Revere's historic ride. Continue following the Freedom Trail to Hull Street and **Copp's Hill Burying Ground** ⑬, the resting place of many Revolutionary heroes. Then head back to Hanover Street to enjoy a well-deserved cappuccino and cannoli.

### TIMING

Allow three to four hours for a walk through the North End. This part of town is made for strolling, day or night. Many people like to spend a day at nearby Quincy Market, then head under the Fitzgerald Expressway to the North End for dinner—the district has an impressive selection of traditional and contemporary Italian restaurants. Families should note that on Saturday afternoons from May to October the Paul Revere House schedules some of the most delightful events for children in the city (what seven-year-old would want to miss out on the mustering of the 10th Regiment Afoot?). And on Sundays, try to catch the ringing of the bells of Old North Church after the 11 AM service (they begin to ring at about 12:10 PM)—the bells today sound as sweet as when Paul Revere rang them on Sabbath mornings as a boy.

## Sights to See

⑬ **Copp's Hill Burying Ground.** An ancient and melancholy air hovers like a fine mist over this Colonial-era burial ground. The extensive North End graveyard incorporates four cemeteries established between 1660 and 1819. Near the Charter Street gate is the tomb of the Mather family, the dynasty of church divines (Cotton and Increase were the most famous sons) who held sway in Boston during the heyday of the old theocracy. Also buried here is Robert Newman, who crept into the steeple of the Old North Church to warn of the British attack the night of Paul Revere's ride. Look for the tombstone of Captain Daniel Malcom; it is pockmarked with musket-ball fire from British soldiers, who used the stones for target practice. ☉ *Apr.–Nov., daily 9–5; Dec.–Mar., daily 9–3. T stop: North Station.*

NEED A
BREAK?

From Copp's Hill head south and down on Snowhill Street; then, at the bottom, jog left briefly on Prince Street and right on Thatcher to arrive at **Pizzeria Regina** (⊠ 11½ Thatcher St., ☎ 617/227–0765) for what some consider the best pizza in the North End—thin-crusted, oily, and wonderful. (Beware Regina's food-court mall outposts, however—not the same animal.) **Galleria Umberto** (⊠ 289 Hanover St., ☎ 617/227–5709) turns out pizza that rivals Regina's, but you have to sample its slices standing up—if you're lucky. It's closed on Sunday.

**Ebenezer Clough House.** Hard by the Old North Church, this house warrants an exercise in imagination. Built in 1712, it is now the only local survivor of its era aside from Old North. Picture the streets lined with houses such as this, with an occasional grander Georgian mansion and some modest wooden-frame survivors of old Boston's many fires—this is what the North End looked like when Paul Revere was young. The home is privately owned and not open to the public. ⊠ *21 Unity St.*

**Hanover Street.** This is one of the North End's two main thoroughfares, named for the ruling dynasty of 18th-century England. Curiously, the label was retained after the Revolution, despite a flurry of patriotic renaming (King Street became State Street, for example). Hanover runs parallel to and one block east of Salem; its business center is thick with pastry shops and Italian cafés. It is also one of Boston's oldest public roads, once the site of the residences of the Rev. Cotton Mather and the Colonial-era patriot Dr. Joseph Warren, as well as a small drygoods store run by Eben D. Jordan—who went on to launch Jordan Marsh.

NEED A
BREAK?

**Caffè Vittoria** (⊠ 296 Hanover St., ☎ 617/227–7606) specializes in cappuccino and other coffee concoctions; its lively ambience and Sinatra-crooning jukebox make it a great spot at any hour. President Clinton has stopped by **Mike's Pastry** (⊠ 300 Hanover St., ☎ 617/742–3050) for the bakery's famous cannoli. Rumor has it that Secret Service agents made additional runs for him while he was in town.

★ ⑫ **Old North Church.** Standing at one end of the **Prado** (☞ Paul Revere Mall, *below*) is a church famous not only for being the oldest one in Boston (built in 1723) but for housing the two lanterns that glimmered from its steeple on the night of April 18, 1775. This is Christ Church, or the Old North, where a middle-aged silversmith named Paul Revere and a young sexton named Robert Newman managed that night to signal the departure by water to Lexington and Concord of the British regulars. Longfellow's poem aside, the lanterns were not a signal *to* Revere but *from* him to the citizens of Charlestown across the harbor. Newman, carrying the lanterns, ascended the steeple (the original tower blew down in 1804 and was replaced; the present one was put up in 1954 after the replacement was destroyed in a hurricane), while Revere began his clandestine trip by rowboat across the Mystic.

Although William Price designed the structure after studying Christopher Wren's London churches, the Old North—still home to an active Episcopal congregation (including descendants of the Reveres)—is an impressive building in its own right. Inside, note the gallery and graceful arrangement of pews (reserved in Colonial times for the families that rented them); the bust of George Washington, pronounced by the Marquis de Lafayette to be the truest likeness of the general he ever saw; the brass chandeliers, made in Amsterdam in 1700 and installed here in 1724; and the clock, the oldest still running in an American public building. The pews—Number 54 was the Revere family pew—

are the highest in America due to the little charcoal-burning foot warmers (used to accommodate parishioners back when). Try to visit when changes are rung on the bells, after the 11 AM Sunday service; recently restored and rehung, they bear the inscription, "We are the first ring of bells cast for the British Empire in North America." Every April 18, descendants of the patriots raise lanterns in the church belfry in a traditional reenactment.

One of the most peculiar mementos in the annals of American history is displayed in the small gift shop and museum next to the church. A glass container holds a vial of tea purportedly decanted from the boots of a participant in the notorious Boston tea party fracas. Other cases display such artifacts as a musket used in the battle of Lexington and a sword carried by Robert Gould Shaw, commander of the black regiment in the Civil War. Delightful souvenirs are for sale here, including bags of maple sugar candy and parchment copies of Longfellow's 1863 poem "Paul Revere's Ride."

Behind the church is the **Washington Memorial Garden,** where volunteers cultivate a plot devoted to plants and flowers favored in the 18th century. The garden is studded with several unusual commemorative plaques, including one for the Rev. George Burrough, who was hanged in the Salem witch trials in 1692; it was his great-grandson, Robert Newman, who had carried the famous pair of lanterns to the steeple. In another niche hangs the "Third Lantern," dedicated in 1976 during the country's bicentennial celebration. ⊠ *193 Salem St.,* ☎ *617/ 523–6676.* ⊙ *Daily 9–5. Sun. services at 9, 11, and 5; Wed. service at 9. T stop: Haymarket, North Station.*

 ☞ ❽ **Paul Revere House.** It is an interesting coincidence that the oldest house standing in downtown Boston should also have been the home of Paul Revere, patriot activist and silversmith. And it *is* a coincidence, as many homes of famous Bostonians have burned or been demolished over the years, and the Revere house could easily have become one of them back when it was just another makeshift tenement in the heyday of European immigration. It was saved from oblivion in 1902 and restored, lovingly though not quite scientifically, to an approximation of its original 17th-century appearance.

The house was built soon after the great fire of 1676, nearly a hundred years before Revere's 1775 midnight ride through Middlesex County (for an in-depth look at the "Son of Liberty," *see* Close-Up: "Listen, My Children, And You Shall Hear . . .", *below*). Revere owned it from 1770 until 1800, although he rented it out during the later part of that period. Pre-1900 photographs show it as a shabby warren of storefronts and apartments. The clapboard sheathing is a replacement, but 90% of the framework is original; note the Elizabethan-style overhang and leaded windowpanes. A few Revere furnishings are on display here, and just gazing at his silverwork brings the great man alive. The **Museum of Fine Arts** (☞ The Fens and Kenmore Square, *below*) has a splendid collection of Revere's silverwork.

Special events are scheduled throughout the year, many designed with children in mind. During the first weekend in December, the staff dresses in period costume and serves up apple cider cake and other Colonial-era goodies, and a silhouette maker shows off his skills. From May to October, there's something going on every Saturday afternoon: a silversmith or broom maker may be on hand, a hammer-dulcimer player could entertain, or the 10th Regiment Afoot—in full antique British regalia—might muster on the premises. And if you go

# "LISTEN, MY CHILDREN, AND YOU SHALL HEAR": ALL ABOUT PAUL REVERE

**THIS IS A TEST.** Paul Revere was (1) a great patriot whose midnight ride helped ignite the American Revolution; (2) a part-time dentist, expert in making false teeth; (3) a silversmith who crafted tea services; (4) a printer who engraved the first Massachusetts state currency; or (5) a talented metallurgist who cast cannons and bells. The only correct response is "all of the above." But there's even more, much more, to this outsize Revolutionary hero—bell ringer for Old North Church, major shareholder in the earliest fire-insurance company in the United States, founder of the coppermills that still bear his name, father of 16 children, coroner, and foreman of the jury of the most sensational murder trial of the day.

Although his life spanned eight decades (1734–1818), Revere is most famous for that one night when he became America's most celebrated Pony Express. *"Listen, my children, and you shall hear / Of the midnight ride of Paul Revere"* are the opening lines of Henry Wadsworth Longfellow's poem, which placed the event at the center of American folklore. Longfellow may have been an effective evangelist for Revere, but he was an indifferent historian. Ever since, scholars have been analyzing the varying accounts of the events of the night of April 18, 1775.

We now know that Revere was not the only midnight rider—William Dawes was also dispatched from Boston. We now know that Revere never looked for the "one if by land" signal from Charlestown: he told Robert Newman to hang two lanterns from Old North's belfry—the redcoats were on the move by water—but by that time, Revere was already on his way to Lexington astride Deacon Larkin's Brown Beauty. Nor did Revere ever raise the alarm in Concord. When he did make a little noise upon arriving, the duty sergeant told him to be quiet! Fischer further states that Revere never uttered the famous cry "The British are coming!" The reason? Bostonians considered themselves British.

**POETIC LICENSE ASIDE,** this tale has become part of the collective American spirit. We dote on learning that Revere forgot his spurs, only to retrieve them by tying a note to his dog's collar, then awaiting its return with the spurs now attached. We're grateful for the temerity he showed in asking a lady to sacrifice her petticoat to muffle the sounds of his oars while crossing the Charles. Little wonder that these tales—which may be less than historically accurate—resonate in the hearts and imagination of America's citizenry, as well as in Boston's streets on the third Monday of every April, Patriot's Day, when Revere's ride is reenacted—in daylight—to the cheers of thousands of onlookers. The clickety-clack of hoofs announces Revere himself, costumed in tricorne, knickers, and Colonial ponytail.

to the house on Patriot's Day, chances are you'll bump into the Middlesex Fife and Drum Corps.

The immediate neighborhood surrounding the Revere house also has Revere associations. The little park in North Square is named after Rachel Revere, his second wife, and the adjacent brick **Pierce-Hichborn House** (☞ *below*) once belonged to relatives of his. The lovely garden connecting the Revere house and the Pierce-Hichborn House is planted with flowers and medicinal herbs favored in Revere's day. ⊠ *19 North Sq.,* ☎ *617/523–2338.* ▣ *$2.50; combined admission for Paul Revere and Pierce-Hichborn houses $4.* ⊙ *Jan.–Mar., Tues.–Sun. 9:30–4:15; Nov.–Dec. and first 2 wks of Apr., daily 9:30–4:15; mid-Apr.–Oct., daily 9:30–5:15. T stop: Haymarket, Aquarium.*

★ ⓫ **Paul Revere Mall** (Prado). This makes a perfect time-out spot from the Freedom Trail. Bookended by two landmark churches—Old North and Bulfinch's St. Stephen's—the mall is flanked by brick walls lined with bronze plaques bearing the stories of famous North Enders of old. An appropriate centerpiece for this lovely cityscape is Cyrus Dallin's equestrian statue of Paul Revere. Despite Longfellow's "Paul Revere's Ride" and such statues as this, the gentle Revere was of stocky build and of medium height—whatever manly dash he possessed must have been in his eyes rather than his physique. That physique served him well enough, however, for he lived to be 83 and saw nearly all his revolutionary comrades buried.

❾ **Pierce-Hichborn House.** One of the city's oldest brick buildings, this structure, just to the left of the **Paul Revere House** (☞ *above*), was once owned by relatives of Revere's mother. (Nearby, at 4 Garden Court Street, a plaque commemorates the site of the former residence of Boston mayor John F. "Honey Fitz" Fitzgerald; his daughter, Rose— mother of President John F. Kennedy—was born there.) ⊠ *29 North Sq.,* ☎ *617/523–2338.* ▣ *Pierce-Hichborn House $2.50; combined admission for Paul Revere and Pierce-Hichborn houses $4.* ⊙ *Daily guided tours 12:30 and 2:30; call ahead to confirm. T stop: Haymarket, Aquarium.*

❿ **St. Stephen's.** Rose Kennedy, matriarch of the Kennedy clan, was christened here; 104 years later, it held mourners at her funeral. This is the only Charles Bulfinch church still standing in Boston and a stunning example of the Federal period to boot. Built in 1804, it was first used as a Unitarian Church; since 1862 it has served a Roman Catholic parish. When the belfry was stripped during a major 1960s renovation, the original dome was found beneath a false cap; it was covered with sheet copper and held together with hand-wrought nails. ⊠ *24 Clark St.,* ☎ *617/523–1230.* ⊙ *Daily 8:30–5. Sun. mass 8:30 and 11; Tues.–Fri. 7:30. T stop: Haymarket.*

**Salem Street.** This ancient and constricted thoroughfare, one of the two main North End streets, cuts through the heart of the neighborhood; it's lined with meat supply stores, hardware stores, an Italian ceramics shop, and more restaurants and cafés.

NEED A BREAK?

The allure of **Bova's Bakery** (⊠ 134 Salem St., ☎ 617/523–5601), a neighborhood institution, is not only its Italian breads and pastries—it's also open 24 hours a day (the deli closes at 1 AM, however). Another modest but pleasant hangout is **Biscotti's** (⊠ 95 Salem St., ☎ 617/ 227–8365).

# CHARLESTOWN

Boston started here. Charlestown was a thriving settlement a year before Colonials headed across the Charles River to found the city proper. Today, the district lures visitors with two of the most visible—and vertical—monuments in Boston's history: the Bunker Hill Monument, which commemorates the grisly battle during the Siege of Boston that became a symbol of patriotic resistance against the British, and the USS *Constitution,* whose indestructible masts continue to tower over the waterfront where she was built more than 200 years ago.

As a neighborhood, Charlestown remains a predominantly Irish-American enclave, with yuppification setting in steadily since the 1980s. The area suffers some notoriety from its reputation as alleged home turf for Irish-led organized crime; a number of bloody murders that remain unsolved—due to the neighborhood's vaunted "code of silence"—haven't helped. But Townies (as old-time Charlestown residents are called) are fiercely proud of their historic, elegantly maintained streets.

The blocks around the Bunker Hill Monument are a good illustration of a neighborhood in flux. Elegantly restored Federal and mid-19th-century town houses stand cheek by jowl with working-class quarters of similar vintage but more modest recent pasts along streets lined with gas lamps. Nearby Winthrop Square also has its share of interesting houses. Farther north along Main Street is City Square, Charlestown's main commercial district, which includes the new City Square Park, with its brick paths and handsome bronze fish sculptures. On Phipps Street you'll find the grave marker of John Harvard, a young minister who in 1638 bequeathed his small library to the fledgling Cambridge College, which was to be renamed in his honor. The precise location of the grave is uncertain, but a monument of 1828 marks its approximate site. John Harvard is also commemorated in the nearby Harvard Mall, a vest-pocket park.

To get to Charlestown, you may take Bus 93 from Haymarket Square, Boston, which stops three blocks from the Navy Yard entrance. A more interesting way to get here is to take the MBTA water shuttle from Long Wharf in downtown Boston, which runs every 15 or 30 minutes year-round.

*Numbers in the text correspond to numbers in the margin and on the Charlestown map.*

## A Good Walk

Charlestown can be reached on foot across the Charlestown Bridge. From **Copp's Hill Burying Ground** (☞ *above*), follow Hull Street to Commercial Street, and turn left to reach the bridge. You come upon the entrance of the **Charlestown Navy Yard** ① on your right after crossing the bridge. Just ahead is the **USS *Constitution*** ② museum and visitor center; next door is the **Visitors Center and Bunker Hill Pavilion.** From here, you may follow the red line of the Freedom Trail to the **Bunker Hill Monument** ③, which is visible from the yard.

### TIMING

Give yourself two to three hours for a Charlestown walk; the lengthy traverse across the Charlestown Bridge calls for endurance in cold weather. You may want to save Charlestown's stretch of the Freedom Trail, which adds considerably to its length, for a second-day outing. You can always save backtracking the historic route by taking the MBTA water shuttle, which ferries back and forth between Charlestown's Navy Yard and downtown Boston's Long Wharf.

## Sights to See

❸ **Bunker Hill Monument.** Three legendary misunderstandings surround this famous monument. First, the Battle of Bunker Hill was actually fought on Breed's Hill, which is where the monument sits today. (The real Bunker Hill is about a half-mile to the north of the monument; it's slightly taller than Breed's Hill.) Second, although the battle is generally considered a Colonial success, Americans actually lost in a Pyrrhic victory for the British redcoats, who lost nearly half of their 2,200 men; American casualties numbered 400 to 600. And third: the famous war cry, "Don't fire until you see the whites of their eyes," may not have been uttered by American colonel William Prescott or general Israel Putnam, but if either one did shout it, he was quoting an old Prussian command made necessary due to the notorious inaccuracy of the musket. No matter. The Americans did employ a deadly delayed-action strategy on June 17, 1775, and conclusively proved themselves to be worthy fighters, capable of defeating the forces of the British Empire.

Among the dead were the brilliant young American doctor and political activist Joseph Warren, recently commissioned as a major general but fighting as a private, and the British major Pitcairn, who two months before had led the redcoats into Lexington. Pitcairn is believed to be buried in the crypt of the Old North Church. Warren lay in a shallow grave on Breed's Hill until the British evacuated Boston in 1776, when his remains were disinterred and buried ceremoniously in the Granary. Today, Warren lies in the Forest Hills Cemetery, his final resting place after his grave was moved by his descendants several more times. How was his body originally identified? Warren's "dentist" recognized his own handiwork in a set of false teeth. The dentist was silversmith Paul Revere, a jack and master of many trades, who had made the teeth's silver springs.

In 1823, a committee was formed to construct a monument on the site of the battle, choosing the form of an Egyptian obelisk as a suitable tribute. Architect Solomon Willard designed a 221-ft-high obelisk constructed of blocks of granite cut from quarries in Quincy. Transportation dilemmas led to the establishment of the country's first commercial railway; the rails were made first of pine, then granite, and finally iron. The Marquis de Lafayette laid the cornerstone of the monument in 1825, but, due to a nagging lack of funds, it wasn't dedicated until 1843. Poet and social reformer Sarah Josepha Hale and other women helped in 1840 with a craft and bake sale that netted $30,000 after a two-week run that filled the Rotunda of Quincy Market. Daniel Webster's stirring words on its dedication have gone down in history: "Let it rise! Let it rise! Till it greets the sun in its coming. Let the earliest light of the morning gild it and painting day, linger and play upon its summit."

The monument's zenith is reached by a flight of 294 steps. There is no elevator, but the views from the observatory are worth the effort of the arduous climb. A statue of Colonel Prescott stands guard at the base. In the lodge at the base, dioramas tell the story of the battle, and ranger programs are conducted regularly. If you are in Boston the week before the 225th anniversary of Bunker Hill Day, June 17, 2000, look for special activities and demonstrations. ☎ *617/242–5641.* 📧 *Free.* ☉ *Lodge daily 9–5; monument daily 9–4:30. T stop: Community College.*

The Charlestown Historical Society runs a **museum** at 43 Monument Square, open May to September. Another Bunker Hill presentation, the multimedia show "Whites of Their Eyes," is shown in the Charlestown

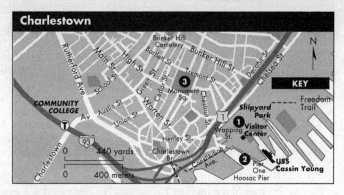

Navy Yard Visitors Information Center near the Navy Yard entrance.
✉ *55 Constitution Rd.*, ☎ *617/241–7576 "Whites of Their Eyes"; 617/
242–5601 visitor center.* ▨ *$3.* ◷ *Apr.–Nov., daily 9:30–5; shows every
½ hr, last show at 4:30.*

**➊  Charlestown Navy Yard.** A National Park Service Historic Site since
closing its doors in 1974, the Charlestown Navy Yard was one of six
established to build warships. For 174 years, as wooden hulls and muzzle-
loading cannons gave way to steel ships and sophisticated electronics,
the yard evolved to meet the changing needs of a changing navy. It is
a virtual museum of American shipbuilding; here are early 19th-century
barracks, workshops, and officers' quarters; a ropewalk (an elongated
building for making rope, not open to the public), designed in 1834
by the Greek Revival architect Alexander Parris and used by the navy
to turn out cordage for more than 125 years; and one of the two oldest dry docks in the United States. Look for special events throughout
2000 to honor the site's 200th anniversary. The USS *Constitution* (☞
*below*) was first to use this dry dock (in 1833). In addition to the ship
itself, check out the *Constitution* Museum, the collections of the Boston
Marine Society, and the USS *Cassin Young*, a World War II destroyer
typical of the ships built here during that era.

**★ ☝ ➋  USS Constitution.** Better known as "Old Ironsides," the USS *Constitution* rides proudly at anchor in her berth at the Charlestown Navy
Yard. The oldest commissioned ship in the U.S. fleet is a battlewagon
of the old school, of the days of "wooden ships and iron men"—when
she and her crew of 200 succeeded at the perilous task of asserting the
sovereignty of an improbable new nation. Once a year—on July 4—
she is towed out for a turnabout in Boston Harbor, the very place her
keel was laid in 1797. To honor her 200th birthday, the majestic ship
set sail from Boston Harbor on July 21, 1997, for the first time since
the 1880s. She anchored off the coast of Marblehead before returning
to her berth later that day.

The venerable craft has narrowly escaped the scrap heap several times
in her long history. She was launched on October 21, 1797, as part of
the nation's fledgling navy. Her hull was made of live oak, the tough-
est wood grown in North America; her bottom was sheathed in copper, provided by Paul Revere at a nominal cost. Her principal service
was during Thomas Jefferson's campaign against the Barbary pirates,
off the coast of North Africa, and in the War of 1812. Of her 42 en-
gagements, her record was 42–0.

The nickname "Old Ironsides" was acquired during the War of 1812
when shots from the British warship *Guerrière* appeared to bounce off
her tough oaken hull. Talk of scrapping the ship began as early as 1830,

but she was saved by a public campaign sparked by Oliver Wendell Holmes's poem "Old Ironsides." A major restoration was done from 1992 to 1996; by now only about 8% to 10% of her original wood remains in place. The keel, the heart of the ship, is original. Today she continues, the oldest commissioned warship in the world, still a part of the U.S. Navy.

The men and women who look after her are regular navy personnel and maintain a 24-hour watch. Sailors, dressed in 1812-era uniforms, show visitors around the ship, guiding them to two of the ship's three below decks: the places at the guns where the desperate, difficult work of naval warfare under sail was performed and, below that, the cramped living quarters. Another treat when visiting the ship: the view of Boston across Boston Harbor is spectacular. ⊠ *USS Constitution,* ☎ *617/242–5670.* ⊡ *Free.* ☉ *Daily 9:30–sunset; 20-min tours, last at 3:30 PM. T stop: Haymarket; then MBTA Bus 92 or 93 to Charlestown City Sq. or Boston Harbor Cruise water shuttle from Long Wharf to Pier 4.*

The *Constitution* **Museum** has artifacts and hands-on exhibits pertaining to the ship—firearms, logs, and instruments. One section takes you step by step through the *Constitution*'s most important battles. Old meets new in a video battle "fought" at the helm of a ship. ⊠ *Constitution Wharf,* ☎ *617/426–1812.* ☉ *Daily 10–5. T stop: Haymarket; then MBTA Bus 92 or 93 to Charlestown City Sq. or Boston Harbor Cruise water shuttle from Long Wharf to Pier 4.*

NEED A BREAK?

Stop for a drink or some food with an international twist at the **Warren Tavern** (⊠ 2 Pleasant St., ☎ 617/241–8142), built in 1780, a restored Colonial neighborhood pub once frequented by George Washington and Paul Revere. It was the first building reconstructed after the Battle of Bunker Hill, which leveled Charlestown.

# DOWNTOWN BOSTON

Boston's commercial and financial districts—the area commonly called downtown—are concentrated in a maze of streets that seem to have been laid out with little logic; they are, after all, only village lanes that happen to be lined with modern 40-story office towers. Just as the great fire of 1872 swept the old financial district clear, the downtown construction over the past two decades has obliterated many of the buildings where Boston businessmen of Silas Lapham's day sat in front of their expansive rolltop desks. Yet many historic sites remain in this thoroughly Manhattanized section of Boston: a good number of them have been linked together to make up a fascinating section of the Freedom Trail.

The area is bordered by **State Street** on the north and by **South Station** and **Chinatown** to the south. **Tremont Street** and the **Common** form the west boundary, and the **harbor** wharves the eastern edge. Locals may be able to navigate the tangle of thoroughfares in between, but very few of them manage to give intelligible directions when consulted, and you're better off trusting a map. The area is confusing, but it is mercifully small.

**Washington Street** (known as "The Wash") is the main commercial thoroughfare of downtown Boston. South of the Old South, Washington is a pedestrian street marked by two venerable anchors of Boston's mercantile district, Filene's and what was once Jordan Marsh and is now Macy's (☞ Chapter 8). William Filene founded his Boston store in 1881 near the site of the present eight-story building (1912). Now a separate corporate entity, Filene's Basement grew to become more famous than its parent store, especially for its yearly wedding gown sales, even though it operated without women's dressing rooms, a lack that necessitated shrewd undergarment planning and tortuous squirming in the aisles. Jordan Marsh was the creation of Eben Jordan, who arrived in Boston from Maine around 1840 with $1.25 in his pocket; he opened Jordan Marsh (Marsh was a partner) in 1851. The huge store expanded rapidly in the 1970s; the entire chain was eventually purchased by the Federated chain, which changed all of the Jordan Marsh stores into Macy's. For Boston shoppers, it was the end of an era.

Street vendors, food carts (including a particularly good burrito bar), flower carts, and gaggles of teenagers and shoppers throng the pedestrian mall outside the two stores.

Downtown is also home to some of Boston's most idiosyncratic neighborhoods. The old Leather District directly abuts **Chinatown,** which is also bordered by the **Theater District,** farther west (and the buildings of the Tufts New England Medical Center), while to the south, the red light of the once brazen and now decaying Combat Zone flickers weakly. The Massachusetts Turnpike and its junction with the Southeast Expressway cuts a wide swath through the area, isolating Chinatown from the South End in much the same way the Fitzgerald Expressway isolates the North End from downtown.

*Numbers in the text correspond to numbers in the margin and on the Downtown Boston map.*

## A Good Walk

After viewing the dramatic interior of **King's Chapel** ① at the corner of Tremont (that's *tre*-mont, not *tree*-mont), visit the burying ground next door, the oldest graveyard in the city. From here, it's two blocks down School Street to the **Old Corner Bookstore Site** ②. From the corner of School Street and Washington turn right (south) to see the **Old South Meeting House** ③, which seethed with revolutionary fervor in the 1770s. A right turn (north) onto Washington Street from the doorstep of the Old South will take you past the Globe Corner Bookstore once again, past Pi Alley (named after the loose type, or "pi," spilled from the pockets of printers when upper Washington Street was Boston's newspaper row—or after Colonial pie shops, depending on which story you prefer to believe), and to the rear of the **Old State House** ④ near the intersection of Court Street. In a traffic island in front is a circle of stones that marks the **site of the Boston Massacre** ⑤. Following State Street east toward the harbor, you pass the **U.S. Custom House** ⑥, one of Boston skyline's most distinct entities with the whimsical blue and orange faces of its clock tower. Then—if you have children in tow—head over to the **New England Aquarium** ⑦ on Central Wharf or skip directly to **Rowes Wharf** ⑧, Boston's most glamorous waterfront development. Turn south on Atlantic Avenue—most likely a solid wall of traffic due to construction of a new underground Central Artery highway nearby—to the foot of Pearl Street where a plaque marks the **site of the original Boston Tea Party** ⑨. The **Boston Tea Party Ship and Museum** ⑩ lies a little farther beyond—cross the Fort Point Channel at Congress Street for a look at the *Beaver II,* a faithful re-creation of the hapless British ship that was carrying tea in 1773. Continue along Congress Street and you come to the 40-ft milk bottle that marks Museum Wharf, home to the **Children's Museum** ⑪ and **Computer Museum** ⑫, conveniently side by side. From here you can make your way back across the Channel toward **Chinatown** (and dinner), passing **South Station** ⑬ and the **Federal Reserve Tower** ⑭.

This section of Boston has a generous share of attractions, so it might be wise to save a full day to spend among the New England Aquarium, the Children's Museum, and the Computer Museum. There are optimum times to catch some sights: the golden dome of the State House shines best under sunny skies, while a stroll along the waterfront at Rowes Wharf is most romantic at dusk. No need to visit the Aquarium at a special hour to catch feeding time—this event happens continuously throughout the day.

## Sights to See

**Boston Harbor Islands State Park.** In 1996, the Boston Harbor Islands—the 31 islands in the inner and outer harbors—were designated a national recreation area, administered by a public-private partnership. The focal point of the park is 28-acre George's Island, on which the pre–Civil War Fort Warren stands, partially restored and partially in ruins. Confederate prisoners were once held here. Other islands include Peddock's Island, which holds the remains of Fort Andrews, and Deer Island, where 200 Native Americans were interned and died during King Philip's War in 1675–76. From May to September, you can reach George's Island on the Boston Harbor Cruises ferry ($8); from June to September, free water taxis run from George's to Gallops, Lovell's, Peddock's, Grape, and Bumpkin islands. Bumpkin and Gallops are small and easily explored within an hour or so; Lovell's and Grape each cover about 60 acres. All the harbor islands are accessible by private boat, with the exception of Thompson's Island, a private research facility. You can fish and hike and picnic—there are plenty of ruins to explore, and beautiful views; Lovell's has a swimming beach with a lifeguard on duty; you can swim unsupervised on Gallops and Grape islands. No dogs are allowed on the islands. (☞ Participant Sports and Fitness *and* Beaches *in* Chapter 7.) ☏ *617/727–7676 park offices; 617/223–8666 for recorded information.* ✉ *Boston Harbor Cruises,* ☏ *617/227–4321.* 🎫 *Trip to George's Island $8.* ☉ *Early June–Sept.* T *stop: Aquarium.*

**⑤ Boston Massacre Site.** Directly in front of the **Old State House** (☞ *below*), a circle of cobblestones (in a traffic island) marks the site of the Boston Massacre, which occurred on the snowy evening of March 5, 1770, when a small contingent of British regular soldiers fired in panic upon a taunting mob of more than 40 Bostonians. Five townsmen died. In the legal action that followed, the defense of the accused soldiers was undertaken by John Adams and Josiah Quincy, both of whom vehemently opposed British oppression but who were devoted to the principle of fair trial. All but two of the nine regulars charged were acquitted; the others were branded on the hand for the crime of manslaughter. Paul Revere lost little time in capturing the "massacre" in a dramatic engraving that soon became one of the Revolution's most potent images of propaganda.

**⑩ Boston Tea Party Ship and Museum.** The *Beaver II*, a handsome replica of one of the ships forcibly boarded and unloaded the night Boston Harbor became a teapot, bobs in the Fort Point Channel at the Congress Street Bridge. The ship was anchored here during the 200th anniversary of the tea party and has remained ever since. Exhibits in the interpretive center on the adjacent pier explain the significance of the events of that cold evening and what led up to it. Then you may be pressed into donning feathers and war paint to reenact the tea drop. One nice touch: a complimentary cup of tea. The site of the actual tea party is marked by a plaque on Pearl Street and Atlantic Avenue (☞ *below*). ✉ *Congress St. Bridge,* ☏ *617/338–1773.* 🎫 *$8.* ☉ *Late*

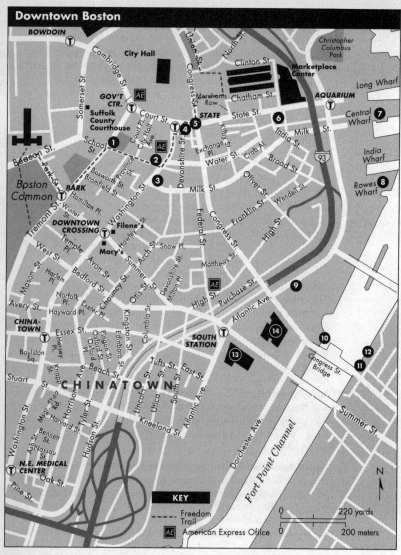

## Downtown Boston

Boston Massacre
Site, **5**

Boston Tea Party Ship
and Museum, **10**

Boston Tea Party
Site, **9**

Children's
Museum, **11**

Computer
Museum, **12**

Federal Reserve
Tower, **14**

King's Chapel, **1**

New England
Aquarium, **7**

Old Corner
Bookstore Site, **2**

Old South Meeting
House, **3**

Old State House, **4**

Rowes Wharf, **8**

South Station, **13**

U.S. Custom
House, **6**

*May–early Sept., daily 9–6; early Sept.–Dec. 1 and Mar.–late May, daily 9–5. T stop: South Station.*

**⑨ Boston Tea Party Site.** Along Atlantic Avenue, a plaque is set into the wall of a commercial building to mark the site of the Boston Tea Party. That this was once Griffin's Wharf is only further evidence of Boston's relentless expansion into its harbor.

**⑪ Children's Museum.** Don't let the name deceive you—this fun museum is not for kids only. Creative hands-on exhibits demonstrate scientific laws, cultural diversity, the human body, and the nature of disabilities. Some of the most popular stops are also the simplest and most delightful: bubble-making machinery, a giant-size mug (big enough to hide a trio of six-year-olds), and a two-story climbing sculpture. In "Teen Tokyo," experience Japanese youth culture, including a Japanese subway car and karaoke booth. "Arthur's World" brings the gregarious aardvark from the PBS series to life. In the toddler room you can let kids under five go free in a fairly safe environment; the attached parent resource room has a great library of books and magazines on parenting issues. The downstairs museum shop overflows with children's books and gifts; upstairs, at Recycle, industrial raw material is sold in bulk. There's also a full schedule of special exhibits, festivals, and performances. ⊠ *300 Congress St.,* ☎ *617/426–6500; 617/426–8855 for recorded information.* ☞ *$7, $1 Fri. 5–9.* ☉ *Mid-June–early Sept., daily 10–7, Fri. 10–9; early Sept.–mid-June, Tues.–Sun. 10–5, Fri. until 9. T stop: South Station.*

**Chinatown.** Boston's Chinatown may be geographically small in the scheme of the city, yet it is home to one of the larger concentrations of Chinese-Americans in the United States. Beginning in the 1870s, Chinese immigrants began to trickle in, many setting up tents in Ping On Alley. The trickle increased to a wave when immigration restrictions were lifted in 1968. As in most other American Chinatowns, the concentration of regional restaurants is a big draw; on Sunday, Bostonians traditionally head for Chinatown to feast on dim sum, the fragrant dumplings that are a popular choice for brunch. Today, the many Chinese establishments—most found along Beach and Tyler streets and Harrison Avenue—are interspersed with Vietnamese, Korean-Japanese, Thai, and Malaysian eateries. A three-story pagoda-style arch at the end of Beach Street welcomes you to the district. The community is centered on the Asian-American Civic Association, housed in the former Quincy School at 90 Tyler Street, built in 1848 to teach arriving Irish and Italian immigrants. An educational landmark, it was the first institution to assign pupils individual desks. Now a statue of Confucius ornaments the front yard, but its civic functions continue. *T stop: Chinatown.*

| NEED A BREAK? | A treasure of a pastry shop in an out-of-the-way part of Chinatown is **May's Cake House** (⊠ 223 Harrison Ave., ☎ 617/350–0210). There's a delightful selection of pastries and treats—be sure to order the little cakes with fresh fruit toppings. |

**Christopher Columbus Park.** It's a short stroll from the financial district to a view of Boston Harbor, once a national symbol of rampant pollution. These days, the harbor is making a slow comeback. Also known as **Waterfront Park**, the green space bordering the harbor and several of Boston's restored wharves is a pleasant oasis with benches and an arborlike shelter. Lewis Wharf and Commercial Wharf (north of the park), which long lay nearly derelict, had by the mid-1970s been transformed into condominiums, apartments, restaurants, and upscale shops. Long Wharf's Marriott hotel was designed to look compatible with the old seaside warehouses. Sailboats and power yachts ride at anchor here. ⊠ *Bordered by Atlantic Ave., Commercial Wharf, and Long Wharf.*

**Combat Zone.** The borders of Chinatown continue to expand—mostly at the expense of the Combat Zone, which has the dubious distinction of being one of the nation's first official red-light districts. It got its name more than 50 years ago when Boston-stationed troops would show up at the local tailor shops for uniform alterations and inevitably tussle with members of other branches of the military there for the same purpose. When the honky-tonk businesses were forced out of Scollay Square, they moved into this run-down area. Seeking to contain the spread of vice, city officials created the Lower Washington Street Adult Entertainment District, as Puritan ghosts shuddered. Today, due to the availability of X-rated tapes at most video outlets, the Combat Zone is a mere shadow of its sleazy self. The old Pilgrim Theater—where onetime Arkansas congressman Wilbur Mills ignited a media scandal by joining stripper Fanny Foxe onstage—is no more. Still, porn entrepreneurs continue to try to open new venues; even owners of the now-defunct Naked i keep attempting to reopen the notorious strip joint. But Chinatown merchants steadily object to the area's prostitution and illegal drug activity, and construction is under way on the major Millennium Place commercial complex on Washington Street at the edge of Chinatown.

☺ ⑫ **Computer Museum.** Given the importance of high tech to the Boston economy, the establishment of this institution was an act akin to the hanging of the *Sacred Cod* in the State House. Standing conveniently next to the **Children's Museum** (☞ *above*), the Computer Museum has more than 170 exhibits in which you can learn about the machines running our lives and about the people who created them. Exhibits include the two-story Walk-Through Computer, a hands-on, interactive exhibit outlining all facets of the information highway, and a gallery to try out the best software for kids. Be sure to beam over to visit celebrity-robot-in-residence R2-D2 from the *Star Wars* trilogy. And get a taste of creating your own reality in a new exhibit that allows young visitors to design fishes for a virtual fish tank. At press time, there were plans to combine the Computer Museum and the Museum of Science (☞ The Old West End, *above*). ⊠ *300 Congress St.,* ☎ *617/426–2800 or 617/423–6758.* ⊡ *$7; half-price Sun. afternoon.* ☉ *Mid-June–Aug., daily 10–6; Sept.–mid-June, Tues.–Sun. 10–5. Open holiday Mondays and Mondays during public school vacations. T stop: South Station.*

⑭ **Federal Reserve Tower.** On Atlantic Avenue, across from South Station, is this striking aluminum-clad building, designed in 1976 by Hugh Stubbins and Associates. Though it's mainly used for offices, it also houses a free art gallery and hosts occasional concerts. ⊠ *600 Atlantic Ave.,* ☎ *617/973–3453.* ☉ *Weekdays 10–4. Tours Fri. 10:30; call 617/973–3451 to schedule.*

❶ **King's Chapel.** Both somber and dramatic, King's Chapel looms over the corner of Tremont and School streets. Its distinctive shape was not achieved entirely by design; for lack of funds, it was never topped with the steeple that architect Peter Harrison had planned. The first chapel on this site was erected in 1688, when Sir Edmund Andros, the royal governor whose authority temporarily replaced the original Colonial charter, appropriated the land for the establishment of an Anglican place of worship. This rankled the Puritans, who had left England to escape Anglicanism and had until then succeeded in keeping it out of the colony.

It took five years to build the solid Quincy granite structure. As construction proceeded, the old church continued to stand within the rising walls of the new, the plan being to remove and carry it away piece by piece when the outer stone chapel was completed. The builders then went to work on the interior, which remains today essentially as they finished it in 1754; it is a masterpiece of elegant proportion and Georgian calm (in fact, its excellent acoustics have made the use of a microphone unnecessary for Sunday sermons). To the right of the main entrance is a special pew, once reserved for condemned prisoners, who were trotted in to hear a sermon before being hanged on the Common. The chapel's bell is Paul Revere's largest and, in his judgment, his sweetest sounding. ✉ *58 Tremont St. (at School St.),* ☎ *617/227–2155.* ☉ *Mid-June–early Sept., Mon. and Thurs.–Sat. 9:30–4, Sun. 1–3; early Sept.–mid-Oct., Mon. and Fri.–Sat. 9:30–3; mid-Oct.–mid-Apr., Sat. 9:30–3; mid-Apr.–mid-June, Mon. and Fri.–Sat. 10–2. Year-round music program Tues. 12:15–1, services on Sun. at 11, Wed. at 12:15. T stop: Park St., Government Center.*

**King's Chapel Burying Ground.** Legends linger in this oldest of the city's cemeteries. Glance at the handy map of famous grave sites (posted at the entrance) and take the path to the right from the entrance and then left by the chapel to the gravestone (1704) of Elizabeth Pain, the model for Hester Prynne in Nathaniel Hawthorne's *The Scarlet Letter*. Note the winged death's head on her stone—it was a common motif on Puritan gravestones, since those ever-dour folks favored reminders that life was harsh and fleeting. Elsewhere, you'll find the grave of William Dawes Jr., who, with Dr. Samuel Prescott, rode out to warn of the British invasion the night of Paul Revere's famous ride; due to Longfellow's stirring poem, Revere's the one who gets all the glory today (which should show you what a good PR agent is worth). Other Boston worthies entombed here were famous for more conventional reasons, including the first Massachusetts governor, John Winthrop, and several generations of his descendants. The prominent slate monument near the entrance to the yard tells (in French) the story of the Chevalier de Saint-Sauveur, a young officer who was part of the first French contingent that arrived to help the rebel Americans in 1778. He was killed in a riot that began when hungry Bostonians were told they could not buy the bread the French were baking for their men, using the Bostonians' own wheat—an awkward situation only aggravated by the language barrier. The chevalier's interment here was probably the occasion for the first Roman Catholic mass in what has since become a city with a substantial Catholic population.

NEED A BREAK?   **Rebecca's Café** (✉ 18 Tremont St., ☎ 617/227–0020), with its fresh salads, sandwiches, and homemade pastries, is a comfortable place to stop for a casual lunch. It's open weekdays 7–7.

**Leather District.** Opposite South Station and nestled into the angle formed by Kneeland Street and Atlantic Avenue is a corner of downtown that has been relatively untouched by high-rise development, the old Leather District; it's probably the best place in downtown Boston to get an idea of what the city's business center looked like in the late 19th century. This was the wholesale supply area for raw materials in the days when the shoe industry was a regional economic mainstay, and a few leather firms are still located here. *T stop: South Station.*

**Memorial to the Irish Famine.** This most Irish of cities got another reminder of its rich immigrant past in 1998 when this memorial was completed. The park memorial consists of two sculptures by artist Robert Shure, one depicting an anguished family on the shores of Ireland, the other a determined and hopeful Irish family stepping ashore in Boston. It's just opposite the Old South Meeting House (☞ *below*).

☝ **❼** **New England Aquarium.** More than just another pretty fish, this aquarium challenges you to really imagine life under (and around) the sea. Seals bark outside the West Wing, its glass-and-steel exterior constructed to mimic fish scales. This facility has a café, a gift shop, and changing exhibits, beginning with "Coastal Rhythms," a look at East Coast ecosystems. Inside the main facility, you'll find penguins, jellyfish, sea otters, a variety of sharks, and other exotic sea creatures—more than 2,000 species in all—some of which make their home in the Aquarium's four-story, 187,000-gallon ocean reef tank, the largest of its kind in the world. Ramps winding around the tank lead to the top level and allow you to view the inhabitants from many vantage points. Don't miss the five-times-a-day feeding time; the procedure lasts nearly an hour and takes divers 23 ft into the tank. Did you know that walruses clang and shrimp snap? Hear these noises in the new "Sounds of the Sea" exhibit. From outside the glassed-off Aquarium Medical Center, you can watch vets treat sick animals—if you've ever pictured an eel in a "hospital bed," here's where you'll see it. At the "Edge of the Sea" exhibit kids can gingerly pick up starfish and other creatures. Learn something about environmental dangers in a multimedia exhibit on sewage systems, or "what happens when you flush." Sea lion shows are held aboard *Discovery*, a floating marine mammal pavilion; and whale-watch cruises (☞ Participant Activities and Fitness *in* Chapter 7) leave from the Aquarium's dock from April to October. There's also a "Science at Sea" educational cruise ($9). Across the plaza is the Aquarium's Education Center; it too, has changing exhibits. On the drawing boards is a new East Wing with a large-format movie theater and a million-gallon open ocean tank. At press time, construction was due to begin in late 1999–early 2000. Just watch your pennies in the gift shop—it seems to have every stuffed marine animal ever made. ⊠ *Central Wharf (between Central and Milk Sts.),* ☎ *617/973–5200; 617/ 973–5277 whale-watching information.* 🎟 *$11; July 4–early Sept. $12.50.* ☉ *July–early Sept., Mon.–Tues., Fri. 9–6, Wed.–Thurs. 9–8, weekends 9–7; early Sept.–June, weekdays 9–5, weekends 9–6. T stop: Aquarium.*

**New England Telephone Building.** It was in a garret on one of the side streets off Scollay Square that Alexander Graham Bell first transmitted a human voice—his own—by telephone. When the building where Bell had his workshop was torn down in the 1920s, the phone company had the room dismantled and reassembled in the headquarters lobby of the New England Telephone Building. There the room looks just as it did on June 3, 1875, when Bell first coaxed his voice across a wire. (His famous call to Thomas Watson, "Come here, I want you," was made nearly a year later in another part of town.) Telephone memorabilia and a 160-ft mural tell the invention's story. ⊠ *185 Franklin St.,* ☎ *617/743–4886.* 🎟 *Free.* ☉ *Weekdays 8:30–5. T stop: Government Center.*

**Old City Hall.** Just outside this sight sits Richard S. Greenough's bronze statue (1855) of Benjamin Franklin, Boston's first portrait sculpture. Franklin was born in 1706 just a few blocks from here, on Milk Street, and attended the Boston Latin School, founded in 1635 near the City Hall site. (The school has long since moved to Louis Pasteur Avenue, near the Fenway.) As a young man, Franklin moved to Philadelphia, where he lived most of his long life. Boston's municipal government settled in to the new City Hall in 1969, and the old Second Empire building now houses business offices and a French restaurant. ⊠ *41–45 School St.*

**②  Old Corner Bookstore Site.** Through these doors, between 1845 and 1865, passed some of the century's greatest literary lights: Thoreau, Emerson, and Longfellow—even Charles Dickens paid a visit. Many of their greatest works were published here by James T. "Jamie" Fields, who in 1830 had founded the seminally important firm of Ticknor and Fields. In the 19th century, the graceful, gambrel-roofed early Georgian structure—built in 1718 on land once owned by religious rebel Anne Hutchinson—also housed the city's leading bookstore. The building is now closed to the public. ⊠ *1 School St. T stop: State St.*

**③  Old South Meeting House.** This is the second-oldest church building in Boston, and were it not for Longfellow's celebration of the Old North in "Paul Revere's Ride," it might well be the most famous. Some of the fieriest of the town meetings that led to the Revolution were held here, culminating in the tumultuous gathering of December 16, 1773, which was called by Samuel Adams to confront the crisis of three ships, laden with dutiable tea, anchored at Griffin's Wharf. The activists wanted the tea returned to England, the governor would not permit it—and the rest is history. To cries of "Boston harbor a tea-pot tonight" and John Hancock's "Let every man do what is right in his own eyes," the protesters poured out of the Old South, headed to the wharf with their waiting comrades, and dumped £18,000 worth of tea into the water.

One of the earliest members of the congregation was an African slave named Phillis Wheately, who had been educated by her owners. In 1773 a book of her poems was printed, making her the first published African-American poet. She later traveled to London, where she was received as a celebrity, but was again overtaken by poverty and obscurity and died at age 31.

The church suffered no small amount of indignity in the Revolution: its pews were ripped out by occupying British troops, and the interior was used for riding exercises by Burgoyne's light dragoons. A century later it escaped destruction in the Great Fire of 1872, only to be threatened with demolition by developers. Aside from the windows and doors, the only original interior features surviving today are the tiered galleries above the main floor. The pulpit is a reproduction of the one used by Colonial divines and secular firebrands. Public contributions saved the church.

In late 1997, the Old South reopened after its first renovation in more than 100 years with increased access for people with disabilities, air-conditioning, and a new permanent exhibition, "Voices of Protest," which highlights Old South as a forum for free speech from Revolutionary days to the present. The renovation also created spaces for changing shows and for educational programs, such as lunchtime lecture series on Thursdays, October to April. ⊠ *310 Washington St.,* ☎ *617/482–6439.* ⊠ *$3.* ⊙ *Apr.–Oct., daily 9:30–5; Nov.–Mar., daily 10–4. T stop: State St., Downtown Crossing.*

**④  Old State House.** This Colonial-era landmark has one of the most elegant facades in Boston, with its State Street gable adorned by a brightly gilded lion and unicorn, symbols of British imperial power. The original figures were pulled down in 1776. For proof that bygones are bygones, we may look not only to the restoration of the sculptures but to the fact that Queen Elizabeth II was greeted by cheering crowds on July 4 during the U.S. bicentennial celebration when she stood on the Old State House balcony (from which the Declaration of Independence was first read in public in Boston and which overlooks the site of the Boston Massacre).

This was the seat of the Colonial government from 1713 until the Revolution, and after the evacuation of the British from Boston in 1776 it served the independent Commonwealth until its replacement on Beacon Hill was completed. John Hancock was inaugurated here as the first governor under the new state constitution. Like many other Colonial-era landmarks, it fared poorly in the years that followed. Nineteenth-century photos show the old building with a mansard roof and signs in the windows advertising a variety of businesses. In the 1830s the Old State House served as Boston's City Hall. When demolition was threatened in the name of improving the traffic flow, the Bostonian Society organized a restoration, after which the Old State House reopened as home to a permanent collection that traces Boston's Revolutionary War history and, on the second floor, changing exhibits.

Immediately outside the Old State House at 15 State Street is a **visitor center** run by the National Park Service; you'll find free brochures and rest rooms. ✉ *206 Washington St.,* ☎ *617/720–3290.* ✇ *$3.* ☉ *Daily 9–5. T stop: State St.*

**⑧ Rowes Wharf.** Take a Beacon Hill redbrick town house, cut loose with white clapboard trim, blow it up to the *n*th power, and you get this 15-story Skidmore, Owings, & Merrill extravaganza, one of the more welcome additions to the Boston Harbor skyline. From under the complex's gateway six-story arch, you can get great views of Boston Harbor and the luxurious yachts parked in the marina. Water shuttles pull up here from Logan Airport—the most spectacular way to enter the city. Enjoy a windswept stroll along the Harborwalk waterfront promenade; from this vantage point, it's easy to forget the intense construction for the Central Artery project nearby on Atlantic Avenue. *T stop: Aquarium.*

**⑬ South Station.** The colonnaded granite structure at the intersection of Atlantic Avenue and Summer Street is the terminal for all Amtrak trains in and out of Boston. Catercorner from it is the terminal for Greyhound, Peter Pan, and other bus lines. Behind the station's grand 1900s facade, a major renovation project has created an airy, modern intermodal transit center. Thanks to its eateries, coffee bars, newsstand, flower stand, and other shops, waiting for a train can actually be a pleasant experience.

**State Street.** In the 19th century, State Street was headquarters for banks, brokerages, and insurance firms; although these businesses have now spread throughout the downtown district, "State Street" retains much the same connotation in Boston that "Wall Street" has elsewhere. The early commercial hegemony of State Street was symbolized by Long Wharf, built originally in 1710 and extending some 1,700 ft into the harbor. If today's Long Wharf does not appear to be that long, it is not because it has been shortened but because the land has expanded around it; State Street once met the water at the base of the Custom House. Landfill operations were pursued relentlessly through the years, and the old coastline is now as much a memory as such Colonial State Street landmarks as Governor Winthrop's 1630 house and the Revolutionary-era Bunch of Grapes Tavern, where Bostonians met to drink and wax indignant at their treatment by the British.

**⑥ U.S. Custom House.** This 1847 structure resembles a Greek Revival temple that appears to have sprouted a tower. It is just that. This is the work of architects Ammi Young and Isaiah Rogers—at least, the bottom part is. The tower (would skyscrapers have looked like this if they could have been built in the 1840s?) was added in 1915, at which time it became Boston's tallest building. To appreciate the grafting job (not Custom House graft, but grafting in the horticultural sense), go inside and look at the great rotunda, surmounted by its handsome dome. The outer surface of that dome was once the roof of the building, but now the dome is embedded in the base of the tower.

The federal government moved out of the Custom Tower in 1987 and sold it to the city of Boston, which, in turn, sold it to the Marriott Corporation, which has converted the building into luxury time-share units. The move disturbed some historical purists, but the units have been selling briskly. Purchase prices start at $20,000 a week, depending on the season. But you don't have to buy a unit to step inside and enjoy the magnificent rotunda and view the maritime prints and antique artifacts now on display, courtesy of the Peabody Essex Museum in Salem. ⊠ *3 McKinley Sq. T stop: Aquarium.*

# THE BACK BAY

In the folklore of American neighborhoods, the Back Bay stands with New York's Park Avenue and San Francisco's Nob Hill as a symbol of propriety and high social standing. You still occasionally hear someone described as coming from "an old Back Bay family" as though the Back Bay were hundreds of years old and its stone mansions the feudal bastions of Puritan settlers from the time they got off the boat.

Nothing could be further from the truth. The Back Bay, at scarcely 125 years old, is one of Boston's newer neighborhoods. Before the 1850s it was a bay, a tidal flat that formed the south bank of a distended Charles River. Boston since time immemorial has been a pear-shaped peninsula joined to the mainland by an isthmus (the Neck) so narrow that in early Colonial times a single gate and guardhouse were sufficient for its defense; today's Washington Street, as it leaves downtown and heads toward the South End, follows the old Neck.

Filling in land along the Neck began in 1850 and resulted in the creation of the South End neighborhood. To the north, a narrow causeway called the Mill Dam (later Beacon Street) was built in 1814 to separate the Back Bay from the Charles. Bostonians began to fill in the shallows in 1858, using gravel brought from West Needham by railroad at a rate of up to 3,500 carloads per day. It took 30 years to complete the filling as far as the Fens. When the work was finished, the original 783-acre peninsula had been expanded by approximately 450 acres. Thus the actual waters of Back Bay became the neighborhood of Back Bay.

More important, city planners were able to do something that had never before been possible in Boston: to lay out an entire neighborhood of arrow-straight streets. Heavily influenced by the then-recent rebuilding of Paris according to the plans of Baron Haussmann, the Back Bay planners created thoroughfares that resemble Parisian boulevards more than they do the mews and squares of London. The main east–west streets—Beacon Street, Marlborough Street, Commonwealth Avenue, Newbury Street, and Boylston Street—were bisected by eight streets named in alphabetical order from Arlington to Hereford. Service alleys run behind the main streets. Though they are used now for waste pickup and parking, they were built so that provisioning wagons could be driven up to basement kitchens—that's how thorough the planning was.

Almost immediately, fashionable families began to decamp from Beacon Hill and the recently developed South End and establish themselves in the brick and brownstone row houses built upon the man-made land. Churches and cultural institutions followed, until by 1900 the streets between the Public Garden and Massachusetts Avenue had become, unquestionably, the smartest, most desirable neighborhood in all Boston. An air of permanence and respectability drifted in as inevitably as the tides once had, and the Back Bay mystique was born.

Some aspects of the Back Bay, such as the way households were distributed, became matters more of natural evolution than of intent. Old families with money congregated on Beacon Street; families with old Boston names but not much money gravitated to tree-lined Marlborough Street; and the nouveau riche tended to build on Commonwealth Avenue. Newbury and Boylston, originally residential rather than commercial streets, were the province of a mix of middle- and upper-middle-class families, as were the cross streets.

The Back Bay remains a living museum of urban Victorian residential architecture. The earliest specimens are nearest to the Public Garden (there are exceptions where showier turn-of-the-century mansions replaced 1860s town houses), and the newer examples are out around the Massachusetts Avenue and Fenway extremes of the district. The height of Back Bay residences and their distance from the street are essentially uniform, as are the interior layouts, chosen to accord with lot width. Yet there is a distinct progression of facades, beginning with French academic and Italianate designs and moving through the various "revivals" of the 19th century. By the time of World War I, when development of the Back Bay was virtually complete, architects and their patrons had come full circle to a revival of the Federal period, which had been out of fashion for only 30 years when the filling began. If the Back Bay architects had not run out of land, they might have gotten around to a revival of Greek Revival.

An outstanding guide to the architecture and history of the Back Bay is Bainbridge Bunting's *Houses of Boston's Back Bay*. A few homes are open to the public.

The Great Depression brought an end to the Back Bay style of living, and today only a few of the houses are single-family residences. Most have been cut up into apartments and, more recently, expensive condominiums. Interior details have experienced a mixed fate—suffering during the years when Victorian fashions were held in low regard—and are at present undergoing careful restoration, now that the aesthetic pendulum has reversed itself and moneyed condo buyers are demanding period authenticity. The blocks and blocks of original facades have survived on all but Newbury and Boylston streets, so the public face of the Back Bay retains much of the original charm and grandeur.

Note: One of the main thoroughfares, Huntington Avenue, which stretches from Copley Square past the Museum of Fine Arts, has been renamed the Avenue of the Arts. However, you're still likely to hear it referred to as Huntington—the old habit dies hard.

*Numbers in the text and margin correspond to numbers on the Back Bay, the South End, and the Fens map.*

## A Good Walk

A walk through the Back Bay properly begins with the **Boston Public Garden** ①, the oldest botanical garden in the United States. After wandering its meandering pathways, venture into the Back Bay through the gate near Arlington and Beacon streets. From here, if you're in the mood for greenery, take the Arthur Fiedler Footbridge to the Esplanade for a river view. Proceed on Beacon Street to the **Gibson House** ② museum. If you are interested in Back Bay mansions, you may wish to visit the Baylies Mansion at 5 Commonwealth Avenue at this point. If not, retrace your steps to Arlington, turn right, and proceed to the **Arlington Street Church** ③ at the corner of Boylston. Then, retrace your steps up Arlington to Newbury Street and turn left; ahead are **Emmanuel Church of Boston** ④ at Number 15 and the **Church of the Covenant** ⑤ at Number 67. At the Church of the Covenant, follow Berkeley back to Commonwealth Avenue. One block to your left is the **First Baptist Church** ⑥. From here you can continue down the **Commonwealth Avenue Mall** to view its sumptuous mansions all the way to Massachusetts Avenue, and return via Newbury Street. Or, at any point before Mass Ave. (as the locals refer to it), you can turn east to reach **Newbury Street** and backtrack along Boston's poshest shopping district, window-shopping all the way. At Dartmouth Street, turn right and head into **Copley Square,** where you will find the **"New" Old South Church** ⑦, **Boston Public Library** ⑧, **Trinity Church** ⑨, and the **John Hancock Tower** ⑩. For more shopping, head for the upscale **Copley Place** ⑪ complex, which can be reached through the Westin Hotel at the corner of Dartmouth Street and the Avenue of the Arts. A walkway takes you over Stuart Street into the shopping galleries. Continue through to the Marriott Hotel, and take another walkway over the Avenue of the Arts to the **Prudential Center** ⑫ for more shopping and viewing the city at the Prudential Center Skywalk. Exit onto Boylston Street and turn left to reach the **Institute of Contemporary Art** ⑬. Continue one block to Mass Ave., turn left, and walk several blocks to the reflecting pool and expansive plaza of the **Christian Science Church Center** ⑭. Just across Mass Ave. at the Avenue of the Arts is **Symphony Hall** ⑮.

TIMING

The Back Bay may be the most well-ordered section of Boston, but it is spread out, so allow three to four hours for leisurely strolls and frequent stops. If you are an indefatigable shopper, give yourself another two hours to cover Newbury Street and/or the shops at Copley Place and the Prudential Center. The reflecting pool at the Christian Science Church is a great time-out spot. Mid-April, the world descends on Copley Square—the finishing line for the Boston Marathon. A week later, magnolia time in Boston arrives (usually the third week of the month)—and nowhere do magnolias bloom more magnificently than along Commonwealth Avenue ("Comm Ave." to locals). In May, the Public Garden bursts with color, thanks to its flowering dogwood trees and thousands of tulips. Set aside a Sunday to enjoy the charms of the district's many historic churches. To keep you oriented, remember the north–south streets are arranged in alphabetical order, from Arlington to Hereford.

## Sights to See

❸ **Arlington Street Church.** Opposite the Park Square corner of the Public Garden, this church was erected in 1861—the first to be built in the Back Bay. Following suit, many of the old downtown congregations relocated to the district's newly filled land and applied their considerable resources to building handsome churches. Often designed in Gothic and Romanesque Revival styles, these churches have aged well and blend harmoniously with the residential blocks, making the Back Bay a great neighborhood for ecclesiastical architecture (☞ **Emmanuel Church, Church of the Covenant, First Baptist Church,** and **Trinity Church,** *below*). Keynoted by its classical portico and modeled after London's St. Martin-in-the-Fields, Arlington Street Church is less pic-

# The Back Bay, the South End, and the Fens

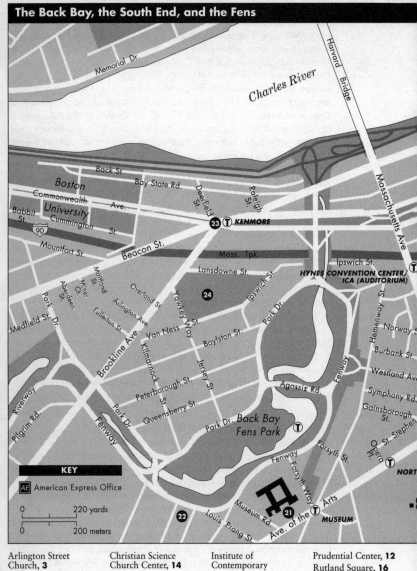

Charles River

Harvard Bridge

Memorial Dr.

Back St.

Bay State Rd.

Boston

Commonwealth Ave.

Babbit St.

Cummington St.

I-90

Mountfort St.

Beacon St.

Deerfield St.

Raleigh St.

Massachusetts Ave.

**23** T **KENMORE**

Mass. Tpk.

Lansdowne St.

Ipswich St.

**HYNES CONVENTION CENTER/ ICA (AUDITORIUM)**

Medfield St.

Maitland St.

Miner Ct.

Aberdeen St.

Fullerton St.

Park Dr.

Brookline Ave.

Overland St.

Arlington Ave.

Yawkey Way

Van Ness St.

Kilmarnock St.

**24**

Baylston St.

Jersey St.

Ipswich St.

Park Dr.

Fenway

Hemenway St.

Norway St.

Burbank St.

Westland Ave

Riverway

Pilgrim Rd.

Park Dr.

Fenway

Peterborough St.

Queensberry St.

Park Dr.

Agassiz Rd.

Symphony Rd.

Gainsborough St.

**Back Bay Fens Park**

T

Fenway

Forsyth St.

Forsyth Way

Opera Pl.

St. Stephen

T

**NORT**

**KEY**

AE American Express Office

0          220 yards

0          200 meters

Museum Rd.

Louis Prang St.

**22**

Ave. of the Arts

**21**

T **MUSEUM**

Arlington Street
Church, **3**

Bay Village, **20**

Boston Center for the
Arts, **19**

Boston Public
Garden, **1**

Boston Public
Library, **8**

Cathedral of the
Holy Cross, **18**

Christian Science
Church Center, **14**

Church of the
Covenant, **5**

Copley Place, **11**

Emmanuel Church of
Boston, **4**

Fenway Park, **24**

First Baptist
Church, **6**

Gibson House, **2**

Institute of
Contemporary
Art, **13**

Isabella Stewart
Gardner Museum, **22**

John Hancock
Tower, **10**

Kenmore Square, **23**

Museum of Fine
Arts, **21**

"New" Old South
Church, **7**

Prudential Center, **12**

Rutland Square, **16**

Symphony Hall, **15**

Trinity Church, **9**

Union Park, **17**

Arthur Fiedler Footbridge

Charles St.

Public Garden

arrow Drive

Back St.

Beacon St.

Berkeley St.

Arlington St.

Clarendon St.

Dartmouth St.

Marlborough St.

Fairfield St.

Gloucester St.

Commonwealth Ave.

The New England Bldg.

Park Sq.

**ARLINGTON**

*COPLEY*

Providence St.

St. James Ave.

Exeter St.

Newbury St.

Copley Sq.

Boylston St.

Blagden St.

Stuart St.

Piedmont St.

Winchester St.

Copley Plaza Hotel

Trinity Pl.

Dalton St.

Belvidere St.

t. Germain St.

learway St.

**PRUDENTIAL**

Harcourt St.

Carleton St.

Yarmouth St.

Buckingham St.

**BACK BAY**

Chandler St.

Tremont St.

Lawrence St.

Appleton St.

Gray St.

E. Berkeley St.

Holyoke St.

Ave. of the Arts

Cumberland St.

St. Botolph St.

Follen St.

Braddock Pkwy.

W. Newton St.

Warren Ave.

Montgomery St.

Canton St.

Dwight St.

Milford St.

Waltham St.

Union Pk.

Shawmut St.

**SYMPHONY**

Massachusetts Ave.

W. Rutland Sq.

Greenwich Pkwy.

Claremont Pk.

Ivanhoe St.

W. Dedham St.

W. Brookline St.

Trumbull St.

Fabin St.

Upton St.

Bradford St.

ASSACHUSETTS AVE.

Columbus Ave.

Rutland Sq.

Concord Sq.

Concord Pl.

Tremont St.

Pembroke St.

Newton St.

Msgr. Reynolds Way

TERN

eastern rsity

Worcester St.

Wellington St.

Newland St.

Shawmut Ave.

Washington St.

Harrison Ave.

N

turesque and more Georgian in character—don't forget to note the beautiful Tiffany stained-glass windows. During the year preceding the Civil War, the church was a hotbed of abolitionist fervor. Later, during the Vietnam War, it became famous as a center of peace activism. ⊠ *351 Boylston St.,* ☎ *617/536–7050.* ⊙ *Weekdays 10–5. Sun. service at 11. T stop: Arlington.*

**Back Bay mansions.** If you like nothing better than to imagine how the other half lives, you'll suffer no shortage of elegant old homes to sigh over in Boston's Back Bay. Most, unfortunately, are off-limits to visitors, but there's no law against gawking from the outside.

Among the grander Back Bay houses is the **Baylies Mansion** (⊠ 5 Commonwealth Ave.), of 1904, now the home of the Boston Center for Adult Education; you can enter to view its first-floor common. Another gem is the **Burrage Mansion** (⊠ 314 Commonwealth Ave.), built in 1899 in an extravagant French château style, complete with turrets and gargoyles, that reflects a cost-be-damned attitude uncommon even among the wealthiest Back Bay families. It now houses an assisted living residence for seniors, and walk-in visitors are not encouraged.

Other mansions of note include the **Cushing-Endicott House** (⊠ 163 Marlborough St.), built in 1871 and later home to William C. Endicott, secretary of war under President Cleveland; this was once dubbed "the handsomest house in the whole Back Bay" by Bainbridge Bunting. The **Oliver Ames Mansion** (⊠ 55 Commonwealth Ave., corner of Massachusetts Ave.) was built in 1882 for a railroad baron and Massachusetts governor. This opulent château is now an office building. The **Ames-Webster House** (⊠ 306 Dartmouth St.), built in 1872 and remodeled in 1882 and 1969, is one of the city's finest houses; it's still a private home.

Two Back Bay mansions are home to organizations that promote foreign language and culture: the **French Library in Boston** (⊠ 53 Marlborough St.) and the German-oriented **Goethe Institute** (⊠ 170 Beacon St.). See the *Boston Globe*'s "Calendar" section on Thursday or the *Boston Herald*'s "Scene" section on Friday for details on lectures, films, and other events held in the handsome quarters of these respected institutions.

★ ❶ **Boston Public Garden.** Although the Boston Public Garden is often lumped together with Boston Common, even in the minds of locals, the two are separate entities with different histories and purposes and a distinct boundary between them at Charles Street. The Common has been public land since Boston was founded in 1630. The Public Garden belongs to a newer Boston; it occupies what had been salt marshes on the edge of the Common's dry land. The marshes supported rope-manufacturing enterprises in the early 1800s, but by 1837 the tract was covered with an abundance of ornamental plantings donated by a private citizen. The area was fully defined in 1856 by the building of Arlington Street, and in 1860 (after the final wrangling over the development of this choice acreage) the architect George Meacham was commissioned to plan the park.

The central feature of the Public Garden is its irregularly shaped pond intended to appear, from any vantage point along its banks, much larger than its nearly 4 acres. The pond has been famous since 1877 for its foot pedal–powered **Swan Boats**, which make leisurely cruises during warm months. They were invented by Robert Paget, who was inspired by the popularity of swan boats made fashionable by Wagner's opera *Lohengrin.* (Paget descendants still run the boats.) The pond is favored by ducks and pairs of swans, and for the price of a few boat rides you can amuse children here for a good hour or more. Near the Swan Boat dock is what has been described as the world's smallest suspension bridge, designed in 1867 to cross the pond at its narrowest point.

The Public Garden has the finest formal plantings in central Boston. The beds along the main walkways are replanted for spring and summer. The tulips during the first two weeks of May are especially colorful, and there is a good sampling of native and European tree species.

The dominant work among the park's statuary is Thomas Ball's equestrian **George Washington** (1869), which faces the head of Commonwealth Avenue at the Arlington Street gate. This is Washington in a triumphant pose as liberator, surveying a scene that, from where he stood with his cannons at Dorchester Heights, would have comprised an immense stretch of blue water. Several dozen yards to the north of Washington (to the right if you're facing Commonwealth Avenue) is the granite and red marble **Ether Monument**, donated in 1866 by Thomas Lee to commemorate the advent of anesthesia 20 years earlier at nearby Massachusetts General Hospital. Other Public Garden monuments include statues of the pioneer Unitarian preacher and transcendentalist William Ellery Channing, at the corner opposite his Arlington Street church; the author (*The Man Without a Country*) and philanthropist Edward Everett Hale, at the Charles Street Gate; and the abolitionist senator Charles Sumner and the Civil War hero Colonel Thomas Cass, along Boylston Street.

The park may be one of the oldest botanical gardens in America, but it also contains a special delight for the young at heart; follow the kids quack-quacking along the pathway between the pond and the park entrance at Charles and Beacon streets to the *Make Way for Ducklings* **bronze statue group** sculpted by Nancy Schon, a tribute to the 1941 classic children's story, beloved for its drawings by Robert McCloskey. ☎ 617/635–4505. ☞ *Swan boats $1.50.* ☉ *Swan boats mid-Apr.–late Sept., daily 10–4. The garden gates are always open, but it's not a good idea to visit after dark. T stop: Arlington.*

★ ❽ **Boston Public Library.** This venerable institution is really two structures in one—a beautiful temple to literature and a valuable research mecca. When the building was opened in 1895, it confirmed the status of architects McKim, Mead & White as apostles of the Renaissance Revival style, while reinforcing Boston's commitment to an enlightened citizenry that goes back 350 years, to the founding of the Public Latin School. Philip Johnson's 1972 skylighted addition emulates the mass and proportion of the original, though not its extraordinary detail; this skylighted annex houses the library's circulating collections.

You don't need a library card to enjoy the old library's magnificent art. Charles McKim saw to it that the interior of his building was ornamented by several of the finest painters of the day. The murals at the head of the staircase, depicting the nine muses, are the work of the French artist Puvis de Chavannes; those in the book-request processing room to the right are Edwin Abbey's interpretations of the Holy Grail legend. Upstairs, in the public areas leading to the fine arts, music, and rare books collections, is John Singer Sargent's marvelous mural series on the subject of Judaism and Christianity, still dazzling, although seriously darkened by time.

You enter the older part of the library from the Dartmouth Street side, passing under the motto *"Omni lux civium"* (Light of all citizens) through the enormous bronze doors by Daniel Chester French, the sculptor of the Lincoln Memorial. Or you can walk around Boylston Street to enter through the newer addition. The corridor leading from the annex opens on to the Renaissance-style **courtyard**—an exact copy of the one in Rome's Palazzodella Cancelleria—around which the original library is built. A patio furnished with chairs rings a flower garden and fountain; from here the bustle of the city seems miles away. Beyond the courtyard is the main entrance hall of the 1895 building, with its immense stone lions by Louis Saint-Gaudens (brother of the more celebrated Augustus), vaulted ceiling, and marble staircase. The corridor at the top of the stairs leads to **Bates Hall,** renovated in 1997 and one of Boston's most sumptuous interior spaces. This is the main reference reading room, 218 ft long with a barrel-arch ceiling 50 ft high. In an ongoing program slated to be completed by 2000, the John Singer Sargent gallery and Edwin A. Abbey rooms are being renovated. ✉ *Dartmouth St. (at Copley Sq.),* ☎ *617/536–5400.* ☉ *Mon.–Thurs. 9–9, Fri.–Sat. 9–5; Sept.–May, also Sun. 1–5. Free guided art and architecture tours Mon. at 2:30, Tues. and Thurs. at 6, Fri. and Sat. at 11, Sun. at 2. T stop: Copley.*

**Boylston Street.** This broad thoroughfare is the southern commercial spine of the Back Bay. The **Hynes Convention Center** (☞ *below*) keeps company with a variety of interesting restaurants and shops, including an F. A. O. Schwarz store with an enormous teddy bear sculpture on the sidewalk in front. Here, too, is the severe, pale gray-stone mass of the **New England Building** (✉ 501 Boylston St.)—housing the first chartered mutual life insurance company in the country. Interesting historical murals embellish the lobby across the street, at 500 Boylston Street, between Berkeley and Clarendon streets, is the company's newer building, a huge postmodern structure with an outdoor courtyard and fountain.

**⑭ Christian Science Church Center.** The world headquarters of the Christian Science faith mixes the traditional with the modern—marrying Bernini to LeCorbusier by combining an Old World basilica with a sleek office complex designed by I. M. Pei. The mother church of the Christian Science faith was established here by Mary Baker Eddy in 1879. Mrs. Eddy's original granite First Church of Christ, Scientist (1894) has since been enveloped by a domed Renaissance Revival basilica, added to the site in 1906, and both church buildings are now surrounded by the offices of the Christian Science Publishing Society, where the *Christian Science Monitor* is produced, and by Pei's complex of church administration structures completed in 1973. You can hear all 13,595 pipes of the church's famed Aeolian-Skinner organ during services. In the publishing society's lobby is the fascinating **Mapparium,** a huge stained-glass globe whose 30-ft diameter can be traversed on a glass bridge (since it was built in the 1930s, don't look for political accuracy: Vietnam is still listed as French Indochina). The Mapparium was closed for renovations in 1999 and due to reopen early in 2000; tours were discontinued during the renovations. Call ahead for the latest information. ✉ *175 Ave. of the Arts,* ☎ *617/450–3790.* ☉ *Mother church Tues.–Sat. 10–4, Sun. 11:15–2; free 30-min tours. On Mon. only, original edifice open for tours. Sun. services 10 AM and 7 PM. Mapparium Mon.–Sat. 10–4. T stop: Prudential.*

**❺ Church of the Covenant.** This 1867 Gothic Revival church at the corner of Newbury and Berkeley streets has more stained-glass windows by Louis Comfort Tiffany than any other structure in the world. It is crowned by a 236-ft-tall steeple—once the tallest in Boston—that Oliver Wendell Holmes called "absolutely perfect." Inside, a 14-ft-high Tiffany lantern, granddaddy to all Tiffany lamps, hangs from a breathtaking 100-ft ceiling. ✉ *67 Newbury St. (enter at church office),* ☎

*617/266–7480.* ⊙ *Mon.–Thurs. 11–3:30. Sun. service at 10. T stop: Arlington.*

**Commonwealth Avenue Mall.** The mall that extends down the middle of the Back Bay's Commonwealth Avenue also has its share of statuary. One of the most interesting memorials, at the Exeter Street intersection, is a portrayal of naval historian and author Samuel Eliot Morison seated on a rock as if he were peering out to sea. The other figures have only tenuous connections to Boston—Norwegian explorer Leif Eriksson and Domingo F. Sarmiento, president of Argentina, and Alexander Hamilton, who tried to block native son John Adams from the presidency. As one *Boston Globe* writer-wag pondered, "Have we forgotten how to hold a grudge?"

However, a dramatic and personal monument was added in 1997 near Dartmouth Street: the **Vendome Monument,** dedicated to the nine firemen who died in 1972 putting out a fire at Back Bay's Vendome Hotel. Designed by Ted Clausen and Peter White, the curved black granite block, 29 ft long and waist-high, is etched with the names of the dead. A bronze cast of a fireman's coat and hat are draped over the granite, as if to say, "The fire is out, we can rest now." Its dedication brought an outpouring of emotion from Bostonians who saw the memorial as honoring the dedication of all firefighters. Just across the street from the monument, at 160 Commonwealth Avenue, is the **Vendome Hotel** itself, which first opened in 1872 and is now used as office space.

**⓫ Copley Place.** Two bold intruders dominate Copley Square—the **John Hancock Tower** (☞ *below*), off the southeast corner, and the even more assertive Copley Place skyscraper, on the southwest. An upscale, glass and brass urban mall, Copley Place, built between 1980 and 1984, includes two major hotels: the high-rise Westin, west, and the Marriott Copley Place, east. Dozens of shops, restaurants, and offices are attractively grouped on several levels surrounding bright, open indoor spaces. The large movie complex is a frequent venue for film festivals, including the popular Boston Film Festival. ☎ *617/369–5000.* ⊙ *Shopping galleries Mon.–Sat. 10–8, Sun. noon–6. T stop: Copley.*

**Copley Square.** For thousands of folks in April, a glimpse of Copley Square is the most wonderful sight in the world; this is where the runners of the Boston Marathon end their 26-mi race. A square now favored by skateboarders (much to the chagrin of city officials), the civic space is defined by three monumental older buildings. One is the stately, bowfront 1912 **Copley Plaza Hotel,** which faces the square on St. James Avenue and serves as a dignified foil to its companions, two of the most important works of architecture in the United States: **Trinity Church** (☞ *below*)—Henry Hobson Richardson's masterwork of 1877—at the left, and the **Boston Public Library** (☞ *above*), by McKim, Mead & White. The John Hancock Building looms in the background. To honor those runners who stagger over the marathon's finish line, bronze statues of the Tortoise and the Hare engaged in their mythical race were cast by Nancy Schon, who also did the much-loved *Make Way for Ducklings* group in the **Boston Public Garden** (☞ *above*).

**❹ Emmanuel Church of Boston.** Built in 1862, this Back Bay brownstone Gothic Episcopal church is popular among classical music–loving worshipers—every Sunday from September to May, a Bach cantata is included as part of the liturgy. Inside the church is the Leslie Lindsey Chapel—a Gothic-style memorial created by parents in memory of their daughter, a young bride who perished with her husband during their honeymoon voyage on the *Lusitania.* Lindsey family descendants still

68

# BOSTON MARATHON: RUNNING FOR THE ROSES

**M**ORE THAN A RACE, more than a social event, the Boston Marathon celebrates the art of endurance. For professionals like Bill Rogers, Joan Benoit Samuelson, Cosmas Ndeti, and Uta Pippig, a marathon victory is the Holy Grail of the running world. For thousands of amateur runners, just finishing the tough 26.2-mi course is a spiritual quest. Though neither the nation's first marathon (from Stamford, Connecticut, to New York City in 1896), nor the largest, the Boston Marathon is the world's oldest continuously run marathon and, many would insist, the most prestigious. An estimated 1 million spectators will throng the race course of the 104th Boston Marathon on April 17, 2000. Special millennial events are being planned for the week prior to the race.

dential Center. In 1986, when the John Hancock became the sponsor, it was moved to its current location (☞ **Copley Square**) in the shadow of the Hancock Tower.

The race's guardian spirit has been the indefatigable John A. Kelley, who ran his first marathon shortly after Warren G. Harding was sworn in as president. Kelley won twice—in 1935 and 1945—and continued to run well into his eighties. Until his retirement in 1992, his arrival at the finish signaled the official end of the race. A double statue of an older Kelley greeting his younger self stands at the route's most strenuous incline—dubbed **"Heartbreak Hill"**—on Commonwealth Avenue in Newton.

Women weren't allowed to race until 1972; until then, the marathon was a bat-

Held every **Patriot's Day** (the third Monday in April), the course passes through Hopkinton, Ashland, Framingham, Natick, Wellesley, Newton, Brookline, and Boston; only the last few miles are run in the city proper. The first marathon, organized by the Boston Athletic Association (BAA), was run on April 19, 1897, when Olympian Tom Burke drew a line in the dirt in Ashland (now the second town on the course) and began a 24½-mi dash to Boston with 15 men. For most of its history, the race concluded on Exeter Street outside the BAA's clubhouse. In 1965, after the Prudential Life Insurance Co. offered financial support, the finish was moved to the front of the Pru-

tleground in the gender wars. In 1966 Roberta Gibb slipped into the throngs under a hooded sweatshirt; she was the first known female participant. In 1967, cameras captured BAA organizer Jock Semple screaming, "Get out of my race," as he tried to rip off the number of Kathrine Switzer, who had registered as K. Switzer. Semple later said he was just angry about the subterfuge. But the marathon's most infamous moment was when 26-year-old Rosie Ruiz came out of nowhere in 1980 to win the women's division. Ruiz apparently joined the race less than 1 mi from the end, and her title was stripped eight days later. Bostonians still quip about her taking the T to the finish.

attend the church and are said to resemble the stained-glass image of young Leslie. ✉ *15 Newbury St.,* ☎ *617/536–3355.* ⊙ *Mon.–Thurs. 10–4 by appointment. Sun. service at 10, Wed. at 6 in the chapel. T stop: Arlington.*

**Exeter Theater.** The massive Romanesque structure was built in 1884 as a temple for the Working Union of Progressive Spiritualists. Beginning in 1914, it enjoyed a long run as a movie theater; as the *A. I. A. Guide to Boston* points out, "it was the only movie theater a proper Boston woman would enter, probably because of its spiritual overtones." It now houses a restaurant. ✉ *26 Exeter St. (at Newbury St.). T stop: Copley.*

**⑥ First Baptist Church.** This 1872 structure, at the corner of Clarendon Street and Commonwealth Avenue, is famed architect Henry Hobson Richardson's first essay in Romanesque Revival. It's marked by its soaring tower, adorned with figures sculpted by Bartholdi, of *Statue of Liberty* fame (his trumpeting angels have earned First Baptist its nickname, "Church of the Holy Bean Blowers"). If you plan to visit on a weekday, you'll need to phone a day in advance for an appointment. ✉ *110 Commonwealth Ave.,* ☎ *617/267–3148.* ⊙ *Weekdays 10–4. Sun. service at 11. T stop: Copley.*

**② Gibson House.** Through the foresight of an eccentric bon vivant, this house provides an authentic glimpse into daily life in Boston's Victorian era. One of the first Back Bay residences (1859), the Gibson House is relatively modest in comparison with some of the grand mansions built during the decades that followed; yet its furnishing, from its circa-1790 Willard clock to gold-trimmed wallpaper to a quaint Turkish pet pavilion, seems sumptuous to modern eyes. Unlike other Back Bay houses, the Gibson family home has been preserved with all its Victorian fixtures and furniture intact. That's the legacy of scion Charles Gibson Jr., a poet, travel writer, and horticulturist, who continued to wear formal attire—morning coat, spats, and a cane—well into the 1940s when he dined daily at the Ritz nearby. As early as 1936, Gibson was roping off furniture and envisioning a museum for the house his grandmother built. His dream was realized in 1957, three years after he died. You can see a full-course setting with a China- trade dinner service in the ornate dining room and discover the elaborate system of servants' bells in the perfectly preserved 19th-century basement kitchen. The house also serves as the meeting place for the New England chapter of the Victorian Society in America and served as an interior for the 1984 Merchant-Ivory film *The Bostonians.* ✉ *137 Beacon St.,* ☎ *617/267–6338.* 🖾 *$5.* ⊙ *Tours May–Oct., Wed.–Sun. at 1, 2, and 3; Nov.–Apr., weekends at 1, 2, and 3. T stop: Arlington.*

NEED A BREAK? You'll find a whiff of Parisian insouciance at the **Café de Paris** (✉ 19 Arlington St., ☎ 617/247–7121), with its strong coffee, ample quiches, and delectable pastries. It's a great spot to people-watch, but do expect less-than-speedy service.

**Hynes Convention Center.** From *Star Trek* confabs to the sports equipment shows, the Hynes plays host to thousands of visitors every week. Designed by Kallmann, McKinnell & Wood, architects of Boston's City Hall, it can hold 22,000 conventioneers. The building's official name is the John B. Hynes Veterans Memorial Convention Center, but everyone just calls it the Hynes. ✉ *900 Boylston St.,* ☎ *617/954–2000 or 617/424–8585. T stop: Hynes Convention Center.*

**⑬ Institute of Contemporary Art.** A 1989 exhibition of Robert Mapplethorpe photographs may have ruffled the feathers of long-time city councillor Dapper O'Neill, but it hardly raised an eyebrow among ICA patrons. Housed in a historic 19th-century police station and firehouse, the ICA has no permanent collection. One month it may present a show on cross-dressing, the next, a retrospective of Annie Leibowitz celebrity portraits, the next, an examination of pop icons Elvis and Marilyn. Videos, installations, and multimedia shows all push the envelope on the concept of "art." The multilevel galleries are compact, and a visit here could easily be combined with a visit to other Boston museums without risk of an art overdose or aesthetic redundancy. ⊠ *955 Boylston St.,* ☎ *617/266–5152.* ☑ *$6, free Thurs. 5–9.* ☉ *Wed.–Sun. noon–5, Thurs. noon–9. Tours weekends at 1 and 3. T stop: Hynes Convention Center.*

**❿ John Hancock Tower.** In the early 1970s, the tallest building in New England became notorious as the monolith that rained glass. Windows were improperly seated in the sills of the stark and graceful reflective blue rhomboid tower, designed by I. M. Pei. After the building's 13 acres of glass were replaced and the central core stiffened, the problem was corrected. Bostonians originally feared the Hancock's stark modernism would overwhelm nearby Trinity Church, but its shimmering sides reflect the older structure's image, actually enlarging its presence. The 60th-floor observatory makes one of the two best vantage points in the city (the other is the **Prudential Center Skywalk;** ☞ *below*), and the "Boston 1775" exhibit shows what the city looked like before the great hill-leveling and landfill operations commenced. Also, several interactive machines let you test your knowledge of Boston trivia, and another machine lets you target the horizon for the names and locations of specific buildings. ⊠ *Observatory ticket office, Trinity Pl. and St. James Ave.,* ☎ *617/247–1977 or 617/572–6429.* ☑ *$5.* ☉ *Apr.– Oct., daily 9 AM–10 PM; Nov.–Mar., Mon.–Sat. 9 AM–10 PM, Sun. 9– 5. T stop: Copley.*

NEED A
BREAK?
The **Small Planet Bar and Grill** (⊠ 565 Boylston St., ☎ 617/536–4477) squeezes in everything from staid cheeseburgers to vegetarian dishes to fresh fish. Food is served until midnight daily.

**Massachusetts Historical Society.** The oldest historical society in the United States (founded in 1791) has paintings, a library, and a 10-million-piece manuscript collection from 17th-century New England. Among these manuscripts are the Adams Papers, which comprise a quarter of a million pages from the letters and diaries of generations of the Adams family, including papers from John Adams and John Quincy Adams (second and sixth American presidents, respectively). The papers are generally available to accredited researchers, but you can take a peek with the help of the librarian. ⊠ *1154 Boylston St.,* ☎ *617/536–1608.* ☑ *Free.* ☉ *Weekdays 9–4:45. T stop: Hynes Convention Center.*

**New England Historic Genealogical Society.** Are you related to Miles Standish or Priscilla Alden? The answer may lie here. Pedigreed New Englanders—as well as those with Irish and Canadian roots—can trace their family trees with the help of the society's collections, which date from the 17th century. An introductory lecture on how to perform your own genealogical study is given every first Wednesday at noon and 7 PM. The society itself dates from 1845. ⊠ *99–101 Newbury St.,* ☎ *617/ 536–5740.* ☑ *$15 fee to use facility.* ☉ *Tues. and Fri.–Sat. 9–4:45, Wed.– Thurs. 9– 8:45; closed Sat. before Mon. holidays. T stop: Copley.*

**❼ "New" Old South Church.** Only in Boston could you call something the New Old South Church with a straight face. Members of the Old

South Meeting House, of Tea Party fame, decamped to this new parish in 1875, a move not without controversy for the congregation. In an Italian Gothic style inspired by John Ruskin and an interior decorated with Venetian mosaics and stained-glass windows, the "new" structure could not be more different from the plainer Meeting House. ✉ *645 Boylston St.,* ☎ *617/536–1970.* ⊙ *Weekdays 9–5. Sun. service at 11; mid-June–mid-Sept. at 10. T stop: Copley.*

**Newbury Street.** Eight-block-long Newbury Street has been compared to New York's 5th Avenue, and certainly this is the city's poshest shopping area, with branches of Chanel, Brooks Brothers, Armani, Burberry, and other top names in fashion. But here the pricey boutiques are more intimate than grand, and people actually live above the trendy restaurants and hair salons. Check out the famous faces in the mural overlooking the public parking lot between Dartmouth and Exeter streets. Toward the Massachusetts Avenue end, cafés proliferate and the stores get funkier, ending with Newbury Comics, Tower Records, and the hipsters' housewares and clothing store, Urban Outfitters (☞ Major Shopping Districts *in* Chapter 8).

| | |
|---|---|
| NEED A BREAK? | Care for a best-seller with your caffe latte? Folks gather at the **Trident Booksellers & Café** (✉ 338 Newbury St., ☎ 617/267–8688) to review mostly New Age best-sellers, look for used-book bargains, and munch on homemade desserts, sandwiches, and soups. It's open until midnight daily. |

⑫ **Prudential Center.** The only rival to the John Hancock's claim on Boston's upper skyline is the 52-story Prudential Tower, built in the early 1960s when the scale of monumental urban redevelopment projects had yet to be challenged. The Prudential Center, which dominates the acreage between Boylston Street and Avenue of the Arts two blocks west of the library, adds considerably to the area's overabundance of mall-style shops and food courts. The "Pru" replaced the railroad yards that blocked off the South End. Its completely remodeled and enclosed shopping mall, connected by a glass bridge to Copley Place, opened at the end of 1993. As for the Prudential Tower itself, Bainbridge Bunting made an acute observation when he called it "an apparition so vast in size that it appears to float above the surrounding district without being related to it." Later modifications to the Boylston Street frontage of the Prudential Center effected a better union of the complex with the urban space around it, but the tower itself will have to float on, vast as ever. Boston's Hynes Convention Center is connected to the Prudential Center, and it also contains a branch of the Greater Boston Visitors Bureau. **Prudential Center Skywalk,** a 50th-floor observatory atop Prudential Center, offers spectacular vistas of Boston, Cambridge, and the suburbs to the west and south—on clear days, you can even see Cape Cod. You can see sailboats skimming the Charles River, the redbrick expanse of the Back Bay, and a great glimpse of the precise abstract geometry of the nearby Christian Science Church's reflecting pool. There are chairs for sitting and noisy interactive exhibits on Boston's history that ease the bite of the admission ticket. ✉ *800 Boylston St.,* ☎ *617/536–4100 weekdays 9–5; 617/859–0648 for Skywalk.* ◻ *Skywalk $4.* ⊙ *Weekdays 8:30–6, Sat. 10–6, Sun. 11:30–6; Skywalk daily 10–10. T stop: Prudential.*

⑮ **Symphony Hall.** With commerce and religion accounted for in the Back Bay by the Prudential Center and the Christian Science headquarters, the neighborhood still has room for a temple to music: Symphony Hall, home of the Boston Symphony Orchestra, the Boston Pops, and frequent guest performers. Symphony Hall was another contribution of McKim, Mead & White to the Boston landscape. But acoustics rather than aesthetics make this hall special for performers and concert goers. Although acoustical science was a brand-new field of research when Professor Wallace Sabine planned the interior, not one of the 2,500 seats is a bad one—the secret is the box-within-a-box design. ⊠ *301 Massachusetts Ave.,* ☎ *617/266–1492; 888/266–1200 box office.* ☉ *Tours by appointment with volunteer office (1 wk notice suggested). T stop: Symphony.*

★ ❾  **Trinity Church.** In his 1877 masterpiece, architect Henry Hobson Richardson brought his Romanesque Revival style to maturity; all the aesthetic elements for which he was famous come together magnificently—bold polychromatic masonry, careful arrangement of masses, sumptuously carved interior woodwork. Today, the church remains the crowning centerpiece of Copley Square. A full appreciation of its architecture requires an understanding of the logistical problems of building it here. Remember, the Back Bay is a reclaimed wetland with a high water table; bedrock, or at least stable glacial till, lies far beneath the wet clay near the surface. Like all older Back Bay buildings, Trinity Church sits on submerged wooden pilings. But its central tower weighs 9,500 tons, and most of the 4,500 pilings beneath the building are under that tremendous central mass. The pilings are checked regularly for sinkage by means of a hatch in the basement. Much to the dismay of churchgoers and Back Bay residents, skateboarders have designated the church steps as the most radical ride in town.

Don't miss the interior. Richardson engaged some of the great artists of his day—John LaFarge, William Morris, and Edward Burne-Jones among them—to execute the paintings and stained glass that make this a monument to everything that was right about the pre-Raphaelite spirit and the nascent aesthetic of Morris's Arts and Crafts movement. LaFarge's brilliant paintings, including the intricate ornamentation of the vaulted ceilings, have been cleaned only once, in the late 1950s, and have never been substantially retouched. Today they look as though the paint were barely dry. Along the north side of the church, note the Augustus Saint-Gaudens statue of Phillips Brooks—the most charismatic rector in New England—who almost single-handedly got Trinity built and decorated. Shining light of Harvard's religious community and lyricist of "O Little Town of Bethlehem," he is shown here—amazingly—with Christ touching his shoulder in approval. ⊠ *Copley Sq.,* ☎ *617/536–0944.* ☉ *Daily 8–6. Sun. services at 8, 9, 11, and 6. Services Mon.–Sat. at 7:30, noon, and 5:30. T stop: Copley.*

# THE SOUTH END

History has come full circle in the South End. Once a fashionable neighborhood created with landfill in the mid-19th century, it was deserted by the well-to-do for the Back Bay toward the end of the 20th century. Solidly back in fashion today, its redbrick row houses in states of refurbished splendor or elegant decay are home to a polyglot mix of ethnic groups and a substantial gay community.

The South End is an anomaly of planning and architecture. It neither rose haphazardly among cow paths and village lanes, like the old sections, nor followed the strict, uniform grid typical of the Back Bay. Bainbridge Bunting called its effect "cellular," and it is certainly more a sum of random blocks and park-centered squares than of bold boulevards and long vistas. An observation often made is that the Back Bay is French-inspired whereas the South End is English. The houses, too, are noticeably different; although they continue the bowfront style, they aspire to a more florid standard of decoration.

Even if the South End was a kind of Victorian Levittown, it is an intimate and nicely proportioned neighborhood that deserved a better reputation than it earned at the outset. Consider the literary evidence: William Dean Howells's Silas Lapham abandoned the South End to build a house on the waterside of Beacon as material proof of his arrival in Boston society. In *The Late George Apley,* John P. Marquand's Brahmin hero tells how his father decided, in the early 1870s, to move the family from his South End bowfront to the Back Bay—a consequence of his walking out on the front steps one morning and seeing a man in his shirtsleeves on the porch opposite. Regardless of whether Marquand exaggerated Victorian notions of propriety (if that was possible), the fact is that people like the Apleys did decamp for the Back Bay, leaving the South End to become what a 1913 guidebook called a "faded quarter."

A more practical reason the South End was relegated to the status of a social backwater was that it was literally out of the way. Railroad tracks separated it from the Back Bay, and disunity between state planners in the Back Bay and their city counterparts in the South End left the two districts with conflicting grid patterns that have never comfortably meshed. The rail tracks are now gone, but the South End is still cut off from the rest of the city by the I–90 underpass, Copley Plaza, and the Prudential Center.

The South End by 1900 was a neighborhood of lower-middle-class families and rooming houses. It had not lost its association with upward mobility, however, and African-Americans, many of them holders of the prestigious Pullman porter jobs on the railroads, began to buy the old bowfronts and establish themselves in the area.

About 25 years ago, middle-class professionals, mostly white, began looking at the South End as though it had just been filled in and built over, and this group didn't care who might be walking around in shirtsleeves. A gentrification process began and continues today.

There is still a substantial African-American community in the South End, particularly along Columbus Avenue and Massachusetts Avenue, which marks the beginning of the predominantly black neighborhood of Roxbury. Boston's gay community also has a large presence in the South End, with most of the gay-popular restaurants and businesses located on Columbus Avenue and Tremont Street between East Berkeley Street and Massachusetts Avenue. Along East Berkeley, neighbors have created a lush community garden. At the north end of the South End, where Harrison Avenue and Washington Street lead to Chinatown, you'll find several Chinese supermarkets.

*Numbers in the text correspond to numbers in the margin and on the Back Bay, the South End, and the Fens map.*

## A Good Walk

Although it would take years to understand the South End completely, you can capture some of its flavor within a few hours. Begin a stroll from Symphony Hall in the Back Bay. Walk down Massachusetts Avenue to Columbus Avenue, turn left, and follow it to the tiny park of **Rutland Square** ⑯ on your right. Continue on Tremont until you turn right on **Union Park** ⑰. Both parks are quiet, shady examples of a more elegant time. Follow Union Park Street across Shawmut to Washington Street for a view of the huge **Cathedral of the Holy Cross** ⑱. If you like, detour to Shawmut Street, a mixture of ethnic outlets and upscale retail spaces. Walk along Shawmut to East Berkeley Street, turn left, and head back to Tremont. On Tremont Street near Clarendon Street is the **Boston Center for the Arts** ⑲. After a break at one of the many trendy restaurants and shops along Tremont Street, retrace your steps on Tremont to Arlington and cross the Massachusetts Turnpike on an overpass to find **Bay Village** ⑳ on your right; it's another 19th-century oasis in the center of Boston.

TIMING

You can walk through the South End in two to three hours. It's a good option on a pleasant day; go elsewhere in bad weather, as most of what you'll want to see here is outdoors.

## Sights to See

⑳ **Bay Village.** It seems improbable that such a fine, serene neighborhood (Edgar Allen Poe was born here) could exist so close to the busy Theater District and the Massachusetts Turnpike. Yet here it is, another Boston surprise. This pocket of early 19th-century brick row houses is near Arlington and Fayette streets. Its quaint window boxes and short, narrow streets make the area seem a toylike replica of Beacon Hill. Note that, owing to the street pattern, it's nearly impossible to drive here, and it's easy to miss on foot.

⑲ **Boston Center for the Arts** (also known as the **Cyclorama Building**). Of Boston's multiple arts organizations, the city-sponsored arts and culture complex is the one that is closest "to the people." Here you can see the work of budding playwrights, view exhibits on Haitian folk art, or walk through an installation commemorating World AIDS Day. The BCA houses three small theaters, the Mills Gallery, and studio space for some 60 Boston-based contemporary artists. It's a bit of a leap from the original purpose of the Cyclorama Building, which was built by William Blackall in 1884 to house a 400- by 50-ft circular painting of the Battle of Gettysburg. After the painting was sent to Pennsylvania, the building was used as a boxing ring, a bicycle ring, and a garage (Alfred Champion invented the spark plug here). The building now hosts frequent antiques shows and fund-raisers. Its distinctive copper dome got a face-lift in 1997, and plans are pending for development of the space next door, created when the old National Theater was razed. ⊠ *539 Tremont St.,* ☎ *617/426–5000; 617/426–7700 for recorded information; 617/426–8835 for Mills Galleries.* 🎫 *Free.* ☉ *Weekdays 9–5; Mills Galleries Wed. and Sun. 1–4, Thurs.–Sat. 1–4 and 7–10. T stop: Back Bay, South End.*

⑱ **Cathedral of the Holy Cross.** Irish Roman Catholics are no longer well represented in the South End, which is ironic, as this enormous 1875 Gothic cathedral dominates the corner of Washington and Union Park streets. It is now used for special occasions (such as the Pope's 1979 visit), and it remains the premier church of the Archdiocese of Boston, New England's largest Catholic church, and the episcopal seat of Bernard Cardinal Law. Check out the *cathedra,* or throne, from which Cardinal Law speaks in his official capacity. ⊠ *Washington St.,* ☎ *617/542–5682.* ☉ *Mass Sun. at 8 and 11, weekdays at 9; in Spanish Sun. at 9, Tues. and Thurs. at 7 PM. T stop: Chinatown, then Bus 49 to Cathedral.*

⑯ **Rutland Square.** Reflecting a time in which the South End was the most prestigious Boston address, this slice of a park, between Columbus Avenue and Tremont Street, is framed by lovely Italianate bowfront houses.

⓱ **Union Park.** Cast-iron fences, Victorian-era town houses, and a lovely grassy area all add up to one of Boston's most charming mini-escapes, dating from the 1850s.

| | |
|---|---|
| NEED A<br>BREAK? | **To Go Bakery** (✉ 312 Shawmut Ave., ☎ 617/482–1015) is a great neighborhood hangout, perfect for a pastry or a sinfully rich dessert. There are only a few tables; on nice days, people congregate outside. |

# THE FENS AND KENMORE SQUARE

The marshland known as the **Back Bay Fens** gave this section of Boston its name, but two quirky institutions give it its character: **Fenway Park**, where hope for another World Series pennant springs eternal, and the **Isabella Stewart Gardner Museum**, the legacy of a bon vivant Brahmin who once attended a concert at Symphony Hall wearing a headband that read, "Oh, You Red Sox." **Kenmore Square**, a favorite haunt for Boston University and Northeastern University students, adds a bit of funky flavor to the mix.

After the outsize job of filling in the bay had been completed, it would have been small trouble to obliterate the Fens with gravel and march row houses straight through to Brookline. But the planners, deciding that enough pavement had been laid between here and the Public Garden, hired none other than Frederick Law Olmsted—cocreator of New York's Central Park—to turn the Fens into a park. Olmsted applied his genius for heightening natural effects while subtly manicuring their surroundings; today's Fens park consists of irregularly shaped reed-bound pools surrounded by broad meadows, trees, and flower gardens.

The Fens mark the beginning of Boston's **Emerald Necklace**, a loosely connected chain of parks designed by Olmsted that extends along the Fenway, Riverway, and Jamaicaway to Jamaica Pond, the Arnold Arboretum, and Franklin Park (for more on the arboretum and Franklin Park, see The Streetcar Suburbs, below). Farther off, at the Boston–Milton line, the vast Blue Hills Reservation offers some of the Boston area's best hiking, scenic views, and even a ski lift.

*Numbers in the text correspond to numbers in the margin and on the Back Bay, the South End, and the Fens map.*

## A Good Walk

With Boston's two most spectacular art museums on this itinerary, a case of museum feet could set in. Happily, both the Museum of Fine Arts and the Isabella Stewart Gardner Museum are surrounded by the sylvan glades of the Fens—a perfect oasis and time-out location when you're suffering from gallery gout. From the intersection of Massachusetts Avenue and Avenue of the Arts, with the front entrance of Symphony Hall on your right, walk down Avenue of the Arts. (A note of caution: this neighborhood becomes deserted at the end of the day, so this outing is not recommended at night.) On your left is the New England Conservatory of Music and, on Gainsborough Street, its recital center, Jordan Hall. Between Avenue of the Arts and the Fenway is the **Museum of Fine Arts** ㉑ and, just around the corner, the **Isabella Stewart Gardner Museum** ㉒. If you prefer to pay homage to the Red Sox: from Symphony Hall, go north on Massachusetts Avenue, turn left on Commonwealth Avenue, and continue until you reach **Kenmore Square** ㉓; from here it's a 15- to 20-minute walk down Brookline Avenue to Yawkey Way and **Fenway Park** ㉔.

TIMING

Although this area can be walked through in a longish afternoon, art lovers could spend a week here—thanks to the glories of the Museum of Fine Arts and the Isabella Stewart Gardner Museum. To cap off a day of culture, plan for an area dinner, then a concert at nearby Symphony Hall. This district is most easily traveled via branches of the MBTA's Green Line; trains operate aboveground on Commonwealth Avenue and Avenue of the Arts.

## Sights to See

★ ㉔ **Fenway Park.** Belief in the "Curse of the Bambino" runs so strong that in 1995 Babe Ruth's daughter felt compelled to publicly dismiss it—to little avail. Red Sox fans will continue to blame the shadow of Babe Ruth—sold as a rookie by the Sox to the New York Yankees—for their beloved team's inability to repeat its 1918 World Series win. Fenway may be one of the smallest parks in the major leagues (capacity almost 34,000), but it is one of the most loved, despite its oddball dimensions and the looming left-field wall, otherwise known as the Green Monster. It was built in 1912 and it still has a real-grass field. Fenway has been bittersweet for the Red Sox, with pennants in 1946, 1967, 1975, and 1986, and a divisional championship in 1988—but long droughts in between. There has been no shortage of heroics: Babe Ruth pitched here when the stadium was new; Ted Williams and Carl Yastrzemski slugged out their entire careers here. The parking may be expensive and the seats a bit cramped, but the air is thick with baseball history. Sadly, Fenway will have to give way to a modern facility; if you want to experience this classic park, don't put off a visit, either for a game or a tour. Yawkey Way is named for the late Tom Yawkey, who bought the team in 1933 as a 30th-birthday present for himself and spent the next 43 years pursuing his elusive grail. ⊠ *4 Yawkey Way, between Van Ness and Lansdowne Sts.,* ☎ *617/267–1700 box office; 617/ 267–8661 recorded information; 617/236–6666 tours.* 🎟 *Tours $5.* ☉ *Tours May–Sept. weekdays at 10, 11 and noon on day game days; additional tour at 2 on non-game or night-game days.*

㉒ **Isabella Stewart Gardner Museum.** A spirited young society woman, Isabella Stewart had come from New York—where ladies were more commonly seen *and* heard than in Boston—in 1860 to marry John Lowell Gardner, one of Boston's leading citizens. "Mrs. Jack" promptly set about becoming the most un-Bostonian of the Proper Bostonians, devoting her life not only to shocking the Brahmins with her flamboyance but also to energetically acquiring art. When it came time finally to settle down with the Old Master paintings and Medici treasures she and her husband had acquired in Europe (with *her* money—she was heir to the Stewart mining fortune), she decided to build the Venetian palazzo of her dreams along Commonwealth Avenue. Always resenting the lack of privacy symbolized by the bay-windowed houses of Beacon Hill—and wanting to escape the prying eyes and raised lorgnettes of Boston grande dames—she built her palace to center on a spacious inner courtyard. On New Year's Day 1903, she threw open the entrance to Fenway Court (to use the museum's original name)—then as now, a monument to one woman's individuality and taste. Today, it probably is America's most idiosyncratic treasure house.

In a city where expensive simplicity was the norm, her palazzo was an amazing sight: a trove of spectacular paintings—including such masterpieces as Titian's *Rape of Europa,* Giorgione's *Christ Bearing the Cross,* Piero della Francesca's *Hercules,* and John Singer Sargent's *El Jaleo*—overflows rooms bought outright from great European houses. Spanish leather panels, Renaissance hooded fireplaces, and Gothic tapestries accent salons; eight "Romeo, Romeo, wherefore art thou, Romeo?" balconies adorn the majestic Venetian courtyard. There is a Raphael Room, a Spanish Cloister, a Gothic Room, a Chinese Loggia, and—to entertain such guests as Henry James and Edith Wharton—a magnificent Tapestry Room for concerts. Throughout the two decades of her residence, Mrs. Jack continued to build her collection under the tutelage of the young Bernard Berenson, who became one of the most respected art connoisseurs and critics of the 20th century.

Mrs. Gardner lived on the top floor at Fenway Court until her death in 1924. When she died, the terms of her will stipulated that Fenway Court remain exactly as she left it—paintings, furniture, everything, down to the smallest object of *virtu* in a hall cabinet. The courtyard, fully protected from the rigors of New England winters by a glass roof, is often decorated with fresh poinsettias at Christmastime, lilies at Easter, chrysanthemums in the fall—just as when Mrs. Jack lived here. Almost everything is just as it was back then.

Well, not quite everything. On March 18, 1990, the Gardner was the target of one of the world's most sensational art heists. Thieves disguised as police officers stole 13 works of art with an estimated value of $200 million from Mrs. Jack's collection. Vermeer's *The Concert* was the most famous painting taken, along with works by Rembrandt, Manet, and Degas. To date, none of the art has been recovered, despite a $1 million reward and reports in the summer of 1997 that an intermediary had glimpsed one of the stolen Rembrandts in a remote warehouse. Because Mrs. Gardner's will prohibited substituting other works for any stolen art, and because of high premiums, the Gardner Museum had chosen not to insure its collections. Empty expanses of wall and small white cards identify the spots where the art once hung; these are studied with great curiosity by museum goers. Today, with more than 2,000 works in the collection and rates dramatically lower because of increasing recoveries of stolen art, the Gardner carries insurance. Mrs. Jack never believed in making a contribution to the Metropolitan Life Insurance Company, putting her faith in her mansion's entry portal, which carries Renaissance-period figures of both St. George and St. Florian, the patron saints protecting believers from theft and fire.

An intimate restaurant overlooks the garden, and in spring and summer tables and chairs spill outside. To fully conjure up the spirit of days past, try to attend one of the concerts still held from September to May in the elegant Tapestry Room. A first-floor gallery has revolving exhibits of historic and contemporary art. ✉ *280 The Fenway,* ☎ *617/ 566–1401 (also for recorded concert information Sept.–May); 617/566– 1088 café.* 🎟 *$10, $11 weekends; concert and galleries $16; café and gift shop free.* ☉ *Museum Tues.–Sun. 11–5, some Mon. holidays; café Tues.–Fri. 11:30–4, weekends 11–4. Weekend concerts at 1:30. T stop: Museum.*

㉓ **Kenmore Square.** Two blocks north of Fenway Park is Kenmore Square, home to fast-food joints, rock clubs, gaggles of university students, and an enormous sign advertising Citgo gasoline. The red, white, and blue neon sign put up in 1965 is so thoroughly identified with the area that historic preservationists have fought, successfully, to save it—proof that Bostonians are an open-minded lot who do not insist that their landmarks be identified with the American Revolution.

In the shadow of Fenway Park is **Lansdowne Street,** a nightlife magnet for students and those whom some (less than affectionately) dub Eurotrash. Choices range from can't-hear-yourself-think dance clubs like Avalon and Axis to "cosmic bowling" (☞ Nightlife *in* Chapter 6). The urban campus of **Boston University** begins farther west on Commonwealth Avenue, in blocks thick with dorms, businesses—including the popular **Nickelodeon movie theater**—and restaurants.

★ ㉑ **Museum of Fine Arts.** When you walk past Cyrus Dallin's *Appeal to the Great Spirit* at this museum's main entrance, between Avenue of the Arts and the Fenway, with its grand stairway and rotunda whose cupola is decorated with frescoes by John Singer Sargent, or through the doors of the newer West Wing, count on staying at this celebrated museum a while if you have any hope of even beginning to see what is here. Eclecticism and thoroughness, often an incompatible pair, have coexisted agreeably at the MFA since its earliest days. From Renaissance and Baroque masters to impressionist marvels to African masks to sublime samples of American Indian pottery and contemporary crafts, the collections are happily shorn of both cultural snobbery and short-sighted trendiness.

Founded in 1870, the museum first had quarters on the upper floors of the Boston Athenaeum, then a Gothic structure on the site where the Copley Plaza Hotel now stands. As the MFA was beginning to outgrow that space, the Fenway area was becoming fashionable, and in 1909 the move was made to Guy Lowell's somewhat severe Beaux Arts building, to which the West Wing, designed by I. M. Pei, was added in 1981. The move helped to cap the half century of expansion of the Back Bay area.

The MFA's vast collection—only a third to two-thirds is on display at any one time—was built from a core of paintings and sculpture from the Boston Athenaeum, historical portraits from the city of Boston, and donations by area universities. The early MFA connoisseurs were as enamored as any cultured Victorians with the great art of European civilizations; nevertheless, they sought out American works as well; today, the MFA's holdings of American art surpass those of all but two or three U.S. museums, supplemented by intensive acquisitions in the early 1990s. It has more than 60 works by John Singleton Copley—Colonial Boston's most celebrated painter—including his amazing *Watson and the Shark,* which depicts a shark attack on a young man in Havana Harbor (Mr. Watson lost his leg but went on to become an 18th-century celebrity and government official). It has major paintings by Winslow Homer, John Singer Sargent (don't miss the stunning portrait of *The Daughters of Edward D. Boit*), Fitz Hugh Lane, and Edward Hopper, as well as a wealth of American works ranging from native New England folk art and Colonial portraiture to New York abstract expressionism of the 1950s and 1960s.

**American decorative arts** are also amply represented, particularly those of New England in the years before the Civil War. Rooms of period furniture, much of it from the matchless Karolik collection, show the progression of taste from the earliest Pilgrim pieces through the 18th-century triumphs of the Queen Anne, Hepplewhite, Sheraton, and Empire styles.

If you think of Paul Revere simply as a sounder of alarms, linger over a gleaming display of his superb silver teapots (more than 13 of them), ornate sauceboats, and other tableware; the patriot was one of the greatest artists ever to turn his hand to silver. An extra pleasure is seeing his silver Liberty Bowl, then viewing the museum's Copley portrait of Revere with the same bowl.

The museum also owns one of the world's most extensive collections of Asian art under one roof. The **Japanese Buddhist art** is the finest outside Japan, and **Chinese porcelains** of the Tang Dynasty are especially well represented. The **Egyptian rooms** display statuary, furniture, and exquisite gold jewelry; a special funerary arts gallery exhibits coffins, mummies, and burial treasures. The gathering of classical treasures proceeds chronologically through the Hellenistic and Roman eras, recalled by marble busts, jewelry, and glassware.

**French Impressionists** abound and are perhaps more comprehensively represented here than at any other New World museum outside the Art Institute of Chicago; many of the 38 Monets, the largest collection of his work outside France, vibrate with color. There are canvases by Renoir, Pisarro, Manet, and the American painters Mary Cassatt and Childe Hassam.

Three important new galleries opened late in 1998; these explore the art of **Africa, Oceania, and the Ancient Americas,** expanding the MFA's emphasis on civilizations outside the Western tradition. Highlights include rare examples of the earliest known figurative sculpture from sub-Saharan Africa, expressive Melanesian works in wood and stone, elegant Olmec jade sculptures, and extraordinary Maya painted ceramics.

The museum has strong collections of textiles and costumes and prints dating from the 15th century, including many works by Dürer and Goya. The museum's collection of antique **musical instruments,** expanded in 1979 by the acquisition of an important group of early keyboard instruments, is among the finest in the world. It includes Benjamin Franklin's keyboard "armonica." (The hours for viewing this collection differ from the regular museum hours; call for the schedule.) The MFA also has a regular concert season (☞ Music *in* Chapter 6).

Fifteen galleries contain the MFA's recently rehung and reorganized European painting and sculpture collection, dating from the 11th to the 20th century. Among the standouts in the Renaissance sculpture gallery on the second floor is Donatello's marble relief *The Madonna of the Clouds.* Also on the second floor is Turner's powerful work *The Slave Ship.* Most striking, however, is the **William I. Koch** (pronounced "coke") **Gallery,** a former tapestry room whose vast 40-ft-high marble walls are now hung—nearly floor to ceiling—with 53 dramatic Renaissance and Baroque paintings by El Greco, Claude Lorraine, Poussin, Rubens, Tintoretto, Titian, Van Dyck, Velázquez, Veronese, and other masters.

The **West Wing,** a handsome, airy, well-lighted space, is used primarily to mount traveling exhibitions, temporary shows drawn from the museum's holdings, and lively contemporary art and photography exhibits. It also has a restaurant, a cafeteria, and a gallery café serving light snacks. In the **Fraser Court,** a charming oasis of green trees and statuary, beverages are served on the terrace from April to October. From October to April, a "Ladies Tea" is served from 2:30 to 4:30 inside near the main entrance. The Morse Study Room for prints, drawings, and photographs, lets you study (by appointment only) more than 200,000 works from the museum's collection. Upcoming scheduled exhibits include *Pharaohs of the Sun* from November 1999 through February 2000; an exhibition of photographs by Edward Weston in spring; and a major Van Gogh portraiture exhibit from summer to early fall.

Outside, on the Fenway Park side of the MFA, the **Tenshin-En** or **Japanese Garden,** the "garden in the heart of heaven," allows visitors to experience landscape as a work of art. An assortment of Japanese and American trees and shrubs combines the elements of the Japanese garden with elements of the New England landscape. A bridge at the center symbolically links longevity on the one side with prosperity on the other. Access to the garden is free with admission to the museum. ⊠ *465 Ave. of the Arts,* ☎ *617/267–9300.* 🎟 *$10; donation Wed. 4–9:45.* ☉ *Entire museum Mon.–Tues., weekends 10–4:45, Wed.–Fri. 10–9:45. West Wing only Thurs.–Fri. 5–10 with admission reduced by $2. 1-hr tours available weekdays. Garden Apr.–Oct., Tues.–Sun. 10–4. T stop: Museum.*

**Northeastern University.** Northeastern students are largely commuters, and their noses are seldom far from the grindstone. For their great numbers, they keep a low local profile. The campus was established in 1898 and now has an enrollment of about 34,000, including part-time students. It is one of the world's largest cooperative-education-plan universities, where students in a wide variety of disciplines alternate periods of classroom study with employment in related professions. Northeastern's engineering school is strong, and the university offers important programs in nursing, computers, business administration, pharmacology, criminal justice, marine sciences, the human development professions, and law—yet another law school in a city of lawyers. Unlike Harvard University or MIT, the school does not have a distinctive, centralized campus. ⊠ *360 Ave. of the Arts,* ☎ *617/373–2000.*

# THE STREETCAR SUBURBS

The expansion of Boston in the 1800s was not confined to the Back Bay and the South End. Toward the close of the century, as the working population of the downtown district swelled and public transportation (first horsecars, then electric trolleys) linked outlying suburbs with the core city, development of the Streetcar Suburbs began. These areas answered the housing needs of the rising native-born middle class as well as the second-generation immigrant families already outgrowing the narrow streets of the North and West Ends.

The landfill project that became South Boston—not to be confused with the South End—is not a true streetcar suburb; its expansion predates the era of commuting. Some of the brick bowfront residences along East Broadway in City Point date from the 1840s and 1850s, but the neighborhood really came into its own with the influx of Irish around 1900, and Irish-Americans still hold sway here. "Southie" is a Celtic enclave, as the annual St. Patrick's Day parade attests.

Inland from Columbia Point are **Dorchester, Roxbury,** and **Jamaica Plain**—rural retreats barely more than a century ago that are now thick with tenements and the distinctive three- or six-family triple-decker apartment houses of Boston's streetcar suburbs. Both Dorchester and Roxbury are almost exclusively residential, tricky to navigate by car, and accessible by the T (the Red or Orange Line) only if you know exactly where you are going. Dorchester and Roxbury are contiguous and border **Franklin Park,** an Olmsted creation of more than 500 acres, noted for its zoo.

Due to its geography, **Brookline** seems like a neighborhood of Boston, but it is a separate civic entity, composed of a mixture of the affluent, the middle-class, and students, proud of their government and school system.

*Numbers in the text and margin correspond to numbers on The Streetcar Suburbs map.*

## A Good Walk

Except for the Arnold Arboretum, the sights covered here aren't particularly walkable from the center of town; your best bet is to make separate trips, either via public transportation or car. If you do have a car, **Castle Island Park** ①, **Dorchester Heights Monument** ②, and the **John F. Kennedy Library and Museum** ③ make a sensible joint excursion, as do the **Franklin Park Zoo** ④ and the **Arnold Arboretum** ⑤, especially if you are not inclined to take the suggested walk to or from it. You'll probably want to make separate trips to the **John F. Kennedy National Historic Site** ⑥, the **Frederick Law Olmsted National Historic Site** ⑦.

If you *do* have the time and stamina for a jaunt of approximately 3½ mi, it is possible to walk almost the entire distance from Arnold Arboretum to **Kenmore Square** (☞ The Fens and Kenmore Square, *above*) within the Emerald Necklace, Boston's loosely connected chain of Olmsted-designed parks. Just follow the Jamaicaway north from its beginning at the circle that marks the northern tip of the arboretum. Within the equivalent of one long block you'll reach Jamaica Pond. Continue along the Jamaicaway through Olmsted Park, past Leverett Pond. From a point just north of here, either Brookline Avenue or the Riverway will take you to the Fens and Kenmore Square. Along the way you will pass many of the spacious freestanding mansions built around the turn of the century along the park borders of Jamaica Plain, when this was the choicest of the streetcar suburbs. Not the least of your pleasures as you move along this stretch will be that you are walking, not driving. The Jamaicaway was one of Boston's first attempts at increasing the pace of traffic, and it worked extremely well for horse-drawn carriages and the slower and narrower early-model automobiles. If you think that Boston still isn't very good at hurrying cars around, remember that, unlike most American cities, it has been inhabited almost exclusively by pedestrians for two-thirds of its history.

TIMING

To enjoy the Streetcar Suburbs—the city at its country best—wait for pleasant weather. The Arnold Arboretum is a great place to see seasonal blooms, with its Lilac Sunday festival and flowering crab apple trees in mid-May and a spectacular rhododendron display in June. Autumn leaves generally peak in October.

# South Boston

**❶ Castle Island Park.** South Boston projects farther into the harbor than any other part of Boston except Logan Airport, and the views of the Harbor Islands from along Day Boulevard or Castle Island are lovely. At L Street and Day Boulevard is the L Street Beach, where an intrepid group called the L Street Brownies swims all year long, including a celebratory dip in the icy Atlantic every New Year's Day. Castle Island Park is no longer on an island, but Fort Independence, when it was built here in 1801, was separated from the mainland by water. The circular walk from the fort around Pleasure Bay, delightful on a warm summer day, has a stunning view of the city's skyline late at night (South Boston is considered one of the city's safest neighborhoods). The statue near the fort is of Donald McKay, whose clipper ships once sped past this point on their way to distant California and the Orient. To get here by the T, take the Red Line to Broadway Station. Just outside the station, catch Bus 9 going east on Broadway, which will take you to within a block of the waterfront. From the waterfront park you can walk the loop, via piers, around the island.

# The "Streetcar Sububs"

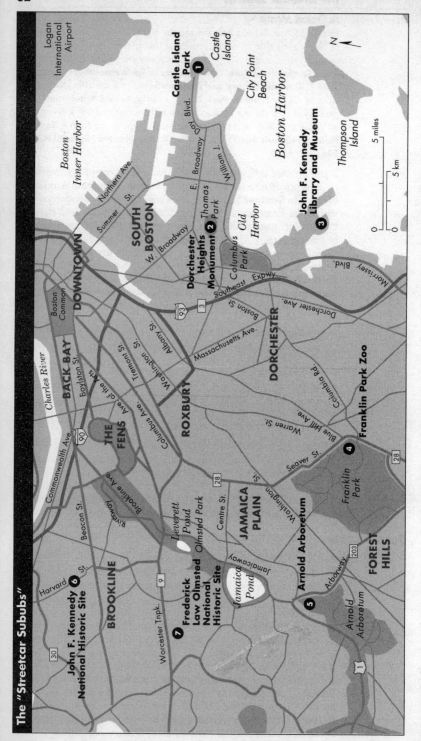

# Dorchester and Roxbury

**❺ Arnold Arboretum.** This 265-acre living laboratory, administered by Harvard University, is incongruously set in a dense urban area. Established in 1872 in accordance with the terms of a bequest from New Bedford merchant James Arnold, it contains more than 4,000 kinds of woody plants, most from the hardy north temperate zone. The rhododendrons, azaleas, lilacs, magnolias, and fruit trees are spectacular when in bloom, and something is always in season from early April through September. In October, the park puts on a spectacular scarlet and neon orange display that will more than satisfy leaf peepers. Peters Hill has a grand view of the Boston skyline and local surroundings. The Larz Anderson bonsai collection has individual specimens more than 200 years old imported from Japan. The visitor center has a 40-to-1 scale model of the arboretum (with 4,000 tiny trees), installed for its 125th anniversary in 1996, plus an exhibit on "Science in the Pleasure Ground," a kind of "green" history of the landscape. The arboretum plans a walking trail to run from the Forest Hills MBTA station through marsh area to the park's Forest Hills Gate, but at press time a completion date had not been set. There are extensive tours and programs, however; call ahead. The arboretum, 6 mi from downtown Boston, is accessible by MBTA Orange Line (Forest Hills stop) or Bus 39 from Copley Square to Centre Street. Walk four blocks south. ⊠ *Rtes. 1 and 203, Arborway,* ☎ *617/524–1718.* ☉ *Grounds daily dawn–dusk; visitor center weekdays 9–4, weekends noon–4. T stop: Forest Hills.*

**❷ Dorchester Heights Monument.** Off Telegraph Street, near the juncture of the South Boston peninsula with the Dorchester mainland, stands the high ground of Thomas Park, where you will find the Dorchester Heights Monument and National Historic Site. In 1776 Dorchester Heights commanded a clear view of central Boston, where the British had been under siege since the preceding year. Here George Washington set up the cannons that Henry Knox, a Boston bookseller turned soldier, and later secretary of war, had hauled through the wilderness after their capture at Fort Ticonderoga. The artillery did its job of intimidation, and the British troops left Boston, never to return. The site has a spectacular view of Boston, and the monument itself is a graceful, white tower; otherwise you may find more history at the Bunker Hill Monument (☞ Charlestown, *above*). ⊠ *Thomas Park (near G St.).* ⊠ *Free.* ☉ *Grounds with interpretive plaques daily. Monument May–Sept., Wed. 4–8, weekends 10–4. T stop: Broadway, then City Point Bus to G St.*

**❹ Franklin Park Zoo.** After a decade of decline, the Franklin Park Zoo has begun to rock and roar. Lions and cheetahs arrived in 1997; gentle giraffes are due in spring 1999. A 4-acre mixed-species area, called Bongo Congo, showcases antelope, zebras, ostriches, ibex, and warthogs. The African Tropical Forest, with its popular gorilla exhibit, continues to be a draw, although the facilities are somewhat outdated. Wallabies, emus, and kangaroos populate the Australian Outback trail; butterflies flit and flutter at Butterfly Landing from May to September. If you see a man in a 10-gallon hat inspecting the zoo on horseback, that may just be director Brian Rutledge, who lives on the grounds. Unfortunately, the zoo continues to struggle with concerns about its location on the outskirts of a high-crime area. The limited Children's Zoo is scheduled for a new site, with construction beginning in late 1999. The park, 4 mi from downtown, is reached by Bus 16 from Forest Hills (Orange Line) or Andrew (Red Line). If you drive, you would hardly guess that the area has a bad reputation, and there's plenty of parking. ☒ *1 Franklin Park Rd.,* ☎ *617/541–5466.* ☎ *$6.* ☉ *Oct.–Mar., weekdays 10–4, weekends 10–6; Apr.–Sept., weekdays 10–5, weekends 10–6.*

**❸**   **John F. Kennedy Library and Museum.** Chronicling a time now passing from memory to history, the library/museum is both a center for serious scholarship and a focus for Boston's nostalgia for her native son. The stark, white, prowlike building (another modernist monument designed by I. M. Pei) at this stunning harbor-enclosed site pays homage to the life and presidency of John F. Kennedy, an Irish-American blessed with distinctive style, intellect, and passion, and to members of his family, including his wife, Jackie, and brother Robert.

The Kennedy Library is the official repository of his presidential papers; the museum displays a trove of Kennedy memorabilia, including re-creations of his desk in the Oval Office and of the television studio in which he debated Richard M. Nixon in the 1960 election. At the entrance, high and dry during the summer months, is the president's 26-ft sailboat; inside, two theaters show a film about his life. The museum exhibits, ranging from the Cuban missile crisis to his assassination, include 20 video presentations. A more recent addition is a permanent display on the late Jackie Kennedy Onassis, including some samples of her distinctive wardrobe and personal mementoes. As a somber note in an otherwise gung-ho museum, continuous videos of the first news bulletin of the assassination and the funeral are shown in a darkened hall. The fourth-floor research facilities are open only to serious researchers. The Steven M. Smith Wing provides space for meetings and events; the facility also includes a store and a small café. ☒ *Columbia Point,* ☎ *617/929–4523.* ☎ *$8.* ☉ *Daily 9–5. T stop: JFK/UMass, then free shuttle bus every 20 mins.*

# Brookline

**❻**   **John F. Kennedy National Historic Site.** This was the home of the 35th president from his birth on May 29, 1917, until 1920, when the family moved to nearby Naples and Abbottsford streets. Mrs. Rose Kennedy provided the furnishings for the restored 2½-story, wood-frame structure. Devoted Kennedyphiles may pick up a brochure for a walking tour of young Kennedy's school, church, and neighborhood. To get here, take the MBTA Green Line to Coolidge Corner and walk north on Harvard Street four blocks. ☒ *83 Beals St.,* ☎ *617/566–7937.* ☎ *$2.* ☉ *Mid-Mar.–Nov., Wed.–Sun. 10–4:30; tours every hr from 10:45. Last tour at 4. T stop: Coolidge Corner.*

**★ ❼**   **Frederick Law Olmsted National Historic Site.** Frederick Law Olmsted (1822–1903), the first person to call himself a "landscape architect," is considered the founder of the profession and the nation's preeminent creator of parks. In 1883 at age 61 while immersed in planning Boston's Emerald Necklace of parks, Olmsted set up his first permanent office at Fairsted, an 18-room farmhouse dating from 1810, to which he added another 18 rooms for his design offices. The site is primarily a mecca for researchers and planners; there are displays of plans and drawings for such high-profile and diverse projects as the U.S. Capitol grounds, Stanford University, and Mount Royal Park in Montreal. You can also tour the design rooms (some still in use for preservation projects) where Olmsted and staff drew up their plans; highlights include a 1904 "electric blueprint machine," a kind of primitive photocopying process. The 1¾-acre site incorporates many trademark Olmstedian designs, including areas of meadow, wild garden, and woodland; Olmsted believed body and spirit could be healed through close association with nature. The site became part of the National Park

Service in 1979; Olmsted's office played an influential role in the creation of this federal agency. In 1916, Olmsted's son, who carried on his father's work here, wrote the words that were to serve as a statement of purpose for legislation establishing the park service that same year: "To conserve the scenery and the natural and historic objects and the wildlife therein and to provide for the enjoyment of the same in such manner and by such means as will leave them unimpaired for the enjoyment of future generations." ⊠ *99 Warren St.,* ☎ *617/566–1689.* ✉ *Free.* ⊙ *Fri.–Sun. 10–4:30, and by appointment; 40-min tours every hr from 10:30. Last tour at 3:30. T stop: Brookline Hills.*

# 3 EXPLORING CAMBRIDGE

Home to Harvard and MIT, Cambridge has more geniuses per capita than any other town in America. Residents are known for their unabashedly liberal politics and willingness to sound off on any topic—opinions fly thick and fast, whether in a classroom or on signs paraded around Harvard Square. The Square is a fascinating cross section, where old-money Cantabrigians mix with backpack-laden students and homeless newspaper hawkers, many of whom are as well-read as the students. In the words of local comic Jimmy Tingle, "It's Cambridge, where even the beggars can be choosers."

By Stephanie
Schorow

Updated by
Robert Kahn

**P**RONOUNCED WITH EITHER PRIDEFUL SATISFACTION
or the occasional smirk, the nickname "The People's
Republic of Cambridge" sums up this independent
city of 95,000 west of Boston. Cambridge not only houses three of the
country's greatest educational institutions—Harvard University, Radcliffe College, and the Massachusetts Institute of Technology (MIT)—
it has a long history as a haven for freethinkers, writers, activists, and
iconoclasts of every stamp. Cambridge also functions as Boston's con-
science; when a new social experiment or piece of progressive legislation appears on the local scene, chances are it grew out of local political
activism. Once a center for publishing, Cambridge has become a high-
tech mecca. Several high-profile companies, including Aspen Technology and Sapient Corporation, have been launched by students and
alumni of MIT.

Yet Cambridge, like Boston, is a city of neighborhoods; the rarefied
air of Harvard Yard and the mansions of Brattle Street are within a
mile of the ethnic enclaves in Central Square and East Cambridge.
Cantabrigians, as residents are known, are a mixed breed, ranging from
French-cuisine doyenne Julia Child to detective novelist Robert Parker
(author of the gritty Spenser books) and William F. Weld, the former
governor. The more than 300,000 students ensure a thicket of cafés,
record stores, music clubs, street-chic boutiques, and bookstores.

The city dates from 1630, when the Puritan leader John Winthrop chose
this meadowland as the site of a carefully planned, stockaded village
he named Newtowne. The site was chosen because it was on a hill 3
mi upriver from the mouth of the Charles and thus safe from attack
by sea. Eight years later the town was renamed in honor of the university in England at which most Puritan leaders had been educated.
In 1636, the Massachusetts Bay Colony established the country's first
college here, which was later named after one of its first benefactors,
John Harvard.

The old Cambridge that took shape around the 17th-century college
was a considerable journey from the several villages that grew up
within its borders. In time they broke away to form Lexington, Watertown, Arlington, and other towns, and in 1846 Cambridge itself was
incorporated as a city. It then included the industrial communities of
Cambridgeport and East Cambridge, which lie below it on the west
bank of the Charles River. By 1900, the population of these communities, made up of Irish, Polish, Italians, and French Canadians, was
eight times that of the Harvard end of town. MIT moved to Cambridge
from Boston in 1916, and after World War II heavy industry was
rapidly replaced by firms engaged in camera manufacturing, electronics, and space research; these activities were in turn succeeded by
software developers in the 1980s and biotechnology in the '90s.

Cambridge, just minutes from Boston by MBTA, is easily reached on
the Red Line train to **Harvard Square.** Although Harvard Square draws
the most tourists, other neighborhood squares exude their own charms.
Inman Square, at the intersection of Cambridge and Hampshire streets,
has a fine concentration of restaurants; Central Square has ethnic
eateries, music clubs, and a burgeoning row of furniture stores; Porter
Square, about 1 mi west of Harvard Square on Massachusetts Avenue,
has several shopping centers, and, within the nearby Porter Exchange,
a mini-mall of Japanese noodle and food shops. Kendall Square, near
MIT, is home to a multiplex showing first-run arthouse films. Still, Harvard Square is the best place to begin.

The area is notorious for limited parking, so do consider taking the T. If you insist on driving, avoid the local circling ritual by pulling into a garage. (The Harvard Square garage is at JFK and Eliot streets; the University Place garage is on University Road at Bennett Street.) Cambridge now has an office of tourism (☞ Visitor Information *in* Smart Travel Tips A to Z).

# HARVARD SQUARE

If elsewhere all roads lead to Rome, in Cambridge the street patterns all point to Harvard Square—which, despite its moniker, is not a classic urban square but instead the name given to the surrounding business district. In addition to being the gateway to Harvard University and its various museums, the square boasts the venerable Passim folk-music club, the House of Blues, two movie theaters, one of the country's first cybercafés, and a tempting collection of shops.

Those familiar with Cambridge will notice a distinct—and by some standards sad—shift in the square's persona. Old and loved mom-and-pop places continue to succumb to the proliferating chain-store competitors. One major loss was the row of local businesses in the old buildings along JFK Street that included the Wursthaus restaurant and the much-loved, nine-stool greasepit, the Tasty Diner. The gutted buildings have become a mall, anchored by an Abercrombie & Fitch clothing store.

If Cambridge, with its influx of people from dozens of countries, is a microcosm of the world, then "the Pit" is that world's vibrating epicenter. Here, in the small plaza atop the main entrance to the Harvard MBTA station, skaters and multipierced punks hang out while fresh-faced students impress their parents with tales of the Ivy League. It's possible to overhear seven or eight languages being spoken along the row of pay phones that lines the sidewalk. On a warm day, street musicians perform next to the browser-fringed newsstand while activists pass out pamphlets promising "God Will Save You."

*Numbers in the text and margin correspond to numbers on the Cambridge map.*

## A Good Walk

A good place to begin your tour is the **Cambridge Information Booth** in **Harvard Square** ① near the MBTA station entrance, where you will find maps and information about the entire city, a guide to local bookstores, and brochures that cover walking tours of Old Cambridge, seasonal events, etc. Walk past the **Wadsworth House** ②, a clapboard house on Massachusetts Avenue that dates from 1726, and enter the dignified hush of **Harvard University**'s ③ Yard. After a stroll through the university's rarefied climes, passing **Widener Library** ④, exit the yard and cross Massachusetts Avenue to view the **Old Burying Ground and the First Parish in Cambridge** ⑤ on the corner of Church Street and Massachusetts Avenue. Through the iron railing of the cemetery, you can make out a number of tombstones. Buried here are the remains of 17th- and 18th-century Tory landowners, slaves, and soldiers. Turn right and cross over to **Dawes Island** ⑥ in the middle of Garden Street to see the historical plaques mounted on signposts and the bronze horseshoes embedded in the sidewalk. Continue up Garden Street to **Christ Church** ⑦, designed in 1761 and still an active parish. The Cambridge Common, across Garden Street, makes a nice place for a picnic or break.

The next portion of this walk is particularly good if you have children. Retrace your steps along Massachusetts Avenue and cross the street near the First Parish. Cut through Harvard Yard, bearing to your left and look for the striking Victorian architecture of **Memorial Hall.** (Ask any student for directions if you're disoriented.) Just past Memorial Hall is Kirkland Street; turn right and follow it to Divinity Avenue, onto which you turn left. At 6 Divinity, you'll find Harvard's **Semitic Museum** ⑧, a fine place to view Egyptian art. At 11 Divinity is the entrance to the extensive **Peabody Museum** and the **Harvard Museum of Natural History** ⑨. If you are inclined toward art, it's about a 15-minute walk through Harvard Yard to Harvard's impressive **Fogg** ⑩ and **Arthur M. Sackler** ⑪ museums on Quincy and Broadway streets, respectively.

In good weather, beginning back at Harvard Square, you can walk along Massachusetts Avenue to reach the bustle and ethnic diversity of urban Central Square, where there are some wonderful Middle Eastern and Indian spots for lunch, and into the warehouselike openness of the Kendall Square area, where the 135-acre campus of the **Massachusetts Institute of Technology** ⑫ dominates the neighborhood. If the weather is poor, take the T Red Line heading inbound from Harvard Square two stops to Kendall Square. The **MIT Museum** ⑬ merits a visit.

TIMING

Budget at least two hours to explore Harvard Square, plus at least three more if you plan to go to either Harvard's cultural and history museums or the art museums. The walk down Massachusetts Avenue to MIT will take an additional 35 to 45 minutes (much less if you catch the T, as suggested above), and you could easily spend an hour or two on the MIT campus admiring its architecture and visiting its museum or the List Visual Arts Center. Even in cold weather the distances between sites should not be off-putting.

## Sights to See

⑪ **Arthur M. Sackler Museum.** The richness of the Orient and artistic treasures of the ancient Greeks, Egyptians, and Romans are a major draw here. Make a beeline for the Ancient and Asian Art Galleries, the permanent installations on the fourth floor, which include Chinese bronzes, Buddhist sculptures, Greek friezes, and Roman marbles. Other exhibits, culled from Harvard's extensive collections, rotate approximately every other month—it's possible to stumble upon works by Picasso, Klee, Toulouse-Lautrec, or Manet. The admission fee also grants you entrance to the Fogg Art Museum (☞ *below*). ⊠ *485 Broadway,* ☎ *617/495–9400.* ⌦ *$5, free all day Wed. and Sat. 10–noon and after 4:30.* ☉ *Mon.–Sat. 10–5, Sun. 1–5.*

OFF THE BEATEN PATH

**Cambridge Multicultural Arts Center.** Ranging from colorfully creepy Mexican Day of the Dead festivals to gospel concerts, from African drumming to Argentine tangos, from Korean dance to Jewish storytelling, the multiethnic events the center hosts are aimed at promoting cross-cultural understanding. Although many events are geared for youngsters, adults also can enjoy lectures, workshops, ongoing art exhibits, and concerts. ⊠ *41 Second St., East Cambridge,* ☎ *617/577–1400.* ⌦ *Gallery free, admission charge for events.* ☉ *Gallery weekdays 9–5; open during events.*

**Cambridge Visitor Information Booth.** At this volunteer-staffed kiosk, just outside the MBTA station entrance, you will find maps, brochures, and guides about the entire city. Material available includes a historic walking tour, an excellent guide to the bookstores in the Square and beyond, and a guide to seasonal events. The booth is supervised by the **Cambridge Tourism office** (⊠ 18 Brattle St., ☎ 617/441–2884 or

800/862–5678). ⊠ *0 Harvard Sq.,* ☎ *617/497–1630.* ☉ *Mon.–Sat. 9–5, Sun. 1–5.*

**❼ Christ Church.** This picturesque structure was designed in 1761 by Peter Harrison, the country's first trained architect. During the Revolution, its mostly Tory congregation fled for their lives and the church was used as a soldiers' barracks during the Siege of Boston. Washington ordered it reopened for services on New Year's Eve, 1775. Step into the vestibule to look for the bullet hole left by either British or Revolutionary forces. The church's historical significance extends to the 20th century; Teddy Roosevelt was a Sunday school teacher here, and Martin Luther King Jr. spoke from the pulpit to announce his opposition to the Vietnam War. ⊠ *0 Garden St.,* ☎ *617/876–0200.* ☉ *Sun.–Fri. 7:30–6, Sat. 7:30–3. Sun. services at 8, 10, 12:30, 5 during academic yr. Services at 8 and 10 in June–Aug.*

**❻ Dawes Island.** Paul Revere, move over. The traffic island in the middle of Garden Street, called Dawes Island, is studded with bronze horseshoes, a bicentennial gift from descendants of William Dawes, a tanner who galloped through Cambridge spreading the alarm "The British are coming," on the eve of the 1775 Battle of Lexington (although, of course, in those days, he wouldn't have used those exact words, as the colonists considered themselves British). Dawes, unlike fellow rider Revere, managed to elude capture by the British. Signs on the island provide additional information. Across Garden Street, through an ornamental arch, is **Cambridge Common,** a public park since 1631. Here, on July 3, 1775, George Washington is said to have taken command of the Continental Army under a large elm. A bronze plaque now marks the site of the "Washington Elm." A striking recent addition is the Irish Famine Memorial by Derry artist Maurice Herron, unveiled in 1997 to coincide with the 150th anniversary of "Black '47," the deadliest year of the potato famine. It shows a desperate Irish mother sending her child off to America. There is also a large memorial to the Civil War, which stands at the Common's center.

**★ ❿ Fogg Art Museum.** Seldom has so much been packed into so small a space. Harvard's most famous art museum is a virtual history of art in the world, stunningly arranged in a way intended to stimulate, not overtax. Opened in 1895, and occupying its current space since 1927, the collection of more than 80,000 works focuses primarily on European, American, and East Asian works. It has notable collections of Italian Renaissance paintings and 19th-century French Impressionists, including Renoir and Monet, plus stunning works by Van Gogh (*Self-Portrait Dedicated to Paul Gauguin,* for instance) and Degas (*The Rehearsal,* with its snapshotlike composition). There are also works by Gauguin, Whistler, Klee, and Kandinsky. The museum has an impressive collection of decorative arts, including American and English silver, and the most curious and distinctly uncomfortable Harvard University "President's Chair," used only at commencement.

A ticket to the Fogg also gains admission to Harvard's **Busch-Reisinger Museum,** in the Werner Otto Hall entered through the Fogg. From the serenity of the Fogg's old masters, you step into the jarring and mesmerizing world of German Expressionists and other 20th-century artists. The museum was founded in 1902 as the university's "Germanic Museum," but its collections now include the modern art considered "degenerate" by the Nazis and art from Central and Northern Europe. ⊠ *32 Quincy St.,* ☎ *617/495–9400.* ☞ *$5, free all day Wed. and Sat. 10–noon.* ☉ *Mon.–Sat. 10–5, Sun. 1–5.*

NEED A
BREAK? **The Broadway Marketplace** (⊠ 468 Broadway, ☎ 617/547–2334) is
the Harvard University of grocery stores—it's where Julia Child does her
grocery shopping. Besides the excellent fresh produce, there's a selection of prepared meals; choose one to be heated up and then grab a
seat for a quick bite.

**Harvard Museum of Natural History.** Many museums promise something for every member of the family; the Harvard museum complex
actually delivers. This vast brick building fulfills the plan of the Swiss
naturalist Louis Agassiz; his idea was to bring under one roof the
study of all kinds of life: plants, animals, and humankind. It contains
three distinct museums within its walls, all accessible through one admission fee. Entrance to the Peabody Museum of Archaeology and Ethnology (☞ *below*) is also included in the fee.

The **Museum of Comparative Zoology** traces the evolution of animals
and humans. You can't miss—literally—the 42-ft-long skeleton of the
underwater *Kronosaurus*. Dinosaur fossils and a zoo of stuffed exotic
animals can occupy young minds for hours.

Oversize garnets and crystals sparkle at the **Mineralogical and Geo-
logical Museum,** founded in 1784. The museum also contains an extensive collection of meteorites.

Perhaps the most famous exhibits of the museum complex are the glass
flowers in the **Botanical Museum,** which were created as teaching
tools that would never wither and die. Renting the audiotape tour will
help you to appreciate fully these 3,000 models of 847 plant species,
meticulously created in glass by a father and son in Dresden, Germany,
who worked continuously from 1887 to 1936. Even more amazing than
the colorful flower petals are the delicate roots of some plants; frequent
signs assure the viewer everything is, indeed, of glass. ⊠ *26 Oxford
St.,* ☎ *617/495–3045.* ⊡ *$5, free Sat. 9–noon.* ☉ *Mon.–Sat. 9–5, Sun.
1–5.*

★ ❶ **Harvard Square.** Gaggles of students, street musicians—known as
buskers—homeless people, end-of-the-world preachers, and political-
cause proponents make for a nonstop pedestrian flow at this most celebrated of Cambridge crossroads. Harvard Square is where
Massachusetts Avenue (locally, Mass Ave.), coming from Boston, turns
and widens into a triangle broad enough to accommodate a brick
peninsula (beneath which the MBTA station is located). Sharing the
peninsula is the Out-of-Town newsstand, a local institution that occupies the restored 1928 kiosk that used to be the entrance to the MBTA
station. Harvard Square is walled on two sides by banks, restaurants,
and shops and on the third by Harvard University.

★ ❸ **Harvard University.** Although its name is often cited to exemplify
Boston-speak, as in "paak the caa in Havaad Yaad," the shade-dappled
expanse of Harvard Yard—the very center of Harvard University—itself exudes peace and gentility. It has been that way for more than 300
years. In 1636 the Great and General Court of the Massachusetts Bay
Colony voted funds to establish the country's first college and a year
later chose Cambridge as the site. Named in 1639 for John Harvard,
a young Charlestown clergyman who died in 1638, leaving the college
his entire library and half his estate, Harvard remained the only college in the New World until 1693, by which time it was firmly established as a respected center of learning. Today, the country's finest
university encompasses various schools or "faculties," including the
Faculty of Arts and Sciences, the medical school, law school, and the
John F. Kennedy School of Government.

**92**

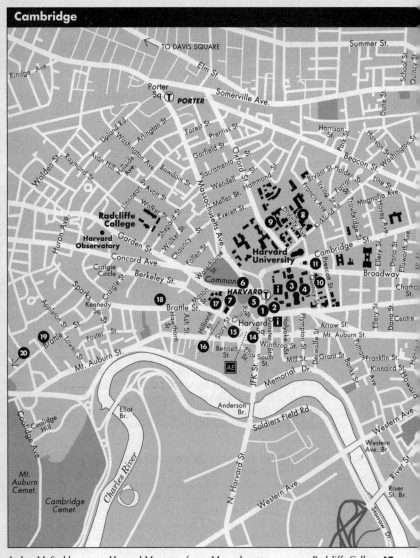

Arthur M. Sackler
Museum, **11**

Brattle House, **15**

Christ Church, **7**

Dawes Island, **6**

Dexter Pratt
House, **16**

Fogg
Art Museum, **10**

Harvard Museum of
Natural History and
the Peabody
Museum, **9**

Harvard Square, **1**

Harvard University, **3**

Hooper-Lee-Nichols
House, **19**

Longfellow National
Historic Site, **18**

Massachusetts
Institute of
Technology, **12**

MIT Museum, **13**

Mt. Auburn
Cemetery, **20**

Old Burying
Ground and the
First Parish in
Cambridge, **5**

Radcliffe College, **17**

Semitic Museum, **8**

Wadsworth House, **2**

Widener Library, **4**

Winthrop Park, **14**

**KEY**

AE American Express Office

0 ——— 550 yards
0 ——— 500 meters

*LECHMERE*

Charlestown Ave.

McGrath Hwy.

Munroe St.
Walnut St.
New St.
Stone Ave.
Washington St.
Linwood St.
Joy St.
Poplar St.
Medford St.
Mansfield St.
Rossmore St.
Meacham St.
Linden St.
Allen St.
Somerville Ave.
Newton Ave.
Concord Ave.
Oak St.
Dickinson St.
Houghton St.
Clarkson St.
nick St.
Webster Ave.
Tremont St.
South St.
Porter St.
Warren St.
Willow St.
Winter St.
Gore St.
Cambridge St.
Otis St.
7th St.
8th St.
Thorndike St.
Spring St.
Hurley St.
3rd St.
Scarappa St.
Fulkerson St.
Charles St.
Bent St.
Roger St.
Binney St.
2nd St.
1st St.
Commercial Ave.
Munroe St.
Athenaeum St.
Longfellow Br.
Cambridge St.
Prospect St.
Hampshire St.
Lincoln St.
Windsor St.
Berkshire St.
York St.
Portland St.
Binney St.
6th St.
5th St.
Fayette St.
Antrim St.
Amory St.
Norfolk St.
Elm St.
Bristol St.
Market St.
Inman St.
Broadway
Harvard St.
*Kendall Sq.*
*KENDALL*
West St.
Lee St.
Clinton St.
Inman St.
Prospect St.
Essex St.
Washington St.
**List Visual Arts Center**
Cardinal St.
Hayward St.
Galileo St.
Amherst St.
**City Hall**
Bishop Richard Allen Dr.
Main St.
**Massachusetts Institute of Technology**
Annex St.
**12**
*CENTRAL* **T** Massachusetts Ave.
**13**
Green St.
Franklin St.
Sidney St.
Landsdowne St.
Cross St.
Memorial Dr.
**MIT Chapel**
**Harvard Bridge**
Western Ave.
Auburn St.
River St.
Pacific St.
Purrington St.
Albany St.
Vassar St.
**Storrow Drive**
Pleasant St.
Magazine St.
Pearl St.
Brookline St.
Waverly St.
Amherst Alley
*Charles River*
Beacon St.
Massachusetts Ave.
Allston St.
Putnam St.
Henry St.
**HYNES CONVENTION CENTER/ ICA (AUDITORIUM)** **T**
Boylston St.

Although the college dates from the 17th century, the oldest buildings in Harvard Yard are of the 18th century; together the buildings chronicle American architecture from the Colonial era to the present. **Holden Chapel,** completed in 1744, is a Georgian gem. The graceful **University Hall** was designed in 1815 by Charles Bulfinch. An 1884 statue of John Harvard by Daniel Chester French stands outside; ironically for a school with the motto of "Veritas" ("Truth"), the model for the statue was a member of the class of 1882, as there is no known contemporary likeness of Harvard himself. **Sever Hall,** completed in 1880 and designed by Henry Hobson Richardson, represents the Romanesque revival that was followed by the classical (note the pillared facade of Widener Library) and the neo-Georgian, represented by the sumptuous brick houses along the Charles River, many of which are now upperclass undergraduate residences. Some of Harvard's four oldest buildings—Massachusetts Hall, Holden Chapel, Hollis Hall, and Harvard Hall—were occupied by patriot regiments during the Revolution. Just north of the Yard is **Memorial Hall,** completed in 1878 as a memorial to Harvard men who died in the Union cause; it is high Victorian both inside and out. It also contains the 1,200-seat Sanders Theater, site of concerts by national and local talent and the festive Christmas Revels. **Memorial Church,** a graceful steepled edifice of modified colonial design, was dedicated in 1932.

Many of Harvard's cultural and scholarly facilities are important sights in themselves; however, be aware that campus buildings are increasingly off-limits to the public. For complete information on the Arthur M. Sackler Museum, the Fogg Art Museum, the Harvard Museum of Natural History, the Peabody Museum, and Widener Library, *see* their separate listings.

The **Harvard University Events and Information Center,** run by students, includes a small library, a video viewing area, computer terminals, and an exhibit space. It also offers maps of the university area and free student-led tours of Harvard Yard. The tour does not include visits to museums, and it does not take you into campus buildings, but it provides a fine orientation—you'll glean interesting tidbits such as the hypothesis that the Harvard Science building, built in the early 1970s with funds partially donated by the Polaroid Corporation, resembles an old Polaroid camera when viewed from above. ⊠ *Holyoke Center, 1350 Massachusetts Ave.,* ☎ *617/495–1573.* ☉ *Mon.–Sat. 9–5. Tours during academic year, weekdays at 10 and 2, Sat. at 2; mid-June–Aug., Mon.–Sat. at 10, 11:15, 2, and 3:15, Sun. at 1:30 and 3.*

**List Visual Arts Center.** Founded by Albert and Vera List, pioneer collectors of modern art, this MIT center has three galleries showcasing exhibitions of cutting-edge art and mixed media. Stark works such as Thomas Hart Benton's painting *Fluid Catalytic Crackers* and Harry Bertoia's altarpiece for the MIT Chapel explore and challenge cultural and socioeconomic conventions. ⊠ *Wiesner Bldg., 20 Ames St.,* ☎ *617/ 253–4680.* ☐ *Free.* ☉ *Oct.–June, Tues.–Thurs. noon–6, Fri. noon–8, weekends noon–6.*

**⑫ Massachusetts Institute of Technology.** Celebrated for both its brains and its cerebral sense of humor, the Massachusetts Institute of Technology occupies 135 acres bordering on the Charles River. The campus may once have been dismissed as "the factory," particularly by its Ivy League neighbor, and its graduates considered confirmed eggheads, but with true "Revenge of the Nerds" flair, MIT and its graduates are sharpening the cutting edge of the information revolution. MIT students are also renowned for their brazen "hacks," or pranks.

Founded in 1861, MIT moved to Cambridge from Copley Square in the Back Bay in 1916, and it has long since fulfilled the predictions of its founder, the geologist William Barton Rogers, that it would surpass "the universities of the land in the accuracy and the extent of its teachings in all branches of positive science." Its emphasis shifted in the 1930s from practical engineering and mechanics to the outer limits of scientific fields. World War II stimulated war research, and MIT has played a major role in producing instrumentation and guidance devices for NASA.

Obviously designed by and for scientists, the MIT campus is divided by Mass Ave. into the West Campus, devoted to student leisure life, and the East Campus, where the heavy work is done. The West Campus has some extraordinary buildings. The **Kresge Auditorium,** designed by Eero Saarinen, with a curving roof and unusual thrust, rests on three, instead of four, points. The nondenominational **MIT Chapel,** a circular Saarinen design, is lighted primarily by a roof oculus that focuses natural light on the altar and by reflections from the water in a small surrounding moat; it is topped by an aluminum sculpture by Theodore Roszak. The serpentine **Baker House** was designed in 1947 by the Finnish architect Alvar Aalto in such a way as to provide every room with a view of the Charles River. Sculptures by Henry Moore and other notable artists dot the campus.

The East Campus, which has grown around the university's original neoclassical buildings of 1916, also has outstanding modern architecture and sculpture, notably the high-rise **Green Building** by I. M. Pei, which houses the Earth Science Center. Just outside is Alexander Calder's giant stabile, entitled *The Big Sail,* designed as a wind baffle so that the revolving doors in Pei's building would function despite unplanned-for wind resistance. Another Pei work on the East Campus is the **Wiesner Building,** designed in 1985, which houses the **List Visual Arts Center** (☞ *above*). The **Great Dome,** which looms over Killian Court, has at various times supported a telephone booth with a ringing phone, a life-size statue of a cow, and a campus police cruiser—all traditional student hacks. Another domed structure is the **Rogers Building** (⌧ 77 Massachusetts Ave.). From its front doors, students can walk throughout the East Campus without ever coming up for air, via a series of hallways and tunnels—the main hallway has been dubbed "the infinite corridor."

The Institute maintains an information center and offers free tours of the campus weekdays at 10 and 2. ⌧ *77 Massachusetts Ave., Bldg. 7,* ☎ *617/253–4795.* ☉ *Weekdays 9–5.*

**⓭ MIT Museum.** A place where art and science meet, the MIT Museum displays photos, paintings, and scientific instruments and memorabilia. A popular ongoing exhibit is the "Hall of Hacks," a look at the pranks MIT students have played over the years; the exhibit includes the campus police cruiser, lights flashing, that was "parked" atop the Great Dome in 1994. Most notable here is a rare photo of Oliver Reed Smoot Jr., a 1958 MIT Lambda Chi Alpha pledge. Smoot's future fraternity brothers used the diminutive freshman to measure the distance of the nearby Harvard Bridge, which spans the Charles. Every 5 ft and 6 inches became "one Smoot." The markings still line the bridge (the frat repaints them every two years), and Boston police actually use them to indicate location when filing accident reports. All told, the bridge is "364.4 Smoots plus 1 ear" long. The museum also has an extensive collection of alluring holograms. ⌧ *265 Massachusetts Ave.,* ☎ *617/ 253–4444.* ⌧ *$3.* ☉ *Tues.–Fri. 10–5, weekends noon–5.*

Administered by the MIT Museum, the **Hart Nautical Gallery** harbors a small but outstanding collection of ship models plus changing exhibits on the history of shipbuilding. ✉ *77 Massachusetts Ave., Bldg. 5, 1st floor,* ☎ *617/253–5942.* ✆ *Free.* ☉ *Daily 9–8.*

**⑤ Old Burying Ground and the First Parish in Cambridge.** Next to the imposing church on the corner of Church Street and Mass Ave. is a spooky-looking Colonial graveyard. You can make out through the iron railing of the cemetery a number of 17th- and 18th-century tombstones of ministers, early Harvard presidents, and Revolutionary War soldiers. The wooden Gothic Revival church, known locally as "First Church" or "First Parish," was built in 1833 by Isaiah Rogers. The church sponsors the popular "Forum" lecture series, with well-known authors and academics speaking each Wednesday. ✉ *3 Church St.,* ☎ *617/876–7772.* ☉ *Church winter, weekdays 8–4; summer, weekdays 8–2. Sun. service at 10:30, church open until 1.*

**Peabody Museum of Archaeology and Ethnology.** With one of the world's outstanding anthropological collections, the Peabody (pronounced *pee*-buh-dee) focuses on Native American and Central and South American cultures; there are also interesting displays on Africa. The Hall of the North American Indian is particularly outstanding, as is the fourth-floor exhibit on Oceania with its Solomon Islands canoe suspended across the ceiling and its festive collection of wooden musical instruments from Borneo. The admission fee includes entrance to the Harvard Museum of Natural History (☞ *above*) as well. ✉ *11 Divinity Ave.,* ☎ *617/495–2248.* ✆ *$5.* ☉ *Mon.–Sat. 9–5, Sun. 1–5.*

**⑧ Semitic Museum.** This Harvard institution serves as an exhibit space for Egyptian, Mesopotamian, and ancient Near East artifacts and as a center for archaeological exploration. No dusty stodginess here: a 1999 exhibit showcased 3,400-year-old cuneiform tablets from the Middle East that relate the charged tale of a head of government whose alleged philandering put him on public trial. (Sound familiar?) Besides the rotating shows, there's a permanent exhibit on the pyramids of Giza. The building also houses the Department of Near Eastern Languages and Civilization. Note that there are no elevators. ✉ *6 Divinity Ave.,* ☎ *617/495–4631.* ✆ *Free.* ☉ *Weekdays 10–4, Sun. 1–4.*

**❷ Wadsworth House.** On the Harvard University side of Harvard Square stands the Wadsworth House, a yellow clapboard structure built in 1726 as a home for Harvard presidents. It served as the first headquarters for George Washington, who arrived on July 2, 1775, to take command of the Continental Army, which he did the following day. The house is closed to the public, as it's now the office of Harvard's library director. ✉ *1341 Massachusetts Ave.*

**❹ Widener Library.** One of the country's largest collections of books (and one of 90 libraries associated with the school), Harvard University's Harry Elkins Widener Library was named for a young book lover who went down with the *Titanic*—it is said that Widener went back to his stateroom to retrieve a first edition of Bacon's *Essays.* The library is not open to the public; people with a "scholarly need" can apply for admission at the privileges office inside. ✉ *Harvard Yard,* ☎ *617/495–2411.*

# BRATTLE STREET/TORY ROW

Brattle Street remains one of New England's most elegant thoroughfares. Elaborate mansions line both sides from where it meets JFK Street to the Fresh Pond Parkway. Brattle Street was once dubbed "Tory Row" because during the 1770s its mansions (numbering seven), on lands that stretched to the river, were owned by staunch supporters of King George. These properties were appropriated by the patriots when they took over Cambridge in the summer of 1775. Many of the historic houses are marked with blue signs, and although only two (the Hooper-Lee-Nichols House and the Longfellow National Historic Site) are fully open to the public, it's easy to imagine yourself back in the days of Emerson and Thoreau as you stroll the brick sidewalks. Less than 2 mi down Brattle Street from Harvard Square stretches the fitting finale of Mt. Auburn Cemetery, an exquisitely landscaped garden cemetery.

*Numbers in the text correspond to numbers in the margin and on the Cambridge map.*

## A Good Walk

Begin your walk at **Winthrop Park** ⑭, a small open space surrounded by bookstores, music shops, clothing stores, and restaurants near the juncture of Mt. Auburn and JFK Street. (You'll see a favorite local sign on the American Express Travel Service office: "Please Go Away Often.") Walk one block along Mt. Auburn as it curves to your right to reach Brattle Street. Proceeding on Brattle Street past a shopping complex, you pass on your left the **Brattle Theater,** followed by the **Brattle House** ⑮, an 18th-century Colonial that now serves as headquarters of the Cambridge Center for Adult Education. Another block, past the three-story Crate & Barrel furniture store, and you pass on the left the yellow **Dexter Pratt House** ⑯, also known as the Blacksmith House, which was immortalized in Longfellow's "The Village Blacksmith." Continue up Brattle just past Hilliard Street. On your left is the Loeb Drama Center, home to the American Repertory Theatre, which takes up nearly the entire block at 64 Brattle Street. Across Brattle Street on your right is **Radcliffe College** ⑰.

Continue on Brattle to the next corner with Ash Street to find the **Stoughton House.** Just one block farther is the **Henry Vassall House,** at the intersection of Hawthorn Street. Across Brattle Street to your right is **Longfellow National Historic Site** ⑱, a mansion built in 1759 by John Vassall Jr. Continuing along Brattle, you'll reach 159, the **Hooper-Lee-Nichols House,** ⑲ one of the few Tory homes open to the public. At 175 Brattle stands the **Ruggles-Fayerweather House,** a white Georgian structure built in 1764 that was taken over by revolutionaries in August 1775 and served as a hospital after the Battle of Bunker Hill. At the corner of Elmwood Avenue and Fresh Pond Parkway is **Elmwood,** another Georgian home.

Continue west, cross the Fresh Pond Parkway, and follow Brattle to where it meets Mt. Auburn Street. **Mt. Auburn Cemetery** ⑳ is a few blocks up on your left. After exploring the cemetery (maps are provided) you can retrace your steps or catch Bus 71 or 73 just outside the cemetery to get back to the Square. Or you can follow Mt. Auburn east, cross over to Memorial Drive on your right, and walk back along the Charles River to JFK Street. This is especially nice on summer Sundays when this section of Memorial Drive is closed to car traffic. The annual Head of the Charles Regatta, held in October, can be seen from along the paths that line the Charles.

### TIMING

If you opt to walk all the way to Mt. Auburn Cemetery (it is about 1½ mi from Longfellow National Historic Site), allot three to four hours for a leisurely stroll. If the weather is raw or rainy, put off the walk for a nicer day.

## Sights to See

⓯ **Brattle House.** This 18th-century, gambrel-roof Colonial once belonged to the Loyalist William Brattle, who moved to Boston in 1774 to escape the patriots' anger, then left in 1776 with the British troops. From 1831 to 1833 it was the residence of Margaret Fuller, feminist editor of *The Dial*; today it is the headquarters of the Cambridge Center for Adult Education and is listed on the National Register of Historic Places. It is one of the seven Tory Houses. ✉ *42 Brattle St.,* ☎ *617/547–6789.* 🎫 *Free.* ☉ *Mon.–Thurs. 9–9, Fri. 9–7, Sat. 9–2. Summer hrs vary.*

**Brattle Theatre.** The square's longtime independent movie house, the Brattle, survived the home-video revolution and now shows foreign, obscure, or classic films, from nouveau to noir. As one employee put it, they're "somewhere between a first-run and a second-run theater." In conjunction with the nearby bookstore WordsWorth, it also hosts free readings by well-known authors. ✉ *40 Brattle St.,* ☎ *617/876–6837.*

> NEED A BREAK?
>
> **Algiers Café** (✉ 40 Brattle St., ☎ 617/492–1557), upstairs from the Brattle Theatre, is a favorite student hangout. Linger over your mint tea and hummus, and don't expect rapid service.

⓰ **Dexter Pratt House.** Also known as the "**Blacksmith House**," the yellow Colonial Dexter Pratt House is now owned by the Cambridge Center for Adult Education. The tree itself is long gone, but this spot inspired Longfellow's lines: "Under a spreading chestnut tree, the village smithy stands." The blacksmith's shop, now commemorated by a granite marker, was next door, at the corner of Story Street. ✉ *56 Brattle St.,* ☎ *617/547–6789.* 🎫 *Free.* ☉ *Mon.–Sat. 9–6.*

> NEED A BREAK?
>
> **The Hi-Rise Pie Company in the Blacksmith House** (☎ 617/492–3003), on the first floor of the Dexter Pratt House, is the perfect stop for a pick-me-up coffee and fresh-baked treat or sandwich. The bakery here was first known as the Window Shop, which evolved during World War II to provide employment for German and Eastern European refugees.

**Elmwood.** A three-story Georgian house built in 1767 by the Colonial governor Thomas Oliver and later home to the Lowell family, Elmwood House is now the residence of Harvard University's president. ✉ *33 Elmwood Ave.*

**Henry Vassall House.** One of the seven Tory houses occupied by wealthy families linked by friendship, if not blood, the house may have been built as early as 1636. In 1737 it was purchased by John Vassall Sr.; four years later he sold it to his younger brother, Henry. It was used as a hospital during the Revolution, and the traitor Dr. Benjamin Church was held here as a prisoner. The house was remodeled during the 19th century. ✉ *94 Brattle St.*

⓲ **Hooper-Lee-Nichols House.** Home to the Cambridge Historical Society, this is one of two Tory-era homes on Brattle Street fully open to the public. (The Emerson family gave it to the society in 1957.) Built between 1685 and 1690, the house has been remodeled at least six times; your tour guide will obligingly pull off false fronts to show layers of the various eras. The downstairs is elegantly, although sparsely, appointed with period books, portraits, and wallpaper. An upstairs bedroom has been preserved to represent the 1850s; in the children's room there's a Victorian dollhouse and other toys. Visits are by tour only. ✉ *159 Brattle St.,* ☎ *617/547–4252.* 🎫 *$5.* ☉ *Tues. and Thurs. 2–5 and Sun. by appointment May–Oct.*

**⑱ Longfellow National Historic Site.** This elegant mansion was once home to Henry Wadsworth Longfellow—the poet whose stirring renditions about the Village Blacksmith, Evangeline, Hiawatha, and Paul Revere's midnight ride thrilled 19th-century America (and who was, surname to the contrary, a short man). Formally called the Vassall-Craigie-Longfellow House after its various occupants, it was built in 1759 by John Vassall Jr. It was one of the seven original Tory Row homes on Brattle Street; George Washington lived here during the siege of Boston from July 1775 to April 1776. Longfellow first boarded here in 1837 and later received the house as a gift from his new father-in-law on his marriage to Frances Appleton, who burned to death here in an accident in 1861. For 45 years Longfellow wrote his famous verses here and filled the house with the exuberant spirit of his own work and that of his literary circle, which included Ralph Waldo Emerson, Nathaniel Hawthorne, and Charles Sumner, an antislavery senator. Even in Longfellow's day, the house was a draw for visitors who wanted to tread the floors where Washington once stood. Across the street is Longfellow Park, created to preserve the view immortalized in the poet's "To the River Charles."

The National Park Service closed the house and park in fall 1998 for renovations that are expected to last through the summer of 2000. For updates on the renovation, you may reach the park service at ☎ 617/566–1689. ⊠ *105 Brattle St.*

**⑳ Mt. Auburn Cemetery.** This was one of the country's first garden cemeteries, and it remains one of the loveliest. Since it opened in 1831, more than 90,000 people have been buried here, among them Henry Wadsworth Longfellow, Mary Baker Eddy, Winslow Homer, Amy Lowell, Dorothea Dix, and Charles Bulfinch. The grave of engineer Buckminster Fuller bears an engraved geodesic dome. In spring, nature lovers and bird-watchers come out of the woodwork to see the warbler migrations and the glorious blossoms. Brochures, maps, and audiotape tours are available at the entrance (though you'll need to bring your own cassette player for the taped tours). Picnicking, jogging, and bicycling are not permitted. ⊠ *Mt. Auburn St.,* ☎ *617/547–7105.* ☉ *Early Apr.–late Oct., daily 8–7; late Oct.–early Apr., daily 8–5. T stop: Harvard; then Watertown (71) or Waverly (73) bus to cemetery.*

**NEED A BREAK?**     Once beyond the vicinity of Harvard Square, Brattle Street lacks eateries, so consider stocking up before your walk at **Darwin's Ltd.** (⊠ 148 Mt. Auburn St., ☎ 617/354–5233), which offers Cambridge-inspired sandwiches and other "comestibles and spirituous provisions."

**⑰ Radcliffe College.** The famed women's college, founded in 1879 and wedded to Harvard University in 1977, was subsumed under Harvard in spring 1999. The college, with its lovely, serene yard, will become an institute for advanced study; it will continue to specialize in gender issues. ⊠ *10 Garden St.*

**Stoughton House.** Built circa 1883, this shingled house was designed by the noted architect H. H. Richardson, who also planned Austin and Sever Halls at Harvard and **Trinity Church** in Boston (☞ Chapter 2). The house is not open to the public. ⊠ *Corner of Ash and Brattle Sts.*

**⑭ Winthrop Park.** Once an 18th-century marketplace and now part and parcel of **Harvard Square** (☞ *above*), the park is a great time-out spot. It is surrounded by shops and restaurants, including Grendel's Den, a favorite student hangout.

# 4 DINING

Victorian Boston's ideal of yeoman food in aristocratic surroundings influenced all America, and all America still imagines Bostonian gentry dining on fish cakes and yesterday's baked beans. Today, in fact, the great dining rooms are gracefully yielding to a flush of creative little bistros. Boston dining can be world class, a world tour, worlds to come, or a world in 10 tables. It's often seafood; sometimes challenging flavors; sometimes comfort food. And the city is still a great place for a lobster dinner whether you like yours simply boiled or nouvelle-fangled wood-grilled with wild seasonings.

Updated by
Robert
Nadeau

**I**T IS ONLY A MYTH THAT THE BOSTONIANS OF HISTORY hated food. Really, it was only unfamiliar food they disdained. Their chowders and codfish cakes, baked beans and apple pies rolled across America and sailed around the world— why would they need anything else to eat? The boiled dinner and breakfast hash that fed the farm hands could be served in fine dining rooms just as well—it was only thrifty common sense.

Their successors and descendants have reversed priorities. Bostonians now want innovative food without formality. They get it in some of the best casual restaurants in the world. Today's Boston certainly has palaces of grand cuisine to rival those of the cultural capitals, but Boston—and especially Cambridge—also has a kind of great restaurant that is similar only to those of San Francisco and New Orleans: restaurants overseen by creative masterminds concocting apparently divinely inspired food, served in very human surroundings by waitstaff who are less suave than enthusiastic and knowledgeable.

Boston now has caught the passion for craft-baked breads, brew-pubs with homemade ales, espresso shops with fine cakes or with computers, and all other exquisite and unique specialties. Ice creams have been central to Boston living for 150 years, and every gourmet restaurant here has a few unusual flavors (☞ introduction *in* Chapter 8).

What Boston diners most enjoy is what every Boston visitor should seek out as well—the fish and shellfish that have always inspired the best Boston cooking. Although the city has many notable restaurants specializing in seafood, you can find at least two or three offerings from the sea *anywhere* you choose to eat. Where the treatments used to be limited to lobsters boiled or baked, fish broiled or fried, nowadays chefs work deftly with sauces. If the chef has pretensions, you may be offered a lobster sausage or wood-roasted lobster with a vanilla sauce. In a Chinese restaurant, the lobster will be stir-fried with ginger and scallion, and the gray sole served with the fried whole fins. Your chowder may be traditional with milk and potatoes or experimentally Caribbean. To get the real flavor of Boston today, eat seafood at a place that's small.

Currently, the New England commercial fishery for cod, haddock, and flatfish has been almost shut down to conserve stocks. But the shortage has provoked a wonderful burst of creative cooking with lesser-known delicacies such as monkfish, wolf fish, tilefish, Chilean sea bass, ocean perch, ocean catfish, skate wings, and squid. Striped bass, once fished to near-extinction, are back on the summer table, followed by New England's seasonal delicacies: harpooned swordfish and tuna steaks, Maine shrimp, bay scallops, steamer clams, and Wellfleet oysters. When lobster prices rise too high, tasty deep-sea crabs appear.

You don't operate a seaport for 350 years without developing a few outside interests, but Boston has acquired an appetite for exotic, foreign cuisines that would have shocked a clipper captain. Anything spicy and different has long been popular in the university culture of Cambridge, but the high immigration of recent decades has given Bostonians and visitors a special chance to taste all the world's delicacies. A few are in settings that evoke the bygone aristocracies—and the cuisines—of Russia, Persia, Thailand, Afghanistan, or Cambodia. Many more serve large immigrant communities from Latin America, Asia, and some countries of Europe and Africa—but welcome the merely curious to their tables.

New England's own food is still widely served in the tourist version, but a young generation of highly trained and well-traveled chefs is reclaiming the regional cuisine by treating the six-state region as though it were a province of France or Italy. It turns out that our wild mushrooms work in a ragout, cheddar makes a fine quiche, and butternut squash or lobster fits into savory ravioli.

Boston is resistant to chain restaurants and puts its own twists on food fads. Yes, it went through a Mediterranean period, followed by a spate of bistros with a little plate of Pan-Asian everything. But the Mediterranean era quickly tuned in to Turkish and Moroccan flavors. And the recent rush of fusion bistros is doing great things with Atlantic seafood. During the restaurant boom of the late 1990s, Boston's chef-owners sponsored their sous-chefs' new concepts, where elsewhere chefs hired anonymous talent and simply chained their way to prominence.

The dominant trend, however, is homegrown. Boston is the special home for small bistro-style restaurants with highly flavored food. Gifted chefs have scattered out among the neighborhoods, infiltrated the established places on the restaurant rows, and now dominate the scene in Cambridge.

To find the best of Boston—gustatorily speaking—follow the roads that radiate out from downtown like the spokes of a giant wheel. Smack inside the hub are the huge, and hugely famous, waterfront seafood restaurants—but go north, or west and south, and you're suddenly into the neighborhoods, home to numerous smaller restaurants on the way up. And beginning in spring 1999, Boston's sidewalks will be increasingly fringed with café tables, as a new city policy authorizes alfresco dining.

Boston's restaurants are nonsmoking; smoking is allowed in bar areas.

For price ranges *see* the dining chart *in* Smart Travel Tips A to Z.

### Restaurant Reservations and Dress Codes

Reservations are always a good idea; we note only when they're essential or when they are not accepted. Book as far ahead as you can, and reconfirm when you get to town. Unless otherwise noted, the restaurants listed are open daily for lunch and dinner. We mention dress only when men are required to wear a jacket or a jacket and tie.

# BOSTON

## Back Bay/Beacon Hill

This upscale neighborhood encompasses Newbury Street, Commonwealth Avenue, and lots of enticing restaurants. Toward Beacon Hill, restaurants and the dining rooms of the large hotels tend to be quite dressy. Around Massachusetts Avenue, the Back Bay's western border, things are looser at the bistros and espresso bars that predominate. Remember that Huntington Avenue was rechristened Avenue of the Arts but that locals may well use the old name.

### Contemporary

**$$$$**  ✕ **Ambrosia.** Chef Tony Ambrose likes his flavors vivid and his platters tall, from an ostrich-meat appetizer to "lobster salad with 22-karat-gold vinaigrette." (You'll literally eat your money.) Take down the French decorations, and the food is haute Yankee, based on native ingredients. The decor is designer-chic: burnished woods, floor-to-ceiling glass windows, and an ever-changing arrangement of modern art on the walls.

⊠ *116 Ave. of the Arts,* ☎ *617/247–2400. Reservations essential. AE, MC, V. No lunch weekends.*

**$$$$** ✕ **Aujourd'hui.** The formula for Aujourd'hui's success has been to speak softly and attract a discreet crowd. This formal dining room of the Four Seasons Hotel has become one of the city's power rooms. The food reflects an inventive approach to regional ingredients and new American cuisine. Some entrées, such as rack of lamb with braised chard caponata and ragout of flageolet beans and pancetta, can be extremely rich, but the seasonal menu also offers "alternative cuisine" and vegetarian choices. Window tables overlook the Public Garden. ⊠ *200 Boylston St.,* ☎ *617/351–2071. Reservations essential. Jacket required. AE, D, DC, MC, V.*

**$$$–$$$$** ✕ **Biba.** Arguably Boston's best restaurant, and surely one of the most
**★** original and high-casual restaurants in America, Biba is a place to see and be seen, from the vividness of the dining room's rambling mural to the huge street-level people-watching windows of the downstairs bar. The menu encourages inventive combinations, unusual cuts and produce, haute comfort food, and big postmodern desserts. Take your time, and don't settle for the "classic lobster pizza" if something like vanilla chicken with chestnut puree is available. The wine list is an adventure. ⊠ *272 Boylston St.,* ☎ *617/426–7878. Reservations essential. AE, D, DC, MC, V.*

**$$–$$$** ✕ **Brew Moon.** Instead of having the usual industrial decor of a brewpub, the flagships of this minichain look like California health-food places. The food tends to have ale as an ingredient and emphasizes the salty and peppery elements that have you ordering more. As always at brewpubs, the darker and stronger ales are best. Save room for serious desserts. Another branch is in Harvard Square, Cambridge. ⊠ *115 Stuart St.,* ☎ *617/742–2739. Cambridge:* ⊠ *50 Church St., Harvard Square,* ☎ *617/499–2739. AE, DC, MC, V.*

**$$–$$$** ✕ **Cena.** Cena (pronounced like Latin, "*kay*-nah") captures the Symphony crowd with a bistro menu of world-beat flavors that quietly drops red meat and barely mentions chicken and cheese. Order the baked polenta with native wild mushrooms, or the udon bowl with sautéed local vegetables, and you'll never miss the meat. They do it with a full palette of vegetables and starches, herbal oils, and exotic spices. ⊠ *14A Westland Ave.,* ☎ *617/262–1485. AE, D, MC, V.*

**$$–$$$** ✕ **Sonsie.** Café society blossoms along Newbury Street, particularly at the elegant Sonsie, where much of the clientele either sips coffee up front or angles for places at the bar. The restaurant is famous for breakfasts (open daily at 7) that extend well into the afternoon for late risers; look for the apple oatmeal pancakes. During warm-weather months, the entire front of Sonsie becomes an open-air café looking out on upper Newbury Street. The dishes on the menu are basic bistro with an American twist, such as sweet pumpkin tamales with spiced pumpkin flan. ⊠ *327 Newbury St.,* ☎ *617/351–2500. AE, DC, MC, V.*

## Continental

**$$$–$$$$** ✕ **Ritz-Carlton Dining Room.** A traditional restaurant in the best sense of the word, the Ritz has subtly modernized the menu while keeping the classic rack of lamb, roast beef hash, broiled scrod, and such seasonal Yankeeisms as shad roe in May and June. The true glory of the Ritz is the service, aristocratic in its detail, democratically offered to all. Second-floor windows provide a commanding view of the Public Garden. All in all, it's the perfect place to allow your grandmother to take you after college graduation. ⊠ *15 Arlington St.,* ☎ *617/536–5700. Reservations essential. Jacket and tie. AE, D, DC, MC, V.*

## French

$$$$     ✕ **L'Espalier.** An elegantly modernized Victorian Back Bay town house
★     is the setting for chef-owner Frank McClelland's intoxicating blend of
new French and newer American cuisine. Grilled New York foie gras
is accompanied by quince anise cranberry compote; Périgord black truffles intensify the poached sole. You can simplify the opulent menu by
choosing a prix-fixe tasting menu, such as the innovative vegetarian
*dégustation*. With two fireplaces and subtle decor in truffle colors, the
downstairs is among Boston's most romantic places—the front salon
is known as the Courtship Room, the back parlor as the Seduction Room.
Upstairs is the Library, more masculine and clubby. ⊠ *30 Gloucester
St.,* ☎ *617/262–3023. Reservations essential. Jacket and tie. AE, D,
DC, MC, V. Closed Sun. No lunch.*

## Japanese

$$–$$$     ✕ **Miyako.** A very competitive sushi bar amid many at this end of Back
Bay, this little spot also offers estimable hot dishes, including *age shu-
mai* (shrimp fritters), *hamachi teriyaki* (yellowtail teriyaki), and *agedashi
dofu* (fried bean curd). Ask for one of the tatami rooms if you have a
big party. ⊠ *279A Newbury St.,* ☎ *617/236–0222. AE, DC, MC, V.*

## Persian

$$–$$$     ✕ **Lala Rokh.** This beautifully detailed and delicious fantasia upon Per-
★     sian food and art focuses on the Azerbaijian corner that is now Northwest Iran. Persian miniatures and medieval maps cover the walls. The
food includes exotically flavored specialties, and dishes as familiar (but
superb here) as eggplant puree, pilaf, kebabs, *fesanjoon* (the classic
pomegranate-walnut sauce), and lamb stews. The staff obviously en-
joys explaining the menu, and the wine list is well selected for foods
that often defy wine matches. ⊠ *97 Mount Vernon St.,* ☎ *617/720–
5511. AE, DC, MC, V. No lunch.*

## Seafood

$$$–$$$$     ✕ **Turner Fisheries of Boston.** On the first floor of the Westin Hotel in
Copley Square, Turner Fisheries is second only to Legal Sea Foods (☞
*below*) in its traditional appeal and has outstripped it in trimmings and
service. Turner broils, grills, bakes, fries, and steams everything in the
ocean but also applies classic and modern sauces, vegetables, and
pasta with panache. Any meal should begin with the creamy chowder
(the restaurant having won Boston's yearly Chowderfest competition
too many times to contend any more). ⊠ *10 Ave. of the Arts,* ☎ *617/
424–7425. Reservations essential. AE, D, DC, MC, V.*

$$–$$$$     ✕ **Legal Sea Foods.** What began as a tiny restaurant upstairs over a
★     Cambridge fish market has grown to important regional status, with
locations in Chestnut Hill, Kendall Square in Cambridge, and now Washington, D.C., and Baltimore. The hallmark, as always, is extra-fresh
seafood. As the organization has matured, it has applied the same standards to the trimmings and the wine list. Once-puritanically simple prepa-
rations have loosened up to include Chinese and French sauces, and
wood-grilling is now the preparation of choice. Rhode Island clam chowder *with tomatoes* has been allowed onto the menu alongside the tra-

ditional Boston milk chowders. The smoked bluefish pâté is one of the finest appetizers anywhere. Dishes come to the table in whatever order they come out of the kitchen, as freshness is held to be more important than the order of courses. If you miss a flight at **Logan Airport,** (✉ Terminal C, ☎ 617/569–4622) a Legal restaurant there can make it the most delicious missed flight of your life. ✉ *26 Park Sq.,* ☎ *617/ 426–4444. Cambridge:* ✉ *5 Cambridge Center, Kendall Sq.,* ☎ *617/ 864–3400. Reservations not accepted. AE, D, DC, MC, V.*

### Steak

$$$$ ✕ **Morton's of Chicago.** A Chicago-based chain with an un-Bostonian display of raw meat and live lobsters, but the best, dry-aged, prime Angus steak in town, Morton's is packed and often noisy. If you brave the 1½-hour Saturday wait, you deserve the 24-ounce porterhouse. ✉ *1 Exeter Plaza,* ☎ *617/266–5858. Reservations essential. AE, DC, MC, V. No lunch.*

$$$–$$$$ ✕ **Grill 23.** Gray business suits predominate at this steak house, and dark paneling, comically oversized flatware, and waiters in white jackets give it a men's-club ambience. Yet seafood, such as the grilled Maine salmon with winter root and truffle hash, outsells beef by a narrow margin. Outstanding is the word for the rotisserie tenderloin with Roquefort mashed potatoes and for the only meat loaf in the world served with mashed potatoes and truffle oil. Break out your jacket and tie. ✉ *161 Berkeley St.,* ☎ *617/542–2255. Reservations essential. AE, D, DC, MC, V. No lunch.*

$$–$$$$ ✕ **Library Grill at the Hampshire House.** Downstairs, usually marked by a massive line of tourists, is the Bull & Finch Pub, the model for the TV sitcom *Cheers.* Upstairs, the Library Grill serves classic steak and lobster in an elegant setting overlooking the Public Garden, making this an apt choice for dinner after the Brahmin tour of Beacon Hill or before the theater. There is valet parking after 5 PM. ✉ *84 Beacon St.,* ☎ *617/227–9600. Reservations essential. AE, D, DC, MC, V.*

## Charlestown

This little neighborhood across Boston Harbor contains the Bunker Hill Monument, the USS *Constitution,* and one culinary landmark, the famous Olives, a standout among otherwise local taverns.

### Mediterranean

$$$–$$$$ ✕ **Olives.** The pacesetting bistro is named for an important Mediter-
★ ranean flavor and for Olivia English, who runs the front of the house. Her husband, Todd English, minds the wood-fired brick oven and the spit-roasting in the kitchen, besides watching over fast-track new enterprises, including a new Olives in Las Vegas and a local line of gourmet pizzerias called Figs. But it was the original that set the local standards for grilled pizza, piled-on platters of delicious things, "vertical food," and such smart signature offerings as the appetizer "Olives tart" with marinated olives, goat cheese, caramelized onions, and anchovies. The crowded seating, noise, long lines, and abrupt service only

## Boston Dining

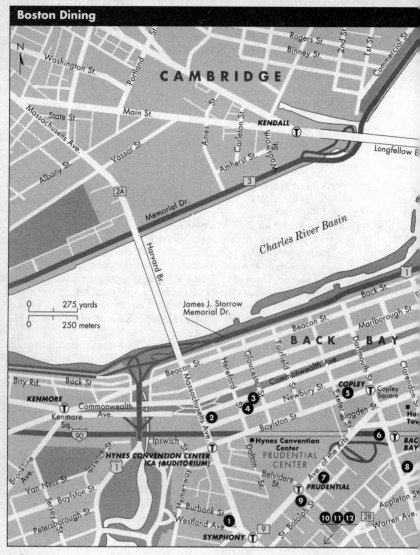

Ambrosia, **7**

Anthony's Pier 4, **36**

Appetito, **17**

Aujourd'hui, **20**

Baja Mexican Cantina, **8**

The Barking Crab Restaurant, **34**

Biba, **21**

Bob the Chef's, **12**

Brasserie Jo, **9**

Brew Moon, **23**

Cena, **1**

Chau Chow, **29**

Chau Chow City, **31**

Claremont Café & Lounge, **11**

Daily Catch, **46**

Durgin Park, **41**

Franklin Cafe, **18**

Grill 23, **14**

Hamersley's Bistro, **15**

Icarus, **16**

Imperial Seafood, **30**

Jae's Café, **10**

Jimmy's Harborside, **37**

Julien, **39**

Jumbo Seafood, **32**

Lala Rokh, **25**

Laurel, **13**

Legal Sea Foods, **22**

Les Zygomates, **27**

L'Espalier, **3**

Library Grill at the Hampshire House, **24**

Locke-Ober Café, **26**

Mamma Maria, **45**

Marcuccio's, **44**

Miyako, **4**

Morton's of Chicago, **5**

New Shanghai, **33**

No-Name Restaurant, **38**

Olives, **43**

Penang, **28**

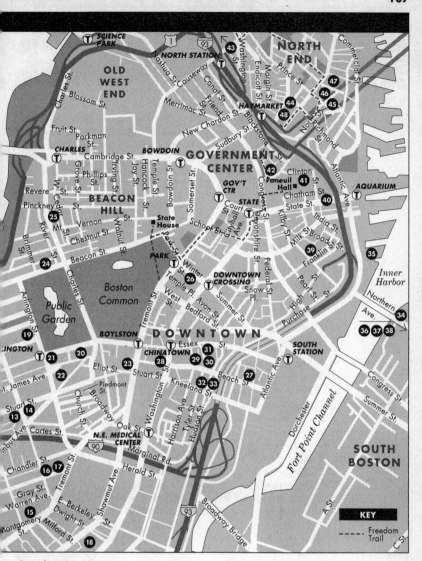

Pomodoro, **47**

Rabia's Ristorante, **48**

Ritz-Carlton Dining
Room, **19**

Rowes Wharf
Restaurant, **35**

Sonsie, **2**

Tatsukichi-Boston, **40**

Turner Fisheries of
Boston, **6**

Union Oyster
House, **42**

add to the legend. Come early or late—or be prepared for an extended wait: reservations are taken only for groups of six or more at 5:30 or 8:30 PM, and there are few nearby alternatives. ⊠ *10 City Sq.,* ☎ *617/ 242–1999. AE, DC, MC, V. Closed Sun. No lunch.*

## Chinatown

Boston's large Chinatown is the focal point for Asian cuisines of all types, from authentic Cantonese and Vietnamese to Malaysian, Japanese, and Mandarin food. Many places are open after midnight while the rest of the city sleeps or lurks. It's definitely worth the adventure, especially if you're tracking down the current rage: live-tank seafood prepared in Hong Kong or Chiu Chow style.

### Chinese

**$–$$$** ✕ **Chau Chow City.** This is the newest, biggest, glitziest, and most versatile production yet from the Chau Chow dynasty, on three floors, with dim sum by day and live-tank seafood by night. Overwhelmed? Order the clams in black bean sauce, the sautéed pea pod stems with garlic, and the honey glazed–walnut jumbo shrimp. ⊠ *83 Essex St.,* ☎ *617/338–8158. AE, D, MC, V.*

**$–$$$** ✕ **Imperial Seafood.** On the first floor is a wonderful (and seldom crowded) Cantonese restaurant specializing in seafood. The livelier second floor is a large, airy dining room with the most extensive dim sum selection in Chinatown. Dim sum denotes both the meal (a veritable Chinese brunch, served daily 8:30–3:30) and the variety of dumplings and buns, tiny spareribs, morsels of pork, chicken, clams, shrimp, and other foods that you select from roving carts and pay for by the item. Pointing is fine. The selection is wider when the restaurant is more crowded with weekend shoppers, mostly suburban Chinese-Americans. ⊠ *70 Beach St.,* ☎ *617/426–8543. AE, MC, V.*

**$–$$** ✕ **Jumbo Seafood.** Although this Cantonese–Hong Kong–style restaurant has much to be proud of, it's happily unpretentious—have a whole sea bass with ginger and scallion and you'll see what all the fuss is about. Non-oceanic offerings are equally outstanding, from the white rice to green vegetables such as stir-fried sugar snap pea tendrils. The Hong Kong influence results in a lot of fried food, of which the "crispy fried calamari with salted pepper" is a standout. The waiters are very understanding, though some don't speak English fluently. ⊠ *5-7-9 Hudson St.,* ☎ *617/542–2823. AE, MC, V.*

**$–$$** ✕ **Chau Chow.** *Chiu Chow* (or *Chaozhou* in China) is the word for ★ people from Shantou (formerly Swatow). They and their wonderful seafood cuisine migrated all over Southeast Asia and around the world, introducing other cultures to clams in black bean sauce, steamed sea bass, gray sole with its fried fins, or any dish with their famous ginger sauce. Chau Chow has expanded to a larger storefront called **Grand Chau Chow,** right across the street, which has live-fish tanks, accepts credit cards, and looks a little nicer on the outside (⊠ *41–45 Beach St.,* ☎ *617/426–6266, AE, D, MC, V*). Your best bet is not to order from the menu per se but to look around at what others are eating and order that way. It's not as rude as it sounds. ⊠ *50–52 Beach St.,* ☎ *617/292–5166. No credit cards.*

**$–$$** ✕ **New Shanghai.** Boston's Chinese restaurants aren't generally of the linen-tablecloth variety found on New York's East Side, but New Shanghai is moving that way. The "old" Shanghai was an island of Mandarin-Szechuan food in the Chinatown sea of southern cuisines; the new one does Szechuan dishes well but has concentrated on Shanghai-style braises and such cold appetizers as red-cooked beef and crisp eels. ⊠ *21 Hudson St.,* ☎ *617/338–6688. AE, MC, V.*

### Malaysian

**$$–$$$** ✗ **Penang.** Penang is a resort island with a history like that of nearby Singapore and an extraordinary cuisine of many influences—Malaysian, Chinese, Indian, Thai, and a bit of British Trader Vic. It all comes together in favorites such as the mashed-taro "yam pot" stir-fries, the house special squid with a dark and spicy sauce, an Indonesian beef curry called *rendang*, and enormous fried coconut shrimp, all paired with umbrella drinks. The open kitchen makes things loud but exciting. ✉ *685–691 Washington St.,* ☎ *617/451–6372. Reservations accepted for 6 or more only. MC, V.*

## Downtown

Boston's downtown scene revs up at lunchtime, but the streets get very quiet after five o'clock, when everyone goes back to the suburbs. The city center is great for after-hours dining, especially around the artist's colony in the former Leather District.

### Continental

**$$$$** ✗ **Locke-Ober Café.** It used to be that the only times the downstairs Men's Café was open to women were the night of the Harvard-Yale game and New Year's Eve, when the nude painting of "Mademoiselle Yvonne" was draped. That changed in 1972, one of the few alterations since Louis Ober's Restaurant Parisien (founded 1875) was merged with Frank Locke's Wine Rooms in 1894. The ancient kitchen struggles to put out traditional Continental favorites, like a flashy steak tartare, and unique Victoriana such as Lobster Savannah (lobster with pimiento, green pepper, mushroom, sherry wine, and Parmesan cheese). If you want to eat here for the experience, stick to simple steaks and seafood. There is valet parking after 6 PM. ✉ *3 Winter Pl.,* ☎ *617/542–1340. Reservations essential. AE, D, DC, MC, V. No lunch weekends.*

### French

**$$$$** ✗ **Julien.** Start with the handsomest dining room in the city—a soar-
★ ing space that used to be the boardroom of the Federal Reserve Bank, with Renaissance Revival gilded cornices and limestone walls. Then serve some of the best French food in Boston, masterminded by French-trained chefs (currently Mark Zapienza and Alain Rayé). A ravioli appetizer is stuffed with frogs' legs and parsley puree, garnished with garlic cream; sautéed Maine lobster comes *en casserole* with white beans, candied tomato, and rosemary. Little wonder Julien has become a favorite with French business travelers and Boston Francophiles. ✉ *Hotel Meridien, 250 Franklin St.,* ☎ *617/451–1900. Reservations essential. Jacket and tie. AE, D, DC, MC, V. Closed Sun. No lunch Sat.*

**$$–$$$** ✗ **Les Zygomates.** *Les zygomates* is the French expression for the
★ muscles on the human face that make you smile—and this combination wine bar–bistro will certainly put them to work. Les Zygomates serves up classic French bistro fare that dares to be simple and simply delicious. The menu beautifully matches the ever-changing wine list, with all wines served by the two-ounce taste, six-ounce glass, or bottle. Most bottles are priced at retail or just a bit above. Les Zygomates offers prix fixe menus at both lunch and dinner. Pan-roasted tuna with red pepper coulis and grilled steak *au bordelaise* with roasted eggplant and garlic typify the taste. ✉ *129 South St.,* ☎ *617/542–5108. Reservations essential. AE, D, DC, MC, V. No lunch weekends.*

### Japanese

**$$–$$$** ✗ **Tatsukichi-Boston.** Sushi and sashimi are specialties, as are pot-cooked dinners and *kushiagi* (deep-fried kebabs). Meals are served in a modern Japanese setting with Western or tatam-room seating. It's a favorite with Japanese business travelers and tourists. ✉ *189 State St.*, ☎ *617/720–2468. AE, D, DC, MC, V. No lunch weekends.*

# Faneuil Hall

Perfect for fueling up for the Freedom Trail, this attraction is a tourist magnet, packed with people eating from its fast-food concessions inside. There are a number of more serious alternatives, though. If you're not on a schedule, and if you've seen enough of Faneuil Hall and want a change of scene, you shouldn't rule out a walk under the expressway to the North End (☞ *below*).

## American

**$$$–$$$$** ✕ **Union Oyster House.** Established in 1826, the Union Oyster House is Boston's oldest continuing restaurant. Our advice is to have what Daniel Webster had—oysters on the half-shell at the ground-floor raw bar, which is the oldest part of the restaurant and still the best. The rooms at the top of the narrow staircase are dark and have low ceilings—very Ye Olde New England—and plenty of non-restaurant history. Uncomfortably small tables and chairs tend to undermine the simple, decent, but expensive food. There is valet parking after 5:30 PM. ✉ *41 Union St.*, ☎ *617/227–2750. AE, D, DC, MC, V.*

**$$–$$$** ✕ **Durgin Park.** You should be hungry enough to cope with enormous portions, yet not so hungry you can't tolerate a long wait. Durgin Park was serving its same hearty New England fare (Indian pudding, baked beans, corned beef and cabbage, and a prime rib hanging over the edge of the plate) back when Faneuil Hall was a working market instead of a tourist attraction. The service is famously brusque bordering on rude bordering on good-natured. ✉ *340 Faneuil Hall Marketplace, North Market Bldg.*, ☎ *617/227–2038. AE, D, DC, MC, V.*

# North End

The North End is Boston's oldest immigrant neighborhood. At the end of the 19th century, Paul Revere's house was a crowded tenement, and at the turn of this one, black-clad Italian grandmothers still push past suburban foodies to get the best of the local groceries. Boston's most authentic Old Country restaurants are here (as you might guess, the smaller the place, the better the kitchen is), along with charming cafés serving up great espresso and cannoli. In recent years, small storefront restaurants have been converting from red-sauce tourist traps to innovative trattoria. Many restaurants here don't take reservations at all, but since they're so close to each other, it's easy to scout among them for a table. In general, the ones with the longest lines are proven winners, but a new restaurant without a line could be the best of all.

## Italian

**$$$–$$$$** ✕ **Mamma Maria.** Despite the clichéd name, Mamma Maria is one of the most elegant and romantic restaurants in the North End, from the smoked-seafood ravioli appetizer to the innovative sauces and entrées to the North End's best desserts; you can't go wrong with the daily tiramisu or specials like chocolate hazelnut cake with a cold champagne sabayon and raspberry compote. ✉ *3 North Sq.*, ☎ *617/523–0077. AE, D, DC, MC, V.*

**$$–$$$$** ✕ **Rabia's Ristorante.** Hidden inside this perfectly good red-sauce spaghetti-and-veal joint is a serious, seasonal seafood restaurant at almost twice the price. Watch the sandwich board outside for specials like soft-shell crabs, yellowfin tuna steak, or frutti di mare and make your move early. Many North End restaurants are cutting out dessert, but Rabia's has made it a strength with a rich tiramisu and chocolate mousse tart. ✉ *73 Salem St.,* ☎ *617/227–6637. Reservations essential. AE, D, DC, MC, V.*

$$$ ✗ **Pomodoro.** Because it's right next door to Daily Catch (☞ *below*),
★ crafty couples can beat the odds against a long wait by splitting up, with one person in line for seafood and the other in line here. This tiny gem of a trattoria is worth the wait, with excellent country Italian favorites such as white beans with various pastas, roasted vegetables, and a fine salad of field greens. Best choice could well be the clam and tomato stew with herbed flat bread—don't forget to enjoy it with a bottle of Vernaccia. They don't serve dessert, but it's easy to find great espresso and pastries in the cafés on Hanover Street. ✉ *319 Hanover St.,* ☎ *617/367–4348. No credit cards.*

$$–$$$ ✗ **Marcuccio's.** Chef Charles Draghi is a pioneer in the use of transparent, highly flavored broth-sauces, as weirdly effective as transparent beer. His rosewater- or lavender-tinged desserts, his veal marsala, and the grilled vegetables among his many antipasti also stand out. There is a tasting menu, so you needn't miss anything. ✉ *125 Salem St.,* ☎ *617/723–1807. MC, V. No lunch.*

### Seafood

$$ ✗ **Daily Catch.** Shoulder-crowding small, this storefront restaurant
★ specializes in calamari dishes, black squid-ink fettuccine, and linguine with clam sauce. You've just got to love this place—for the noise, the intimacy, and, above all, the food. There's something about a big skillet of linguine and calamari that would seem less perfect if served on fine white china. ✉ *323 Hanover St.,* ☎ *617/523–8567. Reservations not accepted. No credit cards.*

# South End

Boston's South End is a highly mixed neighborhood, home to a large number of the city's lesbian and gay professionals, and it is continuing to experience an upscaling trend, with more and better restaurants opening all the time. Eventually, Back Bay prices may infiltrate the South End, but until then, enjoy all the great food at something of a discount—even at the SoHo-like restaurant row at the bend of Tremont Street.

### Contemporary

$$$–$$$$ ✗ **Hamersley's Bistro.** Gordon Hamersley has earned a national rep-
★ utation, thanks to such signature dishes as grilled mushroom-and-garlic sandwich, duck confit, or souffléed lemon custard. He's one of Boston's great chefs and likes to sport a Red Sox cap instead of a toque. His place has a full bar, a café area with 10 tables for walk-ins, and a larger dining room that's a little more formal and decorative than the bar and café, though nowhere near as stuffy as it looks. ✉ *553 Tremont St.,* ☎ *617/423–2700. AE, D, DC, MC, V.*

$$$–$$$$ ✗ **Icarus.** Be ready for an exotic menu of real intensity. Inventive touchstones such as maple-and-bourbon glazed pork chops with sweet potato and leek soufflé, jalapeño sorbet, and polenta with braised exotic mushrooms form the basis of the seasonal menu. The romantic two-tier dining room offers excellent service, and you're within walking distance of the theater district. An extensive wine list complements the fare. Friday nights are spiked with live jazz. ✉ *3 Appleton St.,* ☎ *617/426–1790. Reservations essential. AE, D, DC, MC, V. No lunch.*

$$$ ✗ **Laurel.** A newcomer that's surprisingly quiet and posh for this area,
★ this post-Ritz concept gravitates toward modestly innovative food. Apple-parsnip soup with fried carrots, hand-rolled potato gnocchi, and red snapper wrapped in lettuce have been hits, along with homey desserts like a "cookie jar" served with a glass of milk. ✉ *142 Berkeley St.,* ☎ *617/424–6711. Reservations essential. AE, DC, MC, V.*

$$ ✕ **Franklin Cafe.** Among the dozens of new bistros in Boston, Franklin Cafe has jumped to the head of the class by keeping things simple yet effective. (Its litmus: local chefs gather here to wind down after work.) Beans and lentils as a side-dish/sauce for fish is a typical idea of this unpretentious bar/café. Try anything with the great chive mashed potatoes. No desserts may be keeping it a little too simple, as the café is on a deserted block, not a desserted block. ⊠ *278 Shawmut Ave.,* ☎ *617/ 350–0010. No reservations. AE, MC, V.*

## French

$$$ ✕ **Brasserie Jo.** A little chain action by Alsatian chef Jean Joho, toast
★ of Chicago, hums busily from its classy breakfast through post-Symphony snacks (it's open 'til 1 AM) in a setting evoking '40s Paris. "Brasserie" originally meant brewery—this one is bigger, louder, and more versatile than a bistro. Still, it perfectly carries off classic bistro food like hanger steak and onion soup gratinée as well as beer-friendly Alsatian food such as *choucroûte à l'Alsacienne* (sausages, a cured pork chop, and a pork quenelle, all on a bed of sauerkraut). Serious martinis are on hand, too. ⊠ *120 Ave. of the Arts,* ☎ *617/425–3240. AE, D, DC, MC, V.*

## Italian

$$$ ✕ **Appetito.** Sienese colors and hand-painted murals of people eating and imbibing set off a conditioned reflex for garlic-olive hunger, which this kitchen satisfies with gourmet pizzas, a very good plate of grilled vegetables, and an even better version of spinach gnocchi. It is much less formal than its neighbor Icarus (☞ *above*), so you can use it simply for a pizza stop, a late dessert, or an inexpensive theater restaurant, as it is just enough out of the theater district to make finding parking easier. Brunch is served on Sunday. ⊠ *1 Appleton St.,* ☎ *617/338–6777. Reservations essential. AE, D, DC, MC, V. No lunch.*

## Mediterranean

$$–$$$ ✕ **Claremont Café & Lounge.** In a city full of bistros with limited service and Mediterranean food, this one is exceptional. Every stew and salad is ripe with flavor; even the potent coffee and desserts maintain this intensity. The Peruvian-born owners have started to work a few dishes from that great cuisine into the evening menu, such as *aji de gallina,* a chicken fricasseed in mild chilies and garlic. It opens daily for breakfast at 7:30 and is open for brunch on weekends. ⊠ *535 Columbus Ave.,* ☎ *617/247–9001. AE, MC, V.*

## Mexican

$–$$ ✕ **Baja Mexican Cantina.** Anything-but-traditional Mexican food is served in a postmodern Southwest decor. Start with a margarita made from your choice of premium tequilas. All the Cal-Mex food that follows is quite good, with lots of vegetarian options. If you're health-conscious, go for the salads, relatively low-fat burritos, or the lean hamburger served in a tortilla. ⊠ *111 Dartmouth St.,* ☎ *617/262–7575. AE, D, DC, MC, V.*

## Pan-Asian

$$–$$$ ✕ **Jae's Café and Grill.** Jae's Korean-Californian fusion has a definite way of bringing the taste buds back to life. That's one reason why a young, happening crowd fills the place. They cram the sushi bar, delight in the dishes served in hot-stone pots, and like their rice noodles with barely cooked vegetables. In summer, there's lots of sidewalk seating, the best spots of all. A larger branch in the theater district (⊠ *212 Stuart St.,* ☎ *617/451–7788*) focuses on Korean specialties. ⊠ *520 Columbus Ave.,* ☎ *617/421–9405. AE, DC, MC, V.*

### Soul Food

$$–$$$ ✕ **Bob the Chef's.** Boston's home of genteel soul food and jazz gathers a mellow mix of yuppies and neighborhood families. Given the gentility, take the crabcakes, catfish fingers, chitterlings, and "glorifried" chicken over the ribs or chicken wings, which are baked, not smoked. ⊠ *604 Columbus Ave.,* ☎ *617/536–6204. AE, MC, V. Closed Mon.*

# Waterfront

Tourists flock to Faneuil Hall and the Marketplace almost year-round, so tried-and-true cuisine tends to dominate. Some of Boston's most famous seafood restaurants live on the waterfront, naturally.

## Contemporary

$$$$ ✕ **Rowes Wharf Restaurant.** Rowes Wharf itself is stunning, and the ★ restaurant in the Boston Harbor Hotel takes advantage of this, offering perhaps the city's finest waterfront view. The decor is highly traditional with plush upholstered armchairs, exquisite mahogany paneling, and shaded wall sconces. Chef Daniel Bruce creates scintillating modern menus between the field trips on which he takes his staff to hunt wild mushrooms—his personal passion. Sautéed local wild mushrooms over stone-ground polenta is his signature composition. Roasted Maine lobster and chorizo with sweet corn pudding is the latest thing in dry-heat seafood. The restaurant has Boston's most extensive list of American wines. ⊠ *70 Rowes Wharf,* ☎ *617/439–3995. Reservations essential. Jacket required. AE, D, DC, MC, V.*

## Seafood

$$–$$$ ✕ **Anthony's Pier 4.** This massive theme park of a restaurant rolls along, somewhat uncertainly, hosting celebration dinners for Bostonians and visitors alike. The main drawback: the famous long wait for a table, designed—some complain—to sell drinks. Once seated, you can dine very well on the top-quality seafood if you remember that simple preparations tend to be the best here. Watch for seasonal specials on swordfish, stone crabs, or what now has to be called "fresh schrod" to distinguish the limited New England catch of cod and haddock—Anthony's likes to buy up the best. The wine list is remarkable, and there are scads of older wines at low prices. Reservations are virtually essential. ⊠ *140 Northern Ave.,* ☎ *617/423–6363. Jacket required. AE, D, DC, MC, V.*

$$–$$$ ✕ **Jimmy's Harborside.** Rivaling Anthony's (☞ *above*) for celebrations and power lunches, this exceedingly popular seafood establishment has aged more gracefully. The fish chowder is as fresh and bright-tasting as ever, and simply broiled or fried seasonal fish specials are excellent. You will fish through a lot of cream sauce to find the traditional finnan haddie, however. The wine list is almost all-American, with oversize bottles a specialty, and wisely divided by match-ups, although we would reverse things and have chardonnay with oysters and Riesling with lobster. ⊠ *242 Northern Ave.,* ☎ *617/423–1000. Reservations essential. AE, D, DC, MC, V. No lunch Sun.*

$–$$$ ✕ **The Barking Crab Restaurant.** It is, believe it or not, a seaside clam shack plunk in the middle of Boston with a stunning view of the downtown skyscrapers. An outdoor lobster tent in summer, in winter it retreats indoors to a warm-hearted version of a waterfront dive, with chestnuts roasting on a cozy wood stove. Look for the classic New England clambake—chowder, lobster, steamed clams, corn on the cob—or the spicier crab boil. The fried food lags. ⊠ *88 Sleeper St. (Northern Ave. Bridge),* ☎ *617/426–2722. AE, DC, MC, V.*

**$–$$$**  ✕ **No-Name Restaurant.** Famous for not being famous, the No-Name has been serving fresh seafood, simply broiled or fried, since 1917. Being right on the fish pier has its advantages, but the troubled New England fishing fleet provides fewer fish than it once did. Like they say, it is what it is, but it ain't what it used to be. ⊠ *15½ Fish Pier, off Northern Ave.,* ☎ *617/423–2705. No credit cards.*

# CAMBRIDGE/SOMERVILLE

Among other collegiate enthusiasms, Cambridge has a long-standing fascination with ethnic restaurants. A certain kind of great restaurant has also evolved here, mixing world-class cooking with a studied informality. Famous chefs, attired in flannel shirts, cook with wood fires and borrow flavors from every continent. For posher tastes and the annual celebrations that come with college life (or the end of it), Cambridge also has its share of linen-clothed tables.

### Afghan

**$$–$$$**  ✕ **The Helmand.** The area's first Afghan restaurant is named after a province of Afghanistan south of Kabul. It's run by refugees who came packing an exquisite cuisine, the plans for a lovely room built around a wood hearth, and a vision of service. They also arrived with recipes for three kinds of great rice, some fine sour soups, terrific *aushak* (ravioli stuffed with leeks), the various kebabs you might expect, and an excellent vegetarian menu you might not expect, with a number of choices grilled and stewed in novel ways. ⊠ *143 1st St., Cambridge,* ☎ *617/492–4646. AE, MC, V. No lunch.*

### American

**$**  ✕ **Mr. and Mrs. Bartley's Burger Cottage.** It may be perfect cuisine for the student metabolism: a huge variety of variously garnished thick burgers, french fries, and onion rings. (There's also a competent veggie burger.) The nonalcoholic "raspberry lime rickey," made with fresh limes, raspberry juice, sweetener, and soda water, is the must-try classic drink. Tiny tables in a crowded space make it a convenient place for Phi Beta eavesdropping. ⊠ *1246 Massachusetts Ave., Cambridge,* ☎ *617/354–6559. Reservations not accepted. No credit cards. Closed Sun.*

### Cambodian/French

**$$–$$$**  ✕ **Elephant Walk.** The first manifestation of the popular Cambodian-
★  French restaurant (☞ *below*) moved to larger quarters near Porter Square in 1998 without skipping a bicultural beat. The chef, Langtaine de Monteiro, learned to manage a Cambodian kitchen as the wife of a diplomat and for a time ran a restaurant in Provence. The common element is garlic, from a French appetizer like *moules* (mussels) swimming in garlic butter to superb Cambodian spring rolls, delicate salads, and a red curry of surpassingly fresh flavor. Lately the French dishes have been leaning toward fusion flavors, such as grilled red snapper with lemongrass sauce and an Asian basil coulis. ⊠ *2067 Massachusetts Ave., Cambridge,* ☎ *617/492–6900. AE, D, DC, MC, V.*

### Caribbean

**$$**  ✕ **Rhythm & Spice.** Enjoy mild-mannered Jamaican-style food and soca music in this pretty restaurant, which has become the gathering spot for Boston's growing coterie of African-American academics and their friends. The best food includes the Gundy appetizer (a spread of chopped herrings and apples), gentle curries, and "festival" cakes made with cornmeal. When the live reggae and soca music starts up later in the evening, the dance floor gets hot, hot, hot. ⊠ *315 Massachusetts Ave., Cambridge,* ☎ *617/497–0977. AE, MC, V. No lunch.*

## Chinese

**$–$$**   ✕ **Lucky Garden.** A modest holdover from the first, golden period of Szechuan food in Cambridge, Lucky Garden still serves excellent hot-and-sour soup, *yu hsiang* scallops (with garlic, hot pepper, and ginger), chicken and peanuts, and fried dumplings in a pleasant, comfortable atmosphere. Liquor isn't served. ⊠ *282 Concord Ave.,* ☎ *617/354–9514. AE, D, MC, V.*

**$**   ✕ **Mary Chung Restaurant.** In the 1970s, Szechuan food was all the rage in Cambridge. Mary Chung's was one of the last high-quality restaurants to open and became the chosen spot for a generation of MIT students. When Mary closed down, they set up their own Internet news group to reminisce about the Peking ravioli, *dun-dun* noodles (a cold appetizer of noodles in sesame paste), and other spicy delights. Mary finally had to reopen, and the meatiest "ravs" (hacker-ese for the ravioli) in Boston are back, along with the spicier *suan la chow show* (dumplings in soy soup), and such lesser-known specialties as toothsome chicken velvet (chicken blended with egg whites and stir-fried) and gingery-hot *yu hsiang* broccoli. Reservations are only accepted for parties of at least eight. ⊠ *464 Massachusetts Ave., Central Sq.,* ☎ *617/864–1991. No credit cards.*

## Contemporary

**$$$–$$$$**   ✕ **The Harvest.** The mother of high-profile chefs since the mid-'70s reopened late in 1998, its lavish menu of up-to-date dishes hedged with a little comfort food—mashed potatoes, baked beans, house fries. Start with raw seafood or the elaborately presented New England clam chowder with finnan haddie; then move on to roast monkfish, osso bucco, or roast lamb. Pore over the selection of Very Important Desserts: a tall cylinder of bread pudding, perhaps. The open kitchen makes some noise, but customers at the ever-popular bar don't seem to mind at all. ⊠ *44 Brattle St./1 Mifflin Pl., Cambridge,* ☎ *617/492–1115. Reservations essential. AE, D, DC, MC, V.*

**$$$–$$$$**   ✕ **Salamander.** Take a deep breath as you enter the expansive main
★   dining room—it's enticingly filled with aromas of wood and spice from a visible complex of wood-fired grills and ovens. Entrées are generous and appetizers are eccentric and flavorful, often Asian influenced (menu items change monthly). Favorites are the wood-grilled squid with coconut sauce, the cilantro and couscous crusted monkfish over a seafood tagine, and the pepper tenderloin over a ragout of wild mushrooms. For dessert, the banana wontons are deliciously indescribable; an apple sour-cream walnut cake is baked to order. The service is extremely well paced, and there's a great selection of wines by the glass. ⊠ *1 Atheneum St., Cambridge,* ☎ *617/225–2121. Reservations essential. AE, D, DC, MC, V. Closed Sun.*

**$$$**   ✕ **Blue Room.** Totally hip, funky, and Cambridge, the Blue Room, led by Steve Johnson, the convivial owner-chef, blends a host of ethnic cuisines, with an emphasis on Mediterranean and Latin American small plates. Brightly colored furnishings, counters where you can meet others while you eat, and a friendly staff add up to a good-time place that's serious about the food it serves. Try the seared scallops with hoisin sauce and sesame or perhaps the barrel-aged bourbon crème brûlée with hazelnut biscotti. A word of warning: at peak hours it can be a little too loud. An extraordinary brunch with a buffet of grilled meats and vegetables as well as regular breakfast fare plus a gorgeous array of desserts is served on Sunday. ⊠ *1 Kendall Sq.,* ☎ *617/494–9034. AE, D, DC, MC, V. No lunch Mon.–Sat.*

**$$$**   ✕ **East Coast Grill.** Owner-chef-author Chris Schlesinger built his na-
★   tional reputation on grilled foods and red-hot condiments. The Jamaican jerk, the North Carolina pulled pork, and the habañero-laced "pasta

## Cambridge Dining

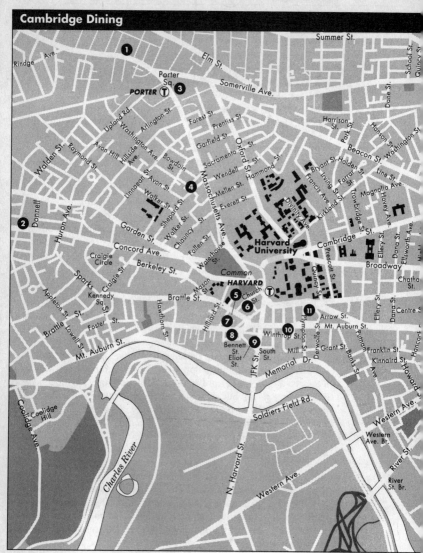

Blue Room, **20**
Border Café, **6**
Casa Portugal, **14**
Casablanca, **5**
Chez Henri, **4**
Cottonwood Café, **3**
East Coast Grill, **13**
Elephant Walk, **1**
Green Street Grill, **16**
The Harvest, **7**

The Helmand, **22**
La Groceria, **18**
Legal Sea Foods, **23**
Lucky Garden, **2**
Mary Chung Restaurant, **17**
Mr. and Mrs. Bartley's Burger Cottage, **11**
Rialto, **8**
Rhythm & Spice, **19**

Salamander, **21**
Sandrine's Bistro, **10**
Sunset Café, **15**
Tanjore, **9**
Union Square Bistro, **12**

N

| 0 | 550 yards |
| 0 | 500 meters |

Walnut St.
**12**
Stone Ave.
Somerville Ave.
Washington St.
E. St.
Medford St.
Mansfield St.
Rossmore St.
Merriam St.
Linden St.
Allen St.
Linwood St.
Poplar St.
Joy St.

**LECHMERE** ⓣ
Charlestown Ave.

Winter St.
Gore St.
Cambridge St.
Otis St.
Thorndike St.
Spring St.
Hurley St.
3rd St.
Scramp St.
Commercial Ave.

Concord Ave.
Oak St.
Webster Ave.
South St.
Porter St.
Warren St.
Willow St.
**15**
Berkshire St.
York St.
Portland St.
8th St.
7th St.
Fulkerson St.
6th St.
Charles St.
**22**
2nd St.
1st St.

Cambridge St.
**13**
**14**
Houghton St.
Tremont St.
Lincoln St.
Windsor St.
Bent St.
Roger St.
Binney St.
Munroe St.
Athenaeum St.
**21**

Hampshire St.
Prospect St.
Amory St.
Antrim St.
Inman St.
Norfolk St.
Elm St.
Market St.
Binney St.
**20**
Bristol St.

West St.
Lee St.
Clinton St.
Bigelow St.
Prospect St.
Essex St.
Pine St.
**Broadway**
Harvard St.

Fayette St.

**KENDALL** ⓣ
Howard St.
Carleton St.
Amherst St.
**23**

Washington St.
**18**
Main St.
**Massachusetts
Institute of
Technology**

**CENTRAL** ⓣ
Bishop Richard Allen Dr.
Green St.
**16**
**17**
**Massachusetts Ave.**
**19**
Ames St.

Western Ave.
River St.
Franklin St.
Auburn St.
Sidney St.
Landsdowne St.
Cross St.
Pacific St.
Purrington St.
Albany St.
Vassar St.
Memorial Dr.

Magazine St.
Pearl St.
Brookline St.
**Harvard
Bridge**
**Storrow
Drive**

Allston St.
Putnam St.
Waverly St.
Amherst Alley
Beacon St.
Massachusetts Ave.
Boylston St.

Henry St.
**Charles River**

**HYNES CONVENTION CENTER/
ICA (AUDITORIUM)** ⓣ

from Hell" are still here, but this restaurant has made an extraordinary play to establish itself in the front ranks of fish restaurants. Spices and condiments are more restrained, and Schlesinger has compiled a wine list bold and flavorful enough to share a table with the highly spiced food. The dining space is completely informal—this is surely the best restaurant in America that also has a motorized wiggling fish as a bathroom joke. Brunch is served on Sunday. ⊠ *1271 Cambridge St.,* ☎ *617/491–6568. AE, D, MC, V. No lunch.*

**\$\$\$**     ✕ **Green Street Grill.** The tables are small, the room is very plain, the
★     service is casual, and the bar next door mixes Bohemians with just-plain drunks, but Caribbean-born co-owner–chef John Levins is one of the living masters of mixing hot spices with other distinctive flavors. A recent example: "beaten & boiled conchmeat simmered in a Scotch bonnet chili pepper, lime & thyme, green plantain, green papaya, wild herb, rum sauce." But expect an entirely different—and elaborate—preparation with Caribbean grouper or Muscovy duck. ⊠ *280 Green St., Cambridge,* ☎ *617/876–1655. AE, DC, MC, V. No lunch.*

**\$\$\$**     ✕ **Union Square Bistro.** This airy room, a floor above the ethnic mar-
★     kets of Union Square, remains true in spirit to the bistro ideal of offering warming foods to small, convivial groups. Former sous-chef Helidomar d'Oliveira has moved into the big toque, and the regulars are celebrating with his neat little Brazilian skewers and addictive *pao de aveijo* (cheese puffs). Although familial service is an official cliché of the bistro movement, Union Square does it with some heart. Brunch is served on Sunday. ⊠ *16 Bow St., Union Sq., Somerville,* ☎ *617/628–3344. Reservations essential. AE, D, DC, MC, V.*

**\$\$–\$\$\$**     ✕ **Cottonwood Café.** This is Tex-Mex pushed to the next dimension. The atmosphere is Nuevo-Wave-o, with exotic architectural touches and rustic Southwestern details. Best of all is the Snake Bite appetizer: deep-fried jalapeños stuffed with shrimp and cheese—impossible to resist yet nearly too spicy-hot to eat. The lunch menu's zuni roll is like a hot sauce–spiked club sandwich in a wrap. The Cambridge café is close to the Porter Square T stop; there's another in Boston's Back Bay. ⊠ *1815 Massachusetts Ave.,* ☎ *617/661–7440; Back Bay:* ⊠ *222 Berkeley St.,* ☎ *617/247–2225. Reservations essential. AE, D, DC, MC, V.*

## French

**\$\$–\$\$\$\$**     ✕ **Sandrine's Bistro.** Chef Owner Raymond Ost goes to his Alsatian
★     roots for flavors easy and intense, but this is a bistro only in the way that little palace at Versailles was a country house. One of the big hits is the *flammenkuche*, the Alsatian onion pizza, but much else is haute cuisine, like the trout Napoleon. ⊠ *8 Holyoke St., Cambridge,* ☎ *617/ 497–5300. AE, MC, V.*

## French/Cuban

**\$\$\$–\$\$\$\$**     ✕ **Chez Henri.** Weird combination, but it works for this comfortable room, with a separate bar serving turnovers, fritters, and grilled three-pork Cuban sandwiches. The dinner menu gets serious with duck tamale with ancho chili, upscale paella, and truly French desserts. Brunch is served on Sunday. ⊠ *1 Shepard St., Cambridge,* ☎ *617/354–8980. AE, DC, MC, V. No lunch.*

## Indian

**\$–\$\$**     ✕ **Tanjore.** From the owners of Rangoli in Allston (☞ *below*) comes this fully regional Indian restaurant, from Sindh to Bengal, with some strength in the novel Western provincial foods (Gujarat, Bombay) with interesting sweet-hot flavors. An extra menu of *nashta,* or Indian tapas, adds to the confusion or the fun, depending on how adventurous you want to be. Some recommendations include *bhel* (a Bombay nashta of fried goodies in a sweet-hot curry), *gofhi char chari* (a Bengali potato and cauliflower entrée), *masala dosa* (Southern Indian curry in a sourdough pancake), and any of the excellent rice dishes, chais, and breads. The staff seems to enjoy explaining these dishes over and over again. The spicing starts mild, so don't be afraid to order "medium." ⊠ *18 Elliot St., Cambridge,* ☎ *617/868–1900. AE, D, MC, V.*

### Italian

**$$–$$$** ✕ **La Groceria.** A trattoria before trattoria was cool, this place draws loyal lovers of Italian food. Instant favorites are the homemade pasta, the table of cold antipasti, veal dishes, and homemade cannoli. ⊠ *853 Main St., Cambridge,* ☎ *617/876–4162. AE, D, DC, MC, V.*

### Mediterranean

**$$$–$$$$** ✕ **Rialto.** The ultraposh Charles Hotel dining room continues a pleasant drift from its Mediterranean beginnings toward more French techniques and more New England ingredients, such as Maine crab cakes and macomber turnips (a mild, white turnip). But the savory tarts and the Tuscan-style sirloin steak with sliced Portobello mushrooms and arugula salad are lifetime commitments. ⊠ *Charles Hotel, 1 Bennett St., Harvard Sq.,* ☎ *617/661–5050. AE, DC, MC, V. No lunch.*

**$$–$$$** ✕ **Casablanca.** Long before *The Rocky Horror Picture Show,* Harvard and Radcliffe types would put on trench coats, lip cigarettes, and head to the Brattle Theatre to see *Casablanca,* rising to recite the Bogart and Bergman lines in unison. Then it was on to this restaurant for more of the same fantasy. The theater and restaurant have both been refurbished, and the restaurant, under chef Ana Sortun, has evolved the best and most authentically Mediterranean food of its long run. Turkish influences have recently crept in, and pan-Mediterranean appetizers delight the crowded bar. Typical entrées include Tunisian spoon lamb with spiced figs, turnips, and couscous, and cod Casablancaise with Moroccan spices. The half-dozen desserts—such as chocolate turnover with ice cream and clove syrup—are substantial. The Casablanca murals by David Omar White are mostly in the lively central bar area. ⊠ *40 Brattle St.,* ☎ *617/876–0999. AE, MC, V.*

### Mexican

**$–$$** ✕ **Border Café.** Reasonably priced Sunbelt fare—Tex-Mex with Cajun and Caribbean influences—and a tightly packed Margaritaville bar scene have the Harvard Square crowd thronging here on weekends. The Cajun shrimp is a favorite, as is the burro (a burrito with enchilada sauce). ⊠ *32 Church St.,* ☎ *617/864–6100. AE, DC, MC, V.*

### Portuguese

**$$–$$$** ✕ **Sunset Café.** The lively atmosphere here may make you feel as
★ though you're attending a giant Portuguese wedding. Entire families come, and on a Friday or Saturday night (when they have guitarists and singers), it's not unusual to see little girls in frilly dresses and little boys in jackets and ties. Specialties include kale soup thickened with potatoes, *mariscada a chefe* (a great seafood combination in a casserole with fine spices), and shrimp Ana María (pan-fried shrimp in seafood stock). The bargain-priced wines on the list include some of the best Dão reds available anywhere outside Portugal. ⊠ *851 Cambridge St.,* ☎ *617/547–2938. AE, D, DC, MC, V.*

**$$** ✕ **Casa Portugal.** The oldest continuing Portuguese restaurant in the Azorean neighborhood east of Inman Square serves specialties such as pork with clams and squid stew simmered to tenderness and complexity. You'll find great fried potatoes (brought to your table with every dinner order), and the Portuguese wines are excellent bargains for the price, too. ⊠ *1200 Cambridge St.,* ☎ *617/491–8880. AE, D, MC, V.*

# BROOKLINE

Going to Brookline is a nice way to get out of town without really leaving town. Although it's surrounded by Boston on three sides, this neighborhood has its own suburban flavor, seasoned with a multitude of historic—and expensive—houses and garnished with a diverse ethnic population that supports a string of sushi bars and an expanding list of kosher restaurants.

### Cambodian/French

$$–$$$  ✕ **Elephant Walk.** Technically this Elephant Walk is in Boston, but psy-
★       chologically it is the gateway to Brookline, carrying on the tradition of its home base in Cambridge (☞ *above*), except it's aboveground, larger, and goes deeper into both modern French platters and what the menu calls "challenging tastes"—such as a dip made from Cambodian shrimp paste. Tease your palate with an exotic assortment of dumpling appetizers, spring rolls that you wrap in fresh lettuce leaves, and mouthwatering coq au vin. The airy atmosphere evokes a British Colonial hotel; the food reminds you of why Phnom Penh was "the Paris of Asia." The desserts, though, are pure Paris. ⊠ *900 Beacon St.,* ☎ *617/247–1500. AE, D, MC, V.*

### Contemporary

$$–$$$  ✕ **Five Seasons.** Lured away from Jamaica Plain, Five Seasons is the best of Boston's macrobiotic restaurants. The new location is twice as big, yet still crowded every night. They've made room for a juice-herbal bar and an open grill—thus more noise to fill the larger spaces between tables. The menu is substantially vegetarian and subtly Japanese-influenced; it offers wonderful fish and chicken dishes. The fried calamari, chowder of the day, sea vegetable salads, and whole grains are highlights. Desserts, under the triple burden of no eggs, no sugar, and no dairy (with an exception made for the option of real whipped cream), are not. ⊠ *1634 Beacon St.,* ☎ *617/731–2500. Reservations not accepted. AE, D, MC, V. No lunch weekends.*

$–$$$   ✕ **Zaftigs.** Here's something different, a contemporary version of a Jewish delicatessen. This food is almost never served without a thick sauce of nostalgia, so it is refreshing to have genuinely lean corned beef, a modest slice of cheesecake, low-sugar homemade borscht, and a lovely whitefish salad sandwich. Of course, a day later you're hungry again. ⊠ *335 Harvard St.,* ☎ *617/975–0075. AE, D, DC, MC, V.*

### Indian

$$     ✕ **Bombay Bistro.** One of Brookline's more pleasing and unusual restaurants, Bombay Bistro offers excellent north Indian cuisine with a couple of hot and spicy south Indian dishes like lamb vindaloo on the menu for good measure. Diners unfamiliar with Indian food should try any of the combination plates, especially the tandoori mix (an assortment of chicken, lamb, and shrimp cooked in a clay oven). The variety of specialty breads is impressive. ⊠ *1353 Beacon St.,* ☎ *617/734–2879. AE, D, DC, MC, V.*

### Irish

$$     ✕ **Matt Murphy's Pub.** There are dozens of Irish pubs in Boston, some catering to Irish expatriates, some serving a well-drawn pint of Guinness. But very few are notable for food, this being a welcome excep-

tion. Matt Murphy's makes real poetry out of thick slabs of bread and butter, giant soups, fish-and-chips served in a twist of newspaper, shepherd's pie, and hot rabbit pie—all served in enormous portions. Don't miss the homemade ketchup with your french fries. ✉ *14 Harvard St., Brookline Village,* ☎ *617/232–0188. No credit cards.*

## Japanese

$$–$$$ ✕ **Fugakyu.** The name sounds awkward in English but in Japanese means "house of elegance." The restaurant's interior hits the mark, with tatami mats, rice-paper partitions, and wooden ships circling a moat around the sushi bar. The menu is elegant and somewhat novel as well, with Boston's first live-tank sashimi, the rare Japanese *matsutake* mushrooms in a vegetarian stir-fry, and appetizers such as *ikura tanzaku* (an orange-on-orange combination of salmon, salmon eggs, and Japanese yam) served in a martini glass. Bento boxes and noodle soups are available at lunch only. ✉ *1280 Beacon St.,* ☎ *617/734–1268. AE, D, DC, MC, V.*

$$–$$$ ✕ **Ginza.** The **Chinatown branch** (✉ 16 Hudson St., Boston, ☎ 617/
★ 338–2261) is thought to have the most advanced sushi in town and serves until 3:30 AM on weekends, but the Brookline location is just as good and gains extra points for its selection of 15 brands of hot sake. Avant-sushi these days include hot spices, fried morsels, boozy marinades, and presentations with props like a martini glass. A quick anthology is the "Ginza Surprise," consisting of a daily assortment of chef's eccentricities, such as "caterpillar maki," with avocado scales. There are lots of good appetizers and hot dinners as well, including teriyaki, tempura, and *nabemono* (one-pot meal). ✉ *1002 Beacon St.,* ☎ *617/ 566–9688. AE, DC, MC, V.*

## Kosher

$–$$ ✕ **Rubin's.** The last kosher Jewish delicatessen in Boston serves a hand-cut pastrami sandwich a New Yorker can respect. (Be sure to order the "Hot Romanian Pastrami.") There are *kasha varnishkes* (buckwheat with bow-tie noodles), hot brisket, and many other high-cholesterol classics but, of course, no real cream for your coffee or dairy desserts. ✉ *500 Harvard St.,* ☎ *617/731–8787. AE, DC, MC, V. Closed Sat. No dinner Fri.*

$ ✕ **Rami's.** This small room is the best of all the falafel restaurants in Boston; its authentic *Zhoug* (Yemenite-style hot sauce) is green with fresh cilantro. The grilled chicken and the *bourekas* (savory pastries) are also stellar. The service tends to be quick and somewhat hurried, but Rami's is still a bit of a home-away-from-home for Israeli expatriates in the neighborhood. ✉ *324 Harvard St.,* ☎ *617/738–3577. No credit cards. Closed Sat. No dinner Fri.*

## Malaysian

$$–$$$ ✕ **Pandan Leaf.** This highly popular Malaysian restaurant has good versions of the *roti canai* appetizer (chicken curry), coconut shrimp, and the yummy taro pots Boston knows from Penang (☞ *above*), plus new specialties of its own: a mild barbecued stingray, sweet-and-spicy fried Indonesian chicken, and a very complicated and delicious raw fish salad served for two or more. Pleasant service warms noticeably when patrons are enthusiastic about the more exotic dishes. ✉ *250 Harvard St.,* ☎ *617/566–9393. AE, MC, V.*

## Russian

**$–$$**   ✕ **Café St. Petersburg.** "Imperial Russian cuisine" is how it's billed, but the sprightly food is even better than how it sounds. Certainly the betuxed servers (in black tie even during lunch) spare us the Dostoevskian gloom. This tiny café is just a great place to eat, from the opening shot of frozen cranberry vodka and the superb "venigret" salad of beets and potatoes to clean-tasting borscht, blini with smoked salmon and salmon caviar, and vegetarian treats such as vegetarian stuffed cabbage with raisins and dill-flavored eggplant caviar. Turkish coffee is the best dessert. There is live music Thursday through Sunday nights and impressive modern Russian art on the walls. ✉ *236 Washington St., Brookline Village,* ☎ *617/277–7100. D, MC, V.*

## Seafood

**$$–$$$**   ✕ **Village Fish.** With one of the few raw bars west of Boston's waterfront, the Village Fish serves nothing but classic seafood, including terrific versions of fried calamari and the best grilled shrimp around. Best seats in the house are either at the bar or at a handful of tables on the bar side. ✉ *22 Harvard St., Brookline Village,* ☎ *617/566–3474. No credit cards.*

## Spanish

**$$–$$$**   ✕ **Taberna de Haro.** Although Boston and Cambridge have fallen for
★   Spanish tapas, this is the first tapas bar to fully capture the modern Spanish spirit of this bar food. At dinner you have a choice of about 30 tapas and a few entrées. Tapas might include grilled white asparagus, *matrimonio* (the wedding being between fresh white anchovies and the familiar brown cured ones), an all-Spanish cheese platter, and *pollo en pepitoria* (chicken legs with enough almond-garlic sauce to employ a lot of bread). The lunchtime paella is cleverly done; to keep the seafood from overcooking, they steam it separately. ✉ *999 Beacon St.,* ☎ *617/277–8272. AE, DC, MC, V.*

## Thai

**$–$$**   ✕ **Sawasdee.** When compared with the other Thai restaurants in the city, this chic dining room holds its own. Multiple curries are the specialty of the house: red, green, or yellow, they pack an aromatic, spicy punch. Other recommendations include the Golden Bags appetizer (a deep-fried tofu pouch stuffed with seafood and vegetables) and the extremely spicy boneless spareribs. ✉ *320 Washington St., Brookline Village,* ☎ *617/566–0720. AE, D, DC, MC, V.*

# ALLSTON/BRIGHTON

Approximately northwest from downtown, this densely packed little enclave of grunge mixes twentysomething college students with immigrants from four continents. In general, the restaurants are homey and cheap, but the best offer a culinary world tour. A number of places allow low-key BYOB; Blanchard's and Marty's on Harvard Avenue are both great wine stores. If you've sampled Boston's past, this is the place to come to taste its future.

## Chinese-Vietnamese

**$$**   ✕ **Ducky Wok.** Despite the silly name, this is an outstanding restau-
★   rant, the first outside Chinatown to feature live-tank seafood, and one of the few Chinese-Vietnamese restaurants whose menu is equally strong with both cuisines. Don't miss the daily tank seafood special, the stir-fried pea pod stems, or the sautéed chicken with lemongrass. ✉ *122–126 Harvard Ave., Allston,* ☎ *617/782–8868. AE, D, MC, V.*

**$–$$**  ✕ **Grasshopper.** Completely vegan versions of Chinese and Vietnamese
★  cuisine work best when not dependent on the fake shrimp, pork, beef,
chicken, or squid. Despite piling on all five kinds of wheat gluten, the
taro nest stands out (it has plenty of veggies), as do any of the noodle
dishes and the jasmine rice. ✉ *1 N. Beacon St., Allston,* ☎ *617/254–
8883. D, MC, V.*

## Contemporary

**$$–$$$**  ✕ **North East Brewing Company.** Bright, hoppy ales and a fresh, rich
stout complement some very good American bistro cooking. The crab
cakes and grilled chicken and potato cakes with squash fritters are immediate knockouts, and the thin-crust pizza is excellent. ✉ *1314 Commonwealth Ave., Allston,* ☎ *617/566–6699. AE, D, DC, MC, V.*

## Indian

**$$**  ✕ **Rangoli.** Most of what Americans think of as Indian food is decid-
edly northern Indian, so Rangoli offers a nice alternative journey into
the hot and spicy (and relatively vegetarian) world of southern Indian
cooking. Specialties include curries wrapped in *dosa* (sourdough pan-
cakes) and *idli sambar* (fiery vegetable soup with soothing dumplings).
If you might like something hot and spicy and crunchy and sweet all
at the same time, the amazing *bhel* appetizer (a novel curry with bits
of fried turnovers worked in) is the dish for you. ✉ *129 Brighton Ave.,
Allston,* ☎ *617/562–0200. AE, D, DC, MC, V.*

## Italian (Contemporary)

**$$$**  ✕ **Uva.** A little piece of the South End in Allston, Uva serves up dishes
★  that land somewhere between new American and new Italian; de-
lightfully, the emphasis is always on the new. Try one of Uva's special
pasta plates, which you construct from dozens of different sauces and
garnishes, or delve into such lively entrées as stuffed veal breast with
sweetbreads. This little bistro has embraced a radical wine-pricing
scheme: $10 over wholesale, which puts $40 and $50 bottles in the
$25 price range (making this a mecca for all wine-lovers). Uva remains
a favorite destination for BU and BC parents after dropping off their
precious college-bound cargo. ✉ *1418 Commonwealth Ave.,* ☎ *617/
566–5670. Reservations essential for 6 or more. AE, D, DC, MC, V.
Closed Sun. No lunch.*

## Korean

**$**  ✕ **Choe's Café.** Although it's housed in a funny-shaped space, Choe's
serves outstanding Korean food and very good sushi. Make a beeline
for the seafood scallion pancake and hot spicy squid. The food is kept
honest by Korean students who drift up from Boston University. ✉
*957 Commonwealth Ave., Allston,* ☎ *617/783–8702. MC, V. No
lunch Sun.*

## South American

**$–$$**  ✕ **Café Brazil.** This little place has a full slate of terrific meaty entrées
from Brazil's Minas Gerais region, including a fine mixed grill and a
couple of fish stews from the neighboring province of Bahia. There is
also a great version of the fried yucca appetizer, *mandioca.* The decor
is basic travel posters, but the down-home Brazilian cooking is almost
as good as a trip to the scenes they depict. ✉ *421 Cambridge St., Allston,* ☎ *617/789–5980. AE, D, MC, V.*

## Thai

**$**  ✕ **Siam Cuisine.** The names of Thai restaurants are hard to keep
straight, but it's not a problem because almost all of them in Allston
are very good. Just watch out for those chili-pepper icons next to certain dishes—they mean spicy and they mean business. Siam Cuisine is
notable both for the food and for the beautifully decorated dining room

# Allston, Brighton, Brookline, and Jamaica Plain Dining

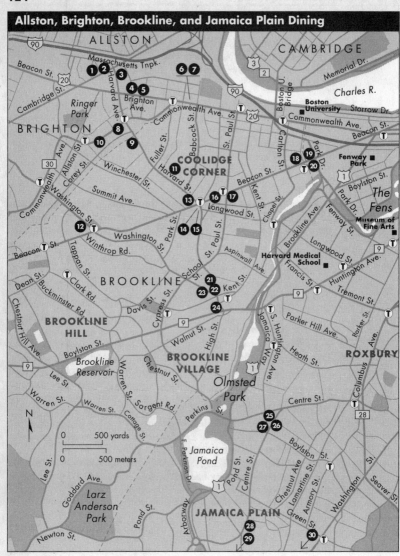

full of large Thai art pieces and antiques. Reserve one of the special floor tables for even more atmosphere. ⊠ *961 Commonwealth Ave.,* ☎ *617/254–4335. AE, MC, V.*

### Vietnamese

$–$$  ✗ **Pho Pasteur.** Here you'll find outstanding Vietnamese food in a less-crowded space than at its Chinatown location. The specialty, *pho* (beef bouillon), arrives in a huge bowl, delicately spiced and full of noodles and a selection of meat garnishes, with side salads you can toss into the bowl as well. For most diners, pho is a full meal. There are also savory rice plates and fine salads (Vietnamese is the one Asian cuisine that gets into salads). For dessert, try the fruit smoothies described as "milkshakes." ⊠ *137 Brighton Ave.,* ☎ *617/783–2340. AE, DC, MC, V.*

# JAMAICA PLAIN

This neighborhood is a kind of mini-Cambridge, multiethnic and filled with radicals, cutting-edge artists, starving college students, and political idealists. There are no large restaurants, so dining out tends to the unusual and is usually pretty affordable.

### American (Contemporary)

$$  ✗ **Black Crow Caffé.** It starts the day as a coffee shop, selling pastries, breads, and rolls with the java. Around lunch time, the Black Crow turns into a jumping sandwich spot. By dinner, it takes on a bistro flair, serving hot Caribbean and Mediterranean dishes and innovative salads from its constantly changing menu. Its progressive, multiethnic atmosphere is the very soul of Jamaica Plain. ⊠ *2 Perkins St.,* ☎ *617/983–9231. AE, MC, V. Closed Mon.*

### Caribbean

$–$$  ✗ **El Oriental de Cuba.** This is a small haven for a large variety of excellent Cuban food, including a healing chicken soup, a classic Cuban sub, superb rice and beans (opt for the red beans over the black beans), sweet "tropical shakes," and the *tostones* (twice-fried plantains) beloved during the cold New England winter by the many Cuban transplants to Boston. It also makes a good breakfast spot. ⊠ *416 Centre St.,* ☎ *617/524–6464. No credit cards.*

### Irish

$–$$$  ✗ **James's Gate.** This rare Irish pub has great food (not all of it Irish), fine contemporary art on the walls (very little of it Irish) yet the look and feel of a real Irish pub (without Irish cottage kitsch). Roam beyond the shepherd's pie and smoked fish-and-cheese "Gate's Plate" to the Thai-style mussels and the veggie quesadillas. Satisfying beers and ales (not all Irish, either) are on draft. On Monday just the bar menu is served. ⊠ *5-11 MacBride St.,* ☎ *617/983–2000. AE, MC, V.*

### Italian (Contemporary)

$$  ✗ **Bella Luna.** This spaced-out menu (sprinkled with sci-fi jokes) has eccentric pizzas and calzones along with Italian standards. For instance, the "Brendan Behan" is topped with goat cheese and roasted red peppers, while the "Diedre Delux" mixes dried cranberries, caramelized onions, and Gorgonzola cheese. Work by local artists lines the walls, while local musicians provide the music. (The weekly schedule could range from jazz to rock.) ⊠ *405 Centre St.,* ☎ *617/ 524–6060. AE, MC, V.*

## Seafood

**$–$$$** ╳ **JP Seafood Café.** So successful they replaced the original fish store with a sushi bar, this neighborhood jewel has one chef for sushi and one for spicier Korean dishes. You'll find top-quality sushi, *jap chae* (stir-fried vegetables with cellophane noodles), a delicious bowl of udon noodle soup with tempura melting in, and a terrific *bi bim bop* (Korean you-mix assorted rice platter) served in a hot stone bowl. ⊠ *730 Centre St.,* ☎ *617/983–5177. AE, DC, MC, V.*

## Soul Food

**$–$$** ╳ **Jake's Boss BBQ.** Right next to Doyle's, Jamaica Plain's great neigh-
★ borhood bar, Jake's fills the food side of the equation with impressive Texas-style smoked meats and some North Carolina pulled pork that Kenton Jacobs picked up during a stint with the East Coast Grill (☞ *above*). The brisket sandwich is perfection of its kind. ⊠ *3294 Washington St.,* ☎ *617/983–3701. DC, MC, V.*

# 5   LODGING

For every cramped dorm room in Boston,
there's a cozy and cosmopolitan hotel room
awaiting. No matter where you hang your
hat, the selection of core-city lodging
options is choice—grande dames like the
Ritz-Carlton, jewel-size B&Bs, and Back Bay
buys accommodate every budget. Many of
the city's hostelries have welcoming lounges,
ideal for enjoying a Paul Revere Alarm over
ice and simply taking in the city's
understated Yankee gentility.

Updated by
Natalie Engler

**A**S THEY GLOWER AT EACH OTHER ACROSS the Public Garden, two of Boston's best and brightest hotels—the dowager Ritz-Carlton and the upstart Four Seasons—typify the diversity and conflict that dominate all aspects of the city. The Ritz, built in 1927, has been here forever, at least by American standards; the Four Seasons sprang up in 1985, polished and relentlessly modern.

Whether you want to spend $300-plus per night on old-fashioned elegance or extravagant modernity, you've come to the right city. The bulk of Boston's accommodations are expense-account territory; nevertheless, there are plenty of great choices among the smaller and older establishments, modern motels, or—perhaps the best option (if you can take early morning small talk)—bed-and-breakfasts. Cheaper than most hotels, and more stylish than most HoJos, B&Bs are becoming increasingly popular in the Boston area and give visitors the chance to experience Boston's famous neighborhoods, from the increasingly hip South End to the hallowed, gaslit streets of Beacon Hill or ethnic enclaves such as Brookline and Cambridge.

Expensive they may be, but many hotels have been plumping up their amenities, giving you more perks for the price. Even in less-expensive establishments, rooms generally come equipped with a hair dryer, iron and ironing board, bathrobe, coffeemaker, in-room modem line, and sometimes even free local calls.

One last thought before waving a sad farewell to deluxe anonymity and committing yourself to breakfast chitchat: check out the promotional packages. Weekend rates at some of the city's best hotels can be far below so-called standard or rack rates and often include free perks like parking, breakfast, or cocktails. If you look hard enough, you can find great deals for family groups, lovers, shoppers, theatergoers, sailors, probably even politicos.

For price ranges, *see* the hotel chart *in* On the Road with Fodor's. These prices are regular weekday rates, and the number of rooms available at this rate may be limited. Assume that all rooms have a private bathroom and that no pets are allowed unless otherwise noted. We note air-conditioning only when it's unusual for the type of property, such as in historic buildings.

Remember that Huntington Avenue was rechristened Avenue of the Arts but that locals may well use the old name.

# HOTELS

With the density of colleges, conventions, and tourist attractions, hotels are generally booked for the spring, summer, and fall (especially in early October during foliage season). When considering prices, remember that room rates rarely include parking, which can cost more than $20 per night.

## Boston

### Back Bay

$$$$    🏨 **Eliot Hotel.** The Eliot is a seriously upscale all-suite hotel. The luxury extends from the split-level marble lobby with its vast chandelier to the hushed pastels of the rooms, each of which has Italian marble bathrooms and two cable-equipped televisions. The Eliot Lounge, the legendary post-marathon hangout, was replaced by Clio, an airy restau-

rant garnering rave reviews for its serene ambience and contemporary French-American cuisine. The Eliot is steps from Newbury Street and a short walk to Kenmore Square. Children under 18 stay free in their parents' room. ⊠ *370 Commonwealth Ave., 02215,* ☎ *617/267–1607 or 800/443–5468,* ℻ *617/536–9114. 95 suites. Restaurant, in-room data ports, minibars, no-smoking rooms, room service, baby-sitting, laundry service and dry cleaning, concierge, meeting rooms, parking (fee). AE, DC, MC, V.*

**$$$$** 🏨 **Fairmont Copley Plaza.** A top-to-bottom renovation completed in
★ early 1998 burnished the opulence of this stately landmark, built in 1912 by Henry Hardenbergh, the architect of the Plaza Hotel and the Dakota in New York City. The public spaces are decidedly grand, with high gilded and painted ceilings, mosaic floors, marble pillars, and crystal chandeliers. Guest rooms have custom furniture from Italy, elegant marble bathrooms, and fax machines. One of the restaurants, now called the Oak Room to match its mahogany-paneled twin in New York's Plaza Hotel, has a dance floor and a raw bar. Despite the imposing Victorian surroundings, the atmosphere is utterly gracious and welcoming, thanks to the multilingual staff. Children under 18 stay free in their parents' room, and pets are welcome. ⊠ *138 St. James Ave., 02116,* ☎ *617/267–5300 or 800/527–4727,* ℻ *617/247–6681. 312 rooms, 67 suites. 2 restaurants, 2 bars, in-room data ports, minibars, no-smoking floors, room service, barbershop, beauty salon, exercise room, baby-sitting, laundry service and dry cleaning, concierge, business services, parking (fee). AE, D, DC, MC, V.*

**$$$$** 🏨 **Four Seasons.** The only hotel in Boston other than the Ritz-Carlton
★ (☞ *below*) to overlook the Public Garden is also, to the Ritz's chagrin, the only five-star hotel in the city. The Four Seasons is famed for luxurious personal service of the sort demanded by guest celebrities such as Alan Alda, Ray Charles, and Luciano Pavarotti. Guest rooms, even with the king-size beds, swim with space; their bathrooms were updated in 1998 with marble the color of cabernet and chocolate. Suites are enhanced with stereos and private bars. An eighth-floor health club includes a whirlpool, sauna, and a heated 51-ft lap pool with a view of the Public Garden. The antiques-filled public spaces are serenely elegant, and Aujourd'hui (☞ Back Bay *in* Chapter 4) is one of Boston's best restaurants. Children stay free in their parents' room and pets are welcome. There's also a complimentary car service that will pick you up or drop you off downtown. ⊠ *200 Boylston St., 02116,* ☎ *617/338–4400 or 800/332–3442,* ℻ *617/423–0154. 216 rooms, 72 suites. 2 restaurants, in-room data ports, in-room safes, minibars, no-smoking floors, room service, indoor pool, health club, baby-sitting, laundry service and dry cleaning, concierge, business services, parking (fee). AE, D, DC, MC, V.*

**$$$$** 🏨 **Lenox Hotel.** When this hotel was renovated in 1997, structural
★ changes to the 1900 building uncovered a trove of period detailing. Now these handsome archways and elaborate moldings help distill the property's historic flavor, particularly in the airily spacious corner rooms, a dozen of which have working fireplaces. Guest rooms have plenty of modern touches too: custom-made traditional furnishings, spacious walk-in closets, and marble baths. The Samuel Adams Brew House (a pub) and the Anago bistro make it easy to stay in in the evenings. Children under 18 stay free in their parents' room. ⊠ *710 Boylston St., 02116,* ☎ *617/536–5300 or 800/225–7676,* ℻ *617/236–0351. 209 rooms, 3 suites. 2 restaurants, bar, in-room data ports, no-smoking floor, room service, exercise room, baby-sitting, dry cleaning, concierge, parking (fee). AE, D, DC, MC, V.*

**$$$$**   ⊞ **Ritz-Carlton.** Despite the attractions of the upstart Four Seasons (☞
★         *above*), many visitors to Boston would never dream of staying anywhere
but the Ritz, thanks to its unmatched location, dignified elegance, and
fierce devotion to its guests' comfort and privacy. Built in 1927 as an
elite club for aristocrats, it is still the hotel of choice for European royalty. White-gloved elevator operators take you to your floor. Standard
rooms throughout are small but stately. Suites in the older section include parlors with woodburning fireplaces and views of the Public Garden, and abundant period details (gilded sconces, the original Ritz clocks).
If you stay in the newer section, you'll trade the garden view for larger
bathrooms with double sinks. The child-with-everything will love the
Junior Presidential Suite's scaled-down kids' bedroom with furniture
and bath fixtures in proportions to suit the smaller set, all for a most
adult-size $695. For decadent shopping you don't even have to go out-
side; there's an inside entrance to the Newbury Street Chanel boutique.
Small pets are welcome. ⊠ *Arlington and Newbury Sts., 02117,* ☎
*617/536–5700 or 800/241–3333,* ℻ *617/536–1335. 233 rooms, 42
suites. Restaurant, bar, lobby lounge, in-room safes, minibars, no-
smoking rooms, refrigerators, room service, beauty salon, exercise
room, baby-sitting, laundry service, concierge, concierge floor, parking (fee). AE, D, DC, MC, V.*

**$$$–$$$$**   ⊞ **Back Bay Hilton.** The 26-story Hilton occupies a corner pocket be-
tween the Prudential Center and the Christian Science Church com-
plex. An expansion completed in mid-1998 added 44 rooms and a
dramatic glassed-in facade to the previously unremarkable building.
The new rooms, decorated with contemporary furnishings in blues, golds,
and burnished maple, have wall-to-wall windows overlooking the
Back Bay and Fenway Park, plus oversize showers. If it's fresh air you
crave, try one of the older rooms, which have windows that open and
balconies. Rooms above the ninth floor have the best views. Continental
breakfast is included. Children under 18 stay free in their parents' room.
Small pets are permitted. ⊠ *40 Dalton St., 02115,* ☎ *617/236–1100
or 800/874–0663,* ℻ *617/867–6104. 380 rooms, 5 suites. Restaurant,
3 bars, in-room data ports, room service, no-smoking floors, indoor
pool, exercise room, dance club, laundry service and dry cleaning, con-
cierge, parking (fee). AE, D, DC, MC, V.*

**$$$–$$$$**   ⊞ **The Colonnade.** Not quite Back Bay, not quite the South End, this
small, nonhectic modern hotel across from the Hynes Convention
Center and next to Copley Place has more personality than some of
the larger business-oriented high-rises on the other side of the avenue.
Three specialty suites cater to politicos, touring authors, and those with
a yen for a baby grand piano. In summer, the rooftop swimming pool
is open. Chicago import Brasserie Jo also found a niche here (☞ South
End *in* Chapter 4). Complete executive services include multilingual
translation and foreign currency exchange; children under 12 stay free
in their parents' room. ⊠ *120 Ave. of the Arts, 02116,* ☎ *617/424–
7000 or 800/962–3030,* ℻ *617/424–1717. 275 rooms, 10 suites.
Restaurant, bar, in-room safes, minibars, pool, exercise room, baby-
sitting, concierge, business services. AE, D, DC, MC, V.*

**$$$–$$$$**   ⊞ **Copley Square Hotel.** If you're a fan of Old World style, you'll ap-
preciate this hotel's quirky turn-of-the-century charm—and its convenient
Back Bay location is an all-around plus. The circa 1891 hotel, one of
the city's oldest, is busy and comfortable, with winding corridors and
repro-antique furniture. The idiosyncratic rooms have a few common
denominators (television, coffeemaker) and some have couches. Chil-
dren under 17 stay free in their parents' room. ⊠ *47 Ave. of the Arts,
02116,* ☎ *617/536–9000 or 800/225–7062,* ℻ *617/267–3547. 143
rooms, 12 suites. 2 restaurants, 2 bars, coffee shop, in-room data*

# In case you want to see the world.

At American Express, we're here to make your journey a smooth one. So we have over 1,700 travel service locations in over 130 countries ready to help. What else would you expect from the world's largest travel agency?

do more

**Travel**

Call 1 800 AXP-3429 or visit
www.americanexpress.com/travel

# In case you want to be welcomed there.

**We're here to see that you're always welcomed at establishments everywhere. That's why millions of people carry the American Express® Card – for peace of mind, confidence, and security, around the world or just around the corner.**

do more

**Cards**

# In case you're running low.

We're here to help with more than 190,000 Express Cash locations around the world. In order to enroll, just call American Express at 1 800 CASH-NOW before you start your vacation.

do more **AMERICAN EXPRESS**

**Express Cash**

# And in case you'd rather be safe than sorry.

We're here with American Express® Travelers Cheques. They're the safe way to carry money on your vacation, because if they're ever lost or stolen you can get a refund, practically anywhere or anytime. To find the nearest place to buy Travelers Cheques, call 1 800 495-1153. Another way we help you do more.

do more **AMERICAN EXPRESS**

**Travelers Cheques**

*ports, in-room safes, no-smoking rooms, room service. AE, D, DC, MC, V.*

$$$–$$$$    🏨 **Marriott Hotel at Copley Place.** You can enter this "megahotel" through any of three impressive entrances: a street-level lobby entrance, a glass skybridge from the Prudential Center/Hynes Auditorium complex, or the Copley Plaza shopping mall. Guest rooms have French Colonial–style dark wood furniture and are decorated in burgundy and green. Some look out toward the Boston Harbor or the Charles River. ✉ *110 Ave. of the Arts, 02116, ☎ 617/236–5800 or 800/228–9290, FAX 617/578–0685. 1,109 rooms, 38 suites. 2 restaurants, 2 bars, sushi bar, in-room data ports, no-smoking floors, room service, indoor pool, health club, video games, dry cleaning, concierge, concierge floors, business services, meeting rooms, parking (fee). AE, D, DC, MC, V.*

$$$–$$$$    🏨 **Radisson 57 Hotel.** The two best reasons to stay at this former Howard Johnson's are the generous size of its rooms and its location in Park Square on the edge of the Theater District. The building itself isn't fancy (it's a 1970s cement high-rise), but it also holds a small theater that hosts off-Broadway shows. All rooms have a sitting area and a private balcony; business-class rooms include a complimentary breakfast, in-room coffee, a daily newspaper, and an in-room movie. Children under 18 stay free in their parents' room. ✉ *200 Stuart St., 02116, ☎ 617/482–1800, FAX 617/451–2750. 356 rooms. 2 restaurants, indoor pool, exercise room, parking (fee). AE, D, DC, MC, V.*

$$$–$$$$    🏨 **Sheraton Boston Hotel & Towers.** These twin 29-story towers are connected to the Hynes Convention Center and the Prudential Tower. At press time the north tower and concierge level in the south tower were closed for renovations until summer 1999. In the meantime the south-tower rooms remain open; modern in both form and function, they have Ethernet access to the Internet and wide windows displaying panoramic city views. (Ask for a room facing the Christian Science Center or the Charles River.) Punch, a cigar bar, is one of the city's few remaining public places for smokers. Small pets are allowed. Children under 17 stay free in their parents' room. ✉ *Prudential Center, 39 Dalton St., 02199, ☎ 617/236–2000 or 800/325–3535, FAX 617/236–1702. 949 rooms, 142 suites. Restaurant, 2 bars, in-room data ports, no-smoking rooms, room service, indoor-outdoor pool, hot tub, exercise room, laundry service and dry cleaning, concierge, concierge floor, business services, parking (fee). AE, D, DC, MC, V.*

$$$–$$$$    🏨 **Westin Copley Place.** You're practically guaranteed a great view from the windows of this 36-story hotel—you can gaze out toward the Charles River, Copley Square, the South End, or the Back Bay. Rooms are large and furnished with oak and mahogany Colonial-style furniture. If you need to work during your stay, they're well prepared; the conference rooms have T-1 and T-3 lines for fast Internet access, and 27 suites include "guest offices" with a fax, copier, and printer, ergonomically designed desk and chair, free local phone calls, and office supplies. A fifth-floor health club features Cybex equipment and more wonderful views; for more material concerns, cross the skybridge that stretches between the hotel and the glossy Copley Place mall. Restaurants include the Palm and the popular Turner Fisheries Bar and Restaurant (☞ Back Bay/Beacon Hill *in* Chapter 4). Small pets are welcome. ✉ *Copley Pl., 02116, ☎ 617/262–9600 or 800/937–8461, FAX 617/424–7483. 755 rooms, 45 suites. 3 restaurants, in-room safes, no-smoking floors, room service, indoor pool, hot tub, sauna, health club, laundry service and dry cleaning, business services, meeting rooms, parking (fee). AE, D, DC, MC, V.*

$$–$$$$    🏨 **Boston Park Plaza Hotel & Towers.** Original decorative plaster moldings and a chandeliered gilt-and-cream lobby with piano bar grace this circa 1927 hotel, which has been visited by every major pres-

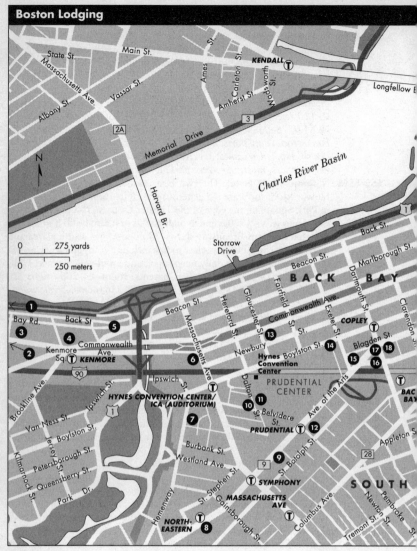

Back Bay Hilton, **10**

Beacon Hill Bed and
Breakfast, **28**

Berkeley
Residence YWCA
Boston, **19**

Best Western Terrace
Inn, **2**

Boston Harbor Hotel
at Rowes Wharf, **37**

Boston Park Plaza
Hotel & Towers, **23**

Chandler Inn, **22**

Clarendon Square
Inn, **20**

The Colonnade, **12**

Copley Square
Hotel, **15**

82 Chandler Street, **21**

Eliot Hotel, **6**

Fairmont Copley
Plaza, **18**

Four Seasons, **26**

Greater Boston
YMCA, **8**

The Gryphon House, **5**

Harborside Inn, **35**

Hilton Boston Logan
Airport, **40**

Holiday Inn Boston
Airport, **39**

Holiday Inn
Express, **44**

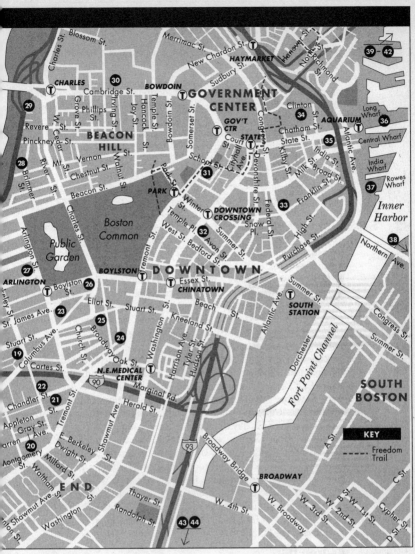

Holiday Inn Select
Boston Government
Center, **30**

Hostelling
International
Boston, **7**

Hotel Buckminster, **4**

Howard Johnson's
Kenmore Square, **3**

Hyatt Harborside at
Boston International
Logan Airport, **41**

John Jeffries House, **29**

Le Meridien Hotel, **33**

Lenox Hotel, **14**

Marriott Hotel at
Copley Place, **16**

Marriott Long
Wharf, **42**

Midtown Hotel, **9**

Newbury Guest
House, **13**

Omni Parker House, **31**

Radisson 57 Hotel, **25**

The Regal Bostonian, **34**

Ritz-Carlton, **27**

Seaport Hotel, **38**

Sheraton Boston
Hotel & Towers, **11**

Susse Chalet Motor
Lodges, **43**

Swissôtel, **32**

The Tremont
Boston, **24**

Westin Copley
Place, **17**

ident since Roosevelt. The Starwood hotel group took over in 1997, and renovations scheduled to be completed in spring 1999 include full soundproofing and enlargement of some of the small rooms. Some will become suites; others will get a pair of bathrooms. The new room interiors have more than a hint of Pottery Barn to them (the designer came from that company); they include dark cherry furniture, full-length mirrors, puffy down comforters, and soothing blue-and-beige or green-and-white color schemes. The location is stellar, one block from the Public Garden and a short walk from Beacon Hill, the Theater District, Newbury Street, and public transportation. Children under 17 stay free in their parents' room. ⊠ *64 Arlington St., 02116, ☎ 617/426–2000 or 800/225–2008, ℻ 617/426–5545. 883 rooms, 60 suites. 2 restaurants, 2 bars, in-room data ports, no-smoking floors, room service, beauty salon, exercise room, theater, laundry service and dry cleaning, concierge, concierge floor, business services, meeting rooms, travel services, parking (fee). AE, D, DC, MC, V.*

**$–$$$**  🏨 **Midtown Hotel.** Comfortable rooms at reasonable rates and a convenient location near the Prudential Center, Symphony Hall, and the Christian Science Center enable this motel-style hotel to hold its own against its large, expensive neighbors. Renovations were wrapped up in 1999; rooms now have a pale gray and cranberry color scheme. Children under 18 stay free in their parents' room. ⊠ *220 Ave. of the Arts, 02115, ☎ 617/262–1000 or 800/343–1177, ℻ 617/262–8739. 157 rooms, 2 suites. Restaurant, in-room data ports, no-smoking rooms, room service, pool, beauty salon, baby-sitting, business services, free parking. AE, D, DC, MC, V.*

**$–$$**  🏨 **Chandler Inn.** This cozy hotel is one of the best bargains in the city. Located near an overpass near the Back Bay, at the end of one of the South End's prettiest streets, it's an easy walk to the T, the Amtrak station, Newbury Street's boutiques, or any of Tremont Street's trendy restaurants. Rooms are small but comfortable with dorm-style furniture and ceiling fans. Try to snag one whose number ends in "08"; these are corner rooms with queen-size beds and views of the Back Bay. Almost half of the rooms are no-smoking. At press time, the hotel planned full renovations for the bathrooms and lobby. Fritz, a popular, gay-friendly sports bar, moonlights as a brunch spot on weekends. The inn often hosts a huge crowd during Gay Pride Week. Small pets are welcome; a Continental breakfast is included. ⊠ *26 Chandler St., 02115, ☎ 617/482–3450, ℻ 617/542–3428. 56 rooms. Restaurant (weekends only), bar. AE, D, DC, MC, V.*

## Beacon Hill

**$–$$**  🏨 **John Jeffries House.** Once a housing facility for nurses, this turn-
★    of-the-century building across from Massachusetts General Hospital is now an elegant four-story inn with a Federal-style double parlor and guest rooms with French country decor. Triple-glazed windows block virtually all noise from busy Charles Circle. Nearly all rooms have kitchenettes, and many have views of the Charles River. All floors are no-smoking. The hotel is an easy walk from public transportation and most of downtown. Continental breakfast is included. ⊠ *14 Embankment Rd., 02114, ☎ 617/367–1866, ℻ 617/742–0313. 23 rooms, 23 suites. Parking (fee). AE, D, DC, MC, V.*

## Downtown

**$$$$**  🏨 **Boston Harbor Hotel at Rowes Wharf.** Travelers who arrive from
★    Logan Airport via water shuttle come straight to the back door of this deluxe harborside hotel, docking amid a slew of luxury yachts and power boats. Everything here is done on a grand scale, starting with the dramatic entrance through an 80-ft archway topped by a rotunda. Guest rooms—decorated in shades of mauve, green, and soft yellow—have

city or water views, and 10 have balconies. At press time, the rooms and lobby were being renovated; the work should be completed by the end of 1999. The Rowes Wharf Restaurant offers a spectacular, if pricey, Sunday brunch as well as seafood and American cuisine. The hotel is within walking distance of Faneuil Hall, the North End, the New England Aquarium, and the Financial District. Pets are welcome. ✉ *70 Rowes Wharf, 02110,* ☎ *617/439–7000 or 800/752–7077,* ℻ *617/ 345–6799. 204 rooms, 26 suites. 2 restaurants, bar, outdoor café, no-smoking rooms, room service, indoor lap pool, beauty salon, spa, health club, concierge, business services, meeting rooms, valet parking. AE, D, DC, MC, V.*

$$$$ 🏨 **Le Meridien Hotel.** Once the Federal Reserve Building, this 1922 Re-
★ naissance Revival landmark in the center of the Financial District still exudes an almost intimidating aura of money and power—everyone seems to be suit-clad even on weekends (does anyone *ever* stay here with kids?), and Julien (☞ Downtown *in* Chapter 4), one of the city's best French restaurants, demands jacket and tie. But there's a hidden light side: the informal Café Fleuri hosts an all-chocolate buffet each Saturday afternoon. The lobby glows with beige marble and royal reds. Most rooms, including some cleverly designed bilevel, skylighted suites, have queen-size or king-size beds; all have a small sitting area. Small pets are permitted. ✉ *250 Franklin St., 02110,* ☎ *617/451–1900 or 800/543–4300,* ℻ *617/423–2844. 309 rooms, 17 suites. 2 restaurants, 2 bars, in-room data ports, minibars, no-smoking floors, room service, indoor pool, health club, laundry service and dry cleaning, concierge, parking (fee). AE, D, DC, MC, V.*

$$$$ 🏨 **The Regal Bostonian.** The small luxury hotel intriguingly blends old
★ and new: the Harkness Wing, built as a warehouse in 1824, has 42 rooms with working fireplaces and exposed beamed ceilings, whereas rooms in the newer wing are done in light woods, crackle finishes, and soft yellows and blues. Every room has live plants and 88 have balconies with window boxes. The hotel is adjacent to Government Center (its restaurant overlooks Quincy Market); request a room facing away from the street if you'd rather not awaken with Quincy Market at dawn. Rates include complimentary access to a nearby health club. Children under 16 stay free in their parents' room. ✉ *Faneuil Hall Marketplace, 02109,* ☎ *617/523–3600 or 800/343–0922,* ℻ *617/523–2454. 152 rooms, 11 suites. Restaurant, lobby lounge, in-room data ports, no-smoking rooms, room service, laundry service and dry cleaning, concierge, valet parking. AE, D, DC, MC, V.*

$$$–$$$$ 🏨 **Omni Parker House.** As the oldest continuously operating hotel in America, the Parker House practically radiates history. The original building opened in 1856 and counted Charles Dickens and actress Sarah Bernhardt among its guests; the current hotel went up in 1927. A 1998 renovation reinstated a Colonial style in both the lobby and guest rooms, and furniture was custom-built to accommodate the guest rooms' small size. A rooftop grand ballroom overlooks the city. The Parker House is known for two things: Parker House rolls and Boston cream pie, both of which were invented here. (The rolls and cream-filled cake are still served in the restaurant, as is a bountiful Sunday brunch.) Appropriately, this historic hotel stands opposite old City Hall, right on the Freedom Trail. ✉ *60 School St., 02108,* ☎ *617/227–8600 or 800/843–6664,* ℻ *617/742–5729. 552 rooms, 26 suites. Restaurant, lounge, in-room data ports, room service, baby-sitting, concierge, business services, valet parking. AE, D, DC, MC, V.*

$$$–$$$$ 🏨 **Seaport Hotel.** Poised on the waterfront, this ultramodern hotel is
★ a gleaming addition to an area undergoing massive revitalization. The crisply elegant lobby is decorated in hunter green, mustard, and carrot hues. Jazz plays over a Bose stereo system. Rooms are huge and

have handcrafted cherry furniture, waterfront views, and marble bathrooms as well as state-of-the-art conveniences such as high-speed Internet access, three phones, conference-call capabilities, and caller identification. Those surprised by an unexpected meeting can order a variety of essentials, ranging from silk scarves to boxer shorts, and have them delivered from nearby Filene's Basement. Weekends a van shuttles guests to Faneuil Hall and the Back Bay. A luxurious health club is complete with a 50-ft heated lap pool with an underwater sound system, Cybex weight machines, and aerobics classes. Children under 18 stay free in their parents' room. Small pets are allowed. ⊠ *1 Seaport La. at the World Trade Center, 02110,* ☎ *617/385–4000 or 877/732–7678,* 🖷 *617/385–4001. 401 rooms, 26 suites. Restaurant, lounge, in-room data ports, in-room safes, room service, indoor lap pool, spa, exercise room, baby-sitting, laundry services, concierge, concierge floor, business services, valet parking. AE, D, DC, MC, V.*

**$$–$$$$** 🏨 **Marriott Long Wharf.** This airy, multitiered redbrick hotel juts out into the bay like a big ship (it's meant to look like one) and is convenient to the Aquarium, Quincy Market, and the North End. The hotel abuts Christopher Columbus Park, whose brick walkways and wisteria-covered arches make it one of the most romantic places to stroll in the city. All of the rooms open onto a five-story-high atrium. A small surcharge ($30) will elevate you into concierge class on the top floor, with free Continental breakfast, cocktail hour, and the best views. Children under 18 stay free in their parents' room, and the hotel offers attractive weekend and vacation packages. ⊠ *296 State St., 02109,* ☎ *617/227–0800 or 800/228–9290,* 🖷 *617/227–2867. 400 rooms, 2 suites. 2 restaurants, no-smoking rooms, room service, indoor pool, sauna, health club, recreation room, laundry service and dry cleaning, concierge, business services, meeting rooms, parking (fee). AE, D, DC, MC, V.*

**$$–$$$$** 🏨 **Swissôtel.** Owned by Swissair, this quietly posh, 22-story hotel relishes its European connections. Half the staff speaks German, and it's the only hotel in Boston to offer DeutscheWelle TV, an English-Spanish-German station that broadcasts from Berlin. Public spaces are impeccably formal, from the handsome mahogany lobby glistening with Waterford crystal chandeliers—even in the elevators—to the regal ballroom. Rooms are appointed with Chippendale reproductions. The Swiss connection crops up again in the café, which serves dishes such as muesli and *bundnertellera* (a dried-beef dish) at breakfast. The hotel is on the edge of the former Combat Zone, a neighborhood that can be slightly dicey at night, but the otherwise excellent location is a short stroll from the shops of Downtown Crossing, Boston Common, the Financial District, and the restaurants of Chinatown. Pets are welcome. ⊠ *1 Ave. de Lafayette, 02111,* ☎ *617/451–2600 or 800/621–9200,* 🖷 *617/451–0054. 501 rooms, 23 suites. Restaurant, bar, in-room data ports, no-smoking rooms, room service, indoor pool, health club, laundry service and dry cleaning, concierge, business services, meeting rooms, parking (fee). AE, D, DC, MC, V.*

**$$–$$$** 🏨 **Harborside Inn.** This 19th-century mercantile warehouse less than
★        a block from Faneuil Hall has been transformed into a plush, sedate inn fitted out with exposed brick and granite walls, hardwood floors, Turkish rugs, and Victorian-style furnishings. An eight-story atrium is surrounded by snug, eclectically shaped rooms with queen-size sleigh beds or cherry four-posters. Continental breakfast is included. Children under 12 stay free in their parents' rooms (though the inn is not especially geared toward families). ⊠ *185 State St., 02109,* ☎ *617/723–7500,* 🖷 *617/670–2010. 52 rooms, 2 suites. Restaurant, café, bar, in-room data ports, no-smoking floors, room service, exercise room, concierge. AE, D, DC, MC, V.*

## Kenmore Square

**$$$–$$$$**
**★** 🏨 **The Gryphon House.** The four-story brownstone may date back to the 19th century, but it's relatively new to the lodging scene, having opened in 1997. Each suite is thematically decorated; for instance, one evokes a Victorian parlor, another a medieval castle. Each is rich with amenities—gas fireplace, wet bar, refrigerator, TV/VCR, CD player, free local calls, private voice mail—but best of all are the enormous bathrooms with oversize Kohler tubs and separate showers. Even the staircase is extraordinary: a 19th-century wallpaper mural, "El Dorado," wraps along the walls. (There is no elevator.) Trompe l'oeil paintings and murals by local artist Michael Ernest Kirk decorate the common spaces and some rooms. Free Continental breakfast is served in the lobby. The rooftop is a prime viewing spot for Fourth of July fireworks. ⊠ *9 Bay State Rd., 02215,* ☎ *617/375–9003,* ℻ *617/425–0716. 8 suites. No-smoking rooms, in-room data ports, free parking. AE, D, DC, MC, V.*

**$$–$$$$** 🏨 **Howard Johnson's Kenmore Square.** Boston University's campus, Fenway Park, and the city's vibrant nightlife scene stretched along Lansdowne Street are all nearby. Most rooms offer balcony views of the city or the Charles River. A major plus is the free parking, a rare commodity in this car-crammed city. Children under 18 stay free in their parents' room. Small pets are allowed. One note of caution: because of its proximity to BU, the hotel can fill up with students, especially during breaks, and they may not share your desire for a peaceful night's sleep (although the hotel claims to control noise levels by concentrating students in one section of the building). ⊠ *575 Commonwealth Ave., 02215,* ☎ *617/267–3100 or 800/654–2000,* ℻ *617/ 424–1045. 170 rooms. Restaurant, lobby lounge, in-room data ports, no-smoking rooms, indoor pool, baby-sitting, free parking. AE, D, DC, MC, V.*

**$–$$** 🏨 **Hotel Buckminster.** Once a residential hotel, the Buckminster is now an economical European-style inn, with maids but no bellhops. The hotel is sparsely furnished and a bit worn around the edges but clean and serviceable. Although the hotel doesn't have its own restaurant, there's a branch of Pizzeria Uno and a sushi restaurant in the same building; Kenmore Square itself has plenty of dining options. It's a short walk from here to the nightlife of Lansdowne Street and the grassy outfield of Fenway Park. ⊠ *645 Beacon St., 02215,* ☎ *617/236–7050 or 800/727–2825,* ℻ *617/262–0068. 120 rooms. AE, D, DC, MC, V.*

## Old West End

**$$–$$$$** 🏨 **Holiday Inn Select Boston Government Center.** A business-class hotel with improvements in the works, this branch sits near Massachusetts General Hospital, state and city offices, and Beacon Hill. A brisk 10-minute walk will take you to Faneuil Hall, the FleetCenter, or the Boston Common. Extensive renovations planned at press time for fall 1999 should spruce up the decor, bringing it closer to the level of the chain's top-of-the-line Crowne Plazas. Meeting space on the 15th floor offers a great view of the city through floor-to-ceiling windows. Continental breakfast is included. Children under 12 stay free in their parents' room. ⊠ *5 Blossom St., 02114,* ☎ *617/742–7630 or 800/465–4329,* ℻ *617/742–4192. 290 rooms, 13 suites. Restaurant, bar, in-room data ports, no-smoking floors, room service, pool, exercise room, coin laundry, dry cleaning, concierge, parking (fee). AE, D, DC, MC, V.*

## Theater District

**$$$–$$$$** 🏨 **The Tremont Boston.** The 15-story Tremont, in the center of the Theater District, is a popular home-away-from-home for the casts of current shows. Built in 1925 as the national headquarters for the Benevolent Protective Order of Elks and transformed into a hotel in the 1950s, the building still retains some hints of its past—look for the original Elks Club brass doorknobs in the guest rooms. The lobby strikes a balance between freshness and formality; there are marble columns and a high, coffered ceiling, but modern furniture keeps it from feeling too grand. Rooms are decorated in royal blue, soft burgundy, and gold; although there are no bathtubs, there are sizable showers. The Tremont is also home to Boston's biggest nightclub, the Roxy (☞ Dance Clubs *in* Chapter 6). ⊠ *275 Tremont St., 02116,* ☎ *617/426–1400 or 800/ 331–9998,* ℻ *617/482–6730. 322 rooms, 25 suites. Restaurant, inroom data ports, no-smoking floors, room service, exercise room, nightclub, laundry service and dry cleaning, concierge, meeting rooms, parking (fee). AE, D, DC, MC, V.*

# Boston Outskirts

## Brighton

**$–$$**  🖭 **Best Western Terrace Inn.** Incongruously sited in a residential neighborhood between Boston University and Boston College, on the line dividing Boston from Brookline, this motel is well priced and well maintained. Twenty-two rooms have kitchenettes, and there's a supermarket two blocks away. A free Continental breakfast is served in the lobby. The T is less than a block away. And with its ethnic shops, cafés, and Olmsted and Kennedy sights [☞ The "Streetcar Suburbs" *in* Chapter 2], Brookline itself is worth exploring. Children under 18 stay free in their parents' room. ⊠ *1650 Commonwealth Ave., 02135,* ☎ *617/566– 6260 or 800/242–8377,* ℻ *617/731–3543. 66 rooms, 6 suites. Free parking. AE, D, DC, MC, V.*

## Dorchester

**$$$**  🖭 **Holiday Inn Express.** If you're passing through town, this could be a convenient option—it's just off the Southeast Expressway. The neighborhood is more commercial than scenic, but you can see the Boston skyline from one of four suites on the sixth floor. (These suites also have whirlpool baths.) Rooms have a burgundy and green color scheme. Although there is no on-premises restaurant, the hotel serves a complimentary Continental breakfast. It's a five-minute walk to public transportation into the city; shuttles to the airport (4 mi away) are free. Children under 18 stay free in their parents' room. ⊠ *69 Boston St., 02125,* ☎ *617/288–3030,* ℻ *617/265–6543. 110 rooms, 8 suites. Laundry service, free parking. AE, D, DC, MC, V.*

**$$**  🖭 **Susse Chalet Motor Lodges.** Bordering on the Boston-Dorchester line, this halved hotel is just off I–93. (The two buildings are a half-mile away from each other.) Renovations completed in 1998 added a fifth floor with 18 suites and an atrium restaurant to the 900 building. Kids can hit the 90-game arcade room. A complimentary shuttle whisks guests to the T to downtown Boston. Children under 18 stay free in their parents' room. ⊠ *800 and 900 Morrissey Blvd., 02122,* ☎ *617/287–9100 or 617/287–9200,* ℻ *617/265–9287 or 617/282–2365. 280 rooms, 28 suites. 3 restaurants, piano bar, pool, coin laundry, free parking. AE, D, DC, MC, V.*

## Logan Airport (East Boston)

**$$$–$$$$**  🖭 **Holiday Inn Boston Airport.** This hotel planned several in-room perks with businesspeople in mind, such as ergonomic desks and chairs and modems. It's 1½ mi from the airport, and so not close to any attractions. For views of Boston or the airport, ask for a room above the seventh floor. The hotel's "Park and Fly" package allows you to leave your car free for up to 10 days, after staying one night at the inn. Children under 18 stay free in their parents' room. ⊠ *225 McClellan Hwy., East Boston 02128,* ☎ *617/569–5250 or 800/798–5849,* ℻ *617/*

*569–5159. 356 rooms. Restaurant, bar, no-smoking rooms, room service, pool, exercise room, airport shuttle. AE, D, DC, MC, V.*

**$$–$$$$** 🏨 **Hilton Boston Logan Airport** At press time, this hotel was slated to open in September 1999 on the grounds of Logan Airport. The designers of the V-shaped, 10-story building had airport convenience in mind, with a 24-hour shuttle service plus direct connection to some terminals via a skybridge. ✉ *75 Service Rd., 02128,* ☎ *617/569–4031,* ℻ *617/561–4485. 600 rooms, 3 suites. Restaurant, lounge, coffee bar, room service, indoor pool, spa, health club, concierge floor, business services, meeting rooms. AE, D, DC, MC, V.*

**$$–$$$** 🏨 **Hyatt Harborside at Boston International Logan Airport.** A 15-story glass structure punctuates this luxury hotel, which perches on a point of land separating Boston Harbor from the Atlantic Ocean. Half of the rooms have sweeping views of either the Boston skyline or the ocean. It's easy to get anywhere from here; the Hyatt operates its own shuttle to all Logan Airport terminals and the Airport T stop, and guests get a discount on the water shuttle that runs between the airport and downtown. All floors but one are no-smoking, and all rooms are soundproof. The restaurant puts on a chocolate buffet each night starting at 5 PM. ✉ *101 Harborside Dr., 02128,* ☎ *617/568–1234 or 800/233–1234,* ℻ *617/567–8856. 270 rooms, 11 suites. Restaurant, bar, in-room data ports, room service, indoor pool, sauna, exercise room, laundry service and dry cleaning, concierge, business services, parking (fee). AE, D, DC, MC, V.*

## Cambridge

**$$$$** 🏨 **Cambridge Center Marriott Hotel.** This modern 26-story hotel in Kendall Square, Cambridge's high-tech district, is just steps from MIT and the subway. It's also a prime location for viewing Fourth of July fireworks. Rooms are decorated in the Marriott chain's signature greens. The city's best cineplex, Kendall Square Cinemas (☞ Film *in* Chapter 6), is a short walk away. Children under 18 stay free in their parents' room. ✉ *2 Cambridge Center, 02142,* ☎ *617/494–6600 or 800/228–9290,* ℻ *617/494–0036. 419 rooms, 12 suites. 2 restaurants, lobby lounge, in-room data ports, no-smoking rooms, room service, indoor pool, sauna, exercise room, dry cleaning, concierge floors, business services, meeting rooms, parking (fee). AE, D, DC, MC, V.*

**$$$$**
**★** 🏨 **The Charles Hotel.** You can't stay much closer to the center of Harvard Square than at this first-class hotel adjacent to the Kennedy School of Government. The interior is contemporary, yet homey, with antiques and work by local artists. Guest rooms are supplied with terry robes, quilted down comforters on every bed, and Bose radios instead of standard-issue alarm clocks; suites have fireplaces. If you're looking for a river or skyline view, ask for something above the seventh floor. If you haven't read any good books lately, "Room Service Books" provides prompt delivery of phone orders from Harvard Square's many bookstores. Kids can also dial up a recorded bedtime story. Both restaurants (☞ Rialto, *in* Dining, Cambridge/Somerville, Mediterranean, *above*) are excellent, and the Regattabar (☞ Jazz Clubs *in* Chapter 6) attracts world-class musicians. ✉ *1 Bennett St., 02138,* ☎ *617/864–1200 or 800/882–1818,* ℻ *617/864–5715. 296 rooms, 44 suites. 2 restaurants, 2 bars, in-room data ports, in-room safes, minibars, no-smoking rooms, room service, pool, spa, health club, nightclub, babysitting, laundry service and dry cleaning, concierge, business services, parking (fee). AE, DC, MC, V.*

**$$$$** 🏨 **Hyatt Regency.** A glass-walled elevator ascends through the central 14-story atrium of this dramatic ziggurat on the Charles River to a revolving rooftop lounge and restaurant. Sixty-six rooms have external

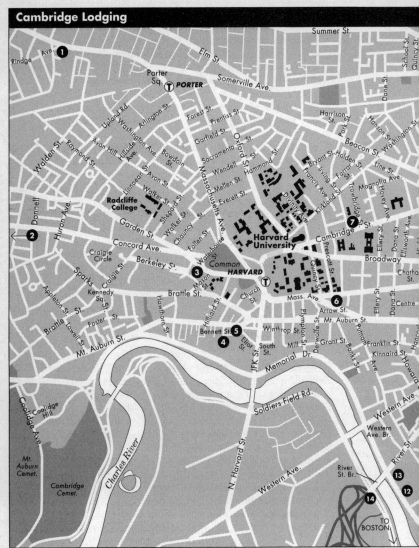

Cambridge Center
Marriott Hotel, **10**

A Cambridge House
Bed and Breakfast, **1**

The Charles Hotel, **4**

Doubletree Guest
Suites, **14**

Harding House, **8**

Harvard Square
Hotel, **5**

Howard Johnson's
Cambridge, **13**

Hyatt Regency, **12**

Inn at Harvard, **6**

Irving House, **7**

Royal Sonesta
Hotel, **11**

Sheraton
Commander, **3**

Susse Chalet Inn, **2**

University Park
Hotel, **9**

private balconies, and 33 have views of Boston across the river. Ask for an "06" room and you'll get a river view and an interior balcony at no extra charge. The indoor-outdoor exercise room includes a retractable glass roof and deck for stationary bikes. A complimentary shuttle makes the rounds of major sights in Boston and Cambridge. Children under 18 stay free in their parents' room. ⊠ *575 Memorial Dr., 02139,* ☎ *617/492–1234 or 800/233–1234,* ℻ *617/491–6906. 469 rooms, 10 suites. 2 restaurants, sports bar, in-room data ports, no-smoking floors, room service, indoor-outdoor pool, health club, bicycles, laundry service and dry cleaning, concierge floor, business center, parking (fee). AE, D, DC, MC, V.*

$$$$ 🏨 **University Park Hotel.** With a remarkable attention to detail, this
★      hotel combines high-tech design and a sense of humor to create a tribute to MIT. The hotel, owned by MIT and managed by Doubletree, is hard by the university. Technology references crop up everywhere—step into one of the elevators and you'll find its carpet patterned with metric symbols. Meeting rooms are named for MIT notables. Maple armoires in the guest rooms are inlaid with recycled computer circuit boards. (Rooms also have floor-to-ceiling windows and ergonomically designed furniture.) Art on loan from the MIT collection and the DeCordova Museum hangs in both the public spaces and guest rooms. In the ultramodern lobby and restaurant, chrome, copper, and zinc pair off with burnished maple, redwood, and oak. If you have a meeting planned on a distractingly beautiful day, you can run up to the third-floor rooftop garden. Children under 18 stay free in their parents' room. ⊠ *20 Sidney St., 02139,* ☎ *617/577–0200 or 800/222–8733,* ℻ *617/ 494–8366. 182 rooms, 28 suites. Restaurant, in-room data ports, no-smoking rooms, room service, exercise room, library, dry cleaning, concierge floors, business services, meeting rooms, parking (fee). AE, D, DC, MC, V.*

$$$–$$$$ 🏨 **Inn at Harvard.** You don't have to be a student or alumnus to enjoy
★      the feeling of a stay at Harvard. This hotel borders Harvard Yard, and its Georgian-style brick exterior mirrors the design of Harvard's own buildings. The lobby opens onto a sculpture-studded living room and atrium. Original 17th- and 18th-century sketches, on loan from the Fogg Art Museum, hang in the guest rooms, along with contemporary watercolors. Oversize windows frame views of Harvard Square or Harvard Yard; many rooms have tiny balconies as well. Guests have access to the Cambridge YMCA a few blocks away in Central Square. ⊠ *1201 Massachusetts Ave., 02138,* ☎ *617/491–2222 or 800/458– 5886,* ℻ *617/491–6520. 109 rooms, 4 suites. Restaurant, in-room data ports, no-smoking floors, room service, dry cleaning, business services, parking (fee). AE, D, DC, MC, V.*

$$$–$$$$ 🏨 **Royal Sonesta Hotel.** The Sonesta's East Cambridge location makes
★      it a good base for visiting the Museum of Science or strolling along the Charles. The 10-floor building offers superb views of Beacon Hill across the Charles River. An impressive collection of modern art spreads throughout the hotel; rooms are mellowed with earth tones. Children under 18 stay free in their parents' room, and the hotel offers great family excursion packages that include boat rides, ice cream, and bicycles. ⊠ *5 Cambridge Pkwy., 02142,* ☎ *617/806–4200 or 800/766– 3782,* ℻ *617/806–4232. 374 rooms, 26 suites. 2 restaurants, 2 bars, in-room data ports, in-room safes, minibars, no-smoking rooms, room service, indoor-outdoor pool, spa, health club, bicycles, dry cleaning, business services, parking (fee). AE, D, DC, MC, V.*

$$$–$$$$ 🏨 **Sheraton Commander.** This sedate brick hotel named for George Washington is near the point where he took command of the Continental Army. It overlooks Cambridge Common and is just a block from Harvard Yard. Rooms are decorated in Colonial style, often with four-

poster beds. Children under 16 stay free in their parents' room. ✉ *16 Garden St., 02238,* ☎ *617/547–4800 or 800/325–3535,* FAX *617/868–8322. 162 rooms, 13 suites. Restaurant, kitchenettes, no-smoking floor, exercise room, concierge, business services, free parking. AE, D, DC, MC, V.*

**$$–$$$$** ⊞ **Howard Johnson's Cambridge.** This hotel's interior may be standard HoJo, but the location gives it an edge. On summer Sundays, the nearby stretch of Memorial Drive is closed to traffic, becoming a favorite place for biking and in-line skating. Try to snag one of the 32 rooms with balconies overlooking the Charles River. Children under 18 stay free in their parents' room. Pets are allowed. ✉ *777 Memorial Dr., 02139,* ☎ *617/492–7777 or 800/654–2000,* FAX *617/492–6038. 203 rooms, 1 suite. 2 restaurants, 2 bars, no-smoking floors, indoor pool, laundry service, free parking. AE, D, DC, MC, V.*

**$$–$$$** ⊞ **Harvard Square Hotel.** Casual and family-friendly, this hotel is an affordable option in a choice location: the heart of Harvard Square. Burgundy and peach decor warms up the rooms. Children under 16 stay free in their parents' room. ✉ *110 Mt. Auburn St., 02138,* ☎ *617/864–5200 or 800/458–5886,* FAX *617/864–2409. 73 rooms. Café, in-room data ports, no-smoking rooms, car rental, parking (fee). AE, D, DC, MC, V.*

**$$**
**★** ⊞ **Doubletree Guest Suites.** Technically, this 15-story hotel, just off Storrow Drive and overlooking the Charles River, is in Boston, but it's actually handier to Cambridge—just a half mile from Harvard Square. Each unit has a living room (with refrigerator and sofa bed), a bedroom with a king-size bed, and a bathroom with a phone. Most suites have views of the Charles River or the Cambridge or Boston skyline. The excellent Sculler's Jazz Club (☞ *Jazz in* Chapter 6) is one of the best places in town to catch a national act. A courtesy van runs to the city's historic sites. Children under 18 stay free in their parents' room. ✉ *400 Soldiers Field Rd., Boston 02134,* ☎ *617/783–0090 or 800/222–8733,* FAX *617/783–0897. 305 suites, 5 bi-level penthouses. Restaurant, bar, in-room data ports, minibars, no-smoking rooms, refrigerators, room service, indoor pool, sauna, exercise room, nightclub, laundry service and dry cleaning, concierge, parking (fee). AE, D, DC, MC, V.*

**$** ⊞ **Susse Chalet Inn.** This is a typical Susse Chalet operation: clean, economical, and spare. It is isolated from most shopping and attractions, being a 10-minute drive from Harvard Square, but it is within walking distance of the Red Line terminus, offering T access to Boston and Cambridge sights. A free Continental breakfast is served in the lobby. ✉ *211 Concord Turnpike, 02140,* ☎ *617/661–7800 or 800/524–2538,* FAX *617/868–8153. 78 rooms. In-room data ports, no-smoking rooms, coin laundry, dry cleaning, free parking. AE, D, DC, MC, V.*

# BED-AND-BREAKFASTS

## Agencies

Despite their names, many of the following agencies also handle apartment, cottage, and house rentals throughout greater Boston and on the North and South shores.

⊞ **ABC: Accommodations of Boston and Cambridge** (✉ 335 Pearl St., Cambridge 02139, ☎ 617/491–0274 or 800/253–5542, FAX 617/547–5478) lists private homes in Cambridge, Boston, and Charlestown.

⊞ **Bed & Breakfast Agency of Boston** (✉ 47 Commercial Wharf, Boston 02110, ☎ 617/720–3540 or 800/248–9262, FAX 617/523–5761) lists 140 guest rooms, private homes, and furnished apartments.

⊡ **Bed & Breakfast Associates Bay Colony Ltd.** (⊠ Box 57166, Babson Park Branch, Boston 02457, ☎ 781/449–5302 or 800/347–5088, FAX 617/449–5958) has more than 150 listings in Boston, Cambridge, the North and South shores, and Cape Cod and the islands.

⊡ **Bed and Breakfast Cambridge and Greater Boston** (⊠ Box 1344, Cambridge 02238, ☎ 617/262–1155 or 800/888–0178, FAX 508/775–2884) lists rooms and unhosted apartments in 60 homes in Cambridge, Boston, and the suburbs.

⊡ **Bed and Breakfast Cape Cod** (⊠ Box 1312, Orleans 02653, ☎ 508/255–3824 or 800/541–6226, FAX 508/775–2884) has 175 lodgings on the Cape, Martha's Vineyard, and Nantucket.

⊡ **Bed and Breakfast Reservations: North Shore/Greater Boston/Cape Cod** (Box 600035, Newtonville 02460, ☎ 617/964–1606; 800/832–2632 outside MA, FAX 617/332–8572) handles vacation rentals and weekly rentals at B&Bs, houses, and apartments. There's a two-night minimum stay.

⊡ **Bettina Network, Inc.** (⊠ Box 380, Cambridge 02238, ☎ 617/497–9166 or 800/347–9166), a national organization, offers a lodging and events service for a network of private homes and inns.

⊡ **Cambridge Discovery** (☎ 617/497–1630), a kiosk in Harvard Square, lists a few dozen B&Bs in the Cambridge area.

⊡ **Citywide Reservations Services** (⊠ 839 Beacon St., Suite A, Boston 02115, ☎ 617/267–7424 or 800/468–3593) books rooms at inns, B&Bs, and hotels all over greater Boston.

⊡ **Host Homes of Boston** (⊠ Box 117, Waban Branch, Boston 02468, ☎ 617/244–1308 or 800/600–1308, FAX 617/244–5156) has listings for about 40 homes in Boston, Cambridge, Brookline, and Newton and around Route 128.

⊡ **New England Bed and Breakfast** (⊠ Box 1426, Waltham 02454, ☎ 617/244–2112) lists 20 homes in Boston, Cambridge, and other New England towns.

## B&Bs

### Boston

$$$–$$$$ ⊡ **Beacon Hill Bed and Breakfast.** Staying at this six-story Victorian row house on Beacon Hill will give you a tiny taste of the elegant Brahmin lifestyle. The front overlooks the Gothic Revival Church of the Advent and a narrow cobblestone street with gaslights. From the rear, bay windows look out on the Charles River Esplanade. The three guest rooms are huge, with built-in bookcases, couches, Victorian antiques, and private bathrooms. Parking is scarce, but shops, restaurants, and the T are all within walking distance. ⊠ *27 Brimmer St., Boston 02108, ☎ 617/523–7376. 3 rooms. Full breakfast. No smoking. No credit cards.*

$$ ⊡ **Clarendon Square Inn.** A gut rehab in 1998 transformed an 1860 row house into an inn with 19-ft by 18-ft marble-fireplaced rooms with private baths containing whirlpools or two-person showers. On the fifth floor is a roof deck with a view of the Boston skyline. The minimum stay is two nights; longer stays are discounted. Continental breakfast is included. Children "of well-behaved parents" are welcome. As with most South End establishments, the Clarendon Square is gay-friendly. ⊠ *198 W. Brookline St., Boston 02118, ☎ 617/536–2229. 3 rooms. Air-conditioning. No smoking. AE, D, MC, V.*

$$ ⊡ **Newbury Guest House.** This elegant redbrick and brownstone row
★ house was built in 1882, opened as a B&B in 1991, and expanded in 1994. It's wildly successful because it's smartly managed, well furnished, and ideally located on Boston's most fashionable shopping street, so be sure to book two to three months in advance. Rooms with queen-

size beds, natural pine floors, and elegant reproduction Victorian furnishings open off a carved oak staircase, and prints from the Museum of Fine Arts enliven the walls. A complimentary Continental breakfast is offered. Limited parking is available at $15 for 24 hours, a good deal for a Boston hotel, especially on Newbury Street. ⊠ *261 Newbury St., Boston 02116,* ☎ *617/437–7666 or 800/437–7668,* FAX *617/262–4243. 32 rooms. Parking (fee). AE, D, DC, MC, V.*

**$–$$$** ⊞ **82 Chandler St.** The 1863 redbrick row house in Boston's South End
★ is just a five-minute walk from Copley Square and Amtrak's Back Bay station. Each room is color-coordinated in green, red, blue, or yellow and is accessible via the four-story main staircase; all are spacious and sunny and have pedestal sinks, Oriental rugs, and private baths. Standard rooms have a discreetly placed kitchen area with refrigerator and microwave oven. The best room—whose wide bay windows overlook downtown—is on the top floor and has a working fireplace and a skylight in the bathroom. There are also two studio apartments, rented out by the week or by month; these have queen-size beds and private baths. One has a television. Continental breakfast is included. Like this alternative, yuppie, racially mixed neighborhood, 82 Chandler is gay-friendly. ⊠ *82 Chandler St., Boston 02115,* ☎ *617/482–0408. 3 rooms, 2 studios. Air-conditioning. No smoking. No credit cards.*

## Boston Outskirts

**$** ⊞ **Beacon Inns.** A B&B budget option, these two guest houses in the streetcar suburb of Brookline, owned by the same family, are convenient to several local colleges, restaurants, and the T, which stops just outside and will get you downtown in 15 minutes. 1087 Beacon Street is a Victorian brick town house with period detailing and large rooms; 1750 Beacon Street was renovated in 1998. Parking is available and inexpensive. ⊠ *1087 and 1750 Beacon St., Brookline 02146,* ☎ *617/566–0088 or 888/575–0088,* FAX *617/397–9267. 1087: 11 rooms, 8 with bath; 1750: 13 rooms, 6 with bath. Parking (fee). AE, MC, V.*

## Cambridge

**$$–$$$$** ⊞ **A Cambridge House Bed and Breakfast.** A gracious 1892 Greek Revival home listed on the National Register of Historic Places, A Cambridge House is on busy Massachusetts Avenue but set well back from the road. Inside, it's a haven of peace and otherworldliness, with richly carved cherry paneling, a grand mahogany fireplace, elegant Victorian antiques, and polished wood floors overlaid with Oriental rugs. The best of the 16 antiques-filled guest rooms is referred to as "the suite" (actually one room), with fabric-covered walls, a working fireplace, and a four-poster canopy bed. Rooms in the adjacent carriage house, however, are small. There's a reservations center here for other host homes in the area. Harvard Square is a distant walk, but public transportation is nearby. ⊠ *2218 Massachusetts Ave., Cambridge 02140,* ☎ *617/491–6300 or 800/232–9989,* FAX *617/868–2848. 16 rooms, 12 with bath. Full breakfast. Free parking. No smoking. MC, V.*

**$$–$$$** ⊞ **Harding House.** It may not be swarming with period details, but this 1867 inn combines the charm of a B&B with the reliability of a hotel. Sunlight streams into the three-story atrium through stained glass and skylights. Rooms have high ceilings but are otherwise standard. Coffee, tea, and cookies are served all day in the dining room. The house is halfway between Harvard and MIT; you can walk four blocks to funky Central Square. Continental breakfast is included. Children under 6 stay free in their parents' room. ⊠ *288 Harvard St., Cambridge 02139,* ☎ *617/876–2888,* FAX *617/497–0953. 14 rooms. Free parking. No smoking. MC, V.*

**$–$$$** ⊞ **Irving House.** A notch above student living, this four-story gray clap-
board B&B is still a bargain. Tucked away on a residential street just
three blocks from Harvard Square, it has two small porches and a sunny
foyer with lace curtains, hardwood floors, and Oriental carpets, giv-
ing it a homier feel than a hotel. Renovations planned at press time
for 1999 will add five much-needed private bathrooms and update eight
old ones. Fresh carpeting and lighting should also help brighten the
place. Continental breakfast is included. Children 6 and under stay free,
and those aged 7–15 stay at a discount. There's even limited free off-
street parking, a real coup in car-clogged Cambridge. ⊠ *24 Irving St.,
Cambridge 02138,* ☎ *617/547–4600,* FAX *617/576–2814. 44 rooms,
10 with shared bath. Air-conditioning, free parking. No smoking. AE,
D, MC, V.*

# HOSTELS

**Greater Boston Council of American Youth Hostels** (⊠ 1020B Com-
monwealth Ave., Boston 02215, ☎ 617/731–5430) provides information
on membership and on hostels in the Boston area.

## Boston

**$** ⊞ **Hostelling International Boston.** Run by American Youth Hostels,
this low-cost option near the Museum of Fine Arts is ideal if you don't
mind sharing space with strangers (although a few private rooms are
available for a higher price). Guests sleep four to six people to a dor-
mitory with shared bath. Linens are provided. The maximum stay is
14 days, and the hostel is open 24 hours. Two fully equipped kitchens
are available. The staff is multilingual. AYH membership is not required.
Member or not, it's best to make reservations. ⊠ *12 Hemenway St.,
02115,* ☎ *617/536–9455,* FAX *617/424–6558. Capacity 205. Lounge,
kitchenette. MC, V.*

# YMCAS AND YWCAS

## Boston

**$** ⊞ **Berkeley Residence YWCA Boston.** Settle in where the Back Bay meets
the South End. This facility has single ($48), double ($74), and triple
($84) rooms for adult women only; nonmembers pay a $2 surcharge.
Long-term stays are $142 per week, which includes breakfast and din-
ner. The desk is staffed around the clock. A dining room serves inex-
pensive meals. Guests have access to an indoor pool. The Back Bay T
station (which also serves Amtrak) is just a block away. For stays of
more than a few nights, you must apply at least one week in advance.
⊠ *40 Berkeley St., 02116,* ☎ *617/482–8850,* FAX *617/482–9692. 200
rooms with shared baths. Lounge, laundry. MC, V.*

**$** ⊞ **Greater Boston YMCA.** This is a great summer option (it's open to
guests only between June and September). The coed facility near the
Museum of Fine Arts has single ($38), double ($56), and triple ($76)
rooms. Besides free breakfast, you'll have in-room TV and excellent
fitness facilities. You must write in advance to reserve a room, espe-
cially if you plan to bring children. ⊠ *316 Ave. of the Arts, 02115,* ☎
*617/536–7800. 180 rooms, most with shared baths. Cafeteria, indoor
pool, sauna, health club, indoor track, coin laundry. MC, V.*

# 6 NIGHTLIFE AND THE ARTS

## INCLUDING CAFÉS AND COFFEEHOUSES

From cafés to concert halls, churches to comedy clubs, Boston offers as wide a variety of entertainment as you'll find in any American metropolis. For devotees of high art, a night out can mean Bach cantatas performed by an early music group at a small church, Beethoven at the BSO, a Broadway-bound show in the Theater District, or a film classic at a Cambridge repertory house. Night crawlers can start the evening at a neighborhood café or bar and move on to one of the city's many comedy, jazz, rock, or dance clubs. Whether it's high culture or low life you're after, New England's liveliest cultural calendar has something to please everyone.

**B**OSTON HAS ALWAYS HAD AN ACTIVE—and traditional—performing arts circuit, but in recent years it has been rewired to reflect the adventurous influence of college students, ethnic immigrants, city newcomers, and the increasingly visible gay community. Good sources of information are the *Boston Globe* "Calendar" section and the weekly listings of the *Boston Phoenix* (both published on Thursday). The Friday Music and Sunday Arts sections in the *Boston Globe* also contain recommendations for the week's top events. *Boston* magazine's "On the Town" feature gives a somewhat less detailed but useful monthly overview.

By Jeanne Cooper

Updated by Anne Stuart

Boston's supporters of the arts are an avid group, and tickets often sell out well in advance, particularly for the increasing number of shows making pre-Broadway stops. If you want to attend a specific performance, it is wise to buy tickets when you make your hotel reservations. Most theaters and music presenters will take telephone orders and charge them to a major credit card, generally with a service fee of several dollars per ticket. If you order far enough in advance, your tickets will be mailed to you; otherwise they will be held at the box office.

**Bostix** is Boston's official entertainment information center and the city's largest ticket agency. It is a full-price Ticketmaster outlet, and, beginning at 11 AM, it sells half-price tickets for same-day performances; the "menu board" in front of the booth announces the available events. Only cash and traveler's checks are accepted. People often begin lining up well before the agency opens. ⊠ *Faneuil Hall Marketplace,* ☎ *617/723–5181 recorded message.* ☉ *Tues.–Sat. 10–6, Sun. 11–4.* ⊠ *Copley Sq., near corner of Boylston and Dartmouth Sts.* ☉ *Mon.–Sat. 10–6, Sun. 11–4.*

**NEXT Ticketing** (☎ 617/423–6398), a Boston-based outlet, handles tickets for shows at the Harborlights and Great Woods outdoor performance centers, the Orpheum Theatre, and Avalon and other nightclubs. The service, which uses a completely automated 24-hour ticket reservation system, also sells tickets online.

**Ticketmaster** (☎ 617/931–2000 or 617/931–2787) allows phone charges to major credit cards, weekdays 9 AM–10 PM, weekends 9–8, with no refunds or exchanges. It also has outlets in local stores; call for nearest address.

Keep in mind that Huntington Avenue has been rechristened Avenue of the Arts but that locals may still use the old name.

# NIGHTLIFE

Boston is a city segregated into neighborhoods, and its nightclubs are divided into crowds. Armani-clad international students head out late, after taking over one of the chichi restaurants on Newbury Street for preclubbing martinis. After dinner, they press $50 bills into the palms of doormen to get in ahead of the queue, and spend 1 AM to 2 AM swilling champagne and grinding to imported techno at a downtown club. Baseball cap–sporting students fill up clubs and pubs along Lansdowne Street, and hipsters bar-hop from Cambridge clubs to Kenmore Square to catch live bands. Some clubs do double duty, scheduling live music early, then packing in a late-night dance crowd. "Theme" nights change frequently, as do clientele, so call first or check Thursday's *Boston Globe* "Calendar" or the *Boston Phoenix*. Cover charges for local acts and club bands generally run from $5 to $15; big-name acts can be double that. Dance clubs average a $5–$10 cover charge.

Most bars open daily for lunch around 11:30. Because Boston retains some vestiges of its puritanical "blue laws," the only places open after the official 2 AM bar-closing time are a few 24-hour IHOPs, restaurants in Chinatown, and all-night diners. Bars may also close up shop early if business is slow or the weather is bad. Blue laws also prohibit bars from offering happy-hour drink specials or encouraging end-of-the-night imbibing by saying "last call." Smokers should be aware that Boston's tough anti-cigarette law bans smoking in restaurants, except in bar areas segregated from main dining areas. Some bars and clubs allow people under 21; some don't; and some alternate. Nearly all accept major credit cards; cash-only places are noted.

## Bars

### Boston

**Atrium Lounge** (✉ Bostonian Hotel, North and Blackstone Sts., ☎ 617/523–3600) is an elegant room overlooking Faneuil Hall Marketplace. A pianist plays nightly from 5 to 9; there's a band or cabaret act on Friday and Saturday nights.

**Bay Tower Room** (✉ 60 State St., ☎ 617/723–1666). By day, it's a private corporate dining room on the 33rd floor of a landmark skyscraper in the Financial District. By night, you can sip a cocktail and watch the sun set through windows two stories high. There's piano music Wednesday–Saturday nights and dancing on Friday and Saturday. (It's closed on Sunday.) It's a jacket-and-tie kind of place.

**Black Rose** (✉ 160 State St., Faneuil Hall, ☎ 617/742–2286). Walking into this Irish pub decorated with family crests, pictures of Ireland, and portraits of the likes of Samuel Beckett, Lady Gregory, and James Joyce is like walking into a pub in Dublin. Its location draws as many tourists as locals, but performances by both traditional and contemporary Celtic performers make it worth braving the crowds.

**Boston Beer Works** (✉ 61 Brookline Ave., Kenmore Sq., ☎ 617/536–2337) is a "naked brewery," with all the works exposed—the tanks, pipes, and gleaming stainless steel and copper kettles used in producing beer. Seasonal brews, in addition to a regular selection, are the draw here for students, young adults, tourists, and fans from nearby Fenway Park. But don't take a first date here; it gets too crowded and noisy for getting-to-know-you chats.

**Bull & Finch Pub** (✉ 84 Beacon St., at Hampshire House, ☎ 617/227–9605) was dismantled in England, shipped to Boston, and reassembled here. This place, the inspiration for the TV series *Cheers,* defines "tourist trap." An crowd of out-of-towners and students often lines up out the door. Live bands and occasional karaoke add to hubbub on weekends.

**Club Café and Lounge** (✉ 209 Columbus Ave., Back Bay/South End, ☎ 617/536–0966) is among the smartest spots in town for gay men and lesbians. The front end of the bar area is popular with suits after work, and there's a stylish contemporary-American restaurant.

**Commonwealth Brewery Co. Ltd.** (✉ 138 Portland St., ☎ 617/523–8383), oldest of Boston's brewpubs, serves a wide selection of ales and tasty barbecue. Choose from an open and noisy upstairs room or a cozier downstairs bar with dartboards and pool tables. It's an easy walk from North Station and the FleetCenter.

**Delux Café & Lounge** (✉ 100 Chandler St., South End, ☎ 617/338–5258) is a perfect spot to mix with locals or to grab a chicken sandwich with homemade chutney. It's decorated with old record album covers and Christmas lights.

**Doyle's Café** (✉ 3484 Washington St., Jamaica Plain, ☎ 617/524–2345) is truly an institution: this friendly, crowded neighborhood Irish pub opened in 1882 and has been a Boston political landmark ever since. Candidates for everything from Boston City Council to the U.S. Senate drop by here to eat corned beef and cabbage, sample one of the 50 brews or single-malt Scotches, and, of course, make speeches and shake hands. Credit cards are not accepted.

**Library Grill at the Hampshire House** (✉ 84 Beacon St., Beacon Hill, ☎ 617/227–9600), above the Bull & Finch Pub (☞ *above*), has the atmosphere of an old Back Bay drawing room, with paneled walls, moose heads, and paintings. There's nightly piano music, a dance combo on Friday and Saturday evenings, and a Sunday jazz brunch.

**Mercury Bar** (✉ 116 Boylston St., Theater District, ☎ 617/482–7799), popular among well-heeled young pros and theatergoers, has a sleek 100-ft bar facing a row of raised, semicircular booths with plush red upholstery and a more private dining room off to the side. Try the extensive tapas menu: anything from mixed olives to sizzling sesame shrimp—food salty or spicy enough to encourage imbibing. Get there early to beat the theater crowd, or call ahead for a reservation.

**Sunset Grill & Tap** (✉ 130 Brighton Ave., Allston, ☎ 617/254–1331) looks at first glance like another unpretentious neighborhood hangout, but it's a beer lover's delight, with nearly 600 varieties to choose from, including more than 100 on tap. Forget about pale domestic brews; try something unpronounceable from a faraway country.

**Top of the Hub** (✉ Prudential Center, Back Bay, ☎ 617/536–1775) is a 52nd-floor lounge with a wonderful view over the entire city; that and the sounds of hip jazz make the pricey drinks worth it.

## Cambridge and Somerville

The **Burren** (✉ 247 Elm St., Somerville, ☎ 617/776–6896) pulls in a devoted local crowd. It's got all the elements of a great Irish bar—Guinness on tap, comfort food such as fish-and-chips and shepherd's pie, and live Irish music nightly—all in a warm, friendly environment.

At the **Cambridge Brewing Co.** (✉ 1 Kendall Sq., Bldg. 100, where Hampshire meets Broadway, ☎ 617/494–1994) microbrewery, try a pint of Cambridge Amber or Charles River porter—or, if you can't decide, a beer sampler. The cavernous joint is cheerful but near-deafening when it fills up; in warm weather, sit outside on the patio. It's a favorite among MIT students and hard-working techies.

**Cantab Lounge** (✉ 738 Massachusetts Ave., near Central Sq., ☎ 617/354–2685) has a local band playing nightly from 9:30 until closing, with a cover charge. Upstairs, Monday and Tuesday are folk and blues nights, and other nights the mix includes rock and jazz. The downstairs bar often hosts poetry slams, open-mike writers' readings, and low-budget cabaret. It's friendly and informal. Credit cards are not accepted.

**Grendel's Den** (✉ 86 Winthrop St., Harvard Sq., ☎ 617/491–1160) is the quintessential college hangout. Though the upstairs restaurant closed in 1999 for renovations, the downstairs bar is little changed since the early 1970s, with the same brick walls and fireplace. And it still offers a "happy hour" when chicken wings, bratwurst sandwiches, and other bar-menu items go for $2. Liquid happy hour runs from 5 to 7:30 PM daily as well as 9 to11:30 PM Sunday–Thursday; there's a $3-per-person drink minimum.

**John Harvard's Brew House** (✉ 33 Dunster St., Harvard Sq., ☎ 617/868–3585) dispenses from behind its long, dark bar a range of ales, lagers, pilsners, and stouts brewed on the premises. It even smells like a real English pub; the food is so-so but plentiful. Stained-glass windows of modern figures add to the mock-antique air.

**Plough & Stars** (✉ 912 Massachusetts Ave., near Central Sq., ☎ 617/441–3455) is a traditional Irish bar with Guinness and Bass on tap and Irish, country, and bluegrass music nightly. It's a comfortable, friendly, noisy place popular with students and a fine place to dine alone. Sometimes there's a cover charge. Credit cards are not accepted.

## Blues/R&B Clubs

**House of Blues** (✉ 96 Winthrop St., Harvard Sq., Cambridge, ☎ 617/491–2583) is co-owned by Dan Aykroyd and the late John Belushi's wife, Judy, plus other celebrity investors. They opened this venue in a ramshackle house in 1992, considering it a local headquarters for blues lovers. In addition to nightly performances by everybody from Taj Mahal to Beverly "Guitar" Watson, there's a gospel brunch on Sunday, plus a museum, store, restaurant, and recording facility. The cover charge varies.

**Johnny D's Uptown** (✉ 17 Holland St., Davis Sq., Somerville, ☎ 617/776–9667) brings an eclectic blend of performers from around the world to play in this restaurant–cum–music hall with a small stage but not a bad seat in the house. Johnny D's headlined swing bands years before they became a country-wide trend; it also lines up Cajun, country, Latin, jazz, blues, and acoustic music and more. Come early for Southern food; stay for the show. Cover varies.

**Marketplace Café** (✉ 300 Faneuil Hall Marketplace, ☎ 617/227–9660) is a "no-cover" treasure in the North Market building amid the bustle of Faneuil Hall. You'll find blues and jazz every night beginning at 9, as well as nouvelle American cuisine.

## Cafés and Coffeehouses

If you just want a cup of coffee, you'll find plenty of Starbucks cafés and Au Bon Pains. However, the atmosphere at most of those establishments won't encourage you to linger. But there is a more welcoming group of cafés and coffeehouses in the city, listed here. Only Club Passim feels like a true old-fashioned coffeehouse, complete with live folk music. At the rest, you can relax in-between or after sightseeing, enjoying your thoughts (or pretending to enjoy those of your date). To eavesdrop on the liveliest conversations—some in Italian—head to the many espresso bars on Hanover Street in the North End.

### Boston

**Caffé Vittoria** (✉ 296 Hanover St., North End, ☎ 617/227–7606) is the biggest and the best of the Italian neighborhood's cafés, with gleaming espresso machines going nonstop. This is a good place to stop for coffee and dessert—think tiramisu, cannoli, gelati—and coffee after a meal in one of the nearby restaurants.

**Other Side Cosmic Café** (✉ 407 Newbury St., ☎ 617/536–9477) perfects the blend of collegiate and funk. Settle in for a good cup of java, a concoction from the fruit and vegetable juice bar, and no-frills soup and sandwiches. The first floor feels like a warehouse; the second floor has low ceilings, red velvet curtains, and mismatched furniture. It's open daily till midnight and does not accept credit cards.

**Roasters** (✉ 85 Newbury St., ☎ 617/867–9967) has outdoor seating for sunny days. Inside is 1930s-sleek, with an art deco–style mural and a huge bay window from which to people-watch while nibbling pastry and sipping coffee roasted on the premises. It's open till 10 PM on weeknights, 11 PM on Friday and Saturday.

**Trident Booksellers Café** (✉ 338 Newbury St., ☎ 617/267–8688) is bohemian-cool with a New Age sensibility. You'll find esoteric books, a great selection of magazines, and a lot of journal-writing. It's open daily till midnight.

## Cambridge

**Algiers Coffee House** (✉ 40 Brattle St., Harvard Sq., ☎ 617/492–1557) is a genuine Middle Eastern café with a choice of strong coffees, teas, and pita-bread lunches. Small, tightly clustered tables fill both floors; upstairs you can peer at the soaring, wood-paneled cathedral ceiling, but nonsmokers should opt for the fresher air downstairs. Service is sluggish; visit when in the mood to linger over conversation or a novel. It's open daily from 8 AM–midnight.

**Club Passim** (✉ 47 Palmer St., Harvard Sq., ☎ 617/492–7679) is one of the country's first and most famous venues for live folk music. The spare, light basement room has tables close together, with wait service, and a separate coffee bar–restaurant counter. It's a nonsmoking venue.

**Someday Café** (✉ 51 Davis Sq., Somerville, ☎ 617/623–3323) is a funky Seattle-style coffeehouse, complete with couches, next to the Somerville Theater right off the Davis Square station on the T's Red Line. The drinks menu is extensive, with Italian sodas and a dozen types of tea alongside the requisite coffees. You can even borrow board games to play. It's open daily 7 AM till 11 PM, except Friday and Saturday, when it closes at midnight; no credit cards are accepted.

**Tealuxe** (✉ Zero Brattle St., Harvard Sq., ☎ 617/441–0077) is a cute-as-a-button "tea bar" with more than 100 different herbal and traditional blends and an assortment of teatime snacks—and just one type of coffee. Savor a cup of Blue Flower Earl Gray or Ginseng Chai. It's open till midnight Thursday–Saturday.

**1369 Coffee House** (✉ 757 Massachusetts Ave., Central Sq., ☎ 617/576–4600) is popular with Cambridge eccentrics and college professors. There are plenty of plugs for laptop work, and the coffee is fresh-brewed in individual pots. It's open 7 AM–11 PM except Sunday, when the hours are 8 AM–10 PM.

# Comedy Clubs

**Comedy Connection** (✉ Faneuil Hall Marketplace, ☎ 617/248–9700) has a mix of local and nationally known acts, seven nights a week (two shows Friday and Saturday), with a cover charge.

**Dick Doherty's Comedy Vault** (✉ 124 Boylston St., Theater District, ☎ 781/938–8088), the flagship of a local comedy-club chain, is tucked away in a former bank vault at Remington's restaurant. It offers sketch, stand-up, and improv comedy. Sunday is open-mike night.

**ImprovBoston** (✉ Back Alley Theater, 1253 Cambridge St., Cambridge, ☎ 617/576–1253) offers performances by the veteran local improv group Guilty Children, Sunday matinee family improvs, and an open-stage cabaret on Thursday nights.

**Nick's Comedy Stop** (✉ 100 Warrenton St., Theater District, ☎ 617/482–0930) presents local comics every night except Monday, and occasionally a well-known comedian pops in. Local boy Jay Leno reportedly got his start here. Reservations advised on weekends; cover charge varies.

# Dance Clubs

**Axis** (✉ 13 Lansdowne St., Kenmore Sq., ☎ 617/262–2424) is one of Boston's largest clubs, with high-energy music and space for more than 1,000 people. Theme nights include Friday's "X Night," a techno session sponsored by hip rock station WFNX, and Sunday's "Gay Night," when Axis and neighboring megaclub Avalon combine and let dancers circulate between the two for one cover charge. Some nights are 18-plus; others are over-21 only. Cover charge varies.

**International** (⊠ 184 High St., Financial District, ☎ 617/542–4747) is a strikingly elegant, multifaceted club in this ordinarily staid neighborhood. Theme nights include jazz, acid jazz, soul, and '70s dance hits. The cover charge varies.

**Joy Boston** (⊠ 533 Washington St., Theater District, ☎ 617/424–7747) draws a fashionable crowd: two levels of wealthy international students and their well-dressed companions move to a techno or acid jazz beat, or occasionally to Greek, Arabic, or Brazilian music—once they make it out of the line to get in. There is a cover charge.

**Man Ray** (⊠ 21 Brookline St., Inman Sq., Cambridge, ☎ 617/864–0400) is the home of Boston's underground scene, where the gothic, glam, and alternative lifestyles indulge in long nights of industrial, house, techno, disco, and trance music. Friday night is "Fetish Night." You needn't participate in the staged spankings—just don't stare. Wear black. It's closed Monday and Tuesday.

The **Roxy** (⊠ 279 Tremont St., Theater District, ☎ 617/338–7699) is Boston's biggest nightclub. The interior resembles an early 20th-century ballroom, but the Roxy is hardly sedate. It throws theme nights such as reggae night, Latin Quarter (salsa and merengue music), swing night (featuring bands such as the Brian Setzer Orchestra and the Squirrel Nut Zippers), and Top 40 night. It also hosts regular magic shows, with an admission charge beyond the usual cover charge.

## Jazz Clubs

Clubs often alternate jazz with other kinds of music; always call ahead for program information and times.

**Regattabar** (⊠ Charles Hotel, Bennett and Eliot Sts., Harvard Sq., ☎ 617/864–1200; 617/876–7777 for tickets) headlines some of the top names in jazz, including Sonny Rollins and Herbie Hancock. Even when there's no entertainment, the spacious, low-ceilinged club is a pleasant (if expensive) place for a drink. Go dressy here.

**Ryles** (⊠ 212 Hampshire St., Inman Sq., Cambridge, ☎ 617/876–9330) has soft lights, mirrors, and greenery to set the mood for first-rate jazz by local and national groups. This is one of the best places for new music and musicians, with a different group playing on each floor. It's open nightly, with a cover charge (no reservations).

**Scullers Jazz Club** (⊠ Doubletree Guest Suites Hotel, 400 Soldiers Field Rd., Allston, ☎ 617/783–0811) hosts well-known acts such as Spyro Gyra, Diana Krall, and Gato Barbieri. Shows are Tuesday through Thursday at 8 and 10 PM and Friday and Saturday at 8:30 and 10:30; reservations are advised. Cover charge varies.

**Turner Fisheries at the Westin** (⊠ Westin Copley Place Hotel, 10 Ave. of the Arts, Copley Sq., ☎ 617/262–9600 or ext. 7425) has live jazz nightly from 8 till midnight. A pianist plays Sunday through Wednesday; Thursday through Saturday the Debra Mann Trio backs varying soloists, and plays till 1 AM. The sleek room is hung with modern art and is adjacent to a handsome oyster bar. There is no cover charge.

**Wally's** (⊠ 427 Massachusetts Ave., ☎ 617/424–1408) is a Boston rarity—a racially well-integrated bar in the South End—with a loyal clientele hooked on jazz and blues. Performers are mostly local musicians. No cover charge.

## Other Attractions

**Cosmic bowling** is a growing trend—it's a souped-up version of bowling, with light shows, videos, loud rock music, and theatrical fog, turning what's long been perceived as a lowbrow pastime into a hip night out. Try it on weekends at **Boston Bowl** (✉ 820 Morrissey Blvd., Dorchester, ☎ 617/825–3800).

**Cybersmith** (✉ 42 Church St., Harvard Sq., Cambridge, ☎ 617/492–5857) is the place to go to check your e-mail, cruise the Web, test-drive CD-ROMs, and play virtual-reality games. You can order—in person or on-line—coffee, juice, sandwiches, and snacks.

**Jillian's** (✉ 145 Ipswich St., Kenmore Sq., ☎ 617/262–0300), a 70,000-square-ft complex on the corner of club-hopping Lansdowne Street, has a pool hall (☞ Billiards *in* Chapter 7) and an arcade with skee ball, pinball, air hockey, and virtual-reality and simulation games (the skiing and snowboarding are particularly addictive). Each floor has a bar. Everything's open until 2 AM.

**Joey & Maria's Comedy Wedding** (✉ Tremont Playhouse, Tremont Hotel, 275 Tremont St., Theater District, ☎ 800/733–5639) is the best-known of the area's many dinner theaters. You'll be a guest at a lavish Italian wedding—dancing, dining on a buffet dinner, then getting drawn into the action as Joey, Maria, and their off-the-wall families are overwhelmed by this special day. Already seen the show? Fast-forward to the next chapter: **Joey & Maria's 25th Wedding Anniversary** (☎ 888/865–2844) in Andover, roughly 35 to 45 minutes by car north of downtown Boston.

# Rock Clubs

**Avalon** (✉ 15 Lansdowne St., Kenmore Sq., ☎ 617/262–2424), known for its state-of-the-art sound and light systems, hosts live concerts; recent performers range from Liz Phair to Seal to the Goo Goo Dolls. After the show, it turns into a dance club, pulling students and twentysomething internationals under the spinning mirror ball. On Sunday, Avalon and next-door Axis co-sponsor a gay night with combined admission to both clubs (☞ Dance Clubs, *above*). Concert show times and cover charges vary. Avalon closes at 2 AM each night.

**Bill's Bar** (✉ 5 Lansdowne St., Kenmore Sq., ☎ 617/421–9678) has live music seven nights a week, including rock, reggae, alternative, and swing. Cover charges vary. Although the club is open until 2 AM, the live music usually ends by midnight.

**Lizard Lounge** (✉ 1667 Massachusetts Ave., Cambridge, ☎ 617/547–0759) has become one of the area's hottest nightspots. National and lesser-known folk, rock, acid jazz, and pop bands perform Thursday through Saturday nights. During the Sunday "poetry jam," a jazz improv trio backs up readers. On Wednesday, there's a music–performance art cabaret. Martinis are a house specialty; upstairs, the Cambridge Common restaurant serves snacks and comfort food (chicken pot pies, curly fries). Cover charge varies; credit cards are not acceptd.

For several years, **Mama Kin** (✉ 36 Lansdowne St., Kenmore Sq., ☎ 617/536–2100) was partly owned by members of the Boston-based rock group Aerosmith (the name comes from an Aerosmith tune). It puts on local bands and artists from other genres. The long, narrow club room, in gothic black and red, has a stage at one end, a CD jukebox, and a custom-built bar with the names of Aerosmith's hit songs inscribed in gold.

The **Middle East Café** (✉ 472 Massachusetts Ave., Central Sq., ☎ 617/497–0576) manages to be both a Middle Eastern restaurant and one of the area's most eclectic rock clubs, with three rooms showcasing live local and national acts. Local phenoms the Mighty Mighty Bosstones got their start here and still perform regularly. Music-world celebs often drop in here when they're in town. There's also belly dancing, folk, jazz, and even the occasional country-tinged rock band. Cover charge varies.

The **Paradise Rock Club** (✉ 967 Commonwealth Ave., near Boston University, ☎ 617/254–3939) is a small club known for having hosted such big-name talent as Soul Coughing and—before they achieved stadium-packing fame—U2 and Pearl Jam. National and local rock, jazz, folk, blues, alternative, and country acts all take their turn here. Inside, two tiers of booths overlook the dance floor, and four bars quench the crowd's thirst. Connected to the Paradise is **M-80,** a DJ-driven dance club that attracts a crowd of Armani-clad real and would-be Euros.

**T.T. the Bear's Place** (✉ 10 Brighton Ave., Central Sq., Cambridge, ☎ 617/492–2327) schedules live rock nightly, showcasing both yet-to-be-discovered talent and nationally known bands such as Smashing Pumpkins and Jane's Addiction. It's also a major literary venue, hosting readings by the Stone Soup poetry collective on Monday nights and a monthly women's poetry slam. It closes at 1 AM.

## Singles

**Buzz Boston/Europa** (✉ 51–67 Stuart St., Theater District, ☎ 617/267–8969), one of the city's trendiest clubs, stands just where the South End gives way to the Theater District. Known as Europa most nights, it attracts a well-heeled, largely Euro crowd who bump and grind on the dance floor. On Saturday it becomes Buzz Boston, catering to a gay crowd. It's 21-plus every night.

**Sonsie** (✉ 327 Newbury St., ☎ 617/351–2500) has no music except a stereo system that conversation by the stylish scenesters often drowns out. The bar crowd, which spills into the sidewalk café, is full of trendy, cosmopolitan types and professionals.

**Trattoria II Panino and Club** (✉ 295 Franklin St., Financial District, ☎ 617/338–1000) attracts a nonstudent, more mature and upscale crowd. (And they dress as such.) The first two floors in this five-floor complex have informal and formal dining, the third has a jazz bar, and the top two are dance floors. There is no cover charge.

# THE ARTS

## Dance

### Ballet

**Boston Ballet** (✉ 19 Clarendon St., ☎ 617/695–6950). The city's premier dance company performs at the Wang Center for the Performing Arts and the Shubert Theatre (☞ *below*) from September through May. In addition to a fine repertory of classical and high-spirited modern works, it presents an elaborate *Nutcracker* every Christmas.

**Ballet Theatre of Boston** (✉ 186 Massachusetts Ave., ☎ 617/262–0961). The company's Cuban-born resident artistic director and choreographer, José Mateo, presides over a young troupe that is building an exciting, contemporary repertory—including an original *Nutcracker*. Performances take place at the Emerson Majestic Theatre (☞ *below*) generally from September through May.

### Contemporary

**Dance Collective** (☎ 617/492–0444) comprises three local choreographers who have explored themes from contemporary life in collaborative works for more than 25 years. They perform at the Green Street Studio in Cambridge, in the Tsai Performance Center at Boston University, and in other local venues—not to mention less conventional spots like store windows and train stations.

**Dance Umbrella** (✉ 515 Washington St., ☎ 617/482–7570) nearly folded from lack of funds in 1999 but struggled through thanks to donations from area corporations and foundations. One of New England's largest presenters of contemporary dance performances, it provides services and advocacy for the area's dance companies and puts together national and international touring companies.

## Folk

**Folk Arts Center of New England** (✉ 1950 Massachusetts Ave., Cambridge, ☎ 617/491–6083) sponsors participatory international folk dancing at locations throughout the city.

**Mandala Folk Dance Ensemble** (☎ 617/868–3641), a popular group of dancers and musicians, performs lively international folk dances in full costume at different venues.

## Multicultural

**Art of Black Dance and Music** (☎ 617/666–1859) performs the music and dance of Africa, Latin America, and the Caribbean at venues across the area.

**Cambridge Multicultural Arts Center** (✉ 41 2nd St., Cambridge, ☎ 617/577–1400) hosts local performers in ethnic music and dance; two galleries showcase the visual arts.

# Film

With its large population of academics and intellectuals, Boston has its share of discerning moviegoers. Several first-run and art-house theaters have closed in recent years, however, and many of the remaining theaters are small or poorly divided into multiplexes. Theaters at suburban malls have better screens, if less adventurous fare. The *Boston Globe* has daily listings in the "Living/Arts" section.

**Boston Public Library** (✉ Copley Sq., ☎ 617/536–5400, ext. 296) regularly screens free family, classic, and documentary films in the Rabb Lecture Hall.

**Brattle Theatre** (✉ 40 Brattle St., Harvard Sq., Cambridge, ☎ 617/876–6837) is a small downstairs cinema offering classic movies, new foreign and independent films, themed series, and directors' cuts. Its sidewalk schedule-posting board is a magnet for students and film buffs.

**Ciné Club at the French Library** (✉ 53 Marlborough St., Back Bay, ☎ 617/266–4351) shows a different French film (usually subtitled) every week, generally on Thursday evening or Friday afternoon or evening. Call for days and times.

**Coolidge Corner Theater** (✉ 290 Harvard St., Brookline, ☎ 617/734–2500) has an eclectic and frequently updated bill of art films, foreign films, cult flicks, and classics. There are also series targeted to families and senior citizens, as well as public events and concerts.

The **Goldwyn/Landmark Kendall Square Cinema**'s (✉ 1 Kendall Sq., Cambridge, ☎ 617/494–9800) well-designed nine-screen theater is devoted to independent and foreign films. There's low-cost validated parking and a concession stand with choices such as biscotti and homemade cookies. Note: 1 Kendall Square stands where Hampshire runs into Broadway, not near the Kendall Square T stop.

**Harvard Film Archive and Film Study Library** (✉ Carpenter Center for the Visual Arts, 24 Quincy St., Cambridge, ☎ 617/495–4700) screens the works of directors not usually shown at commercial cinemas; there are two or more programs daily in the comfortable downstairs theater.

**Loews Harvard Square** (✉ 10 Church St., Harvard Sq., Cambridge, ☎ 617/864–8540) has screenings of everything from new releases to foreign films to *The Rocky Horror Picture Show*.

**Museum of Fine Arts** (✉ 465 Ave. of the Arts, ☎ 617/369–3306 ext. 2, or 617/267–9300) screens international and avant-garde films, early cinema, the work of local filmmakers, and films connected to museum exhibitions in Remis Auditorium.

**Sony Nickelodeon Cinema** (✉ 606 Commonwealth Ave., ☎ 617/424–1500), near Boston University, is one of the few theaters in the city that show first-run independent and foreign films as well as revivals.

# Music

*See also* Blues/R&B Clubs, Jazz Clubs, *and* Rock Clubs *in* Nightlife, *above.*

For its size, Boston is the most musical city in America. Only New York has more events, but it has 10 times the population. Most of the year the music calendar is crammed with both classical and pop events. Jazz, blues, folk, and world music fans have plenty to keep them busy as well. Supplementing appearances by nationally known artists are performers from the area's many colleges and conservatories, which also provide music series, performing spaces, and audiences.

The jewel in Boston's musical crown is the multifaceted Boston Symphony Orchestra, which presents more than 250 concerts annually, led by its music director, Seiji Ozawa, and other distinguished guest conductors. (In Summer 1999, Mr. Ozawa announced plans to leave *the BSO* for the Vienna State Opera after the 2002 season.) The season at Symphony Hall runs from late September to late April. In July and August, the activity shifts to the orchestra's beautiful summer home at the Tanglewood Music Center in Lenox, Massachusetts. A favorite of television audiences, the Boston Pops presents concerts of "lighter music" from May 8 through June 30, followed by outdoor concerts at the Hatch Memorial Shell.

The city has also emerged as the nation's capital of early music performance. Dozens of small groups, often made up of performers who have one foot in the university and another on the concert stage, are rediscovering pre-18th-century composers, whose works they play on period instruments, often in small churches where the acoustics resemble the venues in which some of this music was first performed. The Cambridge Society for Early Music (☎ 617/423–2808) helps promote early music performances and deserves much of the credit for early music's preeminence in Boston's musical scene. If you're a die-hard early music devotee, plan to visit Boston in odd-numbered years, when the biannual Early Music Festival takes over the city for two weeks in June.

## Concert Halls

**Berklee Performance Center** (✉ 136 Massachusetts Ave., ☎ 617/266–1400; 617/266–7455 for recorded information), associated with Berklee College of Music, is best known for its jazz programs but hosts folk, rock, and pop performers as well.

**Boston Conservatory of Music** (✉ 31 Hemenway St., ☎ 617/536–6340, or box office 617/536–3063) presents many free—mostly classical—musical events. Tickets are also available at the box office around the corner at the Fenway.

**Boston University Concert Hall** (✉ Tsai Performance Center, School for the Arts Bldg., 685 Commonwealth Ave., ☎ 617/353–8724), associated with Boston University, presents many free concerts.

The sleek **FleetCenter** (✉ Causeway St., North Station, ☎ 617/624–1000) replaced the beloved but deteriorating Boston Garden (which was finally torn down in 1998). The FleetCenter has better parking, better food, and more seats than its predecessor, as well as unobstructed views for big-name concerts, ice shows, and, of course, Boston Bruins and Boston Celtics games.

**Harborlights** (⌧ Boston Marine Industrial Park, South Boston, ☎ 617/737–6100 or 443–0161), a white tentlike pavilion that was a familiar sight on the downtown waterfront, hosted warm-weather pop, folk, and country acts before being ousted by hotel development. As of press time, plans called for reopening the 5,000-seat venue on a converted wharf just down the street from its former location by mid-1999.

**Hatch Memorial Shell** (⌧ Off Storrow Dr. at Embankment, ☎ 617/727–9548) is a wonderful acoustic shell on the banks of the Charles River where the Boston Pops perform their famous free summer concerts (including their traditional July 4 show, broadcast live nationwide on TV). Local radio stations also put on music festivals here many weekend evenings April through October.

**Isabella Stewart Gardner Museum** (⌧ 280 The Fenway, ☎ 617/734–1359 for schedule information) holds classical concerts by up-and-coming artists in its beautiful Tapestry Room weekends at 1:30 PM, for an additional charge to the museum admission.

**Jordan Hall at the New England Conservatory** (⌧ 30 Gainsborough St., ☎ 617/536–2412) is one of the world's acoustic treasures, ideal for chamber music yet large enough to accommodate a full orchestra. The relatively intimate 1,000-seat hall is home to the **Boston Philharmonic** (☎ 617/868–6696), headed by the charismatic Benjamin Zander, whose informal preconcert talks help audiences better understand what they're about to hear.

**Kresge Auditorium** (⌧ 77 Massachusetts Ave., Cambridge, ☎ 617/253–2826 or 617/253–4003) is MIT's hall for pop and classical concerts.

**Museum of Fine Arts** (⌧ 465 Ave. of the Arts, ☎ 617/369–3306 ext. 4) puts on jazz and concerts in its outdoor courtyard every Wednesday evening from late June through mid-August (bring a blanket and a picnic). The Boston Museum Trio, a Baroque chamber group, and numerous guest artists appear on Sunday afternoons in **Remis Auditorium** from late September to mid-May.

**Orpheum Theatre** (⌧ 1 Hamilton Pl., off Tremont St., ☎ 617/482–0650), a once-ornate theater, is cramped, shabby, and occasionally overheated but nonetheless a popular forum for national and local rock acts avoiding the stadium scene.

**Pickman Recital Hall** (⌧ 27 Garden St., Cambridge, ☎ 617/876–0956) is Longy School of Music's excellent acoustical setting for smaller ensembles and recitals.

**Sanders Theatre** (⌧ Cambridge and Quincy Sts., Cambridge, ☎ 617/496–2222) at Harvard provides a fine stage for local and visiting classical and folk performers. The theater often hosts the Boston Philharmonic; the **Christmas Revels**, a Victorian holiday celebration, delights families there each December.

**Somerville Theatre** (⌧ 55 Davis Sq., Somerville, ☎ 617/625–5700) occasionally interrupts its second-run movie schedule to present blues, folk, world music, and comedy acts such as stand-up satirist Jimmy Tingle. It's two stops from Harvard Square on the Red Line.

**Symphony Hall** (⌧ 301 Massachusetts Ave., ☎ 617/266–1492 or 800/274–8499), one of the world's most perfect acoustical settings, is home to the **Boston Symphony Orchestra,** conducted by Seiji Ozawa for more than 25 years, and the **Boston Pops** (conducted by Keith Lockhart). The hall is also used by visiting orchestras, chamber groups, soloists, and many Boston performing groups. The Pops concerts take place in May and June and around the winter holidays. Rehearsals are sometimes open to the public.

## Chamber Music

Boston is blessed with an impressive array of talented chamber groups, some of them the product of successful undergraduate alliances. Many colleges have their own resident string quartets and other chamber ensembles, and concerts, often free to the public, are given almost every night of the week.

**Alea III** (⊠ 685 Commonwealth Ave., ☎ 617/353–3340), associated with Boston University, presents a season of chamber music performances at the university's Tsai Performance Center.

**Boston Chamber Music Society** (⊠ 286 Congress St., ☎ 617/422–0086), under the artistic direction of Ronald Thomas, gives a 12-concert series each year at Harvard's Sanders Theatre and the New England Conservatory's Jordan Hall.

**Boston Museum Trio** (⊠ 465 Ave. of the Arts, ☎ 617/369–3306 ext. 4), in residence at the Museum of Fine Arts, garners high praise for skilled performances of Baroque chamber music.

**Boston Musica Viva** (⊠ 25 Ave. of the Arts, ☎ 617/353–0556) performs contemporary masterpieces and newly commissioned works at Boston University's Tsai Performance Center.

**Boston Symphony Chamber Players** (⊠ 301 Massachusetts Ave., ☎ 617/266–1492), an outstanding ensemble, comprises members of the Boston Symphony Orchestra.

**Longy School of Music** (⊠ 27 Garden St., Cambridge, ☎ 617/876–0956) often gives free chamber music performances.

## Choral Groups

It's hard to imagine another city's having more active choral groups. Many outstanding choruses are associated with Boston schools and churches. *See* also Church Concerts, *below,* and Early Music Groups, *below,* for additional venues and vocal groups.

**Boston Cecilia** (⊠ 1773 Beacon St., Brookline, ☎ 617/232–4540), dating back to 1875, holds regular concerts at the New England Conservatory's Jordan Hall and is especially noted for its period instrument performances of Handel.

**Cantata Singers** (⊠ Box 375, Cambridge, 02238, ☎ 617/267–6502) perform music dating from the Renaissance to the present.

**Chorus Pro Musica** (⊠ 645 Boylston St., ☎ 617/267–7442), a large chorus with more than 100 singers, appears with various symphony orchestras, often at the Old South Church in Copley Square.

## Church Concerts

Boston's churches offer outstanding music programs. The Saturday *Boston Globe* provides a current listing.

**Emmanuel Church** (⊠ 15 Newbury St., ☎ 617/536–3355) is known as "the Bach church" for its Holy Eucharist services on Sunday at 10 AM. A professional chamber orchestra and chorus performs a Bach cantata each week from mid-September to mid-May.

**King's Chapel** (⊠ 58 Tremont St., downtown, ☎ 617/227–2155) has acoustics so excellent that when local classical performers put on free half-hour organ or vocal concerts each Tuesday at 12:15 PM, they need no microphones.

**Trinity Church** (⊠ Copley Sq., ☎ 617/536–0944) presents a free half-hour organ or choir recital each Friday at 12:15 PM.

## Concert Series

**BankBoston Celebrity Series** (⊠ Statler Bldg., Suite 832, 20 Park Plaza, ☎ 617/482–2595 or 617/482–6661) presents 50 events annually—renowned orchestras, chamber groups, recitalists, vocalists, and dance companies.

*Boston Globe* **Jazz Festival** (☎ 617/523–4047), an annual event sponsored by the city's leading newspaper, brings in prominent jazz musicians and attracts thousands of fans. Performances take place during a week in June, at venues throughout the city.

**Midday Performances** (✉ Federal Reserve Bank of Boston, 600 Atlantic Ave., near South Station, ☎ 617/973–3453) are 40-minute lunchtime programs of music, dance, opera, and such, in the ground-floor auditorium at 12:30 on Thursday.

### Early Music Groups

**Boston Camerata** (✉ 140 Clarendon St., ☎ 617/262–2092) has become a worldwide favorite thanks to its popular recordings. Founded in 1954, it performs a series of medieval, Renaissance, Baroque, and early American vocal and instrumental concerts at various venues.

**Boston Early Music Festival** (✉ Box 2632, Cambridge, 02238, ☎ 617/262–0650) focuses on medieval, Renaissance, and Baroque music, with eight events throughout the year at concert halls and churches. Dozens of concerts, master classes, and lectures culminate in a rarely performed, fully staged Baroque opera. (Past productions have included Hildegard von Bingen's *Ordo Virtutum,* Monteverdi's *Orfeo,* and Purcell's *King Arthur.*)

**Handel & Haydn Society** (✉ 300 Massachusetts Ave., ☎ 617/266–3605), America's oldest musical organization, has a history of performances dating from 1815. It presents instrumental and choral performances at Symphony Hall. The group's holiday-season performances of Handel's *Messiah* are especially popular.

## Opera

**Boston Lyric Opera Company** (✉ 114 State St., ☎ 617/542–6772), based at the Shubert Theatre, stages three full productions each season, usually including one 20th-century work. In recent years, it's performed classics by Mozart and Strauss as well as lesser-knowns. For opera lovers, the Lyric is the only professional show in town; the bankrupt Opera Company of Boston has temporarily shut down until it finds funding and a new home.

## Theater

Boston once played the role of tryout town, a place where producers shaped their productions before taking them on to Broadway. Although fewer shows come to Boston's Theater District in this way today, local troupes are growing in sophistication and number. The rehabilitation of the Boston Center for the Arts has created a range of performance spaces for fledgling troupes, and established companies such as American Repertory Theatre and the Huntington Theatre Company now include pre-Broadway premieres of works by leading playwrights such as David Mamet, August Wilson, and Horton Foote.

### Commercial Theaters

**Charles Playhouse** (✉ 74 Warrenton St., Theater District, ☎ 617/426–6912) is home to two popular and long-running shows. *The Blue Man Group,* a loud, messy, exhilarating trio of playful performance artists painted vivid cobalt, has played here since 1995. Warning: don't dress up, especially if you're sitting close to the stage. Meanwhile, *Shear Madness* (☎ 617/426–5225), a pun-packed interactive whodunit set in a unisex hair salon, has been cracking up audiences for nearly 20 years. The historic theater was formerly a church, a YWCA, a Prohibition-era speakeasy, and a nightclub.

The **Colonial Theatre** (✉ 106 Boylston St., Theater District, ☎ 617/426–9366) opened in 1900; ornate red wallpaper, intricately carved balconies, and stately marble columns evoke its turn-of-the-century glamour. Visiting stars from W.C. Fields to Fanny Brice to Katharine Hepburn have trod its boards—and more recently, the theater welcomed *Fosse,* the tribute to choreographer Bob Fosse, and the Australian dance troupe Tap Dogs.

**Emerson Majestic Theatre** (⊠ 219 Tremont St., Theater District, ☏ 617/824–8000), a 1903 Beaux Arts building, hosts professional and student productions from dance to drama and opera. It's affiliated with nearby Emerson College.

**Huntington Theatre Company** (⊠ 264 Ave. of the Arts, Government Center, ☏ 617/266–0800), occupying a theater opened in 1925 by Henry Jewett's repertory group, is Boston's largest professional resident theater company. Under the auspices of Boston University, with Peter Altman as producing director, the company performs five plays annually, a mix of established 20th-century plays, new works, and classics.

**Loeb Drama Center** (⊠ 64 Brattle St., Harvard Sq., Cambridge, ☏ 617/495–2668) has two theaters, the smaller one an experimental stage. This is the home of **American Repertory Theatre,** the long-established resident professional repertory company. The highly respected ART stages experimental, classic, and contemporary plays; the 1998 season included Debra Winger starring in Paula Vogel's Pulitzer Prize–winning drama *How I Learned to Drive.* ART also puts new works and visiting artists on stage at other venues in Boston and Cambridge.

**Shubert Theatre** (⊠ 265 Tremont St., Theater District, ☏ 617/426–9393), a quietly elegant circa-1910 theater with just 1,700 seats, was closed for years but bounced back with blockbusters such as *Rent* and *Chicago.* Now affiliated with the Wang Center for the Performing Arts, the Shubert has become the home for the Boston Lyric Opera Company (☞ Opera, *above*).

**Wang Center for the Performing Arts** (⊠ 270 Tremont St., Theater District, ☏ 617/482–9393), a huge theater modeled after Paris's Opéra Comique, opened in 1925 as a movie palace. Restructured today for opera, dance, and drama, it stages large-scale productions—notably the Boston Ballet season and Andrew Lloyd Webber extravaganzas—and conducts guided tours of its splendid building.

**Wilbur Theatre** (⊠ 246 Tremont St., Theater District, ☏ 618/423–7440), the smallest of the traditional theater houses in the Theater District, was in and out of foreclosure a few years back but has made a comeback with off-Broadway hits such as *Stomp.*

## Small Theaters and Companies

**Boston Center for the Arts** (⊠ 539 Tremont St., South End, ☏ 617/426–7700) houses more than a dozen quirky low-budget troupes in four performance areas: a basic 40-seat theater, a 90-seat "black box," a fully equipped 140-seat stage, and the massive Cyclorama, built to hold a 360-degree mural of the Battle of Gettysburg (the painting is now at the battlefield). Performances, which go on year-round, range from Coyote Theater, the in-house Equity troupe, to the contemporary SpeakEasy Stage Company, to innovative, explicit one-person shows.

**Harvard's Hasty Pudding Theatricals/Cambridge Theatre Company** (⊠ 12 Holyoke St., Cambridge, ☏ 617/496–8400 or 617/576–7638). The first troupe, the "oldest theatrical organization in the United States," produces one show annually in February and March; it then goes on tour. The troupe also honors a famous actor or actress each spring, presenting an award and conducting a parade around Cambridge. The latter company is a professional company that often uses the Hasty Pudding Theater to present solo artists and to mount its own productions.

**Lyric Stage** (✉ 140 Clarendon St., Back Bay, ☎ 617/437–7172), on the second floor of the YWCA building, presents New England and American premieres as well as the classics. The annual production of *A Child's Christmas in Wales* is a holiday favorite. With new management announced in 1998, theatergoers predict that it will add more daring productions to its lineup in the next year or two.

**New Repertory Theatre** (✉ 54 Lincoln St., Newton Highlands, ☎ 617/332–1646), convenient to the Green Line's D trolley, is often the first repertory company in the area to present popular off-Broadway comedies and dramas, and it's also one of the best.

**Nora Theatre Company** (✉ Harvard Union, Harvard and Quincy Sts., Cambridge, ☎ 617/491–2026) has won local acting and directing awards for its thoughtful stagings of modern drama from Arthur Miller to Terrence McNally.

Since 1974 **Puppet Showplace Theatre** (✉ 32 Station St., Brookline, ☎ 617/731 6400) has drawn on puppeteers from far and near. Performances in the 120-seat theater are given every weekend and holiday weekdays; ticket prices are less than $10.

# 7 OUTDOOR ACTIVITIES AND SPORTS

Boston is a city of sports legends, from basketball stars Larry Bird and Bill Russell to Ted Williams, the last man to bat over .400 in a major league baseball season, and Bobby Orr, the National Hockey League hall-of-famer who still calls Boston his home. And it's the city that still feels the loss of Babe Ruth, who was sold to the Yankees in 1920. Fans pack the bleachers for everything from college football to the Boston Marathon. But sports opportunities aren't just for spectators—you can go biking or ice skating, rowing on the Charles River or running on the Esplanade.

# SPECTATOR SPORTS

By Michele
McPhee

Updated by
Mark Murphy

**E**VERYTHING YOU'VE HEARD about the zeal of Boston fans is true; the home team is what counts here. (In particular, if you're a Yankees fan it's best not to flaunt your partiality within Fenway Park's sacred walls.) Though fans passionately follow the Bruins, Celtics, Patriots, and Red Sox, not one of these teams has won a league title since the Celtics hung up their 16th banner in 1986. Naturally, Bostonians now feel a victory is due. College teams are also followed with enthusiasm, especially Boston College and Harvard football and University of Massachusetts basketball. College hockey fans look forward to the Beanpot Tournament in February.

## Baseball

**Boston Red Sox,** American League (⊠ Fenway Park, ☎ 617/267–1700 for tickets). Baseball season begins early in April and finishes in late September or early October. The Sox won the American League pennant in 1967, 1975, and 1986, though they haven't won a World Series since 1918. (See Dan Shaughnessy's excellent book, *The Curse of the Bambino,* published by Penguin, 1991, for a full explanation of the fix Boston baseball fans are in.) The small ballpark is the country's oldest (Fenway Park and Detroit's Tiger Stadium opened the same day in 1912) and infamously includes the 37-ft-high left-field wall affectionately known as the "Green Monster." Team ownership plans to build a larger, state-of-the-art ballpark, so now is the time to make that Fenway pilgrimage.

## Basketball

**Boston Celtics,** NBA (⊠ FleetCenter, ☎ 617/624–1000; 617/931–2000 Ticketmaster for tickets). Basketball season runs from October to May, though it used to run longer during the Celtics' heyday. The Celts have won the NBA championship 16 times since 1957, the last time in 1986.

**New England Blizzard,** American Basketball League (⊠ Springfield Civic Center, 1277 Main St., Springfield, ☎ 860/522–4667). New England's professional women's team plays occasional exhibition games in Boston, although its home arenas are in Springfield (90 mi west of Boston) and Hartford. The regular season runs from October through February.

## Football

**New England Patriots,** NFL (⊠ Foxboro Stadium, Foxboro, ☎ 800/543–1776). At press time, many of the team's future plans remained uncertain. In spring 1999, the Patriots turned away from an offer to move to Connecticut. Instead, a new stadium has been proposed, which would be built next to the current facility.

**Boston College Eagles** (⊠ Alumni Stadium, Chestnut Hill, ☎ 617/552–3000). With the only Division 1A football program in New England, the BC team annually plays one of the most difficult schedules in the country.

**Harvard University Crimson** (⊠ Harvard Stadium, North Harvard St. and Soldiers Field Rd., Allston, ☎ 617/495–2211). If only to see the stadium, a game here is worth the trip—the experience is akin to watching a football game in a Romanesque coliseum.

## Hockey

**Boston Bruins,** NHL (⊠ FleetCenter, ☎ 617/624–1000; 617/931–2000 Ticketmaster for tickets). The Bruins are on the ice from October until April, frequently on Thursday and Sunday evenings. Talk about patient fans: the Bruins last won a Stanley Cup in 1972.

In February, Boston area college hockey teams (Boston College, Boston University, Harvard, and Northeastern) face off in the annual **Beanpot Hockey Tournament.** It is the most prestigious, and certainly the oldest, of its kind in the nation. Call the FleetCenter for information (☎ 617/624–1000).

## Rowing

Rowing is big in Boston; most of the colleges on both sides of the Charles River have boathouses along the shoreline. The sport's popularity spawned the country's first rowing club, the **Union Boat Club** (☎ 617/742–1520), which is one of several organizations that enter rowers in the world's biggest rowing event, started in 1965, the annual **Head of the Charles Regatta** (☎ 617/864–8415 for information). In mid-October more than 5,000 male and female collegiate rowers from all over the world compete, while thousands of spectators line the shores of the Charles River and use the race as a reason to lounge on blankets and drink beer. (Imbibe with caution; the police have been known to disapprove. Also, be prepared to fight with those legendary local drivers for parking.) The regatta has only been canceled once (1996) for inclement weather.

## Running

Every Patriot's Day (the Monday closest to April 19), fans gather along the Hopkinton-to-Boston route of the **Boston Marathon** to cheer the more than 12,000 runners from all over the world. The race ends near Copley Square in the Back Bay. For information, call the Boston Athletic Association (☎ 617/236–1652).

In October, women runners take the spotlight on Columbus Day for the **Tufts 10K for Women** (☎ 617/439–7700). Starting and ending near the Boston Common, this race typically attracts more than 5,000 entrants and 20,000 spectators.

## Soccer

**New England Revolution,** Major League Soccer (⊠ Foxboro Stadium, Foxboro, ☎ 508/384–9164; 800/946–7287; 617/931–2000 Ticketmaster for tickets). New England's professional soccer team, established in 1996, plays from March to September. There's an unwritten team policy that the players always come out to sign autographs after the games. There's also an interesting, interactive soccer exhibit just outside the stadium's north entrance.

## Tennis

The **Longwood Cricket Club** (⊠ 564 Hammond St., Chestnut Hill, ☎ 617/731–2900) hosts the weeklong U.S. Pro Tennis Championships in midsummer.

# PARTICIPANT ACTIVITIES AND FITNESS

The mania for physical fitness is big in Boston. Lots of people play racquet sports on their lunch hours, and runners and in-line skaters whiz by constantly on the **Storrow Embankment, Memorial Drive Embankment,** or in the **Arnold Arboretum** in Jamaica Plain. Most public recreational facilities, including skating rinks and tennis courts, are operated by the **Metropolitan District Commission** (MDC; ⊠ 20 Somerset St., ☎ 617/727–5114 ext. 555).

## Bicycling

The **Dr. Paul Dudley White Bikeway,** approximately 18 mi long, runs along both sides of the Charles River from Watertown Square to the Museum of Science. For other path locations, call the MDC (☞ *above*).

**Minuteman Bicycle Trail.** The 11-mi trail runs from the Alewife Red Line station in Cambridge through Arlington, Lexington, and Bedford along the bed of an old railroad track. The trail is interrupted by a busy intersection in Arlington Center—be extremely careful on the crossover.

The **Massachusetts Bicycle Coalition (MassBike)** (⊠ 44 Bromfield St., Boston 02178, ☎ 617/542–2453), an advocacy group that works to improve conditions for area cyclists, has information on organized rides and sells bike maps of Boston and the state. Thanks in part to their efforts, for $5 you can buy a permit to take your bike on subway and commuter rail trains, subject to certain time restrictions. Call the Bicycle Coalition for details.

In Boston's South End, **Community Bicycle Supply** (⊠ 496 Tremont St. at E. Berkeley St., ☎ 617/542–8623) rents cycles from April through September.

## Billiards

The **Boston Billiard Club** (⊠ 126 Brookline Ave., ☎ 617/536–7665), near Fenway Park, is comfortably laid-back. It has 42 tables; lessons are available on Monday nights at 7:30.

**Flat Top Johnny's** (⊠ 1 Kendall Sq., Cambridge, ☎ 617/494–9565) is the hippest billiards hall around. Alternative rock, chosen by the tattooed and pierced staff, blares from behind the bar, which has one of the best selections of draft beers in the city. The exposed brick walls show off the art of local painters, and the red felt-topped tables are an attraction if you're tired of headache green. Members of Boston's better local bands often hang out here on their nights off.

**Jillian's Billiard Club** (⊠ 145 Ipswich St., ☎ 617/437–0300) is a semiposh joint near Fenway Park. Professional lessons are available, and the 56-table pool hall also has three bars, a café, darts, shuffleboard, table tennis, a motion simulator, and more than 200 high-tech games.

## Boating

From the Charles River and Inner Harbor to North Washington Street, all types of pleasure boats (except inflatables) are allowed on the waters of Boston Harbor, Dorchester inner and outer bays, and the Neponset River from the Granite Avenue Bridge to Dorchester Bay.

Public landings and floats are located at **North End Waterfront Park** (⊠ Commercial St., Boston Harbor), **Kelly's Landing** (⊠ Day Blvd., South Boston), and at these locations along the Charles River: **Clarendon Street,** Back Bay; **Hatch Shell,** Embankment Road, Back Bay;

**Pinckney Street Landing,** Back Bay; **Brooks Street,** Nonantum Road, Brighton; **Richard T. Artesani Playground,** off Soldiers Field Road, Brighton.

There is another launching area at the **Monsignor William J. Daly Recreation Center** (✉ Nonantum Rd., Brighton, ☎ 617/727–4708) on the Charles River.

**Community Boating** (✉ 21 Embankment Rd., ☎ 617/523–1038), near the Charles Street footbridge that crosses Storrow Drive, has America's oldest public sailing program. From April through October you can have a two-day membership with unlimited boat use for $50 if you are qualified to sail solo. Forty-five-day memberships, during which you may learn to sail solo, are available for $45; a 75-day membership costs $130. Lessons are only available with a membership.

From April through October, rent a canoe, kayak, or shell from **Charles River Canoe and Kayak Center** (✉ 2401 Commonwealth Ave., Newton, ☎ 617/965–5110). A second location (✉ Soldiers' Field Rd., Allston), closer to the city, is open weekends.

The **Jamaica Pond Boat House** (✉ Intersection of Jamaica Way and Pond St., ☎ 617/522–6258), on the outskirts of Jamaica Plain, provides lessons and equipment for rowing and sailing.

## Camping

Of Boston's **Harbor Islands,** Lovell's, Peddock's, Grape, and Bumpkin allow camping with a permit. Camping season runs from July through Labor Day; the bare-bones sites do not have electricity or water. Swimming is available at Lovell's, Grape, and Gallups islands, but lifeguards are on duty only at Lovell's. Pets and alcohol are not allowed on the Harbor Islands. **Boston Harbor Cruises** (✉ 1 Long Wharf, ☎ 617/227–4321) provides boat service to the Harbor Islands. For camping reservations, general Harbor Islands information, and specific questions about islands, contact the **Boston Harbor Islands State Park** (☎ 617/727–7676; ☞ Downtown Boston *in* Chapter 2 ).

## Fishing

You can try freshwater fishing along the shores of the Charles River at **Turtle Pond** (✉ Stony Brook Reservation, Turtle Pond Pkwy., Hyde Park) or at **Jamaica Pond** (✉ Rte. 1, Jamaica Plain), which is stocked with trout and runs an annual one-day fishing contest. For fishing from shore, try the **John J. McCorkle Fishing Pier** (✉ Castle Island) and the pier at **City Point,** both located off Day Boulevard in South Boston. The Boston Harbor Islands (☞ Downtown Boston *in* Chapter 2) also permit fishing. You'll need a Massachusetts fishing license, which can be purchased for $28 at Boston City Hall or Brookline Town Hall.

**Boston Park Rangers** (✉ Boston Parks and Recreation Dept., ☎ 617/635–7383) offer fishing lessons for youth groups at Jamaica Pond. Call for program information and reservations.

## Golfing

**Franklin Park William Devine Golf Course** (✉ Franklin Park, Dorchester, ☎ 617/265–4084), a 6,100-yard, par-70 course, was created in the early 1900s by Donald Ross. It is open year-round, weather permitting. Greens fees are $11 for 9 holes and $19 for 18 holes on weekdays, and $12 and $22, respectively, on weekends (9 holes only after 3 PM on weekends). Fees are $2 to $3 higher for nonresidents of

Boston. The golf course also functions as a family picnic ground and jogging spot for locals.

**George Wright Golf Course** (⊠ 420 West St., ☎ 617/361–8313), another Donald Ross–designed course (1938), offers an even hillier alternative. This 6,096-yard, par-70 course is also open year-round, weather permitting. Weekend greens fees are $24 for residents, $27 for nonresidents, and $21 and $24, respectively, on weekdays. Tee times are necessary on weekends; nine-hole rates aren't available. Nine-hole weekday rates are $12 for residents and $13.50 for nonresidents. Club rentals are $5 for 9 holes and $7 for 18.

The **Massachusetts Golf Association** (⊠ 175 Highland Ave., Needham, ☎ 781/449–3000) represents more than 270 clubs in the state and will provide information on courses that are open to the public as well as on equipment rentals. The office is open weekdays 9–4:30.

## Health Clubs

Several **hotels** (☞ Chapter 5) allow nonguests to use their health club facilities for $10 per day, including the Marriott Hotel at Copley Place, the Sheraton Boston Hotel & Towers, and the Westin Copley Place (all in the Back Bay), Le Meridien Hotel downtown, the Cambridge Center Marriott in Kendall Square, and the Sonesta on Memorial Drive. The Colonnade and Doubletree Guest Suites also allow nonguests to use their pool facilities.

The extensive facilities of the **Greater Boston YMCA** (⊠ 316 Ave. of the Arts, ☎ 617/536–7800) are open for $5 per day (for up to two weeks) to members of other YMCAs in the Boston area; if you have out-of-state YMCA membership, you can use the Boston Y free for up to a week. Nonmembers pay $10 per day or $65 for one month. The site has pools, squash, racquetball courts, cardiovascular equipment, free weights, aerobics, track, and sauna.

The **Cambridge Family YMCA** (⊠ 820 Massachusetts Ave., Cambridge, ☎ 617/661–9622), one of the oldest centers of its kind in the nation, was built in 1893 and incorporated as a YMCA in 1903. The Boston Celtics trained here in the 1960s, and this history is palpable on the court in the pit gym. (The noontime basketball game here draws a cross-section of players from the nearby universities and neighborhoods; it's almost always well attended.) A small jogging track circles overhead. There is also a larger gym on the top floor with a 90-ft basketball court, plus a pool, racquetball and squash courts, cardiovascular equipment, free weights, and aerobics classes. Fees match those of the Greater Boston YMCA (☞ *above*).

The **Boston Athletic Club** (⊠ 653 Summer St., ☎ 617/269–4300) offers use of its facilities, including a pool, to guests of downtown hotels for $20 per day (simply present your hotel key). **Fitcorp** (⊠ 1 Beacon St., ☎ 617/248–9797; ⊠ Prudential Center, ☎ 617/262–2050; ⊠ 350 Longwood Ave., ☎ 617/732–7111; ⊠ 133 Federal St., ☎ 617/542–1010) offers a similar arrangement but does not have a pool; the cost is $12 per day, or $100 for 10 visits.

**Boston Fitness for Women** (⊠ 27 School St., between Tremont and Washington Sts. downtown, ☎ 617/523–3098) has free weights and aerobics and yoga classes. The daily guest fee is $12.

## Hiking

There are excellent footpaths for hikers in the 450-acre **Stony Brook Reservation** (☎ 617/698–1802) in Boston's Hyde Park and West Roxbury sections. A 20-minute drive south of Boston, the **Blue Hills Reservation** (✉ Exit 3, Houghton's Pond, off Rte. 128, Milton, ☎ 617/698–1802) offers 7,000 acres of woodland and about 150 mi of trails, some ideal for cross-country skiing, some designated for mountain biking. Maps ($1) are always available on the headquarters' front porch.

The **Blue Hills Trailside Museum,** operated by the Massachusetts Audubon Society, presents discussions on natural history, live animals, and such special events as organized hikes and walks. ✉ *Exit 2B off Rte. 128 to Rte. 138, Milton,* ☎ *617/333–0690.* ▣ *$3.* ☉ *Tues.–Sun. 10–5.*

The **Boston Harbor Islands** (☞ Downtown Boston *in* Chapter 2) also provide a convenient and off-the-beaten-path venue for beach walks.

## Ice Skating

From late November to early April (weather permitting), skaters can glide across the **Frog Pond** (☎ 617/635–2197) in Boston Common. A warming hut, a concession stand, skate rentals ($5 for adults), lockers ($1), skate sharpening ($6), and lessons are available. Admission is $3 for adults; kids under 14 skate free (kids' rentals are free, too). Frog Pond hours are Monday 10–5, Tuesday–Thursday and Sunday 10–9, and Friday–Saturday 10–10. If the kids get tired of skating, there's a playground adjacent.

In winter, skaters also flock to the frozen waters of the **Boston Public Garden's lagoon.** Ice on one side of the bridge is for figure skating; the other side is for faster-paced ice hockey. **Beacon Hill Skate Shop** (☞ In-Line Skating, *below*) rents skates for use in the Public Garden for $5 per hour or $10 per day.

Outside the city, try the skating rink in **Lars Anderson Park** (✉ 25 Newton St., Brookline, ☎ 617/739–7518); it's at the top of a wooded hill. Admission for Brookline residents is $3 for adults; nonresidents pay $5. Skate rentals cost $4.50. The rink is open from December through March, Wednesday, Friday, and Saturday nights 7:30–9:30, and weekends 10 AM–3 PM.

The MDC operates a total of 19 public ice-skating rinks. For a complete list of rinks and schedules of hours of operation, contact the **Department of Parks and Recreation** (☎ 617/727–9547).

## In-Line Skating

From May through October, **Memorial Drive** on the Cambridge side of the Charles River is closed to auto traffic on Sunday from 11 AM to 7 PM, when the area between the Western Avenue Bridge and Eliot Bridge is transformed into **Riverbend Park.** On the Boston side of the river, the **Esplanade** area offers some excellent skating opportunities.

**Beacon Hill Skate Shop** (✉ 135 Charles St. S, off Tremont St. near the Wang Center for the Performing Arts, ☎ 617/482–7400) rents blades for $5 per hour or $15 per day (you need a credit card for deposit) year-round. Safety equipment is included. **Eric Flaim In-Motion Sports** (✉ 349 Newbury St., ☎ 617/247–3284) also rents in-line skates for $15 per day.

## Jogging

Boston is a runner's city. The most popular—and crowded—jogging routes can be found on both sides of the Charles River: **Memorial Drive** on the Cambridge side and the **Esplanade** on the Boston side. Keep in mind that you'll be sharing the paths with in-line skaters. At **Castle Island** in South Boston (☞ South Boston *in* Chapter 2), skaters and joggers zip past strolling couples and mothers pushing baby carriages. **Jamaica Pond** includes a wooded, 1½-mi-long oval with a number of workout stations.

The **Bill Rodgers Running Center** (✉ Faneuil Hall Marketplace, ☎ 617/723–5612) is a great source of information on local running routes; it also sells running equipment. (Bill Rodgers is a four-time marathon winner.)

## Skiing

**Blue Hills Ski Area** (✉ Blue Hills Reservation, Washington St., Canton, Exit 2B from Rte. 128, just south of Boston city limit, ☎ 781/828–5090 for ticket and ski school information; 781/828–5070 for recorded report on snow conditions) is an MDC-managed downhill facility with a 1,200-ft double chairlift, a J-bar, and two rope tows. Its facilities include seven slopes, snowmaking, a ski school, equipment rentals, and a restaurant.

For serious skiing, **Loon Mountain** (☎ 603/745–8111 or 800/229–5666) and **Waterville Valley** (☎ 603/236–8311 or 800/468–2553) are both about 2½ hours north of Boston in New Hampshire. The **Waterville Valley Chamber of Commerce** (☎ 603/726–3804) is also a good source for ski information.

## Swimming

A small number of **hotel** swimming pools are open to nonguests, including those at the Colonnade and the Doubletree Guest Suites (☞ Chapter 5).

**The Boston Athletic Club** (☞ Health Clubs, *above*) has an eight-lane, 18.3-m (60-ft) heated pool. The central branch of the **Greater Boston YMCA** (☞ Health Clubs, *above*) on the Avenue of the Arts has a 22.9-m (75-ft) heated pool with three wide lap lanes. For outdoor swimming options, *see also* Beaches, *below.*

## Tennis

The MDC maintains tennis courts throughout Boston. No permit is required to use these courts, which operate on a first-come, first-served basis. Call ☎ 617/727–9547 for more information on the following and other **public courts**: **Charlesbank Park** (lighted), along Storrow Drive opposite Charles Street; **North End Park**, Commercial Street; and **Marine Park** (lighted), South Boston.

## Whale-Watching

The **New England Aquarium** (✉ Central Wharf, between Central and Milk Sts., ☎ 617/973–5200; 617/973–5277 for whale-watching information) runs whale-watching cruises between April and October. Several breeds of whale, including humpbacks and minke whales, feed locally during those months, so you're practically guaranteed to see a few—and on a good day you may see dozens. A new boat, *Voyager III*, joined the *Voyager II* in summer 1999. The trip lasts roughly five hours. Be sure to wear rubber-soled shoes and warm clothing.

Whale-watching cruises also run from several waterfront towns outside of Boston (☞ The North Shore *and* South of Boston *in* Chapter 9).

# BEACHES

Boston may be on the ocean, but it is not renowned for its beaches. The harbor is a working harbor, with several million people living nearby, and the water is hardly Bahamas-pure. However, beginning in 1988 the city embarked on a massive cleanup of the harbor waters and opened a brand-new sewage works in 1995. Consequently, public beaches have been spruced up, new facilities added, and the former governor has taken a few well-publicized dips in the once-murky waters, including a head-first dive into the Charles River that made every Bostonian shudder. Most beaches are in relatively family-oriented sections of town and remain largely neighborhood affairs.

The main beaches are **Malibu Beach, Savin Hill Beach,** and **Tenean Beach,** off Morrissey Boulevard, in Dorchester, near the John F. Kennedy Library; and **Carson Beach, Castle Island Beach, City Point Beach, M Street Beach,** and **Pleasure Bay,** off Day Boulevard, in South Boston. The only swimming off the Harbor Islands is at **Lovells Island, Grape Island,** and **Gallups Island** (lifeguards are on duty only at Lovells).

These beaches are open from the end of June to the beginning of September, when lifeguards are on duty daily from 10 to 6. High temperatures and high tide may cause schedule changes. For further information, call the MDC (**Recreation Division:** ☎ 617/727–9547, ext. 450).

Several excellent beaches a short distance from the city make lovely day trips. Among the nicest are **Nantasket Beach** in Hull, **Crane's Beach** in Ipswich, **Plum Island** (☞ Chapter 9) in Newburyport, and **Wingaersheek Beach** and **Good Harbor Beach** in Gloucester. A bit farther away, but well worth the hour to hour-and-a-half drive, are **Duxbury Beach** in Duxbury, **Singing Beach** in Manchester by the Sea, and **Horseneck Beach** in Westport.

# 8 SHOPPING

Boston, Edith Wharton once said, thought she was too fashionable to be serious, whereas New York found her too serious to be fashionable. Today Boston and Cambridge's tens of thousands of students set the dress code—from scrubbed and preppy to the thrift-store slacker look, accessorized with tattoos, piercings, and dyed hair—and there's a store to please them all. Natives and transplants alike wear their pride wherever they go: don't even try to count the T-shirts and sweatshirts you see emblazoned with BOSTON or the name of a college or hometown team. Once you're outfitted like a native, browse through the dozens of bookstores.

Updated by
Stephanie
Schorow

**T**HE LAST FIVE YEARS have shown that Boston residents can shop with the best of them—the city's shopping scene has exploded with both visitor and local business. Now that Boston is a world-class city, the prevailing attitude is that if the world wants to visit, the world wants to shop. Many Bostonians bemoan the proliferation of chain stores; determined shoppers, however, can still find unusual, one-of-a-kind items in idiosyncratic boutiques, craft galleries, and bookstores as well as designer goods whose prices could elicit a nosebleed.

Although they don't exactly sell something you can put in your suitcase, Boston's ice cream stores are a definite local presence. (And they make a great refueling stop during a shopping blowout.) Flavors go far beyond basic vanilla: intense tastes of burnt-caramel or cinnamon could bring tears to your eyes. Many stores have also added nondairy or sugar-substitute choices to their lineup. Among the favorites are **Herrell's** (⌂ 15 Dunster St., Cambridge, ☎ 617/497–2179; ⌂ 224 Newbury St., ☎ 617/236–0857; ⌂ 350 Longwood Ave., Boston, ☎ 617/731–9599); **J. P. Licks Homemade Ice Cream** (⌂ 352 Newbury St., ☎ 617/236–1666; ⌂ 674 Centre St., Jamaica Plain, ☎ 617/524–6740); and **Toscanni Ice Cream** (⌂ 899 Main St., Cambridge, ☎ 617/491–5877; ⌂ 1320 Massachusetts Ave., Cambridge, ☎ 617/354–9350).

Boston's shops and stores are generally open Monday through Saturday from 9 or 10 until 6 or 7; many stay open until 8 one night late in the week, usually Thursday, and open Sunday at 10 or noon and close at 5 or 6. Many mall stores are open until 9 PM weekdays. Most stores accept major credit cards. Traveler's checks are welcome throughout the city (though it may be difficult for a small store to cash a check of large denomination). The state sales tax of 5% does not apply to food, except in restaurants. However, there is a 5% luxury tax on clothes priced more than $175 per item; the tax is levied on the amount in excess of $175. Boston's two daily newspapers, the *Globe* and the *Herald*, are the best places to learn about sales. Unless otherwise noted, stores are in Boston proper. Remember that Huntington Avenue was renamed Avenue of the Arts but that locals will likely use the old name.

## Major Shopping Districts

Boston's shops and department stores are concentrated in the area bounded by Quincy Market, the Back Bay, and downtown. There are few outlet stores in center city, but plenty of bargains nevertheless, particularly in the world-famous Filene's Basement and Chinatown's fabric district. The South End's gentrification spins its own kind of opportunities, from new housewares shops to avant-garde art galleries. In Cambridge, you'll find lots of shopping around Harvard and Central squares, with several independent boutiques migrating west along Mass Ave. toward Porter Square and beyond.

### Boston

**Boylston Street,** in the heart of the Back Bay and parallel to Newbury Street, is home to more than 100 stores, including Talbot's, Eddie Bauer, City Sports, and the flagship store for Willowbee & Kent Travel Company.

At the east end of Boylston Street at Arlington Street is the *très élégant* complex **Heritage on the Garden** (⌂ 300 Boylston St., ☎ 617/426–9500), which contains **Hermès, Saint John's Knits, Sonia Rykiel,** and

**Escada.** At the west end of Boylston Street is the **Prudential Center** complex, where the venerable **Saks Fifth Avenue** moors chain stores such as Ann Taylor, the Body Shop, and Warner Bros. Studio Store.

**Charles Street,** in Beacon Hill, draws antiques and boutique lovers. Some of the city's prettiest shops are here. River Street, parallel to Charles and near the intersection with Chestnut, is also an excellent source for antiques.

**Copley Place** (✉ 100 Ave. of the Arts, ☎ 617/375–4400), an indoor shopping mall that connects the Westin and Marriott hotels in Back Bay, is a blend of the elegant, the glitzy, and the often overpriced. The Neiman Marcus department store anchors more than 90 boutiques, restaurants, and cinemas. To dip into the apparel stratosphere, try on a pair of multi-hundred-dollar pumps at **Bottega Veneta,** drink in the rich leather smell from the briefcases at **Louis Vuitton,** or indulge in a $90 pair of briefs at **Gucci.** Shops on the second level, which include J. Crew, the Gap, Banana Republic, and United Colors of Benetton, are more low-key, in terms of both style and wallet-wallop. There are two galleries of note: the **Artful Hand Gallery** and **Pavo Real Gallery.** A skywalk connects strollers with the shops at the Prudential Center.

**Downtown Crossing,** Boston's downtown shopping area, has a festival feeling year-round in its usually crowded pedestrian mall, with outdoor merchandise kiosks, food carts, street performers, and benches for people-watchers. The city's two largest department stores, **Macy's** and **Filene's** (with the famous **Filene's Basement** beneath it), are here.

**Faneuil Hall Marketplace** (☎ 617/338–2323) continues to buzz despite its strong mall overtones and a surfeit of tourists. There are dozens of shops (mostly chains like Crate & Barrel and Victoria's Secret) plus pushcarts with a variety of wares, street performers, and one of the area's great food experiences, Quincy Market (☞ Government Center *in* Chapter 2). Friday and Saturday are the days to walk through **Haymarket,** a jumble of outdoor fruit and vegetable vendors, meat markets, and fishmongers. **Marketplace Center,** adjacent to Faneuil Hall Marketplace, has more shops and chain stores.

**Newbury Street** is Boston's eight-block-long version of New York's 5th Avenue. Near the Public Garden, Newbury Street is quite upscale, with the most stylish clothing boutiques, some of the most up-to-date art galleries, and the most sparkling jewelry, not to mention formal afternoon tea in the Ritz-Carlton Hotel. Toward Mass Ave., Newbury Street gets funkier with hip clothing stores, ice cream shops, music stores, and bookstores, capped off at Mass Ave. with a branch of Tower Music and Video.

## Cambridge

**CambridgeSide Galleria** (✉ 100 CambridgeSide Pl., ☎ 617/621–8666) is a three-story mall in East Cambridge, accessible from the Green Line Lechmere T stop and a shuttle from the Kendall T stop. The Filene's and Sears make it a good stop for basic clothes and appliance shopping; it's also a big draw for local high school kids.

**Harvard Square** comprises just a few blocks but holds more than 150 stores selling clothes, books and records, furnishings, and a range of specialty items. Three small weatherproof shopping complexes are just off the square: the **Garage** (✉ 38 JFK St.), the **Galeria** (✉ 57 JFK St.), and the **Holyoke Center** (✉ 1352 Massachusetts Ave.). The

Holyoke Center has an outlet for BosTix, where half-price arts and entertainment tickets for Cambridge and Boston venues may be purchased. There's also Harvard Collections, where you can peruse books from the Harvard University Press and sort through tchotchkes that vaguely reflect the collections in Harvard's museums. Farther inside the center, you'll find the Harvard Information office, where you can get information on Harvard programs and tours. A large complex at One Brattle Square houses HMV records and Express, and, for better or worse, you can find a branch of just about any popular chain within a few blocks, including Urban Outfitters, the Body Shop, City Sports, and Crate & Barrel. For book lovers, the **Cambridge Visitor Information Booth** (⊠ 0 Harvard Sq., ☎ 617/497–1630) supplies a wonderful map of bookstores in the area.

**Porter Square,** west on Mass Ave. from Harvard Square, is home to distinctive clothing stores such as **Susanna** (⊠ 1776 Massachusetts Ave., ☎ 617/492–0334) and **Looks** (⊠ 1607 Massachusetts Ave., ☎ 617/491–4251), plus crafts shops, coffee shops, natural food stores, and restaurants. The other direction on Mass Ave. from Harvard Square leads to the funky environs of **Central Square,** which currently has a mix of furniture stores, used-record shops, and ethnic restaurants.

# Blitz Tours

Study the T map or practice your parking maneuvers, and then plunge into one of the following shopping itineraries. These are arranged by special interest; addresses, if not included here, can be found in the store listings below.

## Antiques

Avid antiques shoppers will have their work happily cut out for them. Plan to spend at least three hours on Charles Street, which has more than 30 stores on five blocks. Start at the north end of Charles Street. (This is hard by the Charles/MGH T stop. If you drive, enter this one-way street by the Longfellow Bridge; there's a parking garage almost immediately on the right.) Begin at the elegant **Judith Dowling Asian Art,** followed, in complete contrast, with the cluttered jumble of dealers inside the **Boston Antique Co-op.** Other favorite stops include **Marika's** (⊠ 130 Charles St.), a tangle of American and European objets and furniture with a smattering of Japanese prints, and **Upstairs Downstairs** at the corner of Pickney Street. Across the street is **Eugene Galleries.** At the corner of Mount Vernon Street, turn right and then left on River Street—some small but intriguing galleries are located on this block. Turn left on Chestnut to return to Charles; up a flight of stairs is the engrossing **Devonia: Antiques for Dining.** From here, continue along Charles to Beacon Street and cut through the Public Gardens to Newbury Street to reach **Autrefois Antiques** and the **Brodney Gallery** (⊠ 145 Newbury St.), which carries estate jewelry, silver, and porcelain. Or, for more reasonably priced choices, head to the **Cambridge Antiques Market.** (This is near the Lechmere T stop; by car, go back over the Longfellow Bridge into Cambridge, turn right on Third Street, and continue on to Monsignor O'Brien Highway.)

## Books

Boston is a bibliophile's dream city. For rare, antique, or just plain unusual books, start at **Ars Libri Ltd.** in the South End. From here, head to Newbury Street (by foot, turn right on Waltham, walk three blocks, and cross Tremont, then pick up Clarendon to Newbury) to visit **Avenue Victor Hugo.** Consider taking a break at the **Trident Booksellers**

**and Café,** one of the city's first bookstore-cafés, almost directly across the street. Alternatively, from Ars Libri Ltd., follow Waltham to Tremont, make a right, and head over the turnpike to reach West Street and the **Brattle Bookstore.** From here catch the Red Line T into Harvard Square to browse through the **Harvard Bookstore** and, just around the corner, **Grolier Poetry Bookshop.** Determined book lovers may retrace their steps through Harvard Square and proceed to **Canterbury's Bookshop** (⌧ 1675 Massachusetts Ave.), which has antiquarian and scholarly books. Farther up Mass Ave. is the **Bookcellar** (⌧ 1971 Massachusetts Ave.), a funky basement spot for used books and magazines. About a half mile farther is the ever-popular **Kate's Mystery Books,** where you can find current and hard-to-find mysteries and thrillers.

## Department Stores

**Filene's.** This full-service department store carries a complete line of American men's and women's formal, casual, and career clothing, including designers such as Tommy Hilfiger, Calvin Klein, and Ralph Lauren. Jewelry, shoes, cosmetics, bedding, towels, and luggage are found at the Downtown Crossing store, where escalators connect to the famous Filene's Basement (☞ *below*), a separate business entity. ⌧ *426 Washington St.,* ☎ *617/357–2100;* ⌧ *CambridgeSide Galleria, Cambridge,* ☎ *617/621–3800.*

**Filene's Basement.** It may have spawned suburban outlets, but this is the only store where items are automatically reduced in price according to the number of days they've been on the rack. You can certainly find bargains on designer labels, but many of the items have been marked down for a reason—they're, shall we say, aesthetically challenged. Be prepared to go *mano a mano* with other bargain hunters digging through the tables of merchandise. The basement's wedding gown sales (the big one is usually in November but there are three more during the year) is the bridal equivalent of the running of the bulls—a test of daring and fortitude. You can enter directly from the Downtown Crossing T station. ⌧ *426 Washington St.,* ☎ *617/542–2011.*

**Lord & Taylor.** This is a reliable stop for classic clothing, from casual to elegant, by such designers as Anne Klein and Ralph Lauren, along with accessories, cosmetics, jewelry, and children's clothing. ⌧ *760 Boylston St.,* ☎ *617/262–6000.*

**Macy's.** A plaque outside this building outlines its history; once it was Jordan Marsh, New England's largest department store since the mid-19th century. Its six floors carry men's and women's clothing and shoes, as well as an extensive selection of housewares, furniture, and cosmetics. Although there are top designers and a fur salon, it doesn't feel exclusive; instead, it's a popular family stop for back-to-school clothes. Like Filene's, it has direct access to the Downtown Crossing T station. ⌧ *450 Washington St.,* ☎ *617/357–3000.*

**Neiman Marcus.** The flashy Texas retailer has three levels of glossy-magazine designers such as Jean-Paul Gaultier, Gucci, Salvatore Ferragamo, and Calvin Klein. There are also batteries of cosmetics, housewares, china, and glass. The prices may be high but the personal service is outstanding. ⌧ *5 Copley Pl.,* ☎ *617/536–3660.*

**Saks Fifth Avenue.** Saks runs the gamut from traditional styles (Chanel, St. John's Knits, Armani) to more flamboyant apparel by designers such as Joseph Abboud and Oscar de la Renta, plus accessories and cosmetics. There's also a fur salon and plus-size department, as well as children's clothes (though boys' outfits are limited to toddlers). ⊠ *1 Ring Rd., Prudential Center,* ☎ *617/262–8500.*

# Food Stores

## Baked Goods

**Hi-Rise Bread Co.** Here you can practically walk right into the baking operation. Sample a variety of breads like walnut, olive, or cheddar-pepper loaves, or the house specialty, polka bread, a tough-crusted bread marked with crosshatches. ⊠ *208 Concord Ave., Cambridge,* ☎ *617/876–8766.*

**May's Cake House.** These are the lightest big and little cakes ever to melt in your mouth, topped with fresh fruit in eye-catching patterns. ⊠ *223A Harrison Ave.,* ☎ *617/350–0210.*

**Modern Pastry Shop.** Look beyond the unprepossessing and not-very-modern North End storefront to the tempting array of authentic Italian desserts such as unrivaled biscotti and *torrone* (nougat), which comes in various flavors. ⊠ *257 Hanover St.,* ☎ *617/523–3783.*

**Rosie's Bakery.** This is everyone's sweetheart. Rosie's has tempting cookies, pastries, and cakes, but it's their chocolate chip cookies that consistently win over people's hearts. If you can't get enough, pick up their excellent *Chocolate-Packed, Jam-Filled, Butter-Rich, No Holds-Barred Cookie Book.* ⊠ *2 South Station,* ☎ *617/439–4684;* ⊠ *243 Hampshire St., Cambridge,* ☎ *617/491–9488.*

## Specialty Grocers

**Bread & Circus.** At one of the original health food–gourmet grocery stores, fill a basket with organic fruit, fresh herbs, and other New Age staples, although prices are steep. ⊠ *15 Westland St.,* ☎ *617/375–1010;* ⊠ *186 Alewife Brook Pkwy., Cambridge,* ☎ *617/491–0040;* ⊠ *115 Prospect St., Cambridge,* ☎ *617/492–0070.*

**Cardullo's.** This long-standing shop on Harvard Square purveys exotic imports, sandwiches to go, chocolates, breads, olive oils, cheeses, wines, and beer amid impressive clutter. ⊠ *6 Brattle St., Cambridge,* ☎ *617/491–8888.*

**The 88 Super Market.** Grocery shopping becomes a sensory trip to Asia; the exotic fish, dried mushrooms, and several varieties of noodles make this the perfect place to find special ingredients for a Chinese dinner. ⊠ *50 Herald St.,* ☎ *617/423–1688.*

**Formaggio.** As the name implies, this store is a trove of cheeses, particularly Italian and French cheeses—they can turn up two kinds of Raschera and even the rare Castelmagno. There's also a host of other delectable fare such as exotic jams (like the grapefruit and ginger combo) plus prepared side dishes such as lima beans with a spinach pesto. ⊠ *244 Huron Ave., Cambridge,* ☎ *617/354–4750.*

**Savenor's.** If you're looking for exotic game meats, you've come to the right place; they carry buffalo rump, alligator tail, even rattlesnake. There are plenty of tamer choices, too, as well as outstanding cheeses, breads, and treats such as foie gras and smoked salmon. ⊠ *160 Charles St.,* ☎ *617/723–6328.*

# Specialty Stores

## Antiques

There are some excellent antiques stores on Newbury Street and in the South End, but Charles Street—coincidentally, one of the city's oldest streets—is the place to go for a concentrated perusal of antiquities.

## Boston Shopping

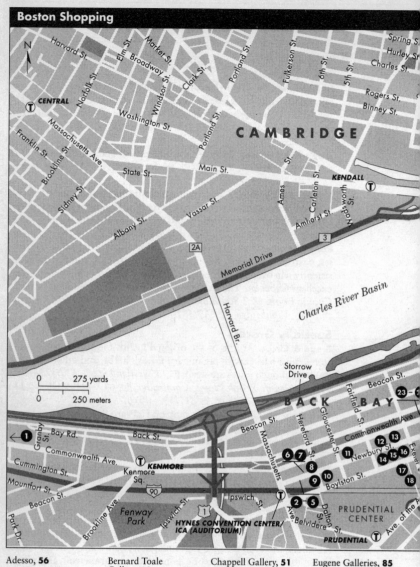

Adesso, **56**
Alan Bilzerian, **47**
Alianza, **19**
Allston Beat, **2**
Alpha Gallery, **48**
Alpha Omega, **37**
April Cornell, **72**
Ars Libri Ltd., **59**
The Artful Hand
Gallery, **36**
Autrefois Antiques, **32**
Avenue Victor Hugo, **8**
Barbara Krakow
Gallery, **49**
Bellezza Home and
Garden, **30**

Bernard Toale
Gallery, **60**
Betsey Johnson, **13**
Bill Rodgers Running
Center, **72**
Black Ink, **80**
Boomerangs, **75**
Boston Antique
Co-op, **79**
Boston City Store, **73**
Brattle Bookstore, **68**
Bromfield Art
Gallery, **61**
Brooks
Brothers, **42, 71**
Buck a Book, **70**
Chanel, **53**

Chappell Gallery, **51**
Chic Repeats, **31**
Childs Gallery, **23**
Churchill Galleries, **81**
Copley Society of
Boston, **20**
Devonia: Antiques for
Dining, **86**
Dorfman Jewels, **50**
Eastern Mountain
Sports, **1**
The 88 Super
Market, **58**
El Paso, **21**
Emporio Armani, **15**
Eric Flaim In-Motion
Sports, **6**

Eugene Galleries, **85**
F. A. O. Schwarz, **41**
Filene's, **69**
Filene's Basement, **69**
Fresh, **29**
Gallery NAGA, **40**
Genovese/Sullivan
Gallery, **62**
Gianni Versace, **52**
Giorgio Armani, **44**
Globe Corner
Bookstore, **35**
Guild of Boston
Artists, **22**
Haley and Steele, **38**

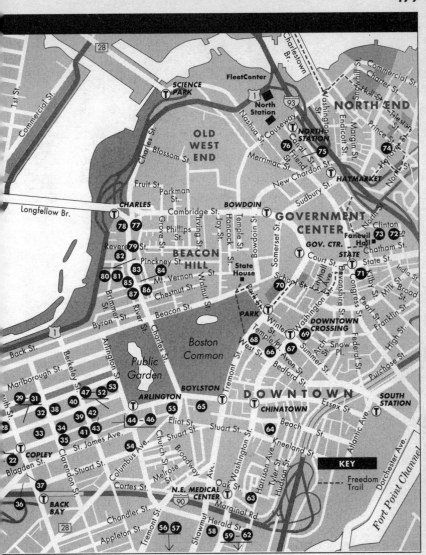

# Cambridge Shopping

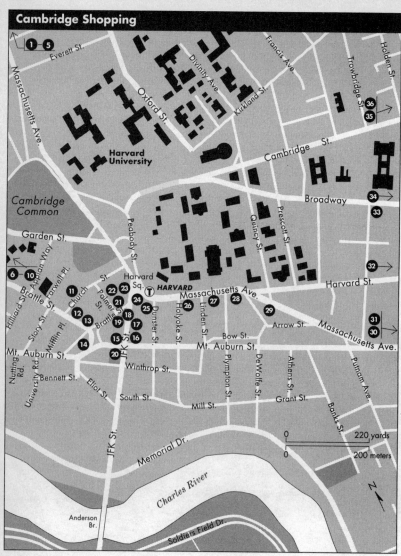

Everett St.

Massachusetts Ave.

Oxford St.

Divinity Ave.

Francis Ave.

Holden St.

Trowbridge St.

Kirkland St.

**Harvard University**

Cambridge St.

Broadway

*Cambridge Common*

Garden St.

Peabody St.

Quincy St.

Prescott St.

Harvard St.

Appian Way

Farwell Pl.

Brattle St.

Hilliard St.

Story St.

Church St.

Palmer St.

Harvard St.

**HARVARD**

Harvard Sq.

Massachusetts Ave.

Massachusetts Ave.

Arrow St.

Dunster St.

Holyoke St.

Linden St.

Bow St.

Brattle St.

Mifflin Pl.

Mt. Auburn St.

Mt. Auburn St.

Plympton St.

DeWolfe St.

Athens St.

Banks St.

Putnam Ave.

Nutting Rd.

University Rd.

Bennett St.

Eliot St.

Winthrop St.

South St.

Mill St.

Grant St.

JFK St.

Memorial Dr.

*Charles River*

Anderson Br.

Soldier's Field Dr.

0    220 yards
0    200 meters

N

**Autrefois Antiques.** A good source of country French and some Italian 18th- and 19th-century antiques and furniture, Autrefois also stocks Chinese lamps and vases, ivory, and silver. ⊠ *125 Newbury St.,* ☎ *617/424–8823;* ⊠ *130 Harvard St., Brookline,* ☎ *617/566–0113.*

**Boston Antique Co-op.** A flea market–style collection of dealers occupies two floors, carrying everything from vintage photos and paintings to porcelain, silver, bronzes, and furniture. ⊠ *119 Charles St.,* ☎ *617/227–9810 or 617/227–9811.*

**Cambridge Antique Market.** Off the beaten track this may be, but it has a selection bordering on overwhelming: four floors of dealers and pieces ranging from 19th-century furniture to vintage clothing, as well as plenty of reasonably priced items. Parking can be tricky. ⊠ *201 Monsignor O'Brien Hwy., Cambridge,* ☎ *617/868–9655.*

**Churchill Galleries.** This elegant setting shelters fine period furniture, paintings, and decorative objects. ⊠ *103 Charles St.,* ☎ *617/722–9490.*

**Consignment Galleries.** Sift through truly affordable used and antique furniture and collectibles—china, glass, silver, jewelry, and some amazing odds and ends. Prices go down the longer the item remains unsold. ⊠ *2044 Massachusetts Ave., Cambridge,* ☎ *617/354–4408.*

**Devonia: Antiques for Dining.** Some of the fabulous china sets here are fit for a queen—literally, as they were designed for royalty. Feast your eyes on a 1910 Dresden handpainted lattice setting for 12 or a 20-piece Davenport dessert set from 1830. ⊠ *43 Charles St.,* ☎ *617/523–8313.*

**Eugene Galleries.** This store is chockablock with prints, etchings, old maps, city views, and books; pick up a 19th-century print of the Old South Church or other Boston landmarks. ⊠ *76 Charles St.,* ☎ *617/227–3062.*

**Judith Dowling Asian Art.** Unlike that of many other antiques-shop owners, Judith Dowling's sophistication results from spareness and restraint. High-end Asian artifacts range from Japanese pottery to scrolls, painted screens, cabinets, and other furnishings. ⊠ *133 Charles St.,* ☎ *617/523–5211.*

**Shreve, Crump & Low.** The old-money jewelry store also has 18th- and 19th-century English and American furniture and silver, Chinese export porcelain, crystal, and decorative lamps. There's an extensive collection of clocks and watches, an excellent selection of diamonds, and exclusive lines such as Scott Potter's decoupage glassware. ⊠ *330 Boylston St.,* ☎ *617/267–9100.*

**Upstairs Downstairs.** This feels akin to an upscale country store; Victorian paintings hang next to needlepoint armchairs, while cabinets, chests, and other furniture are all neatly arranged. The staff is particularly friendly. ⊠ *93 Charles St.,* ☎ *617/367–1950.*

## Art Galleries

Although Newbury Street has the highest concentration of galleries in the city, a neighborhood in the South End, dubbed SoWa (for South of Washington), has emerged as a hotspot for aspiring contemporary artists. The Fort Point Channel area, near South Station, also percolates with studios.

**Alpha Gallery.** This gallery specializes in 20th-century American and European painting, sculpture, and master prints. ⊠ *14 Newbury St.,* ☎ *617/536–4465.*

**Barbara Krakow Gallery.** Contemporary American and European paintings, photographs, drawings, and prints are shown here. ⊠ *10 Newbury St., 5th floor,* ☎ *617/262–4490.*

**Bernard Toale Gallery.** This contemporary art space is one of the more recent immigrants from Newbury Street to the burgeoning artistic district in the South End. Toale showcases more experimental works in his new digs, including oil paintings, photographs, and installations. ⊠ *450 Harrison Ave.,* ☎ *617/482–2549.*

**Bromfield Art Gallery.** This small, cooperative operation mounts month-long shows of its members' work, including oil and acrylic paintings and charcoal and pastel drawings. ⊠ *560 Harrison Ave.,* ☎ *617/451–3605.*

**Chappell Gallery.** This petite, distinctive space displays contemporary art glass by American, Canadian, Japanese, and Czech artists. With colorful vases and glowing liquid forms, the gallery reveals just how powerful a medium "the fluid canvas" can be. ⊠ *14 Newbury St.,* ☎ *617/236–2255.*

**Childs Gallery.** With a wide chronological reach, Childs carries paintings, prints, drawings, watercolors, and sculpture from the 16th to the 20th century. ⊠ *169 Newbury St.,* ☎ *617/266–1108.*

**Copley Society of Boston.** After more than a century, this nonprofit membership organization continues to present the works of well-known and aspiring New England artists. ⊠ *158 Newbury St.,* ☎ *617/536–5049.*

**Gallery NAGA.** Here you'll find contemporary paintings, sculpture, and furniture in a striking space: the Church of the Covenant. ⊠ *67 Newbury St.,* ☎ *617/267–9060.*

**Genovese/Sullivan Gallery.** After a decade in business, this gallery moved to the South End in early 1997—one of the pioneers in this neighborhood. It shows paintings, sculpture, and installations by nationally known contemporary artists. ⊠ *47 Thayer St.,* ☎ *617/426–9738.*

**Guild of Boston Artists.** This nonprofit gallery sells representational watercolors, oils, graphics, and sculpture by guild members. ⊠ *162 Newbury St.,* ☎ *617/536–7660.*

**Haley and Steele.** With nary an abstract in sight, this gallery specializes in 19th-century British sporting, historical New England, and marine prints. ⊠ *91 Newbury St.,* ☎ *617/536–6339.*

**Judi Rotenberg Gallery.** These dealers represent painters Zygmund Jankowski, Oliver Balf, Roz Farbush, Charles Movalli, Jason Berger, and Harold and Judi Rotenberg, and sculptor Marianna Pineda. ⊠ *130 Newbury St.,* ☎ *617/437–1518.*

**Nielsen Gallery.** This gallery showcases established and aspiring artists, as well as representative and abstract paintings and prints. ⊠ *179 Newbury St.,* ☎ *617/266–4835.*

**Pucker Gallery.** The rotating shows here mount contemporary paintings, sculpture, ceramics, and prints. ⊠ *171 Newbury St.,* ☎ *617/267–9473.*

**Rolly-Michaux.** An impressive cache of 20th-century works includes paintings, graphics, silk screens, and sculpture by artists such as Moore, Calder, Picasso, Chagall, Miró, and Matisse. ⊠ *290 Dartmouth St.,* ☎ *617/536–9898.*

**Vose Galleries.** Established in 1841, Vose specializes in 19th- and 20th-century American art, including the Hudson River School, Boston School, and American Impressionists. ⊠ *238 Newbury St.,* ☎ *617/536–6176.*

## Books

If Boston and Cambridge have bragging rights to anything, it would be to their independent bookstores, many of which stay open late into the evening. Many stores sponsor author readings and literary programs. Besides these unique spots, there are all the major chains: **Barnes & Noble** (⊠ *395 Washington St.,* ☎ *617/426–5184;* ⊠ *660 Beacon St.,* Kenmore Sq., ☎ *617/267–8484);* **Borders** (⊠ *24 School St.,* ☎ *617/*

557–7188); **B. Dalton** (✉ 100 CambridgeSide Pl., Cambridge, ☎ 617/
252–0019); **Doubleday** (✉ 800 Boylston St., ☎ 617/536–2606).

**Ars Libri Ltd.** The rare and wonderful books on display make it easy
to be drawn in. The airy space is filled with books on photography
and architecture, out-of-print art books, monographs, and exhibition
catalogs. ✉ *560 Harrison Ave.,* ☎ *617/357–5212.*

**Avenue Victor Hugo.** These two crowded floors of used books can di-
vulge some eye-opening finds (a signed edition of Longfellow), plus fiction, art books, and a great selection of old magazines, some of which
go back to the 1800s. ✉ *339 Newbury St.,* ☎ *617/266–7746.*

**Brattle Bookstore.** The late George Gloss built this into Boston's best
used- and rare-book shop. Today, his son, Kenneth, fields the queries
from passionate book lovers. If the book they want is out of print, Brattle has it or can probably find it. ✉ *9 West St.,* ☎ *617/542–0210 or
800/447–9595.*

**Buck a Book.** They stick to their word here; this is the ultimate discount bookstore, with overstocked fiction, nonfiction, and children's
books. "Better" books run $3 and up, but there is always a find for a
buck. ✉ *125 Tremont St.,* ☎ *617/357–1919;* ✉ *38 Court St.,* ☎ *617/
367–9419;* ✉ *30 JFK St., Cambridge,* ☎ *617/492–5500.*

**Globe Corner Bookstore.** Hands down, these are the best sources for
domestic and international travel books and maps; they also carry very
good selections of books about New England and by New England authors. ✉ *500 Boylston St.,* ☎ *617/859–8008;* ✉ *28 Church St., Cambridge,* ☎ *617/497–6277.*

**Grolier Poetry Bookshop.** Proprietor Louisa Solano is an outspoken pro-
ponent of all things poetic. The store, founded in 1927, specializes in
the writings of those whose vice is verse. ✉ *6 Plympton St., Cambridge,*
☎ *617/547–4648.*

**Harvard Bookstore.** The intellectual and academic community is well
served here, with new titles upstairs and used and remaindered books
downstairs. ✉ *1256 Massachusetts Ave., Cambridge,* ☎ *617/661–1515.*

**Harvard Coop Society.** Begun in 1882 as a nonprofit service for students and faculty, the Coop is now managed by Barnes & Noble. Although the main store has a thick selection of books and textbooks
(many discounted), there are plenty of things beyond calculus tomes.
Downstairs is a children's book section; one adjoining annex sells
clothes, hats, and even umbrellas with the Harvard insignia; and another annex sells cards, stationery, and housewares, most on the order
of dorm furnishings. ✉ *1400 Massachusetts Ave., Cambridge,* ☎ *617/
499–2000;* ✉ *MIT, 3 Cambridge Center,* ☎ *617/499–3200.*

**Kate's Mystery Books.** A favorite Cambridge haunt, Kate's is a good
place to find mysteries by local writers; look for the authors in person
at one of the shop's frequent readings and events. ✉ *2211 Massachusetts
Ave., Cambridge,* ☎ *617/491–2660.*

**New Words.** New England's largest and oldest women's bookstore stocks
works about and by women; it also sells gifts, stationery, and children's
books. ✉ *186 Hampshire St., Cambridge,* ☎ *617/876–5310.*

**Trident Bookseller and Café.** Browse through an eclectic collection of
books, tapes, and magazines; then settle in with something from the
café menu. It's open until midnight daily, making it a favorite with students. ✉ *338 Newbury St.,* ☎ *617/267–8688.*

**We Think the World of You.** This store in the heart of the South End's
gay neighborhood has gay- and lesbian-oriented books and publications ranging from novels to travel to cooking and exercise. It's also a

great source of posted information for the neighborhood's active gay community and for readings by local and nationally known gay and lesbian authors. ⊠ *540 Tremont St.,* ☎ *617/423–1965.*

**WordsWorth.** One of the biggest bookstores in Harvard Square has about 100,000 titles, most of them discounted. It's easy to get lost among the narrow stacks. Just down the block is **Curious George Goes to WordsWorth** (⊠ 1 JFK St., ☎ 617/498–0062), an annex devoted entirely to children's books and an eclectic selection of book-related toys and activity sets. ⊠ *30 Brattle St., Cambridge,* ☎ *617/354–5201.*

## Clothing

The terminally chic shop on Newbury Street, the hip hang in Harvard Square, and everyone goes downtown for the real bargains.

**Alan Bilzerian.** Satisfying the Euro crowd, this store sells luxe men's and women's clothing by fashionista darlings such as Gaultier, Yohji Yamamoto, and Anne Demeulemeester. ⊠ *34 Newbury St.,* ☎ *617/536–1001.*

**Allston Beat.** Loud in every sense, with rock music thumping through speakers and in-your-face skirts, shirts, tights, and accessories on display, this place has had local street cred for years. It's a favorite place for students to get their now-uniform Doc Martens. ⊠ *348 Newbury St.,* ☎ *617/421–9555.*

**Betsey Johnson.** This is the place to take your teenage daughter—if you dare—to finger leopard-print tops and short, flirty dresses. Skirts are short enough for Ally McBeal. ⊠ *201 Newbury St.,* ☎ *617/236–7072.*

**Brooks Brothers.** To many, Brooks is synonymous with the Wasp good life; its men's and women's clothes run to old faithfuls such as navy blazers, seersucker in summer, and crisp oxford shirts. ⊠ *46 Newbury St.,* ☎ *617/267–2600;* ⊠ *75 State St.,* ☎ *617/261–9990.*

**Chanel.** Located at No. 5 in honor of its famous perfume, this branch of the Parisian couture house carries suits, separates, bags, shoes, and, of course, a selection of little black dresses (from $2,000 to $3,000). ⊠ *5 Newbury St.,* ☎ *617/859–0055.*

**Gianni Versace.** The gold Medusa-head logo and brilliant colors still emblazon the men's and women's clothing and accessories (upstairs) and silk-covered pillows, dishes, and other home furnishings (downstairs). ⊠ *12 Newbury St.,* ☎ *617/536–8300.*

**Giorgio Armani.** This top-of-the-line Italian couturier is known for his carefully shaped jackets, soft suits, and mostly neutral palette. **Emporio Armani** (⊠ 210 Newbury St., ☎ 617/262–7300) sells sportier versions, in addition to jeans, children's clothes, and housewares. The café next door, which spills out onto the sidewalk in warm weather, is popular with the store's international clientele. **A/X Armani Exchange** in the Copley Place mall is even more casual, selling denim, sweaters, and T-shirts. ⊠ *22 Newbury St.,* ☎ *617/267–3200.*

**Jasmine/Sola.** Culling from both coasts, Jasmine shows the work of current designers from New York and Los Angeles. The Cambridge store includes the Sola and Sola Men shoe boutiques. ⊠ *329 Newbury St.,* ☎ *617/437–8466;* ⊠ *37A Brattle St., Cambridge,* ☎ *617/354–6043.*

**Jos. A. Bank Clothiers.** Bostonians head here for reasonably priced classic men's and women's apparel. ⊠ *399 Boylston St.,* ☎ *617/536–5050.*

**Louis, Boston.** Elegantly tailored designs and a wide selection of imported clothing and accessories highlight the latest Italian styles. Subtly updated classics come in everything from linen to tweed. Visiting celebrities might be trolling the racks along with you. ⊠ *234 Berkeley St.,* ☎ *617/262–6100.*

**Serendipity.** Women can outfit themselves for casual Fridays here, with comfortable, loose styles by Eileen Fisher or natural-fiber clothes by Flax. ⊠ *229 Newbury St.,* ☎ *617/437–1850;* ⊠ *1312 Massachusetts Ave., Cambridge,* ☎ *617/661–7143.*

## Crafts

**Alianza.** These are some of Newbury Street's finest crafts, including intricate glasswork, eye-catching ceramics, and innovative jewelry. Seasonal shows might focus on sculptural clocks or whimsical teapots. ⊠ *154 Newbury St.,* ☎ *627/262–2385.*

**The Artful Hand Gallery.** American artisans' work is showcased here, with jewelry, glass, pottery, lamps, and furniture ripe for discovery. ⊠ *36 Copley Pl. (at 100 Ave. of the Arts),* ☎ *617/262–9601.*

**Cambridge Artists' Cooperative.** The items here—ceramics, weavings, jewelry, leatherwork—can be expensive, but they're truly one of a kind. ⊠ *59A Church St., Cambridge,* ☎ *617/868–4434.*

**Fresh Pond Clay Works.** This store exhibits the work of local and nationally known ceramic artists. ⊠ *368 Huron Ave., Cambridge,* ☎ *617/492–1907.*

**Society of Arts and Crafts.** Having hit the century mark in 1997, this is one of the country's oldest nonprofit crafts organizations. It displays an excellent assortment of ceramics, jewelry, leather, glass, woodwork, and furniture by some of the country's finest craftspeople. ⊠ *175 Newbury St.,* ☎ *617/266–1810;* ⊠ *101 Arch St.,* ☎ *617/345–0033.*

## Gifts

**Bellezza Home and Garden.** These Italian bowls, plates, vases, and tiles are exquisitely painted. ⊠ *129 Newbury St.,* ☎ *617/266–1183.*

**Black Ink.** A wall full of funky rubber stamps stretches above unusual candles, cookie jars, and other home accessories. **Black Ink @ Home** (⊠ 370 Broadway, ☎ 617/576–0707) goes further into home territory with industrial-style lamps, furniture, and rugs. ⊠ *101 Charles St.,* ☎ *617/723–3883.*

**Fresh.** You won't know whether to wash with these soaps or nibble on them. The shea butter–rich bars come in scents like clove-hazelnut and orange-cranberry; although they may cost $6 to $7 each, they carry the scent to the end. ⊠ *121 Newbury St.,* ☎ *617/421–1212.*

**Loulou's Lost & Found.** Reproduction jazz-era tableware, salt and pepper shakers, and other items from old ships and hotels could have you itching to start a Grand Tour. **Loulou's Tealuxe** outlet (⊠ Brattle St., Cambridge, ☎ 617/441–0077) also sells 140 premium teas and tea accessories; you can stop here for a cup of organic peppermint or mandarin-cinnamon tea. ⊠ *121 Newbury St.,* ☎ *617/859–8593.*

**Women's Educational and Industrial Union.** Look for the large gold swan above the door; inside are cards, gifts, decorative items, children's clothing, and accessories sold on behalf of the social and educational organization. ⊠ *356 Boylston St.,* ☎ *617/536–5651.*

## Home Furnishings

A home-furnishings hot spot has emerged in an area bounded by the South End, Back Bay, and the Theater District.

**Adesso.** French-, Dutch-, and Italian-designed chairs, sofas, cabinets, and mirrors are joined by equally sharp lighting by Philippe Starck. ⊠ *200 Boylston St.,* ☎ *617/451–2212.*

**April Cornell.** You may enjoying browsing through the Cambridge location, but the Faneuil Hall outlet is the better place to find bargains on lovely printed table linens and bedding. (You'll be choosing from discontinued lines, but the prices are excellent.) You'll also find unusual women's clothing, hats, pottery, and accessories at both locations. ⊠ *Faneuil Hall Marketplace, North Market Bldg.,* ☎ *617/248–0280;* ⊠ *43 Brattle St., Cambridge,* ☎ *617/661–8910.*

**Kitchen Arts.** Here's where to find all sorts of stylish gadgets, gizmos, and doodads. ⊠ *161 Newbury St.,* ☎ *617/266–8701.*

**Koo de Kir.** Break with the blond-wood school with this offbeat selection of furniture, lamps, candles, wine racks, table settings, and other urban necessities. ⊠ *34 Charles St.,* ☎ *617/723–8111.*

**Mohr & McPerson.** This store is a visual Asian feast; cabinets, tables, chairs, and lamps from Japan, India, China, and Indonesia fill the huge space. The Moroccan painted furniture is particularly impressive. Also impressive are the prices—if you suffer from sticker shock, visit the store's Cambridge location, a nearby annex with discounted stock. ⊠ *81 Arlington St.,* ☎ *617/338–1288;* ⊠ *290 Concord Ave., Cambridge,* ☎ *617/354–6662.*

**Repertoire.** Celeste Cooper, the company's artistic director, adds her own furniture to the selection of sofas, chairs, and tables by international designers; there are also table settings from the likes of Richard Ginori and Calvin Klein. ⊠ *114 Boylston St.,* ☎ *617/426–3865.*

**Sweet Peas Home.** Strong accents of color and whimsy characterize the handpainted furniture, vases, mirrors, candles, and folk art figures. ⊠ *216 Clarendon St.,* ☎ *617/247–2828.*

**Zoe.** Form meets function in these contemporary home accessories, which include lamps, shelves, and tables—check out the granite indoor fountains or funky aluminum candlesticks. ⊠ *279 Newbury St.,* ☎ *617/ 375–9133;* ⊠ *554A Tremont St.,* ☎ *617/556–9966.*

## Jewelry

**Alpha Omega.** Rarefied and reasonably priced timepieces (Rolex, Breitling, Chronoswiss, and Rado) pack these stores. ⊠ *Prudential Center,* ☎ *617/424–9030;* ⊠ *57 JFK St., Cambridge,* ☎ *617/864–1227.*

**Dorfman Jewels.** This elegant shop glows with first-class watches, pearls, and precious stones. ⊠ *24 Newbury St.,* ☎ *617/536–2022.*

**Shreve, Crump & Low.** ☞ Antiques, *above.*

**Tiffany & Co.** This is 5th Avenue come to Boston, with the finest in gems and precious metal jewelry as well as flatware, crystal, china, stationery, and fragrances. ⊠ *Copley Pl. (at 100 Ave. of the Arts),* ☎ *617/ 353–0222.*

**Twentieth Century Limited.** Every kind of rhinestone concoction imaginable seems to be here—perfect for the bauble babe in your life. ⊠ *73 Charles St.,* ☎ *617/742–1031.*

## Odds and Ends

**Boston City Store.** This assortment of Boston souvenirs and memorabilia is delightfully off-kilter—everything from vintage street signs to surplus parking meters and hard hats. Profits from the store support neighborhood youth programs; it is closed Sundays. Enter on the north side of the hall. ⊠ *Faneuil Hall basement,* ☎ *617/635–2911.*

**North End Fabrics.** If you're handy with a needle, stop in here for a full range of materials: imported laces, fun furs, satins, and woolens. ⊠ *31 Harrison Ave.,* ☎ *617/542–2763.*

**Out-of-Town News.** Smack in the middle of Harvard Square is a staggering cross section of the world's newspapers and magazines. The stand is open daily 6 AM–11:30 PM and until midnight on Friday and Saturday. ⊠ *Zero Harvard Sq., Cambridge,* ☎ *617/354–7777.*

## Records, Tapes, and Compact Discs

As befitting a town with more than 20 colleges, music of all kinds is never far away, including a hot market in used vinyl.

**HMV.** It's the British rival to Tower Records: a large selection of CDs and tapes of every sort, with listening stations to sample the wares. ⊠ *24 Winter St.,* ☎ *617/357–8444;* ⊠ *1 Brattle Sq., Cambridge,* ☎ *617/ 868–9696.*

**Mystery Train.** For musical rarities and oddities, make tracks to these racks of used and collectible CDs, tapes, and vinyl. ⊠ *306 Newbury St.,* ☎ *617/536–0216;* ⊠ *1208 Massachusetts Ave., Cambridge,* ☎ *617/536–0216;* ⊠ *403 Massachusetts Ave., Cambridge,* ☎ *617/547–9976.*

**Newbury Comics.** This local outpost for new rock-and-roll carries an especially good lineup of independent pressings. Frequent sales keep prices down. ⊠ *332 Newbury St.,* ☎ *617/236–4930;* ⊠ *36 JFK St., Cambridge,* ☎ *617/491–0337.*

**Stereo Jack's.** "Stereo" Jack Woker got his nickname way before the CD was born. His store stocks used and new vinyl records and CDs, particularly jazz, blues, and classical. ⊠ *1686 Massachusetts Ave., Cambridge,* ☎ *617/497–9447.*

**Tower Records Video Books.** Tower distinguishes itself by having not just a good selection but entire discographies. Three enormous floors stock every kind of music imaginable, plus books, magazines, and videos. ⊠ *360 Newbury St.,* ☎ *617/247–5900;* ⊠ *95 Mt. Auburn St., Cambridge,* ☎ *617/876–3377.*

## Shoes

**El Paso.** Here you'll find cowboy boots both wild—look for the green and white or the orange and white—and sober, plus belts and cowboy shirts. ⊠ *154 Newbury St.,* ☎ *617/536–2120.*

**John Fluevog Shoes.** Many club goers have at least one pair of Fluevogs in their closets. The store may make you nostalgic for the days of disco with its lines of Lucite-heeled shoes, tall boots, and even high-stacked, crepe-soled sneakers. ⊠ *302 Newbury St.,* ☎ *617/266–1079.*

**Helen's Leather Shop.** Choose from half a dozen brands of boots (Lucchese, Larry Mahan, Dan Post, Tony Lama, Justin, and Frye); then peruse the leather sandals, jackets, briefcases, luggage, and accessories. ⊠ *110 Charles St.,* ☎ *617/742–2077.*

## Sporting Goods

**Bill Rodgers Running Center.** You can get completely outfitted here with shoes, clothes, and running accessories. Happily, you don't need to be a sports champion to get good pointers from the attentive staff. ⊠ *North Market, Faneuil Hall Marketplace,* ☎ *617/723–5612.*

**Eastern Mountain Sports.** The stock includes everything from tents and sleeping bags to weight-lifting equipment—and a wide selection of casual clothing. ⊠ *1041 Commonwealth Ave., Brighton,* ☎ *617/254–4250.*

**Eric Flaim In-Motion Sports.** Some of the skaters zipping down the Esplanade may well have made a stop here to buy or rent Rollerblades and other in-line skates. ⊠ *349 Newbury St.,* ☎ *617/247–3284.*

**Hilton's Tent City.** This out-of-the-way store in an old building is stuffed to the gills with an excellent selection of hiking, backpacking, and camping equipment, boots and clothing, and hard-to-find items. ⊠ *272 Friend St.,* ☎ *617/227–9242.*

**Marathon Sports.** A shop for serious runners, Marathon is known for its personalized service and advice for choosing the perfect running shoe. ⊠ *1654 Massachusetts Ave., Brookline,* ☎ *617/354–4161.*

**Niketown.** A kind of temple to marketing hype, this huge, flashy setting hawks high-tech sports apparel, gear, and shoes. ⊠ *200 Newbury St.,* ☎ *617/267–3400.*

## Thrift Shops

**Boomerangs.** Clothing, home furnishings, and collectibles are sold in this airy space at bargain rates; all proceeds go to the AIDS Action Committee. ⊠ *60 Canal St.,* ☎ *617/723–2666.*

**Chic Repeats.** Run by the Junior League of Boston, this store sells donated or consigned clothing of high quality, often with designer labels. ⊠ *117 Newbury St.,* ☎ *617/536–8580.*

**The Garment District.** This warehouselike building is crammed with vintage, used, and new clothing and accessories. Students crowd the store year-round, and everyone comes here at Halloween searching for that perfect costume. ⊠ *200 Broadway, Cambridge,* ☎ *617/876–9795.*

**Keezer's.** Since 1895, this shop has been the secret to many a man's success when he wanted formal for a informal price. Pick up new or used suits, tuxedos, ties, shirts, and pants. It also has formal wear for rent. ⊠ *140 River St., Cambridge,* ☎ *617/547–2455.*

## Toys

**F. A. O. Schwarz.** A branch of the famed New York toy emporium has all kinds of toys—trains, dolls, stuffed animals, games, and other intriguing playthings—of the highest quality, at the highest prices. The giant teddy bear sculpture outside is a popular photo spot. ⊠ *440 Boylston St.,* ☎ *617/266–5101.*

**Henry Bear's Park.** This charming neighborhood children's store carries books, toys, dinosaurs, party favors, games, Gund bears—but nothing that hints of violence. ⊠ *361 Huron St., Cambridge,* ☎ *617/ 547–8424;* ⊠ *81 Union St., Newton Centre,* ☎ *617/969–8616.*

# 9 SIDE TRIPS

## WEST OF BOSTON, THE NORTH SHORE, SOUTH OF BOSTON

If your vision of an ideal New England includes pre-Revolutionary inns, seriously scenic surroundings, and towns right out of a Currier & Ives print, then head west for the historic towns of Lexington and Concord and nearby Walden Pond. Heading north leads you to the ocean, and cozy inns, seafood stands, crafts shops, art galleries, and coastal walks that offer a relaxing contrast to Boston's urbanity. In Salem, revisit the sites important to the witch trials. South of Boston, travel back in time at Plimoth Plantation, an unerring re-creation of New England's first settlement in 1627, seven years after the *Mayflower* landed.

**S**OME OF THE MOST IMPORTANT SITES in early American history are within shouting distance of Boston. Whether you spend a day or a long weekend visiting these places, you will come away with an enriched sense of history—a deeper view made possible after walking across a dewy battlefield, ducking through the abbreviated door frame of a 300-year-old house, strolling through the woods or along the seashore, or envisioning inhabitants of bygone eras that, truth be told, are much closer to our own than we typically imagine.

Updated by
Carolyn Heller

You might begin at the beginning, 40 mi south in Plymouth, where a living history center known as Plimoth Plantation re-creates the 17th-century everyday life of the Pilgrims. The quintessential New England towns of Lexington and Concord offer a glimpse of the American Revolution as well as homes of and small museums devoted to some of the country's first literary luminaries—Ralph Waldo Emerson, Nathaniel Hawthorne, Louisa May Alcott, and Henry David Thoreau. Walden, the pond that occasioned the eponymous book, is now a state park. A national historic park in the town of Lowell commemorates the Industrial Revolution. About 35 mi north of Boston, you'll find "the other Cape"—Cape Ann, home to Gloucester, the oldest seaport in the United States, and charming Rockport, crammed with crafts shops and art galleries. Elsewhere on the North Shore, there's Salem, overcome by witchcraft hysteria in the 17th century. And don't miss Newburyport, with its redbrick town center and rows of Federal mansions.

## Pleasures and Pastimes

### By the Sea

Bostonians usually visit the North Shore for its beaches, especially those around Gloucester and Rockport. Others enjoy discovering the pretty New England coastal towns with colorful clapboard cottages, narrow streets, and antiques stores; these are found in greatest concentration inland around Essex—but there are plenty sprinkled elsewhere on Cape Ann as well.

Many of the area's attractions—swimming, boating, and fishing—focus on the water: deep-sea fishing trips are plentiful and surf casting is popular, as is freshwater fishing in the Parker and Ipswich rivers. If you prefer to observe sea life rather than fish for it, take a whale-watching trip. Several breeds of whale feed locally between May and October, so you're practically guaranteed to see a few—and on a good day you may see upward of 40. Organized boat trips leave from many of the coastal towns; they usually last three to four hours, including travel time to and from the whales' feeding grounds.

### Dining

The North Shore offers these destinations' most distinctive dining. In addition to the plethora of seafood restaurants big and small, look for traditional "seafood in the rough" eating places. These establishments serve generous, inexpensive seafood on paper plates, often at wooden picnic tables and frequently outdoors. Menus favor plenty of fried fish dishes and usually fried clams, "invented" in Essex at the turn of the century. In many Boston-area suburbs, upscale contemporary restaurants are increasingly common; it's also possible to sample food that reflects the region's many immigrant groups, including Portuguese, Italian, Greek, and Asian. For price ranges *see* the Dining chart *in* On the Road with Fodor's.

## Literary Haunts

The area west of Boston is particularly rich with literary landmarks. In Concord alone, you may visit in one afternoon Alcott's Orchard House, Nathaniel Hawthorne's Wayside, the Ralph Waldo Emerson House, and Henry David Thoreau's Walden Pond. North of Boston, in Salem, is Hawthorne's House of Seven Gables. Though you might not associate the Beats with this region, Jack Kerouac's grave is in his hometown, Lowell.

## Lodging

In the areas around Concord and Lexington, you'll find country inns and bed-and-breakfasts—many with a delightful personal touch. The North Shore, meanwhile, is home to distinctive seaside inns. Some are converted sea captains' mansions, others were once grand summer homes, a few were built as hotels. The best successfully combine country and oceanside ambience. Cedar shingles, ships' lanterns, and pineapple motifs (a pineapple on the doorstep showed that seafarers were safely returned from exotic lands) combine with patchwork quilts, shining hardwood floors, and open fireplaces to offer some outstanding accommodations. Less expensive options—waterfront motels and bed-and-breakfast homes—are also widely available in summer. But be sure to make reservations early. The North Shore tourist season ends earlier than those in other areas, with many places closing down from late October until April or May. We note air-conditioning only when it's unusual for the type of property, such as historic buildings. For price ranges, *see* the hotel chart *in* On the Road with Fodor's.

## The Spirit of 1775

To better understand the Boston Tea Party, the Battle of Bunker Hill, and the "Massacre," visit Lexington and Concord, the towns where Boston's, and the country's, freedom trail truly began in 1775. These communities quietly embody the region's character traits: charm, reserve, fierce independence, and, above all, deep pride in their history. (But be warned: even in traditional New England, quaintness does beget some development.) Here history is a multifaceted experience; you can explore Revolutionary battlegrounds, taverns, and houses as well as several excellent museums that emphasize both content and context.

# WEST OF BOSTON

West of Boston lie a group of historic sites known by every American schoolchild as the birthplace of the American Revolution. Synonymous with patriotism, daring deeds, and heroic horsemanship, the quintessential New England towns of **Lexington** and **Concord** are where the Revolution's first military encounters took place.

If your interests lean more toward literature and philosophy, you'll find abundant evidence here of an intellectual revolution as well. Lofty thinkers Thoreau and Emerson, and writers Nathaniel Hawthorne and Louisa May Alcott, turned Concord into a think—and literary—tank. These famed figures of American culture were nurtured in these unassuming small towns, now comfortable green commuter suburbs.

**Lincoln, Sudbury,** and **Waltham**—also west of Boston—offer a number of other attractions, although they lack the historic and literary significance of either Lexington or Concord.

Farther west and north, **Lowell** underwent still another revolution—the Industrial Revolution—and its legacy is considerably less picturesque. But despite its derelict mills and canals, and its high quotient

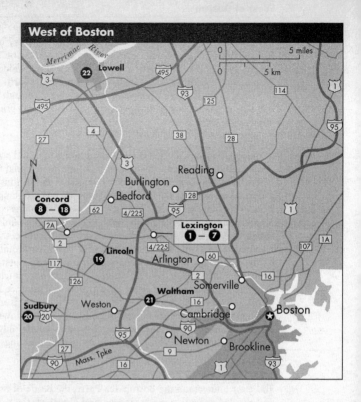

West of Boston

of crime and poverty, Lowell offers an imaginatively restored down-town area, including a large, compelling urban national park.

## Lexington

*Numbers in the margin correspond to points of interest on the Lex-ington map.*

*16 mi northwest of Boston.*

The discontent smoldering in the British-ruled American colonies burst into action in Lexington on April 19, 1775. On the previous night, pa-triot leader Paul Revere alerted the town that British soldiers were ap-proaching. As the British advance troops, led by Major John Pitcairn, arrived in Lexington on their march toward Concord, a small group of militiamen, known as the Minutemen, were waiting to confront the redcoats in what became the first skirmish of the Revolutionary War.

The events of the American Revolution are very much a part of present-day Lexington, a modern suburb that now sprawls out from the his-toric sites near the town center. Although the downtown area is generally lively, with its ice cream and coffee shops, boutiques, and a great little movie theater, the town is especially animated each Patriot's Day (the Monday nearest April 19), when groups of costume-clad "Min-utemen" re-create battle maneuvers and "Paul Revere" reenacts his mid-night ride. In 2000 the town will have an especially elaborate reenactment to celebrate the 225th anniversary of the events; a series of battles and ceremonies will involve more than 1,500 participants—including units from Britain.

The real Paul Revere roused patriots John Hancock and Sam Adams—who were in Concord to attend the Provincial Congress then in ses- sion—from their sleep at the eight-room **Hancock-Clarke House,** a parsonage built in 1698. Revere rode out from Boston on the night of April 18, 1775 to "spread the alarm" that the British were approaching "through every Middlesex village and farm." Both Hancock and Adams fled to avoid capture. The house, a 10-minute walk from Lexington Common, displays the pistols of the British major John Pitcairn as well as period furnishings and portraits. A 20-minute tour is offered. ✉ *36 Hancock St.,* ☎ *781/861–0928.* 🎫 *$4; $10 combination ticket for the Hancock-Clarke House, Buckman Tavern, and Munroe Tavern.* ☉ *Mid-Apr.–Oct., Mon.–Sat. 10–5, Sun. 1–5.*

❷ The Minutemen gathered at the **Buckman Tavern** (1690) on the morning of April 19, 1775. A 35-minute tour takes in the tavern's seven rooms. Display items include an old front door with a hole made by a British musket ball. ✉ *1 Bedford St.,* ☎ *781/862–5598.* 🎫 *$4; $10 combination ticket for the Hancock-Clarke House, Buckman Tavern, and Munroe Tavern.* ☉ *Mid-Apr.–Oct., Mon.–Sat. 10–5, Sun. 1–5.*

❸ Minuteman captain John Parker assembled his men out on **Battle Green,** a 2-acre, triangular piece of land, to await the arrival of the British, who were marching from Boston toward Concord to "teach rebels a lesson." (The Minutemen were so called because they were able to prepare themselves at a moment's notice.) Parker's role is com-
❹ memorated in Henry Hudson Kitson's renowned sculpture, the **Minuteman Statue,** standing at the tip of the Green, facing downtown Lexington. Because it's in a traffic island, it doesn't present a natural photo op. The **Revolutionary Monument,** near the *Minuteman* statue, marks the burial site of Minutemen killed that day. Captain Parker's command that morning to his 77 men, who formed two uneven lines of defense, is emblazoned on the **Line of Battle boulder,** to the right of the *Minuteman* statue: "Stand your ground, don't fire unless fired upon; but if they mean to have war, let it begin here." The British major John Pitcairn ordered his troops to surround the Minutemen and disarm them but not to fire. A shot did ring out, and the rest is history. Two questions remain unanswered: Who fired that first shot? And why did Parker, a seasoned veteran of the French and Indian Wars, position his men behind the two-story, barnlike meetinghouse that stood on the spot where the *Minuteman* statue stands today? (A memorial behind the statue marks the site.) From there, the Minutemen weren't able to see the British advancing, much less make a show of resistance. Indeed, why didn't Captain Parker tell his men to take to the hills overlooking the British route? It was an absurd situation: 77 men against 700, turning it into one of history's most notorious mishaps. Even in modern times, the green has been the site of patriotic public gatherings: in 1942, residents gathered to pledge support for the Allies, and during the 1960s, it saw demonstrations on civil rights and the Vietnam War. The pleasant **Lexington Visitor Center** nearby has a diorama of the 1775 clash on the green, plus a gift shop. *Visitor Center (Lexington Chamber of Commerce):* ✉ *1875 Massachusetts Ave.,* ☎ *781/ 862–1450.* ☉ *Mid-Apr.–Oct., daily 9–5; Nov.–mid-Apr., generally weekdays 10–3, weekends 10–4.*

As April 19 dragged on, British forces met far fiercer resistance in Concord. Dazed and demoralized after the battle at Old North Bridge (☞
❺ Concord, *below*), the British backtracked and regrouped at the **Munroe Tavern** (1695) while the Munroe family hid in nearby woods; then the troops retreated through what is now the town of Arlington and, after a bloody battle there, returned to Boston. The tavern is 1 mi east of Lexington Common. ✉ *1332 Massachusetts Ave.,* ☎ *781/674–9238.* 🎫 *$4; $10 combination ticket for the Hancock-Clarke House, Buck-*

# Lexington

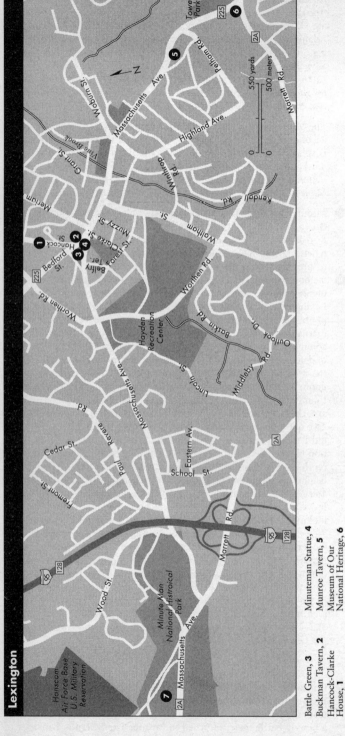

Battle Green, **3**
Buckman Tavern, **2**
Hancock-Clarke
House, **1**
Minute Man
National Historic
Park Visitor Center, **7**

Minuteman Statue, **4**
Munroe Tavern, **5**
Museum of Our
National Heritage, **6**

# Finally, a travel companion that doesn't snore on the plane or eat all your peanuts.

**MCI WORLDCOM** · *WorldPhone®*

123 456 7891 2345
J.D. SMITH

When traveling, your MCI WorldCom Card is the best way to keep in touch. Our operators speak your language, so they'll be able to connect you back home—no matter where your travels take you. Plus, your MCI WorldCom Card is easy to use, and even earns you frequent flyer miles every time you use it. When you add in our great rates, you get something even more valuable: peace-of-mind. So go ahead. Travel the world. MCI WorldCom just brought it a whole lot closer.

You can even sign up today at www.mci.com/worldphone or ask your operator to make a collect call to 1-410-314-2938.

## EASY TO CALL WORLDWIDE

1. Just dial the WorldPhone access number of the country you're calling from.
2. Dial or give the operator your MCI WorldCom Card number.
3. Dial or give the number you're calling.

| | |
|---|---|
| **Australia ◆**<br>To call using OPTUS<br>To call using TELSTRA | **1-800-551-111**<br>**1-800-881-100** |
| **Bahamas/Bermuda** | **1-800-888-8000** |
| **British Virgin Islands** | **1-800-888-8000** |
| **Costa Rica ◆** | **0-800-012-2222** |
| **Denmark** | **8001-0022** |
| **Norway ◆** | **800 -19912** |
| **India**<br>For collect access | **000-127**<br>**000-126** |
| **United States/Canada** | **1-800-888-8000** |

For your complete WorldPhone calling guide, dial the WorldPhone access number for the country you're in and ask the operator for Customer Service. In the U.S. call 1-800-431-5402.

◆ Public phones may require deposit of coin or phone card for dial tone.

## EARN FREQUENT FLYER MILES

**American Airlines®**
**AAdvantage®**

**Continental Airlines**
**OnePass**

**▲ Delta Air Lines**
**SkyMiles®**

**MILEAGE PLUS.**
**United Airlines**

**U·S AIRWAYS**
**DIVIDEND MILES**

MCI WorldCom, its logo and the names of the products referred to herein are proprietary marks of MCI WorldCom, Inc. All airline names and logos are proprietary marks of the respective airlines. All airline program rules and conditions apply.

**MCI WORLDCOM**

# Fodor's

Distinctive guides packed with up-to-date expert advice
and smart choices for every type of traveler.

**Fodor's.** For the world of ways you travel.

*man Tavern, and Munroe Tavern.* ⊙ *Mid-Apr.–Oct., Mon.–Sat. 10–5, Sun. 1–5.*

★ ⑥ Ironically, the **Museum of Our National Heritage,** devoted to the nation's cultural heritage and located in one of its oldest towns, is housed in a contemporary brick-and-glass building. This small but dynamic institution superbly displays items and artifacts from all facets of American life, putting them in social and political context. An ongoing exhibit, "Lexington Alarm'd," illustrates Revolutionary-era life through everyday household objects. Another ongoing exhibit highlights the country's fraternal organizations. The museum also hosts lectures, family programs, and films; there's a well-stocked gift shop. ⊠ *33 Marrett Rd. (Rte. 2A at Massachusetts Ave.),* ☎ *781/861–6559.* ▦ *Free; donation suggested.* ⊙ *Mon.–Sat. 10–5, Sun. noon–5.*

⑦ If you're headed for Concord, stop at the **Minute Man National Historical Park Visitor Center,** formerly the Battle Road Visitor Center, in the 800-acre Minute Man National Historical Park that extends into Lexington, Concord, and Lincoln. The center's exhibits and film focus on the Revolutionary War. ⊠ *Rte. 2A, ½ mi west of Rte. 128,* ☎ *781/862–7753.* ⊙ *Mid-Apr.–Oct., daily 9–5; Nov.–mid-Apr., daily 9–4.*

OFF THE
BEATEN PATH

**ARLINGTON** – Although seldom mentioned in the same breath as Lexington and Concord, Arlington—now a bustling suburb between Cambridge and Lexington—played an important role in Revolutionary history. As the redcoats retreated during that fateful battle on April 19, 1775, Minutemen peppered them with musket fire from behind stone walls and pine trees. The bullet-ridden **Jason Russell House** marks the spot where 10 Minutemen and more than 20 British soldiers were killed during the Battle of the Foot of the Rocks. Today, the interior displays period kitchenware, spinning wheels, even a stray cannonball. Adjoining the Jason Russell House, a modern barn-shaped structure houses the **George Abbott Smith History Museum,** with changing exhibits illustrating Massachusetts and Arlington history. Displays include a Revolutionary-era musket, a statement of town expenses from 1811, and photos of historic area homes. The museum has a longer visiting season than the unheated Jason Russell House, staying open through December; from January to mid-April you can visit by prior appointment. ⊠ *7 Jason St., at Massachusetts Ave.,* ☎ *781/648–4300.* ▦ *$2.* ⊙ *Mid-Apr.–Oct., Tues.–Sat. 1–5. Tours available.*

## Dining

$–$$$ ✗ **Dabin.** This relaxing restaurant serves traditional Japanese and Korean fare. Lunch specials include udon or soba noodles, sushi combinations, and *bento* boxes of tempura, Korean-style grilled beef, or broiled salmon. It's just one block off Massachusetts Avenue. ⊠ *10 Muzzey St.,* ☎ *781/860–0171. AE, D, MC, V.*

$ ✗ **Bertucci's.** Part of a popular chain, this Italian restaurant offers good food, reasonable prices, a large menu, and a family-friendly atmosphere. Specialties include ravioli, calzones, and a wide assortment of brick-oven baked pizzas. ⊠ *1777 Massachusetts Ave.,* ☎ *781/860–9000. AE, D, MC, V.*

## Outdoor Activities and Sports

### BICYCLING

During warm weather, Lexington fills with bicyclists—taking a break for an ice cream fix—from the nearby **Minuteman Trail,** an 11-mi biking, in-line skating, and jogging path that follows an abandoned railroad route running from Cambridge (near Alewife Station) through

Arlington and Lexington to Bedford. A trail map is available at the **Lexington Visitor Center** (☞ *above*).

## Concord

*Numbers in the margin correspond to points of interest on the Concord map.*

*About 10 mi west of Lexington, 21 mi northwest of Boston.*

Concord's historical prominence has both military and literary claims. Today it's a modern suburb with a busy center filled with arty shops, places to eat, and (recalling the town's literary connections) old bookstores. Autumn lovers, take note: Concord is a great place to start a fall foliage tour. From Boston, head west along Route 2 to find harvest stands and do-it-yourself apple-picking around Harvard and Stow.

To reach Concord from Lexington, take Routes 4/225 through Bedford and Route 62 west to Concord; or pick up Route 2A west from Massachusetts Avenue at the Museum of Our National Heritage or by taking Waltham Street south from Lexington Center. Following Route 2A is a longer but charming drive that takes you through parts of the **Minute Man National Historical Park,** a two-parcel park with more than 800 acres straddling Lexington, Concord, and Lincoln. Stop off at the point where Revere's midnight ride ended with his capture by the British; it's marked with a boulder and plaque. The park contains many of the sites important to Concord's role in the Revolution, such as the Old North Bridge (☞ *below*), Fiske Hill, and Hartwell Tavern, plus two visitor centers. (If you're headed for Concord center, bear right onto Lexington Road off of Route 2A shortly after the Hartwell Tavern.) The park is crossed by Battle Road, which roughly follows the path the British took to and from Boston during the battle of Lexington and Concord. (You can attempt to drive it; pick up a map at the park visitor center and watch for the distinctive signs.) The National Park Service has also built a 5-mi trail for bikes and foot, the **Battle Road Trail,** which lets the more intrepid see the park sans auto. *North Bridge Visitor Center,* ✉ *174 Liberty St.,* ☎ *978/369–6993.* 🎫 *Free.* ☉ *Early May–Nov., daily 9–5:30; Nov.–early May, daily 9–4.*

You can reach the North Bridge section of the park by water if you rent a canoe at the **South Bridge Boat House** and paddle along the Sudbury and Concord rivers. ✉ *496 Main St.,* ☎ *978/369–9438.*

Although the initial Revolutionary War sorties were in Lexington, word of the American losses spread rapidly to surrounding towns: when the British marched into Concord, more than 400 Minutemen were waiting. A marker set in the stone wall along Liberty Street, behind the Old North Bridge Visitors Center, announces: "On this field the Minutemen and militia formed before marching down to the fight at the bridge."

❽ At the **Old North Bridge,** ½ mi from Concord center, the Concord Minutemen turned the tables on the British in the morning of April 19, 1775. The Americans did not fire first, but when two of their own fell dead from a redcoat volley, Major John Buttrick of Concord roared, "Fire, fellow soldiers, for God's sake, fire." The Minutemen released volley after volley, and the redcoats fled. Daniel Chester French's famous statue *The Minuteman* (1875) honors the country's first freedom fighters. The lovely wooded surroundings give a sense of what the landscape was like in more rural times.

Of the confrontation, Ralph Waldo Emerson wrote in 1837: "By the rude bridge that arched the flood / Their flag to April's breeze unfurled /

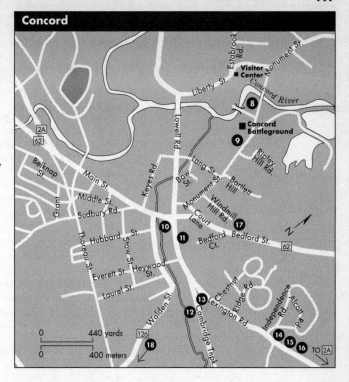

Concord

Here once the embattled farmers stood / And fired the shot heard round the world." (The lines are inscribed at the foot of *The Minuteman*) statue. Hence, Concord claims the right to the "shot," believing that native son Emerson was, of course, referring to the North Bridge standoff. Park Service officials skirt the issue, saying the shot could refer to the battle on Lexington Green, when the very first shot rang out from an unknown source, or to Concord when Minutemen held back the redcoats in the Revolution's first major battle, or even to the Boston Massacre. What's important is Emerson's vision that here began the modern world's first experiment in democracy.

**9** The Reverend William Emerson, ancestor of Ralph Waldo Emerson, watched rebels and redcoats battle from behind his home, the **Old Manse,** within sight of the Old North Bridge. The house, built in 1770, was occupied by the family except for a period of 3½ years, when renter Nathaniel Hawthorne lived and wrote short stories here. Furnishings date from the late 18th century. To see the interior you'll need to join a tour; these run throughout the day and last 40 minutes, with a new tour starting within 15 minutes of when the first person signs up. ⊠ *269 Monument St.,* ☎ *978/369–3909.* ⌛ *$5.50.* ☉ *Mid-Apr.–late Oct., Mon.–Sat. 10–5, Sun. noon–5.*

NEED A
BREAK?

If your sweet tooth needs indulging, stop at the **Sally Ann Food Shop** (⊠ 73 Main St., ☎ 978/369–4558), a popular bakery selling cookies (try the tart lemon poppyseed), muffins, and danishes. You can also put together a picnic around the corner at the **Cheese Shop** (⊠ 31 Walden St., ☎ 978/369–5778), a specialty grocer, wine retailer, and deli.

**10** The **Wright Tavern,** built in 1747, served as headquarters first for the Minutemen, then the British, both on April 19. It is closed to the public. ⊠ *2 Lexington Rd.*

⑪ Now displaying a series of rotating art exhibits, the **Jonathan Ball House,** built in 1753, was a station on the Underground Railroad for runaway slaves during the Civil War. Ask to see the secret room. The garden and waterfall are refreshing sights. ⊠ *Art Association, 37 Lexington Rd.,* ☎ *978/369–2578.* ☜ *Free.* ☉ *Tues.–Sat. 10–4:30.*

The 19th-century essayist and poet Ralph Waldo Emerson, grandson of William Emerson, lived briefly in the Old Manse in 1834–35, then ⑫ moved to what is known as the **Ralph Waldo Emerson House,** where he lived until his death in 1882. Here he wrote the *Essays* ("To be great is to be misunderstood"; "A foolish consistency is the hobgoblin of little minds"). Except for items from Emerson's study, now at the nearby Concord Museum (☞ *below*), the Emerson House furnishings have been preserved as the writer left them, down to his hat resting on the newel post. You must join one of the half-hour-long tours to see the interior. ⊠ *28 Cambridge Turnpike, at Lexington Rd.,* ☎ *978/369–2236.* ☜ *$5.* ☉ *Mid-Apr.–late Oct., Thurs.–Sat. 10–4:30, Sun. 2–4:30.*

⑬ The original contents of Emerson's private study are in the **Concord Museum,** just east of the town center. In a 1930 Colonial Revival structure, the museum houses 15 period rooms, ranging in decor from Colonial to Empire. It has the world's largest collection of Thoreau artifacts, including furnishings from the Walden Pond cabin, as well as a diorama of the Old North Bridge battle, Native American artifacts, and one of two lanterns hung at Boston's Old North Church on the night of April 18, 1775. ⊠ *200 Lexington Rd. (entrance on Cambridge Turnpike),* ☎ *978/369–9763.* ☜ *$6.* ☉ *Apr.–Dec., Mon.–Sat. 9–5, Sun. noon–5; Jan.–Mar., Mon.–Sat. 11–4, Sun. 1–4.*

⑭ The dark brown exterior of Louisa May Alcott's family home, **Orchard House,** poses a sharp contrast to the light, wit, and energy so much in evidence inside. Named for the apple orchard that once surrounded it, Orchard House was the Alcott family home from 1857 to 1877. Here Louisa wrote *Little Women,* based on her life with her three sisters, and her father, Bronson, founded his school of philosophy; the building remains behind the house. (Earlier, Bronson, along with Emerson, Thoreau, and English reformer Charles Lane, had established a Utopian community at Fruitlands, a farm farther west in rural Harvard.) Because Orchard House had just one owner after the Alcotts left and because it became a museum in 1911, many of the original furnishings remain, including the semicircular shelf-desk where Louisa wrote *Little Women.* Portraits and watercolors by May Alcott (the model for Amy) abound; in her room you can see where she sketched figures on the walls—the Alcotts encouraged such creativity. The gift shop has a generous selection of Alcott books. ⊠ *399 Lexington Rd.,* ☎ *978/369–4118.* ☜ *$5.50.* ☉ *Apr.–Oct., Mon.–Sat. 10–4:30, Sun. 1–4:30; Nov.–Mar., weekdays 11–3, Sat. 10–4:30, Sun. 1–4:30; closed Jan. 1–15.*

Nathaniel Hawthorne lived at the Old Manse in 1842–45, working on stories and sketches; he then moved to Salem (where he wrote *The Scarlet Letter*) and later to Lenox (*The House of the Seven Gables*). In 1852 he returned to Concord, bought a rambling structure called ⑮ **The Wayside,** and lived here until his death in 1864. The subsequent owner, Margaret Sidney (author of *Five Little Peppers and How They Grew*), kept Hawthorne's tower-study intact. Prior to Hawthorne's ownership, the Alcotts lived here, from 1845 to 1848. To see the interior, you'll need to take one of the 45-minute-long tours. ⊠ *455 Lexington Rd.,* ☎ *978/369–6975 or 978/369–6993.* ☜ *$4.* ☉ *Mid-May–Oct., Thurs.–Tues. 10–5.*

**⑯** A Concord curiosity, the yard of the privately owned **Grapevine Cottage** has the original Concord grapevine, the grape that the Welch's jams and jellies company made famous. In 1983, Welch's moved its corporate headquarters from New York to Concord to bring the company "back to its roots." A plaque on the fence tells how Ephraim Wales Bull began cultivating the Concord grape. The cottage is closed to the public. ⊠ *491 Lexington Rd.*

**⑰** Each Memorial Day, Louisa May Alcott's grave in the nearby **Sleepy Hollow Cemetery** is decorated in commemoration of her death. Like Emerson, Thoreau, and Nathaniel Hawthorne, Alcott is buried in a section of the cemetery known as **Author's Ridge.** ⊠ *Bedford St. (Rte. 62),* ☎ *978/318–3233.* ☉ *Generally, daily 7–dusk.*

**⑱** A trip to Concord can also include a pilgrimage to **Walden Pond,** Henry David Thoreau's most famous residence. Here, in 1845, at age 28, Thoreau moved into a one-room cabin—built for $28.12½—on the shore of this 100-ft-deep kettle hole, formed 12,000 years ago by the retreat of the New England glacier. Living alone for the next two years, Thoreau discovered the benefits of solitude and the beauties of nature. "Thank God they can't cut down the clouds," he once remarked; such sentiments made him into the philosophical godfather of the 20th-century ecological movement. Thoreau later published *Walden* (1854), a collection of essays on observations he made while living here. The site of that first cabin—only discovered a few decades ago—is staked out in stone. A full-size, authentically furnished replica of the cabin stands about ½ mi from the original site, near the Walden Pond State Reservation parking lot. Even when it's closed, you can peek through its windows. Its sparseness is stirring, even if—truth be told—Thoreau was not actually that far from civilization: the railroad ran nearby and he could walk into town. Nevertheless, standing at the pond, particularly in cold weather when the tourist throngs are gone, you may be moved to "simplify, simplify" your life.

Modern conservationists have fought long and hard, as did Thoreau, to keep commercial development at bay. One only has to notice the huge sanitary landfill just ¼ mi from the park's entrance to realize that Thoreau's legacy meant little when a fast buck was to be made. Now, however, through the Walden Woods Project, about 90 acres of the area surrounding the 333-acre Walden Pond Reservation have been set aside in perpetuity. (The group battled a developer who sought to open an office park across Route 2 from the pond.)

Now, as in Thoreau's time, the pond is a delightful summertime spot for swimming, fishing, and rowing, and there's hiking in the nearby woods. To get to Walden Pond State Reservation from the center of Concord—a trip of only 1½ mi—take Concord's Main Street a block west from Monument Square, turn left onto Walden Street, and head for the intersection of Routes 2 and 126. Cross over Route 2 onto Route 126, heading south for ½ mi. The entrance to the state reservation is on the left. Parking is extremely tight in summer; it's a good idea to call ahead to find out the next hour at which the lot will open again (only a certain number of visitors are allowed in at a time). ⊠ *Rte. 126,* ☎ *978/369–3254.* ◪ *Free; parking across road from pond, late May–early Sept., $2 per vehicle; early Sept.–late May, free parking.* ☉ *Daily until approximately ½ hr before sunset. Replica of Thoreau's cabin late May–mid-Oct., daily 1–3.*

## Dining and Lodging

**$$–$$$**   ✕ **Walden Grille.** In this old brick firehouse turned dining room, satisfy your appetite with tempting contemporary dishes. Lighter options include salads (such as rare lamb over arugula) and sandwiches (try grilled chicken with red pepper rémoulade or the hummus and cucumber wrap). Heartier entrées may range from wild mushroom ravioli to grilled shrimp with risotto-polenta cakes. ⊠ *24 Walden St.,* ☎ *978/371–2233. AE, D, DC, MC, V.*

**$$$–$$$$**   ✕🏠 **Colonial Inn.** Traditional fare—from prime ribs to scallops—is served in the gracious dining room of this 1716 inn (reservations are essential). Rooms in the main inn have Colonial elegance, with exposed beams and antique furniture. The 1960s Prescott Wing has a cozier, more modern country-inn-floral feel. ⊠ *48 Monument Sq., 01742,* ☎ *978/369–9200 or 800/370–9200,* 𝖥𝖠𝖷 *978/371–1533. 49 rooms. Restaurant, 2 bars, laundry service. AE, D, DC, MC, V.*

**$$–$$$$**   🏠 **Hawthorne Inn.** This rambling pink stuccoed Victorian B&B, just across busy Lexington Road from the Wayside (☞ *above*), has an eclectic, homey feel—antique four-poster and canopy beds and handmade quilts are mixed with African masks and contemporary sculpture. Rooms vary in size from petite to moderate; the larger ones have bay-windowed nooks. Owners Gregory Burch (he did many of the sculptures) and Marilyn Mudry (she made the quilts) provide magazines and poetry books for guests to peruse by the fire in the cozy common room. Continental breakfast is included. ⊠ *462 Lexington Rd., 01742,* ☎ *978/369–5610,* 𝖥𝖠𝖷 *978/287–4949. 7 rooms. Breakfast room, air-conditioning (in summer). AE, D, MC, V.*

# Lincoln

*Numbers in the margin correspond to points of interest on the West of Boston map.*

⑲ *15 mi from Boston, west of I–95 and mostly south of Rte. 2.*

Lincoln is an elegant suburb that preserves more than 7,000 acres of land in conservation areas and is home to several interesting sites. From Concord, continue south on Route 126, past Walden Pond, into Lincoln.

🐾   The Massachusetts Audubon Society's **Drumlin Farm** is a 180-acre working New England farm with domestic and wild animal exhibits, nature trails, hayrides, and a gift shop. ⊠ *South Great Rd., Rte. 117,* ☎ *781/259–9807.* 🎟 *$6.* ☉ *Mar.–Oct., Mon. holidays and Tues.–Sun. 9–5; Nov.–Feb., Mon. holidays and Tues.–Sun. 9–4.*

The **DeCordova Museum and Sculpture Park** is worth a morning or afternoon, especially on a sunny day when you can walk around the modern sculptures set on 30 acres of parkland overlooking Sandy Pond. Indoors, the museum offers rotating contemporary art exhibitions emphasizing the work of New England artists. Outdoor concerts take place on weekends in warm weather. ⊠ *51 Sandy Pond Rd.,* ☎ *781/259–8355.* 🎟 *Museum $6, grounds free.* ☉ *Museum Tues.–Sun. 11–5 and selected Mon. holidays; grounds daily.*

The **Codman House,** originally a two-story, L-shaped Georgian structure set amid agricultural fields, was more than doubled in size in 1797–98 by John Codman. (The design for the expansion is attributed to Charles Bulfinch.) The house is preserved with evidence of every period, from the original Georgian paneled rooms to a Victorian dining room, and it is run under the supervision of the Society for the Preservation of New England Antiquities (SPNEA). Codman also landscaped the grounds to resemble those of an English country estate. ⊠ *Cod-*

*man Rd. (off Rte. 126),* ☎ *781/259–8843.* 🎟 *Guided tours $4, grounds free.* ☉ *June–mid-Oct., Wed.–Sun. 11–5; last tour departs at 4 PM. Grounds open year-round.*

The **Gropius House** was the family home of the architect Walter Gropius (1883–1969), director of the Bauhaus, the celebrated modernist school of design in Germany, from 1919 to 1928. This was the first building he designed on his arrival in the United States in 1937. He used components available from catalogs and building-supply stores in a revolutionary manner; the results were faithful to the Bauhaus principles of functionality and simplicity. The house is under the supervision of SPNEA. Tours are given on the hour. ✉ *68 Baker Bridge Rd. (off Rte. 126),* ☎ *781/259–8098.* 🎟 *Guided tours $5.* ☉ *June–mid-Oct., Wed.–Sun. 11–5; mid-Oct.–May, weekends 11–5.*

## Sudbury

**②⓪** *8 mi southwest of Lincoln, 20 mi west of Boston on Rte. 20.*

Sudbury, a developing suburban community with a busy commercial strip along Route 20, actually has a strong literary tie. Here you'll find **Longfellow's Wayside Inn,** which was restored, beginning in 1923, by auto titan Henry Ford. Known originally in the 1700s as How's Inn, the tavern became forever linked with the name of the poet Henry Wadsworth Longfellow when his *Tales of a Wayside Inn* was published in 1863. The inn is far from a museum, though—you can still get a traditional meal and a bed for the night (☞ Dining and Lodging, *below*). Within walking distance of the inn are a working reproduction of an 18th-century **gristmill**; the 1798 **schoolhouse** that "Mary" and her "little lamb" reportedly attended (moved here from Sterling, Massachusetts, by Henry Ford in 1926); and the **Martha-Mary Chapel,** which Henry Ford built in 1940 in memory of his mother-in-law and his mother. The chapel is now frequently used for weddings.

OFF THE BEATEN PATH

Heading back east toward Boston, about 10 mi from Sudbury along Route 20 in Weston—a rich, rambling country suburb characterized by gracious homes on large rural lots—stop at the **Cardinal Spellman Philatelic Museum,** on the campus of Regis College. More than 3½ million stamps are displayed—everything from Walt Disney–theme stamps to flower stamps. ✉ *235 Wellesley St.,* ☎ *781/894–6735.* 🎟 *$5.* ☉ *Thurs.–Sun. noon–5.*

In springtime, garden-loving Bostonians make the trip to the **Garden in the Woods** to glimpse the first blossoming trees, wildflowers, and shrubs. Run by the New England Wild Flower Society, the 45-acre garden has nearly 3 mi of trails and is planted with more than 1,600 kinds of plants, 200 of them rare or endangered. Even in summer and fall, the majestic trees and naturalistic woodland landscapes can be a welcome escape from an urban overdose. Self-guiding booklets are available, and informal guided walks are given at 10 AM every day except Sunday. The garden also offers numerous garden and wildflower classes and workshops. The garden is about 1mi south of Route 20; there are detailed directions on the recorded message. ✉ *180 Hemenway Rd., Framingham,* ☎ *508/877–7630; 508/877–6574 recorded information.* 🎟 *$6.* ☉ *Mid-Apr.–mid-June, daily 9–5; extended hrs to 7 PM in May; mid-June–Oct., Tues.–Sun. 9–5. Last admission 1 hr before closing.*

### Dining and Lodging

**$$** ✕⊡ **Longfellow's Wayside Inn.** Billed as America's oldest operating inn, the Wayside was built as a two-room homestead in 1702; owner David How expanded the building and began offering lodging in 1716. Guest rooms are furnished with Colonial-style antiques; a full breakfast is included. In the dining room, guests can begin with a "coow woow," a rum drink reputed to be America's first cocktail, and continue with Yankee pot roast, baked stuffed fillet of sole, or other New England classics. ⊠ *Wayside Inn Rd. (off Boston Post Rd./Rte. 20), 01776, ☎ 978/443–8846 or 800/339–1776, ℻ 978/443–8041. 10 rooms. Restaurant, bar, air-conditioning. AE, D, DC, MC, V.*

## Waltham

㉑ *12 mi west of Boston on Rte. 20 near the Charles River.*

Waltham's role today is primarily as a commuter suburb of Boston on the Charles River and a base for high-tech companies along Route 128, but back in 1813, the local Boston Manufacturing Company experimented with an "industrial revolution" of its own: producing a product—machine-made cloth—from start to finish under one roof. When it became obvious that the waters of the Charles were inadequate to supply enough energy to produce cloth on the scale intended, however, Boston Manufacturing moved its operations north to Lowell, on the Merrimack River. The **Charles River Museum of Industry** houses a history of American industry, from 1800 to the present, with an emphasis on steam-powered machinery. Exhibits include automobile manufacturing, watchmaking, and power looms. At press time, the museum planned to open a new telecommunications gallery and public Internet center in 1999. ⊠ *154 Moody St. (the parking lot is around the corner; take Pine St. to Cooper St.), ☎ 781/893–5410. ☞ $4. ⊗ Mon.–Sat. 10–5.*

Besides its landmarks of the industrial revolution, Waltham's past has another side, captured in two well-preserved pieces of architecture. One, the **Lyman Estate,** or the Vale, was built in 1793 by Theodore Lyman, a wealthy Boston merchant and entrepreneur. The Salem architect Samuel McIntire designed the elegant country house and the surrounding grounds in accordance with English design principles. An enthusiastic horticulturist and gentleman-farmer, Lyman erected **greenhouses** for the cultivation of exotic fruits and flowers. Many of the camellias and grapevines growing here today are more than 100 years old. The property is run under the supervision of SPNEA, which has a **Conservation Center** here. The house, substantially enlarged in 1882, is rented out for special events. ⊠ *185 Lyman St. (off Beaver St.), ☎ 781/891–7095 greenhouses; 781/893–7232 house. ☞ Greenhouses $2 donation suggested. ⊗ Greenhouses Mon.–Sat. 9–4; house by appointment for groups of 10 or more only.*

Waltham's other distinctive building is **Gore Place,** a 22-room Federal-period mansion built in 1805, accented by a "flying staircase" that spirals three full flights. Built as the country house of Governor Christopher Gore, it's now a museum devoted to Early American and European antiques. (The house's interior is shown only through its guided tours.) The 45 acres of grounds comprise cultivated fields, gardens, and woodlands. ⊠ *52 Gore St. (off Main St./Rte. 20 on the Waltham-Watertown line), ☎ 781/894–2798. ☞ $5; grounds free. ⊗ Mid-Apr.–mid-Nov., tours Tues.–Sat. 11–5, Sun. 1–5 (last tour leaves at 4); mid-Nov.–mid-Apr., tours by appointment only. Grounds open daily dawn–dusk.*

### Dining

$$$–$$$$ ✕ **Il Capriccio.** Waltham is earning notice as an emerging suburban restaurant district; this contemporary Italian spot helps build that reputation. The menu successfully blends the innovative—foie gras ravioli, wild boar sausage with grilled polenta—with updated Italian classics, such as seafood risotto and braised rabbit with black olives. ⊠ *888 Main St. (at Prospect St.),* ☎ *781/894–2234. AE, D, DC, MC, V.*

$–$$ ✕ **Carambola.** Under the same ownership as the Cambridge-based Elephant Walk restaurant (☞ Cambridge/Somerville *in* Chapter 4), Carambola serves delicious Cambodian food in a comfortable, tropically decorated room. Specialties include *soupe phnom-penh* (brimming with rice noodles, sliced pork, and fried garlic), a fragrant lime-cured beef salad, and chicken sautéed with lemongrass. ⊠ *663 Main St. (near Moody St.),* ☎ *781/899–2244. AE, D, DC, MC, V.*

## Lowell

🏻 *30 mi northwest of Boston.*

Everyone knows that the American Revolution began in Massachusetts. But the Commonwealth, and in particular the Merrimack Valley, also nurtured the Industrial Revolution. Lowell's first mill opened in 1823; by the 1850s, 40 factories employed thousands of workers and produced 2 million yards of cloth every week. By the mid-20th century, much of the textile industry had moved South, but the remnants of redbrick factories and murky canals remain as testaments to Lowell's role in American industrial history. The **Lowell National Historical Park** tracks the history of a gritty era when the power loom was the symbol of economic power and progress. It encompasses several blocks in the downtown area, including former mills turned museums, a network of canals, and a helpful visitor center. In addition to the park-managed sights—the Boott Cotton Mills Museum, the Working People Exhibit, and Boarding House Park (☞ *below*)—the city includes several noteworthy, privately run museums.

Part of Lowell's fascinating character stems from its broad ethnic diversity, a legacy of the days when immigrants from all over North America and Europe came to work in the textile mills. (The current influx is from Cambodia, but it was a Chinese immigrant, Dr. An Wang, who established a computer company here.) Lowell now holds a city celebration for the Cambodian New Year every April. One major ethnic group to migrate to Lowell in its mill days was the French-Canadians; a noted son of French-Canadian Lowell was the late Beat poet and novelist Jack Kerouac, born here in 1922. Kerouac's memory is honored in the Eastern Canal Park on Bridge Street, where plaques bear quotes from his Lowell novels and from *On the Road.* Every October "Lowell Celebrates Kerouac" offers academic symposia, music, and coffee-house poetry. Why October? "I was going home in October. Everyone goes home in October," he wrote in *On the Road.* His grave is in **Edson Cemetery,** 2 mi south of the Lowell Connector, the highway linking Lowell with I–495.

The **National Park Visitor Center** in the Market Mills Complex offers a thorough orientation to the city. The 1902 Market Mills building was the headquarters of the Lowell Manufacturing Company at the height of Lowell's mill days. Since the city's museums and historic sights spread out in three directions from the visitor center (and there's a parking lot), it's a good starting point. Pick up a self-guiding brochure for a walking tour that highlights aspects of local history, from the ubiquitous "mill girls" (young women who toiled up to 13 hours a day in factories) to the city's 5½ mi of canals. Park rangers offer guided tours on foot year-round and on turn-of-the-century trolleys and canal barges in summer and fall. ⊠ *246 Market St.,* ☎ *978/970–5000.* 🎫 *Free, except for trolley and barge tours.* ⊙ *Daily 9–5.*

The **Boott Cotton Mills Museum,** about a 10-minute walk northeast from the visitor center, is the first major National Park Service museum devoted to the history of industrialization. You know you're in for an unusual museum experience when you're handed ear plugs with your admission ticket. (You'll want the plugs for walking through an authentic re-creation of a 1920s weave room, complete with the deafening roar of 88 working power looms. Today's visitors are luckier than the workers, who were never issued protective ear gear.) Other exhibits at the Boott Mills complex, which dates from the mid-19th century, include weaving artifacts, cloth samples, video interviews with workers, and a large, meticulous scale model of 19th-century production. Images have not been prettified; the textile worker's grueling life is shown with all its grit, noise, and dust. ⊠ *400 block of John St.,* ☎ *978/970–5000.* 🎫 *$4.* ⊙ *Daily 9:30–5.*

Just outside the Boott Cotton Mills Museum is **Boarding House Park,** an open space bordered by the former boarding houses where many millworkers lived and dotted with contemporary sculptures and structures that pay homage to working men and women.

The **Working People Exhibit,** in a restored Boott Mills boardinghouse, records the triumphs, sorrows, and daily experiences of both women millworkers and immigrants. Upstairs, there's a poignant display of letters and books belonging to several mill girls; downstairs, a kitchen and parlor show how they lived; there's even a display on the food they gulped down during 30-minute breaks in their grueling work days. Immigrants, from the Irish to Cambodians, are celebrated with photos, video, and historical artifacts. ⊠ *40 French St.,* ☎ *978/970–5000.* 🎫 *Free.* ⊙ *June–Oct., daily 9–5; Nov.–May, daily 1–5.*

**NEED A BREAK?** For coffee, quiche, and muffins baked on the premises, stop at the **Coffee Mill** (⊠ 23 Palmer St., ☎ 978/458–8852), a storefront café and sandwich shop.

The **New England Quilt Museum** is a small but charming museum that displays historic and contemporary examples of quilting, banishing forever doubts about whether quilting is an art form. ⊠ *18 Shattuck St.,* ☎ *978/452–4207.* 🎫 *$4.* ⊙ *Tues.–Sat. 10–4. Call for Sun. hrs.*

The **Sports Museum of New England** provides an option for partners of quilt enthusiasts (☞ New England Quilt Museum, *above*) who'd rather view basketballs than blankets. The small collection includes sports memorabilia, uniforms, and photographs from New England athletes past and present. ⊠ *25 Shattuck St.,* ☎ *978/452–6775.* 🎫 *$3.* ⊙ *Tues.–Sat. 10–5, Sun. noon–5.*

The **Brush Art Gallery,** in the Market Mills Complex, mounts changing exhibitions and hosts open studios of artists creating weaving, papermaking, painting, and sculpture. ⊠ *256 Market St.,* ☎ *978/459–7819.* ⊙ *Tues.–Sat. 11–5, Sun. noon–4, and by appointment.*

The **American Textile History Museum,** a short walk southwest along Dutton Street from the **National Park Visitor Center** (☞ *above*), enhances the city's position as a major interpreter of the Industrial Revolution. Housed in a former Civil War–era mill, the museum's collection of working machines ranges from an 18th-century water wheel to an 1860s power loom to a 1950s "weave room" where fabrics are still made. Designs are drawn from the museum's extensive collection of period textiles, and some museum-produced products, such as blankets and tablecloths, are for sale on-site. ⊠ *491 Dutton St.,* ☏ *978/ 441–0400.* ☞ *$5.* ☉ *Tues.–Fri. 9–4, weekends, holidays 10–4.*

Two blocks northwest of the **National Park Visitor Center** (☞ *above*) is the birthplace and museum of American artist James McNeill Whistler. Despite Whistler's claim that he was a Baltimore native, the Lowell Art Association purchased the gray clapboard Whistler house (built in 1823) to preserve the painter's roots in his real hometown. Inside, the **Whistler House Museum of Art** displays the museum's permanent collections, including a number of Whistler's etchings, as well as works by late-19th- and early 20th-century American representational artists. The **Parker Gallery** in an adjacent building has temporary exhibits of contemporary and historic arts. Hour-long tours are available. ⊠ *243 Worthen St.,* ☏ *978/452–7641.* ☞ *$3.* ☉ *Mar.–Oct., Wed.–Sat. 11–4, Sun. 1–4; Nov.–Feb., Wed.–Sat. 11–4.*

### Dining

$$ ✕ **The Olympia.** Lowell's diverse population includes a large Greek-American community. Specialties at this family-run Greek restaurant—a favorite of employees at the nearby museums—include lamb, moussaka, and fish dishes. ⊠ *457 Market St.,* ☏ *978/452–8092. MC, V.*

## West of Boston A to Z

### Arriving and Departing

BY BUS

The **MBTA** (☏ 617/222–3200) operates buses to Lexington from Alewife station in Cambridge. Buses 62 and 76 make the trip in 25–30 minutes.

BY CAR

To get to Lexington by car from Boston, it's possible to follow Massachusetts Avenue through Cambridge and Arlington into Lexington, but this route is slow and heavily trafficked. Alternatively, take Memorial Drive in Cambridge to the Fresh Pond Parkway, then Route 2 west. Exit Route 2 at Routes 4/225 if your first stop is the Museum of Our National Heritage; from Routes 4/225, turn left on Mass Ave. For Lexington center, take the Waltham Street/Lexington exit from Route 2. Follow Waltham Street just under 2 mi to Mass Ave.; you'll be just east of the Battle Green. The drive takes about 30 minutes. To reach Concord or Lincoln by car, continue west on Route 2. Or take I–90 (the Massachusetts Turnpike) to I–95 north, and then exit at Route 2, heading west. Driving time is 40–45 minutes.

The fastest way to reach Sudbury or Waltham from Boston is the Massachusetts Turnpike westbound, then I–95 north to Route 20 (head west for Sudbury and east for most Waltham addresses). Allow about 40–50 minutes to reach Sudbury, 30 minutes to get to Waltham.

Lowell lies near the intersection of I–495 and Route 3. From Boston, take I–93 north to I–495. Go south on I–495 to Exit 35C, the Lowell Connector. Follow the Lowell Connector to Exit 5B, Thorndike Street. Travel time is 45 minutes to an hour.

BY TRAIN

The **"purple line,"** the T's commuter rail, runs from North Station (⊠ 150 Causeway St., ☏ 617/222–3200) to Concord in about 40 minutes and to Lowell in about 45 minutes. The Lowell station is about ½ mi from the historic attractions; public shuttle buses run between the station and downtown every half hour weekdays 6–6, Saturday 10–4.

## Getting Around

Lexington is easily accessible by the MBTA and bus service and compact enough to be explored on foot. The sights in Concord, however, are more spread out, so either plan to visit by car or wear substantial walking shoes. The historic sections of Lowell are all easily reached on foot from the National Park Visitor Center. Lincoln, Sudbury, and Waltham are not considered walking towns; plan to visit by car.

## Guided Tours

**Brush Hill/Gray Line Tours** (⊠ 435 High St., Randolph 02368, ☎ 781/986–6100 or 800/343–1328; 14 S. Charles St., Boston, ☎ 617/236–2148) offers several daily motorcoach tours from the Transportation Building in downtown Boston (with pickups at several area hotels) to Lexington's Battle Green and Concord's Old North Bridge area, generally late March through mid-November.

Rangers for **Lowell National Historical Park** (☞ Lowell, *above*) offer guided walking tours year-round and on turn-of-the-century trolleys and canal barges in summer and fall. Contact the National Park Visitor Center for information (⊠ 246 Market St., ☎ 978/970–5000).

## Contacts and Resources

EMERGENCIES

**Police** (☎ 911).

**Emerson Hospital** (⊠ 133 Ornack [off Rte. 2], Concord, ☎ 978/369–1400). **Newton-Wellesley Hospital** (⊠ 2014 Washington St. [Rte. 16], Newton, ☎ 617/243–6000).

**Walgreen's** has locations in Lexington (⊠ 60 Bedford St.,, ☎ 781/863–1110) and in Waltham (⊠ 15 Main St., ☎ 781/642–1793), which stay open weekdays till 10, weekends till 9. **CVS Pharmacy** (⊠ 191 Sudbury Rd., Concord, ☎ 978/369–8661) is open weekdays till 10, weekends till 9.

## Visitor Information

**Concord Chamber of Commerce** (⊠ 2 Lexington Rd., Concord, ☎ 978/369–3120) is open daily 9:30–4:30. **Lexington Chamber of Commerce and Visitor Center** (⊠ 1875 Massachusetts Ave., Lexington, ☎ 781/862–1450) is open mid-April–October, daily 9–5; November–mid-April, generally weekdays 10–3, weekends 10–4. **National Park Visitors Center** (⊠ 246 Market St., Lowell, ☎ 978/970–5000) is open daily 9–5.

# THE NORTH SHORE

The slice of Massachusetts's Atlantic Coast known as the North Shore extends past grimy docklands, through Boston's well-to-do northern suburbs, to the picturesque **Cape Ann** region, and beyond Cape Ann to Newburyport, just south of the New Hampshire border. In addition to miles of fine beaches, the North Shore encompasses **Marblehead**, a quintessential New England sea town; **Salem**, which thrives on a history of witches, millionaires, and the maritime trades; **Gloucester**, the oldest seaport in America; quaint, colorful **Rockport**, crammed with crafts shops and artists' studios; and **Newburyport**, with its red-brick center and rows of clapboard Federal mansions. Bright and bustling during the short summer season, the North Shore is calmer between November and June, with many restaurants, inns, and attractions operating during reduced hours or closing down entirely. It's worth calling ahead off-season.

# The North Shore

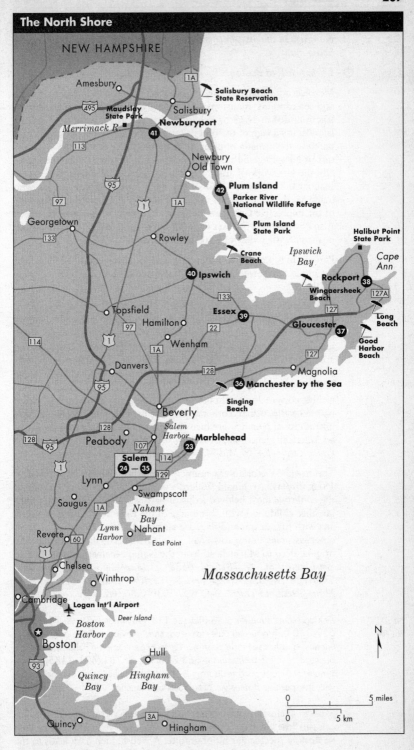

NEW HAMPSHIRE

Amesbury

Maudslay
State Park

495

1A

Salisbury

Salisbury Beach
State Reservation

**Newburyport**
41

Merrimack R.

113

Newbury
Old Town

95

97

Georgetown

1

1A

42 **Plum Island**

Parker River
National Wildlife Refuge

Plum Island
State Park

133

Rowley

Crane
Beach

*Ipswich
Bay*

Halibut Point
State Park

*Cape
Ann*

40 **Ipswich**

133

Rockport 38

127A

Wingaersheek
Beach

127

Topsfield

97

Hamilton

22

**Essex** 39

**Gloucester**
37

Long
Beach

1

Wenham

1A

128

127

Good
Harbor
Beach

114

95

Danvers

128

Magnolia

36 **Manchester by the Sea**

Singing
Beach

128

Beverly

95

128

Peabody

*Salem
Harbor*

107

**Salem**

24 — 35

**Marblehead**
23

114

129

Lynn

Swampscott

1A

Saugus

*Nahant
Bay* Nahant

Revere

60

*Lynn
Harbor*

East Point

1

Chelsea

Winthrop

*Massachusetts Bay*

Cambridge

Logan Int'l Airport

*Deer Island*

*Boston
Harbor*

N

**Boston**

Hull

93

*Quincy
Bay*

*Hingham
Bay*

0          5 miles

0          5 km

Quincy

3A

Hingham

# Marblehead

*Numbers in the margin correspond to points of interest on the North Shore map.*

**㉓** *17 mi north of Boston.*

Marblehead, with its narrow and winding streets, old clapboard houses, and sea captains' mansions, retains much of the character of the village founded in 1629 by fishermen from Cornwall and the Channel Islands. It's a sign of the times that today's fishing fleet is small compared to the armada of pleasure craft anchored in the harbor. This is one of New England's premier sailing capitals, and Race Week (usually the last week of July) attracts boats from all along the Eastern seaboard. The proud spirit of the ambitious merchant sailors who made Marblehead prosper in the 18th century can still be felt in many of the impressive Georgian mansions that line the downtown streets. Also downtown is **Crocker Park** (⊠ Front St.), a lovely place for a walk or picnic with a view of Marblehead harbor.

Parking in town can be difficult; try the lot at the end of Front Street, the lot on State Street by the Landing restaurant, or the metered areas on the street.

The Chamber of Commerce (☞ North Shore A to Z, *below*) has a complete visitor guide with a suggested walking tour of the city. Plaques on homes note the date of construction and the original owner. A few mansions are owned and operated by the town historical society and are open to the public. One exquisite example of Marblehead's 18th-century high society is the **Jeremiah Lee Mansion.** Colonel Lee was one of the wealthiest people in the colonies in 1768, and although few furnishings original to the house remain, the mahogany paneling, hand-painted wallpaper, and other appointments, as well as a fine collection of traditional North Shore furniture, provide a glimpse into the life of an American gentleman. ⊠ *161 Washington St.,* ☎ *781/631–1069.* ☞ *Guided tours $4.* ☉ *Mid-May–Oct., Mon.–Sat. 10–4, Sun. 1–4.*

The town's Victorian-era municipal building, **Abbott Hall,** built in 1876, displays Archibald Willard's painting *The Spirit of '76,* one of the country's most beloved icons of patriotism. Many visitors, familiar since childhood with this image of the three Revolutionary veterans with fife, drum, and flag, are surprised to find the original in an otherwise unassuming town hall. Other artifacts on display include the original deed to Marblehead from the Nanapashemet Indians. ⊠ *188 Washington St.,* ☎ *781/631–0528.* ☉ *May–Oct., Mon.–Tues. and Thurs. 8–5, Wed. 7:30–7:30, Fri. 8–1, Sat. 9–6, Sun. 11–6; Nov.–Apr., Mon.–Tues. and Thurs. 8–5, Wed. 7:30–7:30, Fri. 8–1.*

NEED A BREAK?

Pick up picnic supplies at **Truffles** (⊠ 114 Washington St., ☎ 781/639–1104), a gourmet café/take–out shop serving tasty salads, sandwiches, and house-made pastries. Or to experience the fisherman's Marblehead, visit the **Driftwood** (⊠ 63 Front St., ☎ 781/631–1145), a simple, red-clapboard restaurant by the harbor where you can get excellent, inexpensive homestyle breakfasts and lunches.

Most of exclusive, estate-filled Marblehead Neck (a finger of land locals call "the Neck") is privately owned, but you're free to explore **Castle Rock,** a spectacular bit of granite. A well-hidden path leads to the small, rocky point jutting into the Atlantic. The spot got its name from the adjacent house—a large, stone manor locally known as the Castle. Look for the wrought-iron fence in the 300 block of Ocean Avenue.

## Dining and Lodging

**$–$$** ✕ **King's Rook.** At this cozy café and wine bar, the crisp single-serving pizzas include one with goat cheese, roasted red peppers, and caramelized onions, and another loaded with veggies. The restaurant also serves elegant sandwiches like the curried egg salad with raisins and the over-stuffed turkey. The signature dessert, lemonberry-jazz, layers lemon cream, Maine blueberries, and lemon mousse on a shortbread crust. ✉ *12 State St.,* ☎ *781/631–9838. MC, V. No dinner Mon.*

**$$$–$$$$** 🏠 **Marblehead Inn.** This rambling Victorian mansion sits on the main road between Salem and Marblehead. The two-room suites have living rooms, bedrooms (some with pineapple four-poster beds), and kitchenettes. Continental breakfast is included. ✉ *264 Pleasant St. (Rte. 114), 01945,* ☎ *781/639–9999 or 800/399–5843. 9 suites. Free parking. AE, MC, V. No smoking.*

**$$–$$$$** 🏠 **Harbor Light Inn.** Staying here is much like stepping into a mental
★ picture of a typical New England inn. There's a strong appeal to tradition in the stately antiques, four-poster and canopy beds, carved arched doorways, and wide-board floors. There are modern pluses, too; several guest rooms have fireplaces, whirlpool tubs, or skylights. Continental breakfast is included, as well as afternoon tea and wine and cheese on Saturday night. ✉ *58 Washington St., 01945,* ☎ *781/631–2186,* 𝐅𝐀𝐗 *781/631–2216. 21 rooms. Pool, meeting room. AE, MC, V.*

**$–$$** 🏠 **Harborside House.** A ship's carpenter built this house in 1850; current owner Susan Livingston, a considerate and interesting host, has lived here for more than 30 years. The downstairs living room has a working brick fireplace; there's also a deck, a porch, a garden patio, and a sitting room with TV. Bedrooms have polished wide-board floors; one overlooks Marblehead harbor and its hundreds of sailboats. Continental breakfast is included. ✉ *23 Gregory St., 01945,* ☎ *781/ 631–1032. 2 rooms. Free parking. No credit cards. No smoking.*

## Outdoor Activities and Sports

BEACHES

Marblehead is not known for sprawling beaches, but the ones it does have are well maintained and mostly used by "'headers" (natives of Marblehead) for family outings or quick ocean dips. **Deveraux Beach** (✉ Ocean Ave. before the causeway to Marblehead Neck), the most spacious, has some sandy and some pebbled areas, as well as a playground. Parking is $5 for nonresidents.

BOATING

Marblehead is one of the North Shore's pleasure-sailing capitals, but don't count on finding mooring space here. Like many nearby communities, the town has long waiting lists. The town **harbormaster** (☎ 781/631–2386) can inform you of nightly fees at public docks when space is available.

# Salem

*Numbers in margin correspond to points of interest on the Salem map.*

*16 mi northeast of Boston, 4 mi west of Marblehead.*

Salem unabashedly calls itself "Witch City." During the town's wildly popular October "Haunted Happenings," museums and businesses transform into haunted houses, graveyards, or dungeons, as the town celebrates its spooky past. Witches astride broomsticks decorate the police cars; numerous witch-related attractions and shops, as well as resident witchcraft practitioners, recall the city's infamous connection with the witchcraft hysteria and trials of 1692. The incident began in January 1692 when several Salem-area girls fell ill and accused several

**210**

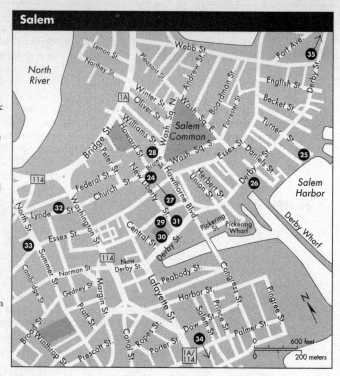

townspeople of bewitching them. As the accusations spiraled, more than 150 men and women were charged with practicing witchcraft, a crime punishable by death. After the resulting trials later that year, 19 innocent people were hanged and one was pressed to death for refusing a trial. The present-day commercialization—some would say trivialization—of the event led in part to the dedication of a somber, reflective monument, the Salem Witch Trials Memorial (☞ *below*).

Witchcraft aside, Salem's charms include compelling museums, trendy waterfront stores and restaurants, and a wide common with a children's playground. Settled in 1626, the town has a rich maritime tradition; frigates out of Salem opened the Far East trade routes and generated the wealth that created America's first millionaires. Among its native sons were writer Nathaniel Hawthorne, navigator Nathaniel Bowditch, and architect Samuel McIntire.

**②** A good place to start your Salem tour is the large **National Park Service Visitor Center,** which has a wide variety of booklets and pamphlets, including a "Maritime Trail" and "Early Settlement Trail" for Essex County, as well as a free 27-minute film. ✉ *2 New Liberty St.,* ☎ *978/ 740–1650.* ☉ *Daily 9–5.*

One way to explore Salem is to follow the 1¾-mi Heritage Trail (painted in red on the sidewalk) around town. If you prefer, the **Salem Trolley** leaves every hour for a guided tour from near the National Park Visitor Center. You may get off and back on the trolley en route. *Trolley Depot, 191 Essex St.,* ☎ *978/744–5469.* ✉ *$9.* ☉ *Apr.–Oct., daily 10–5; Nov. and Mar., weekends 10–4.*

**★ ②** The **House of the Seven Gables,** immortalized in the classic novel by Nathaniel Hawthorne, should not be missed. Highlights of the house tour are the period furnishings, a secret staircase, and the garret containing an antique scale model of the house. The complex of 17th-century buildings includes the small house where Hawthorne was born in 1804; it was moved from its original location elsewhere in Salem. ⊠ *54 Turner St. (off Derby St.),* ☎ *978/744–0991.* ✉ *Guided tours $7.* ☺ *May–Nov., daily 10–5; Dec.–Apr., Mon.–Sat. 10–5, Sun. noon–5; closed first 2 wks in Jan.*

**㉖** A short walk along Derby Street, near Derby Wharf, is the 9¼-acre **Salem Maritime National Historic Site,** which is run by the National Park Service. The site focuses on Salem's heritage as a major seaport with a thriving overseas trade; it includes the 1762 home of Elias Derby, America's first millionaire; the 1819 Customs House, made famous in Nathaniel Hawthorne's *The Scarlet Letter*; the 1671 Narbonne-Hale House; and three sites relating to sea trade: the 1819 Public Stores, the 1826 Scale House, and the West India Goods Store. A replica of *The Friendship*, a 171-ft, three-masted 1797 trader merchant vessel, was scheduled to open in 2000. ⊠ *174 Derby St.,* ☎ *978/740–1660.* ✉ *Guided tours $3, site free.* ☺ *Daily 9–5.*

<table>
<tr><td>NEED A<br>BREAK?</td><td>The **Salem Beer Works** (⊠ 278 Derby St., ☎ 978/745–2337), a micro-brewery restaurant, offers eclectic American cuisine and fresh-brewed beers in a historic merchants' warehouse.</td></tr>
</table>

**㉗** Salem's vast, dazzling maritime riches are the focal point of the **Peabody Essex Museum,** which celebrated its 200th anniversary in 1999. The East India Hall Galleries on Liberty Street are filled with maritime art and history and spoils of the Asian export trade—ranging from 16th-century Chinese blue porcelain to an entire Japanese carrying litter to Indian colonial silver. **Plummer Hall** on Essex Street contains New England portraits and Revere silver. Scrimshaw, a whale's jaw, and boat models illustrate Salem's seafaring past. ⊠ *East India Sq.,* ☎ *978/745–9500 or 800/745–4054.* ✉ *$8.50, good for two consecutive days.* ☺ *Mon.–Sat. 10–5, Sun. noon–5; closed Mon. Nov.–late May.*

**㉘** For an informative, if somewhat hokey, introduction to the 1692 witchcraft hysteria, visit the **Salem Witch Museum.** A half-hour exhibit re-creates key scenes, using 13 sets, life-size models, and a taped narration. The museum also sells an interesting pamphlet on the events that led to the witch trials. ⊠ *Washington Sq. N,* ☎ *978/744–1692.* ✉ *$4.50.* ☺ *Sept.–June, daily 10–5; July–Aug., daily 10–7.*

**㉙** The **Salem Witch Trials Memorial,** dedicated in 1992 on the 300th anniversary of the witchcraft trials, honors those who died not because they were witches but because they refused to confess. This melancholy space, next to the central burial ground, provides an antidote to the relentless marketing of the merry-witches motif. A stone wall is studded with 20 stone benches, each inscribed with a victim's name. Look for the flagstones at one end of the plot that are engraved with protestations of innocence, sometimes cut off in mid-sentence. Black locust trees, reputedly the kind used for the hangings, are planted here. The monument was dedicated by Holocaust survivor Elie Wiesel, who drew parallels at the ceremony to other historic atrocities. ⊠ *Off Liberty St., near corner of Charter St.* ☺ *Daily.*

**㉚** The **Salem Wax Museum of Witches and Seafarers** offers a multimedia presentation of sights and sounds culled from a century of Salem's **㉛** tragedies and triumphs. At the **Salem Witch Village** across the street (and managed by the wax museum) you can learn about historic and modern witchcraft's spiritual and religious practices. ⊠ *282–288 Derby St.,* ☎ *978/740–2929.* ✉ *$4.50 each, $7.95 for a combination* *ticket.* ⏱ *Nov.–Apr., daily 9–5; May–June and Sept., daily 9–6; July–Aug. and Oct., daily 9–7.*

❷ The **Witch Dungeon Museum** features a guided tour of dungeons where accused witches were kept and a continuous live reenactment of one trial, as adapted from 1692 transcripts. ✉ *16 Lynde St.,* ☎ *978/741–3570.* 🎫 *$4.50.* ⏱ *Apr.–Nov., daily 10–5; evening hours around Halloween.*

❸ No witch ever lived at the **Witch House,** the former home of witch-trial magistrate Jonathan Corwin, but more than 200 accused witches were questioned on the premises. It's the only remaining structure with direct ties to the 1692 trials; decor remains authentic to the period. Tours are offered. ✉ *310½ Essex St.,* ☎ *978/744–0180.* 🎫 *$5.* ⏱ *Mid-Mar.–June and Sept.–Nov., daily 10–4:30; July–Aug., daily 10–6.*

☕ ❹ At the **Salem 1630 Pioneer Village** costumed "interpreters" help recreate the Salem of the early 17th century, when it was a fishing village and the Commonwealth's first capital. Replicas of thatched-roof cottages, period gardens, and wigwams have been constructed at the site. ✉ *Forest River Park (follow Rte. 114 east, then turn left onto West Ave.),* ☎ *978/744–0991.* 🎫 *$5.* ⏱ *Generally Apr.–Nov., Mon.–Sat. 10–5, Sun. noon–5.*

☕ ❺ **Salem Willows Park**—some distance from the historic sites—has picnic grounds, beaches, food stands, amusements, games, boat rentals, and fishing bait. ✉ *Eastern end of Derby St.*

---

OFF THE BEATEN PATH

**DANVERS** – Although Salem became famous as the witch-trials city, it is Danvers (formerly Salem Village), several miles northwest of present-day Salem, that has the real relics of the witchcraft episode. The house where the black slave Tituba told her tales to two impressionable girls—helping to begin the whole sorry business—has long been demolished, but its foundations were excavated in 1970; they can be viewed behind 67 Center Street. (Park around the corner; there's no place to stop on Center Street.) A monument to the victims was dedicated in 1992 near 178 Hobart Street.

Also in Danvers, the **Rebecca Nurse Homestead** was the home of aged, pious Rebecca, a devout churchgoer whose accusation of being a witch caused shock waves in the community. Her trial was a mockery (she was first pronounced innocent, but the jury was urged to change its verdict), and she was hanged in 1692. Her family secretly buried her body somewhere on the grounds of this house, which has period furnishings and 17th-century vegetable and herb gardens. ✉ *149 Pine St.,* ☎ *978/774–8799.* 🎫 *$3.50.* ⏱ *Mid-June–early Sept., Tues.–Sun. 1–4:30; early Sept.–Oct., weekends 1–4:30 or by appointment; May–mid-June, by appointment.*

---

## Dining and Lodging

$$–$$$  ✕ **Chase House.** On Pickering Wharf overlooking the harbor, this restaurant is extremely busy in summer. The menu emphasizes steaks, seafood, and pasta. A house specialty is the baked lobster stuffed with still more lobster and, for the abstemious, the "heart-healthy" scrod. ✉ *Pickering Wharf,* ☎ *978/744–0000. AE, D, DC, MC, V.*

$$–$$$  ✕ **The Grapevine.** This inviting bistro opposite Pickering Wharf serves contemporary northern Italian fare. At lunch, look for "pizettes," pastas, and risottos. The dinner menu may include lamb scallopini sautéed with green peppercorns, shrimp, and roasted garlic ravioli, or balsamic-glazed pork chops with Vidalia home fries, as well as vegetarian selections. ✉ *26 Congress St.,* ☎ *978/745–9335. AE, MC, V.*

$$$ ✕⊡ **Hawthorne Hotel.** This imposing redbrick structure stands on the green, just a short walk from the commercial center, the waterfront, and other attractions. Guest rooms are appointed with reproduction 18th-century antiques, armchairs, and desks. The hotel's formal, chandelier-bedecked restaurant, Nathaniel's, is one of the more elegant eateries in Salem; the ambitious menu includes lobster, swordfish in mustard cream, prime rib, and poached sole on spinach with a champagne cream sauce. There's live entertainment on weekends in the bar. ⊠ *18 Washington Sq. W, 01970,* ☎ *978/744–4080 or 800/729–7829,* ␗ *978/745–9842. 83 rooms, 6 suites. Restaurant, bar, lounge, exercise room, meeting rooms. AE, D, DC, MC, V.*

$$–$$$ ⊡ **Inn at Seven Winter St.** Built in 1871, this inn has been restored to a Victorian-era appearance. Rooms are spacious and well furnished, with heavy mahogany and walnut antiques. Some open to a deck, some have whirlpool tubs, some have marble fireplaces. The one-room studio has a microwave and refrigerator; the suites have kitchens. Rates include a Continental breakfast buffet. It's better suited for couples than for families. ⊠ *7 Winter St., 01970,* ☎ *978/745–9520 or 800/932–5547,* ␗ *978/745–0523. 7 rooms, 2 suites, 1 studio. Breakfast room, free parking. AE, MC, V. No smoking.*

$–$$ ⊡ **Amelia Payson Guest House.** This elegantly restored 1845 Greek Revival house has been converted into a bright, airy bed-and-breakfast; it is near all historic attractions. The pretty rooms are decorated with floral-print wallpaper, brass and canopy beds, nonworking marble fireplaces, and white wicker furnishings. The downstairs parlor has a grand piano. Rates include Continental breakfast. ⊠ *16 Winter St., 01970,* ☎ *978/744–8304. 3 rooms, 1 studio. Breakfast room, free parking. AE, MC, V. No smoking.*

## Nightlife and the Arts

The **North Shore Music Theatre** (⊠ 62 Dunham Rd., Beverly, ☎ 978/922–8500) puts on celebrity concerts, musicals, and children's theater from May through December.

## Shopping

Salem is the center for a number of offbeat shops related to the city's witchcraft history. The best-known supernatural store is **Crow Haven Corner** (⊠ 125 Essex St., ☎ 978/745–8763), the former haunt of Laurie Cabot, once dubbed Salem's "official" witch. Her daughter, Jody, now presides over crystal balls, herbs, tarot decks, healing stones, and books about witchcraft. The **Broom Closet** (⊠ 3 Central St., ☎ 978/741–3669) stocks dried herbs, aromatic oils, candles, tarot cards, New Age music, and witchcraft supplies. **Pyramid Books** (⊠ 214 Derby St., ☎ 978/745–7171) stocks New Age publications.

Somewhat more conventional are the waterside gift and antiques shops on restored **Pickering Wharf.** The **Pickering Wharf Antique Gallery** (☎ 978/741–3113), a 4,000-square-ft former theater-in-the-round, now houses about 30 dealers.

# Manchester by the Sea

*Numbers in the margin correspond to points of interest on the North Shore map.*

**36** *29 mi northeast of Boston, 13 mi northeast of Salem, via Beverly on Rte. 127.*

Manchester became a fashionable summer community for well-to-do urbanites in the mid-19th century. Today, the town is a small seaside commuter suburb built around a picturesque harbor. Bostonians still visit for its lovely, long **Singing Beach,** so called because of the whistling noise your feet make against the white sand. The beach has lifeguards, food stands, and rest rooms, but no parking; either take the commuter train from Boston or park in the private pay lot ($15 per day for non-residents) by the railroad station. It's a ½-mi walk to the beach.

### Lodging

**$–$$** ⌂ **Old Corner Inn.** Built in 1865 and once used as the summer residence of the Danish Embassy, this inn has bedrooms with bird's-eye maple floors, four-poster beds, brass gaslight-era fixtures, featherbeds, and claw-foot tubs. Some rooms have working fireplaces. Although the country location is attractive, it's a mile walk from the village center and about 1½ mi from the beach. An apartment with bedroom, sitting room, private bath, and kitchenette is available. Continental breakfast is included in the rate. ⊠ *2 Harbor St., 01944,* ☎ *978/526–4996. 8 rooms, 5 rooms with bath, 1 apartment. AE, MC, V.*

## Gloucester

**❸⓻** *37 mi from Boston, 8 mi from Manchester.*

On Gloucester's fine seaside promenade is a famous statue of a man steering a ship's wheel, his eyes searching the horizon. The statue, which honors those "who go down to the sea in ships," was commissioned by the town citizens in 1923 in celebration of Gloucester's 300th anniversary. The oldest seaport in the nation (and one with some of the North Shore's best beaches), this is still a major fishing port. One portrait of Gloucester's fishing community can be found in Sebastian Junger's 1997 book, *A Perfect Storm,* about a Gloucester fishing boat caught in "the storm of the century" in October 1991.

The creative side of the town's personality is illuminated by the **Rocky Neck** neighborhood, the first-settled artists' colony in the United States. Its alumni include Winslow Homer, Maurice Prendergast, Jane Peter, and Cecilia Beaux. Today Rocky Neck remains home to many artists; its galleries are usually open daily 10 AM to 10 PM during the busy summer months. From downtown, head down East Main Street.

**Hammond Castle Museum,** a stone "medieval" castle built in 1926 by the inventor John Hays Hammond Jr. contains medieval-style furnishings and paintings. The Great Hall houses an organ impressive for its 8,200 pipes. From the castle you can also see "Norman's Woe Rock," made famous by Longfellow in his poem "The Wreck of the Hesperus." The museum often closes to host weddings or special events, particularly on summer and fall weekends; call ahead. ⊠ *80 Hesperus Ave. (south side of Gloucester off Rte. 127),* ☎ *978/283–2080 or 978/283–7673.* ⌂ *$6.* ☼ *Late May–early Sept., daily 9–6; early Sept.–late May, weekends 10–4; closed last 2 wks in Oct.*

The **Cape Ann Historical Museum** has the nation's largest collection of paintings by the 19th-century master Fitz Hugh Lane, plus works by other artists associated with Cape Ann, including Winslow Homer and Maurice Prendergast, in a furnished Federal-period house. The museum's Maritime and Fisheries galleries house wooden boats, fishing equipment, ship models, and other artifacts from the town's fishing tradition. ⊠ *27 Pleasant St., off Main St.,* ☎ *978/283–0455.* ⌂ *$4.* ☼ *Mar.–Jan., Tues.–Sat. 10–5.*

The **Sargent House Museum** was home to sea merchants and high-minded community leaders. The Georgian house was built in 1782 for writer and activist Judith Sargent Murray and her husband John Murray, founder of Universalism in America. It's furnished with 1790s textiles, personal items, and china; there are also works by Judith's great-great nephew, John Singer Sargent. ⊠ *49 Middle St.,* ☎ *978/281–2432.* 🖼 *$3.* ☉ *Late May–mid-Oct., Fri.–Mon. noon–4.*

## Dining and Lodging

**$$$** ✕ **White Rainbow.** The dining room in this excellent restaurant is in
★ the basement of a downtown store, and candlelight provides a romantic atmosphere. The contemporary American specialties include Maui onion soup, grilled filet mignon, lobster, and fresh fish of the day. ⊠ *65 Main St.,* ☎ *978/281–0017. AE, D, DC, MC, V.*

**$$–$$$** ✕ **Thyme's on the Square.** A cozy, bistro-style restaurant on the road to Rocky Neck, with high ceilings, large windows, and walls covered with paintings, it offers creative American cuisine. Choices from the changing menu may include an appetizer of cod cakes with arugula and warm bacon dressing; linguine with lobster, shrimp, and artichoke hearts; and grilled vegetable gratin with wild mushroom etouffée. ⊠ *197 E Main St.,* ☎ *978/282–4426. AE, D, MC, V.*

**$–$$** 🏨 **Cape Ann Motor Inn.** On the sands of Long Beach, the Cape Ann operates year-round and offers guest rooms with balconies and ocean views. Half the rooms have kitchenettes equipped with appliances and cooking paraphernalia. The Honeymoon Suite has a full kitchen, a fireplace, a whirlpool bath, a king-size bed, and a private balcony. Rates include a Continental breakfast. Pets are welcome. ⊠ *33 Rockport Rd., 01930,* ☎ *978/281–2900 or 800/464–8439,* 🖷 *978/281–1359. 30 rooms, 1 suite. AE, D, MC, V.*

**$–$$** 🏨 **Cape Ann's Marina Resort.** This year-round hostelry less than a mile from Gloucester really comes alive in summer, when a full-service restaurant, a whale-watch boat, and deep-sea fishing excursions operate on and from the premises. The rooms, with views of the water, have color TVs, balconies, and air-conditioning, should the Atlantic breezes be insufficient. ⊠ *75 Essex Ave., 01930,* ☎ *978/283–2116 or 800/626–7660,* 🖷 *978/281–4905. 52 rooms. Restaurant (mid-Apr.–mid-Nov.), indoor pool. AE, D, MC, V.*

**$–$$** 🏨 **Vista Motel.** The name is apt, because every room in this motel perched atop a small, steep hill overlooks the sea and Good Harbor Beach, just a few minutes' walk away. Some rooms have decks, all have refrigerators, and 20 also have a two-burner stove and cooking equipment. ⊠ *22 Thatcher Rd., 01930,* ☎ *978/281–3410. 40 rooms (30 in winter). Refrigerators, pool. AE, MC, V.*

## Nightlife and the Arts

The **Hammond Castle Museum** (⊠ 80 Hesperus Ave., ☎ 978/283–2080) has a summer chamber-music concert series. The **Gloucester Stage Company** (⊠ 267 E. Main St., ☎ 978/281–4099) is a nonprofit professional group that stages new plays and revivals May–September. The **Rhumb Line** (⊠ 40 Railroad Ave., ☎ 978/283–9732) has good food and live entertainment every night but Tuesday, with rock-and-roll on Friday and Saturday and jazz on Sunday.

## Outdoor Activities and Sports

BEACHES

Gloucester has some of the best beaches on the North Shore. Parking costs about $10 on weekdays and about $15 on weekends, when the lots often fill by 10 AM. **Wingaersheek Beach** (⊠ Exit 13 off Rte. 128) is a picture-perfect, well-protected cove of white sand and dunes, with the white Annisquam lighthouse in the bay. **Good Harbor Beach** (⊠ Signposted from Rte. 127A) is a huge, sandy, dune-backed beach with a rocky islet just offshore. **Long Beach** (⊠ Off Rte. 127A on Gloucester-Rockport town line) is another excellent place for sunbathing; parking here is only $5.

BOATING

If you prefer sailing, consider a sail along the harbor and coast aboard the 65-ft schooner **Thomas E. Lannon,** crafted in Essex in 1996 and modeled after the great boats built a century ago. There are two-hour and half-day sails, as well as sunset and Sunday brunch cruises. It's best to make a reservation in advance. ⊠ *37 Rogers St., Seven Seas Wharf,* ☎ *978/281–6634.*

FISHING

Gloucester has a great fishing tradition, and many fishermen in the town's busy working harbor offer fishing trips, generally May through October. (Gear is provided.) Try **Captain Bill's Deep Sea Fishing/Whale Watch** (⊠ 33 Harbor Loop; mailing address: 9 Traverse St., ☎ 978/283–6995) for full- and half-day excursions. **Coastal Fishing Charters** (⊠ Rose's Wharf, 415 Main St., ☎ 978/283–5113), under the same ownership as Cape Ann Whale Watch, operates day and evening fishing trips and kids' trips in Gloucester harbor. The **Yankee Fishing Fleet** (⊠ 75 Essex Ave., ☎ 978/283–0313 or 800/942–5464) conducts deepsea fishing trips.

WHALE-WATCHING

*See* North Shore A to Z, *below,* for a list of whale-watch boat operators.

# Rockport

③⑧ *41 mi northeast of Boston, 4 mi northeast of Gloucester on Rte. 127.*

Rockport, at the very tip of Cape Ann, derives its name from the local granite formations, and many Boston-area structures are made of stone cut from its long-gone quarries. Today, the town is a tourist center, with hilly rows of colorful clapboard houses, historic inns, and artists' studios. The town has wisely refrained from going overboard with T-shirt emporia and other typical tourist-trap landmarks. Shops sell good crafts, clothing, and cameras, and the restaurants serve quiche, seafood, or home-baked cookies rather than fast food. The best time to visit Rockport is during the uncrowded off-season, when many of the shops remain open. Walk out to the end of Bearskin Neck for an impressive view of the Atlantic and the old, weather-beaten lobster shack known as "Motif No. 1" because of its popularity as a subject for amateur painters. Other sights include the **Rockport Art Association Gallery** (⊠ 12 Main St., ☎ 978/546–6604), open all year, which displays the best work of local artists.

## Dining and Lodging

$$     ✕ **Brackett's Oceanview Restaurant.** A big bay window in this quiet, homey restaurant allows an excellent view across Sandy Bay. The menu includes scallop casserole, fish cakes, and other seafood dishes. ⊠ *27 Main St.,* ☎ *978/546–2797. AE, D, DC, MC, V. Closed Nov.– late Mar.*

$$     ✕ **My Place by the Sea.** This restaurant is perched right at the tip of Bearskin Neck, with a lower deck on rocks over the ocean. The menu offers New England seafood specialties such as lobster, plus steaks, pasta, salads, and sandwiches. ⊠ *Bearskin Neck,* ☎ *978/546–9667. AE, D, DC, MC, V. Closed Nov.–Mar.*

$     ✕ **Portside Chowder House.** This great little hole-in-the-wall is one of the few restaurants in Rockport that remain open year-round. The tiny dining room with wood beams and low ceilings has partial sea views. Chowder is the house specialty; also offered are lobster and crab plates, salads, burgers, and sandwiches. The seafood is caught and served fresh daily. ⊠ *Bearskin Neck,* ☎ *978/546–7045. No credit cards. Reduced hrs in winter.*

**$$–$$$$**   ★   ⚗ **Yankee Clipper Inn.** The imposing Georgian mansion that forms the main part of this perfectly located inn sits surrounded by gardens on a rocky point jutting into the sea. Guest rooms vary somewhat in size, but most are spacious. Furnished with antiques, they contain four-poster or canopy beds, and all but one have an ocean view. In the Quarterdeck, a newer building across the lawn, all rooms have fabulous sea views; the decor here is more modern, and rooms are spacious with large picture windows. The Bullfinch House across the street is an 1840 Greek Revival house, tastefully appointed with antique furnishings but with less-grand views. Rates include full breakfast in season. ✉ *96 Granite St., 01966,* ☎ *978/546–3407 or 800/545–3699,* 𝔽𝔸𝕏 *978/546–9730. 27 rooms, 6 suites. Restaurant, pool. AE, D, MC, V. Closed mid-Dec.– Mar. 1.*

**$$–$$$**   ★   ⚗ **Addison Choate Inn.** This historic inn sits inconspicuously among private homes, just a minute's walk from the center of Rockport. The sizable rooms, with large tile bathrooms, are beautifully decorated; the navy-and-white captain's room contains a canopy bed, handmade quilts, and Oriental rugs. Other rooms—all with polished pine floors— have their share of antiques and local seascape paintings. In the third-floor suite, huge windows look out over the rooftops to the sea. Two comfortably appointed duplex stable-house apartments have skylights, cathedral ceilings, and exposed wood beams. Rates include breakfast and afternoon tea. ✉ *49 Broadway, 01966,* ☎ *978/546–7543 or 800/ 245–7543,* 𝔽𝔸𝕏 *978/546–7638. 5 rooms, 1 suite, 2 apartments. Dining room, pool. D, MC, V. No smoking.*

**$$–$$$**   ⚗ **Seacrest Manor.** This distinctive 1911 clapboard mansion, surrounded by large gardens, sits atop a hill overlooking the sea; the inn's motto is "decidedly small, intentionally quiet." Two elegant sitting rooms are furnished with antiques and leather chairs; one has a huge looking glass salvaged from the old Philadelphia Opera House. The hall and staircase are hung with paintings—some depicting the inn—done by local artists. Guest rooms vary in size and character and combine simple traditional and antique furnishings; some have large, private decks. Rates include full breakfast and afternoon tea. ✉ *99 Marmion Way, 01966,* ☎ *978/546–2211. 8 rooms, 6 with bath. Dining room, 2 lounges. No credit cards. Closed Dec.–Apr. 1. No smoking.*

**$–$$**   ⚗ **Bearskin Neck Motor Lodge.** Set almost at the end of Bearskin Neck, this small gray-shingled motel is within a short hike of many gift and crafts shops and eateries. Rooms are comfortably but simply appointed with plain wood furnishings, but their real attraction is the view: all face the water. From the windows and private balconies all you see is the ocean, and at night you can hear it rolling in—or thundering—against the rocks below. You can sun or read on the motel's large deck. ✉ *64 Bearskin Neck, 01966,* ☎ *978/546–6677. 8 rooms. No credit cards. Closed mid-Dec.–Mar. 30.*

**$–$$**   ⚗ **Inn on Cove Hill.** This Federal building set on a picturesque hillside dates from 1791. Its construction was reportedly paid for with gold from a pirate's booty. Some of the guest rooms are small, but all are cheerful and pretty, with wood floors, bright, floral-print paper, Oriental rugs, patchwork quilts, and old-fashioned beds—some brass, others canopy four-posters. Rates include Continental breakfast. ✉ *37 Mt. Pleasant St., 01966,* ☎ *978/546–2701 or 888/546–2701. 11 rooms, 9 with bath. MC, V. Closed late-Oct.–Apr. No smoking.*

**$–$$**   ★   ⚗ **Sally Webster Inn.** Sally Webster was a member of Hannah Jumper's so-called hatchet gang, which smashed up the town's liquor stores in 1856 and turned Rockport into the dry town it remains today. Sally lived in this house for much of her life, and the guest rooms are named for members of her family. They contain rocking chairs; nonworking brick fireplaces; pineapple four-poster, brass, canopy, or spool beds; and pine wide-board floors covered with Oriental rugs. Rates include a Continental buffet breakfast. ⊠ *34 Mt. Pleasant St., 01966,* ☎ *978/546–9251 or 877/546–9251. 8 rooms. Dining room, lounge. D, MC, V. Closed late Dec.–Feb. 1. No smoking.*

### Nightlife and the Arts

During the **Rockport Chamber Music Festival** (⊠ Box 312, 01966, ☎ 978/546–7391), held from mid-June to mid-July, musicians and music lovers gather for classical concerts held at the Rockport Art Association Gallery (☞ *above*).

### Shopping

An artist's colony, Rockport has a tremendous concentration of **studios** and **galleries** selling the work of local artists. Most of these are on Main Street near the harbor and on Bearskin Neck. The *Rockport Fine Arts Gallery Guide,* available from the Rockport Chamber of Commerce (☞ Visitor Information, *below*), lists some 30 reputable galleries in town.

## Essex

**39** *30 mi northeast of Boston, 12 mi west of Rockport. Head west out of Cape Ann on Rte. 128, turning north on Rte. 133.*

The small, picturesque town of Essex, once an important shipbuilding center, is surrounded by salt marshes and is filled with antiques stores and seafood restaurants. The **Essex Shipbuilding Museum,** which is still a working shipyard, has exhibits on 19th-century shipbuilding, including displays of period tools and ship models. ⊠ *66 Main St. (Rte. 133),* ☎ *978/768–7541.* ☞ *$4.* ☼ *Late May–late Oct., Mon.–Sat. 10–5, Sun. 1–5; late Oct.–late May, weekends 1–4.*

To explore the area's salt marshes, rivers, and local wildlife, take a 1½-hour narrated cruise on the *Essex River Queen,* run by **Essex River Cruises.** ⊠ *Essex Marina, 35 Dodge St.,* ☎ *978/768–6981 or 800/748–3706,* ☼ *Apr.–Oct., daily.*

### Dining

$$–$$$ ✕ **Jerry Pelonzi's Hearthside.** This 250-year-old converted farmhouse is the epitome of coziness; its small dining rooms have exposed beams and open fireplaces. Entrées include baked stuffed haddock, seafood casserole, sirloin steak, lobster, and chicken. ⊠ *109 Eastern Ave. (Rte. 133),* ☎ *978/768–6002. AE, MC, V.*

$$$ ✕ **Tom Shea's.** Picture windows in this expanded two-story, cedar-shingle restaurant overlook the salt marsh. Seafood is the main fare, including shrimp in coconut-beer batter, scallop-stuffed sole, Boston scrod, lobster, and, of course, the fried clams for which Essex is famous. ⊠ *122 Main St. (Rte. 133),* ☎ *978/768–6931. AE, D, MC, V.*

$–$$ ✕ **Woodman's of Essex.** Back in 1916, Lawrence "Chubby" Wood-
★ man dipped a shucked clam in batter and threw it into the french fryer as a kind of joke, apparently creating the first fried clam in town. Today, this large wooden shack with unpretentious booths is *the* place for seafood in the rough. The menu includes lobster, a raw bar, clam chowder, and fried clams. ⊠ *121 Main St. (Rte. 133),* ☎ *978/768–6451 or 800/649–1773. No credit cards.*

### Shopping

Essex is a popular antiquing destination. Most of the shops are along Route 133 (Main Street). The **White Elephant** (⊠ 32 Main St., ☎ 978/768–6901) is one of the region's largest consignment shops, offering furniture, china, and collectibles; **Chebacco Antiques** (⊠ 38 Main St.,

☎ 978/768–7371) concentrates on American pine and county furniture. **Howard's Flying Dragon Antiques** (✉ 136 Main St., ☎ 978/768–7282) is a general antiques shop with statuary and glass as well.

# Ipswich

🔟 *36 mi north of Boston, 6 mi northwest of Essex.*

Quiet little Ipswich, settled in 1633 and famous for its clams, is said to have more 17th-century houses standing and occupied than any other place in America; more than 40 were built before 1725. Information and a booklet with a suggested walking tour are available at the **Visitor Information Center** (☞ Visitor Information *in* North Shore A to Z, *below*). Among the noteworthy homes are the circa-1650 **John Whipple House** (✉ 1 South Village Green ), with large fireplaces and wide-board floors, and the **John Heard House** (✉ 54 S. Main St.), a 1795 Federal-style house. The houses and visitor center are run by the Ipswich Historical Society.

☘ At **Goodale Orchards,** a short drive from Crane Beach (☞ Outdoor Activities and Sports, *below*), you can pick whatever fruit is in season and buy apples and other produce, as well as feed the friendly barnyard animals. The small winery here produces hard cider and fruit wines; you can watch the regular cider being made with wood presses in the back of the barn. ✉ *123 Argilla Rd.,* ☎ *978/356–5366.* ☉ *May–Dec.*

## Dining and Lodging

$$–$$$  ✕ **Stone Soup Cafe.** It may be hard to believe that a hole-in-the-wall in an industrial park could be this good, but this restaurant is booked nearly a year in advance for dinner. There are two seatings of six tables a night for lobster bisque, porcini ravioli, or whatever else the chef is inspired to cook based on the finds at the farm stand that day. If you can't book ahead, stop in for breakfast or lunch. ✉ *20 Mitchell Rd. (off Rte. 1A),* ☎ *978/356–4222. Reservations essential for dinner. No credit cards. Closed Sun.–Mon. No dinner Tues.–Wed.*

$  ✕ **Clam Box.** No visit to Ipswich is complete without a sampling of the town's famous clams, and where better than at a restaurant shaped like a box of fried clams? Since 1932, locals and tourists have come to this casual spot for excellent clams, fries, and onion rings. ✉ *246 High St. (Rte. 1A),* ☎ *978/356–9707. No credit cards.*

$$–$$$$  🏨 **Miles River Country Inn.** Staying in this sprawling Colonial home
★  lets you really stretch out—acres of lawns and gardens spread around the inn. (In winter you can cross-country ski right from the front door.) The guest rooms, living room, and sunporch are all comfortably furnished with country-style antiques. Breakfast often includes eggs from the hens of the gracious innkeepers, Gretel and Peter Clark, and honey from Gretel's beehives. ✉ *823 Bay Rd. (Rte. 1A), 01936,* ☎ *978/468–7206. 8 rooms, 6 with bath. AE, MC, V. Air-conditioning.*

## Nightlife and the Arts

**Castle Hill** (✉ Argilla Rd., ☎ 978/356–7774), a 59-room Stuart-style mansion built in 1927, holds an annual summer festival of pop, folk, and classical music, plus a jazz ball and winter-holiday concert.

## Outdoor Activities and Sports

BEACHES

★  **Crane Beach,** one of the North Shore's most beautiful beaches, is a sandy, 4-mi-long stretch backed by dunes and a nature trail. There are lifeguards and changing rooms. Public parking is available. ✉ *290 Argilla Rd.,* ☎ *978/356–4354.* 🅿 *Apr.–early Sept., parking $10 weekdays, $15 weekends; early Sept.–Mar., parking $5.* ☉ *Daily 8–sunset.*

Several small islands can be explored by taking a **Crane Island Tour** (✉ ☎ 978/356–4351) across the Castle Neck river. You can take a hay-wagon tour of Hog Island, view sets from the 1996 film *The Crucible* (filmed here and in nearby Essex), and admire the many birds and wildlife protected at this refuge. The tour lasts two hours; the boats to the island leave at 10 and 2. (The boat ride takes under 10 minutes.)

### HIKING

The Ipswich area, with its miles of unique salt marshes, is one of the best places to hike on the North Shore. The Massachusetts Audubon Society's **Ipswich River Wildlife Sanctuary** has a variety of trails through marshland hills, where there are remains of early Colonial settlements as well as abundant wildlife. Get a self-guiding trail map from the office. The Rockery Trail takes you to the perennial rock garden and the Japanese garden; the map details a further 10 mi of walking trails. You can also fish in the Parker and Ipswich rivers, both of which are stocked with trout each spring. ✉ *87 Perkins Row, Topsfield (southwest of Ipswich, 1 mi off Rte. 97),* ☎ *978/887–9264. Office and trails closed Mon.*

### POLO

The one spectator sport of note on the North Shore is polo. The very grand **Myopia Hunt Club** (☎ 978/468–4433 or 978/468–7956 for polo schedules in season), one of the most exclusive clubs in America, stages polo matches (open to the public) on weekends Memorial Day through October at its grounds along Route 1A in Hamilton, just south of Ipswich.

*En Route*     South of Ipswich and Hamilton, stop at the lovely **Sedgwick Gardens at Long Hill** (✉ Essex St. [Rte. 22], Beverly, ☎ 978/921–1944), at the former summer home of Ellery Sedgwick, editor of the *Atlantic Monthly* from 1909 to 1938. The 114-acre property encompasses numerous gardens, a lotus pool, a Chinese pagoda, and a woodland path lined with unusual plants. It's open daily 8–dusk; admission is free. If you've brought the kids, detour to the ☺ **Wenham Museum** (✉ 132 Main St. [Rte. 1A], Wenham, ☎ 978/468–2377) to check out the extensive antique doll collection and the large room full of model trains. Admission is $4, and it's open Tuesday–Sunday 10–4 and on some Monday holidays.

# Newburyport

**㊶** *38 mi north of Boston, 12 mi north of Ipswich on Rte. 1A.*

Newburyport's High Street is lined with some of the finest examples of Federal-period (roughly, 1790–1810) mansions in New England. The city was once a leading port and shipbuilding center; the houses were built for prosperous sea captains. You'll notice widow's walks perched atop many of the houses.

Although Newburyport's maritime significance ended with the decline of the clipper ships, an energetic downtown renewal program has brought new life to the town's brick-front center. Renovated buildings house restaurants, taverns, and shops that sell everything from nautical brasses to antique Oriental rugs. The civic improvements have been matched by private restorations of the town's housing stock, much of which dates from the 18th century, with a scattering of 17th-century homes in some neighborhoods.

Newburyport is a good walking city, and there is all-day free parking down by the water. A stroll through the **Waterfront Park and Promenade** gives a super view of the harbor and the fishing and pleasure boats that moor here. Turn left as you leave the parking lot to reach the **Custom House Maritime Museum.** Built in 1835 in Classical Revival style, it contains exhibits on maritime history, ship models, tools, and paintings. ⊠ *25 Water St.,* ☎ *978/462–8681.* ⊡ *$3.* ⊙ *Apr.–Dec., Mon.– Sat. 10–4, Sun. 1–4.*

**42** A causeway leads from Newburyport to a narrow spit of land known as **Plum Island,** which harbors a summer colony (rapidly becoming year-round) at one end. The **Parker River National Wildlife Refuge** is at the other end of Plum Island. The refuge has 4,662 acres of salt marsh, freshwater marsh, beaches, and dunes; it is one of the few natural barrier beach–dune–salt marsh complexes left on the Northeast coast. There are exhilarating opportunities for bird-watching, surf fishing, plum and cranberry picking, and swimming. The refuge is such a popular place in summer, especially on weekends, that cars begin to line up at the gate before 7 AM. Only a limited number of cars are let in, although there's no restriction on the number of people using the beach. ☎ *978/ 465–5753.* ⊡ *$5 per car; $2 for bicycles and walk-ins.* ⊙ *Dawn–dusk. Beach sometimes closed during endangered species nesting season in spring and early summer. No pets.*

### Dining and Lodging

**$$$** ✕ **Scandia.** This restaurant is well known locally for its fine cuisine; **★** house specialties include Caesar salad prepared table-side and a veal and lobster sauté. The Sunday brunch has hot entrées, cold salads, crepes, waffles, and omelets. There are just 15 tables, so try to snag a reservation. ⊠ *25 State St.,* ☎ *978/462–6271. AE, D, DC, MC, V.*

**$$–$$$** ✕ **David's and Downstairs at David's.** These two restaurants at the Gar-**★** rison Inn (☞ *below*) are top-of-the-line for both food and service (though they're under separate management). If you dine upstairs in the formal room—furnished with chandeliers and damask-covered chairs—you may have a difficult time choosing among entrées such as sautéed lobster, scallop and shrimp with roasted vegetables, crisp ravioli in rich lobster cream sauce, and sautéed breast of duck. Downstairs at David's is less formal, with a tavern offering some of the same dishes served upstairs, as well as steaks, burgers, and full- or half-portions of seafood and pasta. Both supply supervised child care for $5 per youngster, allowing kids to play and eat while parents enjoy their meals in peace. ⊠ *11 Brown Sq.,* ☎ *978/462–8077. AE, D, MC, V.*

**$** ✕ **East End Seafood Restaurant.** For a true dining "in the rough" experience, visit this restaurant just south of Newburyport in the village of Rowley. Dining is on wooden picnic tables, and the fare is deep-fried seafood. It closes at 8 PM. ⊠ *Corner Rte. 1A and Railroad Ave., Rowley,* ☎ *978/948–7227. No credit cards.*

**$$–$$$** ⊞ **Clark Currier Inn.** This 1803 Federal mansion with an elegant "good **★** morning" staircase (so called because two small staircases join at the head of a large one, permitting people to greet one another on their way down to breakfast) has been restored with care, taste, and imagination, making it one of the best inns on the North Shore. Guest rooms are spacious and furnished with antiques, including one with a glorious, late 19th-century sleigh bed. Rates include Continental breakfast and afternoon tea. ⊠ *45 Green St., 01950,* ☎ *978/465–8363. 8 rooms. AE, D, MC, V. Air-conditioning, library, garden. No smoking.*

**$$–$$$** ⊞ **Garrison Inn.** This four-story Georgian redbrick building is set back from the main road on a small square. Guest rooms vary in size; all are furnished with Colonial reproductions. The best rooms are the two-level suites with working fireplaces. ⊠ *11 Brown Sq., 01950,* ☎ *978/ 499–8500,* ℻ *978/499–8555. 16 rooms, 8 suites. AE, MC, V.*

## Nightlife

The **Grog Shop** (⊠ 13 Middle St., ☎ 978/465–8008) hosts blues and rock bands several nights weekly.

## Outdoor Activities and Sports

FISHING

Surf casting is popular—bluefish, pollack, and striped bass can be taken from the ocean shores of Plum Island; if you enter the refuge with fishing equipment in the daylight you can obtain a free permit to remain on the beach after dark. You don't need a permit to fish from the public beach at Plum Island; the best spot is around the mouth of the Merrimack River. You can get fishing tackle at **Surfland Bait & Tackle** (⊠ 28 Plum Island Turnpike, ☎ 978/462–4202).

HIKING

At the **Parker River National Wildlife Refuge** (⊠ Plum Island, ☎ 978/465–5753), deer and rabbits share space with thousands of ducks and geese, many of them migrating. The 2-mi Hellcat Swamp Trail cuts through the marshes and sand dunes, taking in the best of the sanctuary. Trail maps are available at the office on Sunset Drive, ½ mi south of the bridge onto Plum Island.

WHALE-WATCHING

*See* North Shore A to Z, *below,* for a list of whale-watch tour operators.

# North Shore A to Z

## Arriving and Departing

BY BOAT

A boat leaves Boston for Gloucester daily between Memorial Day and Labor Day at 10 AM; the trip takes about 2½ hours, and the return boat leaves Gloucester at 3 PM. On weekends in June and daily from June to Labor Day, the Gloucester boat will also stop at Salem Willows Park. For information, call **A. C. Cruise Lines** (⊠ 290 Northern Ave., Pier 1, Boston, ☎ 617/261–6633 or 800/422–8419).

**Harbor Express** commuter boats (☎ 617/376–8401) make the one-hour trip between Boston's Long Wharf (near the Aquarium subway station) and Salem daily in the summer and fall.

BY BUS

The **Cape Ann Transportation Authority** (CATA, ☎ 978/283–7916) covers the Gloucester, Rockport, and Essex region with buses and water shuttles.

The **Coach Company** bus line (☎ 800/874–3377) runs an express commuter bus between Boston and Newburyport on weekdays.

**Massachusetts Bay Transportation Authority (MBTA)** buses (☎ 617/222–3200 for schedules) leave daily from Boston's Haymarket Station for Marblehead and Salem. Travel time is about 1 to 1¼ hours.

BY CAR

The primary link between Boston and the North Shore is Route 128, which splits off from I–95 and follows the coast northeast to Gloucester. To pick up Route 128 from Boston, take I–93 north to I–95 north to Route 128. If you stay on I–95, you'll reach Newburyport. A less direct route is Route 1A, which leaves Boston via the Callahan Tunnel; once you're north of Lynn you'll pass through several pretty towns. Beyond Beverly, Route 1A travels inland toward Ipswich and Essex; at this point, Route 127 follows the coast to Gloucester and Rockport.

From Boston to Salem or Marblehead, follow Route 128 to Route 114 into Salem and on to Marblehead. A word of caution: This route is confusing and poorly marked, particularly returning to Route 128. An alternative route to Marblehead: follow Route 1A north, and then pick up Route 129 north along the shore through Swampscott and into Marblehead.

Approximate driving times from Boston to Salem, about 35–40 minutes; to Gloucester, 50–60 minutes; to Newburyport, about 50–60 minutes. Many of the smaller roads connecting the North Shore communities (Routes 1A, 133, 127) do double duty as the towns' main streets.

### BY TRAIN

**MBTA** trains travel from Boston's North Station to Salem (25–30 minutes), Manchester (40–50 minutes), Gloucester (55–60 minutes), Rockport (70 minutes), Ipswich (50–55 minutes), and Newburyport (60–65 minutes). Call ☎ 617/222–3200 for schedules.

## Getting Around

If you don't have a car, Marblehead, Salem, Rockport, and Newburyport are the most accessible of the North Shore towns; many of the historic sights, museums, and shops are within walking distance. Attractions in the other North Shore communities are more spread out and are better explored by car.

## Guided Tours

**Brush Hill/Gray Line Tours** (⊠ 435 High St., Randolph 02368, ☎ 781/986–6100 or 800/343–1328; 14 S. Charles St., Boston, ☎ 617/236–2148) runs a Salem and Marblehead tour out of Boston, generally late May through October.

**Essex River Cruises** (☞ Essex, *above*) organizes narrated cruises of nearby salt marshes and rivers.

### WHALE-WATCHING

The most popular special-interest tours on the North Shore are whale-sighting excursions, which are generally offered from May through October. Some of the more reputable whale-watch operations include **Cape Ann Whale Watch** (⊠ Rose's Wharf, 415 Main St., Box 345, Gloucester 01930, ☎ 978/283–5110 or 800/877–5110); **Captain Bill's Whale Watch** (33 Harbor Loop; mailing address: 9 Traverse St., Gloucester 01930, ☎ 978/283–6995); **Newburyport Whale Watch** (⊠ 54 Merrimac St., Newburyport 01950, ☎ 978/465–9885 or 800/848–1111); and **Yankee Whale Watch** (⊠ 75 Essex Ave., Gloucester 01930, ☎ 978/283–0313 or 800/942–5464).

## Contacts and Resources

### EMERGENCIES

**Police** (☎ 911).

**Beverly Hospital** (⊠ 85 Herrick St., Beverly, ☎ 978/922–3000).

**CVS Pharmacy** (⊠ 53 Dodge St., Beverly, ☎ 978/927–3291) is open 24 hours a day. **Walgreen's** (⊠ 201 Main St., Gloucester, ☎ 978/283–7361) is open until 10 weeknights, 6 on weekends.

### STATE PARKS

Of the numerous parks in the area, the following have particularly varied facilities: **Halibut Point State Park** (⊠ Rte. 127 to Gott Ave., Rockport, ☎ 978/546–2997). **Maudslay State Park** (⊠ Curzon Mill Rd., Newburyport [I–95 to Rte. 113 east; then left on Noble St.], ☎ 978/465–7223). **Parker River National Wildlife Refuge** (⊠ Plum Island, off Rte. 1A, Newburyport, ☎ 978/465–5753). **Plum Island State Reser-**

**vation** (⊠ Off Rte. 1A, Newburyport, ☎ 978/462–4481). **Salisbury Beach State Reservation** (⊠ Rte. 1A, Salisbury, ☎ 978/462–4481).

## Visitor Information

The umbrella organization for the whole region is the **North of Boston Visitors and Convention Bureau** (⊠ 17 Peabody Sq., Peabody 01960, ☎ 978/977–7760 or 800/742–5306). The following cover more specific areas.

**Cape Ann Chamber of Commerce** (⊠ 33 Commercial St., Gloucester 01930, ☎ 978/283–1601). **Greater Newburyport Chamber of Commerce and Industry** (⊠ 29 State St., Newburyport 01950, ☎ 978/462–6680). **Ipswich Visitor Information** (⊠ 20 S. Main St., Ipswich 01936, ☎ 978/356–8540). **Marblehead Chamber of Commerce** (⊠ 62 Pleasant St., Box 76, Marblehead 01945, ☎ 781/631–2868). **National Park Service Visitor Information** (2 New Liberty St., Salem 01970, ☎ 978/740–1650). **Rockport Chamber of Commerce Visitor's Booth** (Box 67, 3 Main St., Rockport 01966, ☎ 978/546–6575). **Salem Chamber of Commerce and Visitor Information** (⊠ 32 Derby Sq., Salem 01970, ☎ 978/744–0004 or 800/777–6848). **Salem Maritime National Historic Site** (⊠ 174 Derby St., Salem 01970, ☎ 978/740–1660). **Salisbury by the Sea Chamber of Commerce** (⊠ Town Hall, Beach Rd., Salisbury 01952, ☎ 978/465–3581 or 800/779–1771).

# SOUTH OF BOSTON

The towns south of Boston make an enjoyable day trip or a convenient stop on your way down to the Cape or Martha's Vineyard. If you're a history buff or are seeking to give children an educational experience they won't soon forget, take the 40-mi trip south to **Plymouth**, the community locals proudly call "America's Home Town." Here you can see the monument you've heard about since childhood—Plymouth Rock. A couple of miles down the road at Plimoth Plantation you can stroll through a re-creation of a 17th-century Puritan village that puts new meaning into the word *authentic*, or walk the decks of the *Mayflower II*. Most important, with its historical accuracy, Plymouth dispels many myths about the first English settlers. The truth, you're likely to find, is far more fascinating.

If you're more ambitious, take a drive into the seafaring towns of **New Bedford** and **Fall River**. In Fall River, history has taken a macabre turn with the ever-burgeoning interest in the Trial of the Century—the 19th century, that is. Fall River is the hometown of Lizzie Borden—who was accused, and acquitted, of dispatching her parents with "40 whacks"— and Borden history has become a cottage industry here. New Bedford is a center of seafaring history.

## Plymouth

*Numbers in the margin correspond to points of interest on the South of Boston map.*

**43** *40 mi south of Boston.*

On December 26, 1620, 102 weary men, women, and children disembarked from the *Mayflower* to found the first permanent European settlement north of Virginia. (In fact, Virginia was their intended destination, but storms pushed the ship off course.) Of the settlers, just a third were members of the Separatist church, now known as the Pilgrims. Before coming ashore, the expedition's leaders drew up the Mayflower Compact, a historic agreement binding the group to the

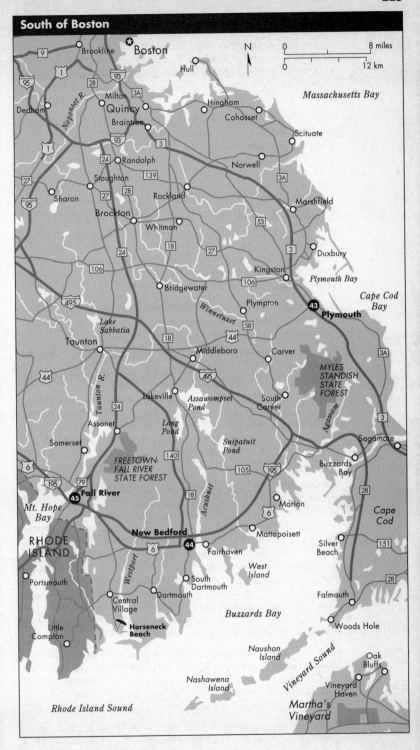

law of the majority. This compact was the basis for the colony's later government. After a rough start (half of the original settlers died during the first winter), the colony stabilized and grew under the leadership of Governor William Bradford. Two other founding fathers—military leader Myles Standish and John Alden—acquired mythical status via a poem by Longfellow, "The Courtship of Miles Standish."

Today, Plymouth is characterized by narrow streets, clapboard mansions, shops, and antiques stores. Some commercial names would make the Pilgrims shudder: The John Alden Gift Shop, Mayflower Seafoods, and, incongruously, Pocahontas Gifts, Sportswear and Sundries. (She was from Virginia.) But it's easy to overlook these and admire the picturesque waterfront—the view from the harbor is spectacular. The town also offers a parade, historic-house tours, and other activities to mark Thanksgiving.

A variety of **historic statues** dot the town, including ones of William Bradford on Water Street, a Pilgrim maiden in Brewster Gardens, Massasoit (chief of the local Wampanoag tribe) on Carver Street, and the largest freestanding granite statue in the country, the *National Monument to the Forefathers,* on Allerton Street.

Several historic houses are also open for visits, including the 1640 **Sparrow House,** Plymouth's oldest structure. ⊠ *42 Summer St.,* ☎ *508/ 747–1240.* ▭ *$2.* ☉ *Apr.–Dec., Thurs.–Tues. 10–5.*

The 1749 **Spooner House,** home to the same family for 200 years, has guided tours, historic recipes, and a garden. ⊠ *27 North St.,* ☎ *508/ 746–0012.* ▭ *Donation.* ☉ *June–Oct., Tues.–Thurs. 10–3:30 or 4.*

Like Plimoth Plantation (☞ *below*), the **Mayflower II,** an exact replica of the 1620 *Mayflower,* is manned by staff in period dress. The ship was built in England through research and a bit of guesswork, then sailed across the Atlantic in 1957. ⊠ *State Pier,* ☎ *508/746–1622.* ▭ *$5.75 or as part of Plimoth Plantation fee.* ☉ *Apr.–Nov., daily 9–5; July–Aug., daily 9–7.*

A few dozen yards from the *Mayflower II* is **Plymouth Rock,** popularly believed to have been the Pilgrims' stepping stone when they left the ship. Given the stone's unimpressive appearance—many visitors are dismayed that it's little more than a boulder—and dubious authenticity (as explained on a nearby plaque), the grand canopy overhead seems a trifle ostentatious. Across the street from Plymouth Rock is **Cole's Hill,** where the company buried their dead—at night, so the Native Americans could not count the dwindling numbers of survivors. Just past the hill, on what was once called locally First Street, is the site of the original settlement; in 1834, the street was named Leyden Street in honor of the Dutch city that sheltered the Pilgrims. Look for plaques designating the locations of the original lots.

For a more traditional view of the Pilgrims, visit the **Plymouth National Wax Museum,** on the top of Cole's Hill. It contains 26 scenes with 180 life-size models that tell the settlers' story. ⊠ *16 Carver St.,* ☎ *508/ 746–6468.* ▭ *$5.* ☉ *Mar.–May and Nov., daily 9–5; June and Sept.– Oct., daily 9–7; July–Aug., daily 9–9.*

From the waterfront sights, it's a short walk to one of the country's oldest public museums. The **Pilgrim Hall Museum,** established in 1824, transports visitors back to the time before the Pilgrims' landing, with items carried by those weary travelers to the New World. Included are a carved chest, a remarkably well preserved wicker cradle, Myles Standish's sword, John Alden's Bible, Native American artifacts, and the remains of the *Sparrow Hawk*, a sailing ship that was wrecked in 1626. There are also changing exhibits. ⊠ *75 Court St. (Rte. 3A),* ☎ *508/746–1620.* ☞ *$5.* ☉ *Feb.–Dec., daily 9:30–4:30.*

Imagine an entire museum devoted to a Thanksgiving side dish. But the Ocean Spray–operated **Cranberry World** is amazingly popular. For one thing, it's free. After viewing details of how the state's local crop is grown, harvested, and processed, you can sip juices and sample products made from *Vaccinium macrocarpon* (the Latin name for cranberries). In October, you can see harvesting techniques and attend local cranberry festivals. ⊠ *225 Water St.,* ☎ *508/747–2350.* ☞ *Free.* ☉ *Mid-Apr.–Nov., daily 9:30–5.*

NEED A
BREAK? Sample some cranberry wine—it's oddly refreshing, and free—at the **Plymouth Bay Winery** (⊠ Village Landing Marketplace, 170 Water St., ☎ 508/746–2100), open March–December. For more substantive fare, the **Lobster Hut** (☎ 508/746–2270), open year-round (except January) on Town Wharf at the waterfront, offers seafood in classic breaded and fried style, plus sandwiches and luncheon specials.

★ ☙ Over the entrance of the **Plimoth Plantation** is the caution: "You are now entering 1627." Believe it. Against the backdrop of the Atlantic Ocean, a Pilgrim village has been painstakingly re-created, from the thatched roofs, cramped quarters, and open fireplaces to the long-horned livestock. Throw away your preconception of white collars and funny hats; through ongoing research, the Plimoth staff has developed a portrait of the Pilgrims that's more complex than the dour folk in elementary school textbooks. Listen to the accents of the "residents," who never break out of character. You might see them plucking ducks, cooking rabbit stew, or tending garden. Feel free to engage them in conversation about their life, but expect only curious looks if you ask about anything that happened later than 1627.

Elsewhere on the plantation is **Hobbamock's Homestead,** where descendants of the Wampanoag Indians re-create the life of a Native American who chose to live near the newcomers. In the **Carriage House Craft Center** visitors may see such items created using the techniques of 17th-century English craftsmanship—that is, what the Pilgrims might have imported. (You can also buy samples.) At the **Nye Barn,** you can see goats, cows, pigs, and chickens bred from 17th-century gene pools or bred to represent animals raised in the original plantation. The visitor center has gift shops, a cafeteria, and multimedia presentations. Dress for the weather, since many exhibits are outdoors. Admission tickets are good for two consecutive days; if you have time, you may want to spread out your plantation visit to take in all the sights. ⊠ *Warren Ave. (Rte. 3A),* ☎ *508/746–1622.* ☞ *$18.50 (includes entry to Mayflower II); Plantation only, $15.* ☉ *Apr.–Nov., daily 9–5.*

## Dining and Lodging

$$–$$$ ✕ **Bert's Cove.** This local landmark, just off the entrance to Plymouth Beach, has great ocean views along with a menu listing choices from veal medallions, sirloin steak, and risotto to fresh seafood. ⊠ *140 Warren Ave., Rte. 3A,* ☎ *508/746–3330. AE, D, MC, V.*

$$ ✕ **Iguana's.** A good spot for both lunch and late-night dining, Iguana's serves fajitas, burritos, and other Mexican-Southwestern fare, plus burgers, sandwiches, and chicken, steak, and rib dishes. There's a bar, a patio, ocean views—and a live iguana. ⊠ *Village Landing Marketplace, 170 Water St.,* ☎ *508/747–4000. AE, DC, MC, V.*

**$–$$** ✕ **The All-American Diner.** The look is nostalgia—red, white, and blue with movie posters. The specialty is beloved American foods—omelets and pancakes for breakfast; burgers, salads, and soups for lunch. ✉ *60 Court St.,* ☎ *508/747–4763. DC, MC, V. Closed dinner.*

**$–$$** ✕▥ **John Carver Inn.** This three-story Colonial-style redbrick building with a massive pillared facade is just a few steps from Plymouth's main attractions. The public rooms and dining rooms are lavish, with period furnishings and stylish drapes. The rooms are more matter-of-fact, but ask for one of the six environmentally sensitive alpine rooms, which have filtered air and water and in-room exercise equipment. At its Hearth 'n Kettle Restaurant, a huge menu of American favorites, including hearty sandwiches and a broad range of seafoods, is served by a staff dressed in Colonial attire. At press time, the inn was planning additions for 1999: a new indoor pool with a *Mayflower* ship model and a water slide, as well as six two-room suites with fireplaces and whirlpool baths. ✉ *25 Summer St., 02360,* ☎ *508/746–7100 or 800/ 274–1620,* ℻ *508/746–8299. 79 rooms. Restaurant, bar, pool, meeting rooms. AE, D, DC, MC, V.*

**$–$$** ▥ **Governor Bradford Motor Inn.** The waterfront location here (directly across from the *Mayflower II*) is a big plus. Rooms are motel-basic, each with two double beds, a small refrigerator, and free HBO. ✉ *98 Water St., 02360,* ☎ *508/746–6200 or 800/332–1620,* ℻ *508/747– 3032. 94 rooms. No-smoking rooms, refrigerators, pool. AE, D, MC, V.*

# New Bedford

🄸🄸 *45 mi southwest of Plymouth, 50 mi south of Boston.*

New Bedford is home to the largest fishing fleet on the East Coast. Although much of the town is industrial, the restored historic district near the water is a delight. It was here that Herman Melville set his masterpiece, *Moby-Dick,* a novel ostensibly about whaling. The city's whaling tradition is commemorated in the **New Bedford Whaling National Historical Park,** encompassing 13 blocks of the waterfront historic district. The park visitor center, housed in an 1853 Greek Revival former bank, provides maps and information about whaling-related sites. ✉ *33 William St.,* ☎ *508/991–6200.* ☉ *Daily 9–4.*

The **New Bedford Whaling Museum,** established in 1902, is the largest American museum devoted to the 200-year history of whaling. Peruse the incredible collection of scrimshaw, then climb aboard an 89-ft, half-scale model of the 1826 whaling ship *Lagoda*—the world's largest ship model. A 22-minute film depicting an actual whaling chase is shown daily. In 1998, the museum acquired the bones of a 66-ft blue whale that had been killed in a collision with a ship near Newport, Rhode Island. You can watch the scientists and sculptors rebuild the whale skeleton, which will be displayed in a new addition to the museum that is scheduled for completion in 2000. ✉ *18 Johnny Cake Hill,* ☎ *508/ 997–0046.* ▱ *$4.50.* ☉ *Late May–early Sept., Fri.–Wed. 9–5, Thurs. 9–8; early Sept.–late May, daily 9–5.*

**Seaman's Bethel,** the small chapel described in *Moby-Dick,* is across the street from the whaling museum. ✉ *15 Johnny Cake Hill,* ☎ *508/ 992–3295.*

## Dining

**$$$** ✕ **Davy's Locker.** A huge seafood menu is the main draw at this spot overlooking Buzzards Bay. Choose from more than a dozen shrimp preparations or a healthy choice entrée—dishes prepared with olive oil, vegetables, garlic, and herbs. For landlubbers, chicken, steak, ribs, and the like are also served. You can park or dock your boat at the restaurant's private pier. ⊠ *1480 E. Rodney French Blvd.,* ☎ *508/992–7359. AE, D, MC, V.*

$–$$ ✕ **Antonio's.** If you'd like to sample the traditional fare of New Bedford's large Portuguese population, friendly unadorned Antonio's serves up hearty portions of pork and shellfish stew, *bacalau* (salt cod), and grilled sardines, often on plates piled high with crispy fried potatoes and rice. ⊠ *267 Coggeshall St., (near intersection of I–195 and Rte. 18)* ☎ *508/990–3636. No credit cards.*

# Fall River

⑤ *54 mi south of Boston, 15 mi northwest of New Bedford.*

Every schoolchild can recite this rhyme of woe: "Lizzie Borden took an axe / And gave her mother 40 whacks. / When she saw what she had done, / She gave her father 41." And yet Lizzie, the maiden daughter of the town's prominent banker, was found innocent of the 1892 bludgeoning deaths of her father and stepmother in the most sensational trial of its time. She went on to spend the rest of her life quietly in Fall River, today a fading port and factory town. The Borden tragedy continues to draw the curious, although the city's burgeoning factory-outlet centers also attract bargain-hunters.

The best place to learn about the Borden case is the **Fall River Historical Society,** which has the world's largest collection of Borden artifacts, including courtroom evidence, photographs, and the handleless hatchet suspected to be the murder weapon. The Greek Revival–style mansion also displays artifacts related to Fall River's days as home of the world's largest cotton cloth manufacturer. Another exhibit illustrates 19th-century mourning practices. Tours are available. ⊠ *451 Rock St.,* ☎ *508/679–1071.* ⚏ *$5.* ☉ *Apr.–May, Oct.–Nov., Tues.–Fri. 9–4:30; June–Sept. and Dec., Tues.–Fri. 9–4:30, weekends 1–5.*

If you're strong of heart and stomach, you may also want to take in the **Lizzie Borden Bed & Breakfast Museum** (☞ *Lodging, below*). In 1996, the Borden home, the site of the murders, was transformed into a B&B. Even if you don't spend the night here, you can still drop by to see the display of Lizzie-related items. ⊠ *92 Second St.,* ☎ *508/675–7333.* ⚏ *$7.50.* ☉ *Daily 11–3, tours every ½ hr.*

Another Lizzie highlight is the **Borden burial plot** in the Oak Grove Cemetery on Prospect Street. Lizzie's home after her acquittal was at **306 French Street** (a private residence), where she lived until her death in 1927.

A visit to Fall River can skirt Lizzie Borden's sad saga entirely. The town's industrial docks and enormous factories recall the city's past as a major textile center in the 19th century and early decades of the 20th century. It also served as a port; today the most interesting site is **Battleship Cove,** a "floating" museum complex docked on the Taunton River. The cove is home to the 35,000-ton battleship USS *Massachusetts;* the destroyer USS *Joseph P. Kennedy, Jr.;* a World War II attack sub, the USS *Lionfish;* two PT boats from World War II; and a Cold War–era, Russian-built warship. ⊠ *5 Water St. at Davol St., off Rte. 79,* ☎ *508/678–1100 or 800/533–3194.* ⚏ *$9.* ☉ *Daily 9–4:30.*

From May through October, the **HMS Bounty,** built for the 1962 film *Mutiny on the Bounty,* is docked adjacent to Battleship Cove. Visitors can participate in sails organized by the Tall Ship Bounty Foundation; call for details. ☎ *508/673–3886.* ⚏ *$5.* ☉ *Daily 10–6; call ahead, as ship is often on sail.*

The **Fall River Carousel,** built in the 1920s, was rescued from the defunct Lincoln Amusement Park in 1992 and moved to Battleship Cove. The glorious restoration is now housed dockside. ⊠ *Battleship Cove,* ☎ *508/324–4300.* ▤ *Rides 75¢.* ☺ *Mid-Apr.–May and early Sept.– late Oct., weekends noon–4; June, daily noon–6; July–early Sept., daily noon–8.*

Also at riverside, the **Fall River Heritage State Park** tells the story of Fall River's industrial past, focusing on the city's textile mills and their workers. The park has a visitor center, sailboat rentals, a summer concert series, and exhibits. ⊠ *200 Davol St. W,* ☎ *508/675–5759.* ▤ *Free.* ☺ *June–early Sept., daily 10–6; early Sept.–May, daily 10–4.*

Two blocks from Battleship Cove, the **Marine Museum at Fall River** celebrates the age of sail and steamship travel, especially the lavishly fitted ships of the Old Fall River Line, which operated until 1937 between New England and New York City. The museum also contains the 28-ft-long, 1-ton model of the *Titanic* used in the 1952 movie. ⊠ *70 Water St.,* ☎ *508/674–3533.* ▤ *$4.* ☺ *Weekdays 9–5, Sat. noon–5, Sun. noon–4.*

### Dining and Lodging

$–$$    ✕ **Waterstreet Café.** This casually sophisticated café, with exposed brick and sponge-painted walls, serves hummus and tabouleh roll-ups, falafel, and other Middle Eastern–inspired salads and sandwiches. Other specialties include "something fresh in a shell over linguine" (pasta with clams or mussels), "Greek Island Shrimp" sautéed with artichoke hearts and feta cheese. It's just across the street from the Marine Museum. ⊠ *36 Water St.,* ☎ *508/672–8748. AE, MC, V.*

$$$–$$$$    ▥ **Lizzie Borden Bed & Breakfast Museum.** Could you stand to sleep in the same house where Lizzie Borden's father and stepmother met a bloody end? Choose from one of the four original bedrooms, two of which are suites, or two rooms converted from attic space. A full breakfast and a house tour are included. Nonguests may tour the place between 11 and 3. Overnight guests must be 12 or older; it's also a no-smoking property. ⊠ *92 Second St., 02721,* ☎ 𝔽𝔸𝕏 *508/675–7333. 4 rooms, 2 suites. AE, D, MC, V.*

### Shopping

Fall River is home to more than 70 brand-name factory outlet stores, clustered at Exit 8A from I–195, housed in original granite mills that once turned out cotton. The largest of these outlet centers is **Quality Factory Outlets** (⊠ 638 Quequechan, ☎ 508/677–4949).

## South of Boston A to Z

### Arriving and Departing

BY BUS

**American Eagle Motorcoach Inc.** (☎ 800/453–5040) offers service from Boston to New Bedford. **Plymouth & Brockton Street Railway** (☎ 508/746–0378) links Plymouth and the South Shore to Boston's South Station with frequent bus service. From the Plymouth bus depot, take the **Plymouth Area Link** buses (☎ 508/746–0378) to the town center or to Plimoth Plantation.

BY CAR

To get to **Plymouth,** take the Southeast Expressway I–93 south to Route 3 (toward Cape Cod); Exits 6 and 4 lead to downtown Plymouth and Plimoth Plantation, respectively. To get to **Fall River,** take I–93 to Route 24 south to I–195. To **New Bedford,** follow I–93 to Route 24 south to Route 140 south, and continue to I–195. Allow about one hour from Boston to any of these three cities, about one hour from

Plymouth to either Fall River or New Bedford, and about 15–20 minutes between New Bedford and Fall River.

BY TRAIN
**MBTA** (☎ 617/222–3200) commuter rail service is available to Plymouth. Travel time is about one hour. From the station, take the **Plymouth Area Link** buses (☞ By Bus, *above*) to the historic attractions.

## Guided Tours
**Colonial Lantern Tours** (✉ Box 3541, Plymouth 02361, ☎ 508/747–4161 or 800/698–5636) offers guided evening tours April through November of the original Plymouth plantation site and historic district, as well as a nightly "Blood, Gore, and Ghosts" tour highlighting Plymouth's more macabre history.

**Brush Hill/Gray Line Tours** (✉ 435 High St., Randolph 02368, ☎ 781/986–6100 or 800/343–1328; 14 S. Charles St., Boston, ☎ 617/236–2148) runs tours from Boston to Plymouth, generally late-May through October.

WHALE-WATCHING
**Capt. John Boats** (☎ 508/746–2643) offers several daily whale-watch cruises from from Plymouth Town Wharf April to November. **Andy Lynn Boats** (☎ 508/746–7776), also at Plymouth Town Wharf, offers daily trips May through October.

## Contacts and Resources
EMERGENCIES
**Police** (☎ 911 or dial township station).
**CVS Pharmacy** (✉ 2100 Acushnet Ave., New Bedford, ☎ 508/995–2653) is open until 10 weeknights and 9 weekends. **CVS Pharmacy** (✉ 317 State Rd., Manomet [Plymouth], ☎ 508/224–3312) is open until 9 Monday through Saturday and until 6 on Sunday.
**St. Luke's Hospital** (✉ 101 Page St., New Bedford, ☎ 508/997–1515).
**Jordan Hospital** (✉ 275 Sandwich St., Plymouth, ☎ 508/746–2000).

STATE PARKS
**Fort Phoenix State Beach Reservation** (✉ Green St., Fairhaven, off Rte. 6, ☎ 508/992–4524), the site of the Revolutionary War's first naval battle, has a small beach. The more than 5,000 acres of **Freetown-Fall River State Forest** (✉ Slab Bridge Rd., Assonet, Exit 10 off Rte. 24, ☎ 508/644–5522) include picnic areas and 25 mi of unpaved roads for cross-country skiing, snowmobiling, and motorcycling. **Horseneck Beach State Reservation** (✉ Rte. 88, Westport, ☎ 508/636–8816) draws summer crowds to its 2-mi sandy beach. **Myles Standish State Forest** (✉ Cranberry Rd., South Carver, Exit 5 off Rte. 3, ☎ 508/866–2526) has more than 16,000 acres for hiking, biking, swimming, picnicking, and canoeing. Several ponds are stocked with bass, perch, and pickerel.

## Visitor Information
**Bristol County Convention and Visitors Center** (✉ 70 N. Second St., Box 976, New Bedford 02741, ☎ 508/997–1250).
**Destination Plymouth** (✉ 225 Water St., Suite 202, Plymouth 02360, ☎ 800/872–1620). **Fall River Chamber of Commerce** (✉ 200 Pocasset St., Fall River 02721, ☎ 508/676–8226). **New Bedford Chamber of Commerce** (✉ 794 Purchase St., New Bedford 02742, ☎ 508/999–5231). **Plymouth Waterfront Visitor Information Center** (✉ 180 Water St. [at Rte. 44], 02360, ☎ 508/747–7525).

# BOOKS AND FILMS

## Books

Boston's history and culture have been the delight of scholars and critics ever since Harvard opened its doors in 1636. "The Hub" best comes alive, however, in the pages of novelists.

### Art, Architecture, and Culture

Check out the art catalog *John Singleton Copley in America* (1995); Henry Russell Hitchcock's masterful study, *The Architecture of Henry Hobson Richardson and His Times* (1961); and Percy Miller's famous studies, *The New England Mind* (1939) and *The American Transcendentalists* (1957). For the last word on Boston Brahmins, see Cleveland Amory's *The Proper Bostonians* (1947). *Frederick Law Olmsted and the Boston Park System* (1982) is an oversize, richly detailed look at Boston's "emerald necklace" of Olmsted-designed parks. A picture book, *Running: One Hundred Years of the Boston Marathon* (1995) by Hugh R. Higdon, captures the excitement of the race. And then there's *Fenway* (1999), which evokes the historic, tear-to-the-eye ballpark.

### History and Biography

Native son Samuel Eliot Morison is one of Boston's best-known historians. Just a few of his works are *One Boy's Boston* (1962), *The Intellectual Life of Colonial New England* (1956), and the celebrated *The European Discovery of America* (1974). Important volumes on the powdered-wig era include *The Baron of Beacon Hill: A Biography of John Hancock* (1979) by William M. Fowler, Jack Shepherd's *The Adams Chronicles* (1975), Catherine Drinker Bowen's *John Adams and the American Revolution* (1955), and *The Minute Men and Their World* (1976) by Robert Gross. Two of the most beautifully written works on Boston's Colonial era are devoted to America's best-known messenger: *Paul Revere and the World He Lived In* by Esther Forbes (1942) and the groundbreaking *Paul Revere's Ride* by David Hackett Fischer (1994). For a brilliant new biography of the multifaceted Revere, see *A True Republican: The Life of Paul Revere* (1998) by Jayne E. Triber. On the most colorful events of the period, see *The Devil in Massachusetts: A Modern Enquiry into the Salem Witch Trials* (1949) by Marion Starkey, *A Delusion of Satan: The Full Story of the Salem Witch Trials* (1995) by Frances Hill, *The Boston Massacre* (1976) by Hiller B. Zobel, and Benjamin Labaree's *The Boston Tea Party* (1964). *Emerson Among the Eccentrics,* by Carlos Baker (1996), is a collective biography of the 19th-century west-of-Boston literary and philosophical crowd that included Thoreau and the Alcotts. For a look at one of Boston's wonderfully unconventional figures, try *The Art of Scandal: The Life and Times of Isabella Stewart Gardner* (1998) by Douglass Shand-Tucci.

### Literature

The great classics remain Henry James's *The Europeans* and *The Bostonians,* William Dean Howells's *A Modern Instance* and *The Rise of Silas Lapham,* and George Santayana's *The Last Puritan.* The Salem witch trials inspired two interpretations of more recent vintage: Arthur Miller's stirring play, *The Crucible* (1953)—recently made into a movie starring Daniel Day-Lewis and Winona Ryder—and the Newbery award winner *The Witch of Blackbird Pond* (1958) by Elizabeth George Speare. Other American classics invoking Boston-area towns include Nathaniel Hawthorne's *The House of Seven Gables* and *The Scarlet Letter,* Henry David Thoreau's *Walden,* and Louisa May Alcott's *Little Women.* Fiction set in Boston includes Gerald Green's *The Last Angry Man,* Edwin O'Connor's *The Last Hurrah,* Sylvia Plath's *The Bell Jar,* May Sarton's *Faithful Are the Wounds,* J. Anthony Lukas's *Common Ground,* and Scott Turow's *One L.* Several other good reads are Alice Adams's *Superior Women,* James Carroll's *Mortal Friends* and *The City Below,* Jean Stafford's *Boston Adventure,* and John Updike's *Couples.* The mystery writers Jane Langton and Robert B. Parker locate their novels in the Boston area.

# Films

Boston attracts filmmakers with both its historical significance and its vibrant urban neighborhood life. Books are, not surprisingly, an important source of inspiration for many of the major movies set here. In *Friends of Eddie Coyle* (1973), directed by Peter Yates, Robert Mitchum plays a small-time hood facing a return to jail who sells information about stolen guns to the government while simultaneously supplying guns to bank robbers. *The Paper Chase* (1973) dramatizes a student's first year at Harvard's law school; John Houseman won an Oscar for his performance as his notoriously difficult professor. Sidney Lumet's *The Verdict* (1982) stars Paul Newman as a lawyer facing up to issues he has avoided throughout his career. Jack Nicholson waxes Mephistophelean in a fantasy about three New England widows in *The Witches of Eastwick* (1987), directed by George Miller. *Blown Away* (1994), di-rected by Stephen Hopkins, ratchets up the suspense as a Boston police bomb-squad officer discovers a plot to kill him when one of his colleagues is blown up dismantling a device. In *Amistad* (1997), directed by Steven Spielberg, the story of a mutiny aboard a slave ship in 1839 and the courtroom drama that ensues, the Massachusetts State House is a significant location. Academy Award–winning *Good Will Hunting* (1997), directed by Gus Van Sant, depicts the struggle of a physics genius to acknowledge his gift at the cost of leaving his Southie roots; besides the shots of the Public Garden and MIT, it's rich with local spots like South Boston's L Street Tavern and the now-closed (and much-mourned) Tasty Diner. The romantic comedy *Next Stop Wonderland* (1998) follows the not-quite-crossing paths of a nurse and an employee at the New England Aquarium; Emerson's quote about "the hobgoblin of little minds" comes into play.

# INDEX

## Icons and Symbols

★ Our special recommendations

✕ Restaurant

🏨 Lodging establishment

✕🏨 Lodging establishment whose restaurant warrants a special trip

🦆 Good for kids (rubber duck)

☞ Sends you to another section of the guide for more information

⊠ Address

☎ Telephone number

☉ Opening and closing times

🎟 Admission prices

Numbers in white and black circles ③ ❸ that appear on the maps, in the margins, and within the tours correspond to one another.

## A

A Cambridge House Bed and Breakfast 🏨, 145
Abbott Hall, 208
Abiel Smith School, 22, 26
Acorn Street, 18, 19
Addison Choate Inn 🏨, 217
African Meeting House, 18, 19, 22
Air travel, x–xi
with children, xv–xvi
luggage, xxiii
Airports and transfers, xi–xii
Alea III, 159
Algiers Café ✕, 98
Algiers Coffee House, 152
All-American Diner ✕, 228
Allston, 122–125
Ambrosia ✕, 102–103
Amelia Payson Guest House 🏨, 213
American Express, xxii
American Textile History Museum, 204–205
Ames-Webster House, 64
Ancient and Honorable Artillery Company of Massachusetts, 36
Annual Spring New England Flower Show, 13
Anthony's Pier 4 ✕, 113
Antiques, 14, 175, 177, 181
Antonio's ✕, 229
Apartment rentals, xxi
Appalachian Mountain Club, 19, 21
Appetito ✕, 112
Appleton Mansions, 21

## B

Baby-sitting, xv
Back Bay, 6, 59–72, 102–105, 128–134
Back Bay Hilton 🏨, 130
Back Bay mansions, 64
Baja Mexican Cantina ✕, 112
Baker House, 95
Bakeries, 177
Ballet, 14, 155
Ballet Theatre of Boston, 155
BankBoston Celebrity Series (concerts), 159
Barking Crab Restaurant ✕, 113
Bars, 11, 149–151
Baseball, 13, 164
Basketball, 164
Bates Hall, 66
Battle Green, 193
Battle of Fort Wagner, 14
Battle reenactments, 13
Battleship Cove, 229
Bay Tower Room (bar), 149
Baylies Mansion, 64
Beaches, 171, 190, 209, 213–214, 215, 219–220
Beacon Hill, 6, 16–30, 102–105, 134
Beacon Hill Bed and Breakfast 🏨, 144
Beacon Hill Skate Shop, 169
Beacon Inns 🏨, 145
Beacon Street, 18, 21
Beanpot Hockey Tournament, 13, 165
Bearskin Neck Motor Lodge 🏨, 217
Beaver II (ship replica), 50

Aquarium, 50, 56, 170
Arboretum, 13, 81, 83, 166
Archaeological museum, 89, 96
Arlington, 195
Arlington Street Church, 61, 64
Arnold Arboretum, 13, 81, 83, 166
Art galleries, 181–182, 204, 205, 216
Art museums, 61, 69–70, 74, 75, 76–77, 78–80, 89, 90, 94, 95–96, 200, 201, 205, 211
Art of Black Dance and Music, 156
Arthur M. Sackler Museum, 89
Arts, 148, 155–162, 213, 215, 218, 219
Atrium Lounge, 149
August Moon Festival, 14
Aujourd'hui ✕, 103
Avalon (rock club), 154
Axis (dance club), 152–153

Bed-and-breakfasts, xxi, 143–146, 191, 200, 209, 213, 214, 221, 229, 230
Bella Luna ✕, 125
Berkeley Residence YMCA Boston 🏨, 146
Berklee Performance Center, 157
Bert's Cove ✕, 227
Bertucci's ✕, 195
Best Western Terrace Inn 🏨, 138
Biba ✕, 103
Bicycling, 166, 195–196
Big Apple Circus, 13
Big Dig, 5
Billiards, 166
Bill Rodger's Running Center, 170
Bill's Bar (rock club), 154
Biscotti's (coffeehouse), 45
Black Crow Caffé ✕, 125
Black Heritage Trail, 22, 26
Black History Month, 13
Black Rose (bar), 149
Blacksmith House, 97, 98
Blackstone Block, 37
Blue Hills Ski Area, 170
Blue Hills Reservation, 169
Blue Hills Trailside Museum, 169
Blue Room ✕, 115
Blues clubs, 151
Blues festival, 14
Boarding House Park, 204
Boat and ferry travel, xii–xiii, 222
Boating, 166–167, 196, 209, 216, 218
Bob the Chef's ✕, 113
Bombay Bistro ✕, 120
Book fair, 14
Bookstores, 175–176, 182–184
Boott Cotton Mills Museum, 204
Borden, Lizzie, 229
Border Café ✕, 119
Boston Athenaeum, 18, 21, 23
Boston Athletic Club, 168, 170
Boston Ballet, 155
Boston Beer Works (bar), 149
Boston Billiards Club, 166
Boston Bruins, 14, 165
Boston Camerata (early music group), 160
Boston Cecilia (choral group), 159
Boston Celtics, 14, 164
Boston Center for the Arts (Cyclorama Building), 74, 161
Boston Chamber Music Society, 159
Boston College Eagles, 164